The George Bell-Alphons Koechlin Correspondence

The Selected Letters and Papers of George Bell, Bishop of Chichester

GEORGE KENNEDY ALLEN BELL (1883–1958) was a figure of distinctive importance in many of the great political and religious landscapes by which we have come to recognize the history of the European 20th century. He was a priest of the Church of England, a chaplain to an Archbishop of Canterbury, a Dean of Canterbury and then, for almost thirty years, Bishop of Chichester. Bell played a significant role in the development of that church, but his most distinctive contribution lay in the evolution of the international ecumenical movement. Bell became a leading light in the Life and Work movement and then the World Council of Churches, and a crucial bridge not only between the Church of England and other churches but between British Christianity and the churches of the world at large. In this context he came to know intimately Nathan Söderblom, Dietrich Bonhoeffer, Willem Visser't Hooft and Eivind Berggrav.

In the context of the unfolding history of the Third Reich, Bell worked to support the persecuted, playing an important part in the German Church Struggle and also organizing relief work to support refugee families who sought to escape abroad. He saved many lives. During the Second World War Bell repeatedly challenged British military and diplomatic policy, particularly over the obliteration bombing of German cities, and by his own secret initiatives he became a ready emissary of the German resistance against Hitler. Throughout his life Bell also sought to promote a new relationship between religion and the arts, commissioning new work from the composer Gustav Holst and new drama from John Masefield, T.S. Eliot and Christopher Fry. He was, at the last, a figure of the 20th-century world, a friend of Gandhi and Radhakrishnan, of the pastor Martin Niemöller, the constitutional lawyer Gerhard Leibholz and the artist Hans Feibusch.

The Selected Letters and Papers of George Bell, Bishop of Chichester seeks to represent the many, interrelating dimensions of the career of a man whom the German pastor Heinrich Grűber considered as great a presence in his lifetime as Albert Schweitzer, Martin Buber and Martin Luther King.

Published:

The George Bell-Gerhard Leibholz Correspondence: In the Long Shadow of the Third Reich, 1938–1958, edited by Gerhard Ringshausen and Andrew Chandler

Forthcoming:

George Bell in the House of Lords, 1938–1958, edited by Andrew Chandler

The George Bell-Alphons Koechlin Correspondence

The German Church Struggle in an International Perspective, 1933–1954

Edited by
Gerhard Ringshausen and Andrew Chandler

BLOOMSBURY ACADEMIC
LONDON • NEW YORK • OXFORD • NEW DELHI • SYDNEY

BLOOMSBURY ACADEMIC
Bloomsbury Publishing Plc, 50 Bedford Square, London, WC1B 3DP, UK
Bloomsbury Publishing Inc, 1359 Broadway, New York, NY 10018, USA
Bloomsbury Publishing Ireland, 29 Earlsfort Terrace, Dublin 2, D02 AY28, Ireland

BLOOMSBURY, BLOOMSBURY ACADEMIC and the Diana logo are trademarks of
Bloomsbury Publishing Plc

First published in Great Britain 2024
Paperback edition published 2026

Copyright © Gerhard Ringshausen and Andrew Chandler, 2024

Gerhard Ringshausen and Andrew Chandler have asserted their right under the Copyright, Designs and Patents Act, 1988, to be identified as Editors of this work.

For legal purposes the Acknowledgements on p. viii constitute an extension of this copyright page.

Cover images: [left] Alphons Koechlin-Thurneysen (© UB Basel, Portr BS Koechlin A 1885, 3); [right] Dr George Kennedy Allen Bell (©Topical Press Agency / Stringer / Getty)

All rights reserved. No part of this publication may be: i) reproduced or transmitted in any form, electronic or mechanical, including photocopying, recording or by means of any information storage or retrieval system without prior permission in writing from the publishers; or ii) used or reproduced in any way for the training, development or operation of artificial intelligence (AI) technologies, including generative AI technologies. The rights holders expressly reserve this publication from the text and data mining exception as per Article 4(3) of the Digital Single Market Directive (EU) 2019/790.

Bloomsbury Publishing Plc does not have any control over, or responsibility for, any third-party websites referred to or in this book. All internet addresses given in this book were correct at the time of going to press. The author and publisher regret any inconvenience caused if addresses have changed or sites have ceased to exist, but can accept no responsibility for any such changes.

A catalogue record for this book is available from the British Library.

A catalog record for this book is available from the Library of Congress.

ISBN: HB: 978-1-3500-4699-3
PB: 978-1-3504-5516-0
ePDF: 978-1-3500-4700-6
eBook: 978-1-3500-4701-3

Typeset by Deanta Global Publishing Services, Chennai, India

For product safety related questions contact productsafety@bloomsbury.com.

To find out more about our authors and books visit www.bloomsbury.com and sign up for our newsletters.

The situation seems to be worse in Germany. . . . It is an extremely difficult and delicate situation. One does not want to make a false step; nor does one want by inaction to give the appearance of weakness or betrayal.

– George Bell to Alphons Koechlin, 4 October 1937

Contents

Acknowledgements	viii
Introduction	1
The presentation of the text: Editorial conventions	13
The letters, with annual chronologies	15
Appendices	311
Bibliography	323
Index	329

Acknowledgements

Our many thanks are owed to the staff at the Basel University Library and at Lambeth Palace Library in London. We also owe much to Lisa-Marie Meyer for her work on the transcriptions from the Basel archive. We are most grateful to the late Hans Florin and to Ev. Florin, Charlotte and David Evans and Nicholas Frayling for financial support. We acknowledge our many thanks to our editor, Rhodri Mogford, and to his colleagues at Bloomsbury, and to Mahesh Meiyazhagan and the staff at Deanta in Chennai. We continue to owe much to Ellen Ringshausen in Lüneburg and to the Chandler family in Chichester.

Introduction

What is the place in history of the letters of George Bell and Alphons Koechlin? The ecumenical movement of the twentieth century has all too often disappeared inside the margins of church histories which still seek to thrive in confessional and national categories. Meanwhile, the presence of Christian churches in the affairs of the world has seldom been much acknowledged by historians of politics. All of this would have surprised, and disappointed, both men, for they certainly believed that their work together represented a direct involvement with issues that were fundamental, and vital, to their age. For the unfolding history of the Third Reich created not merely a German, but an international, history. The National Socialist State created controversies which not only attracted observers in all countries but, indeed, often converted them into active participants. In no area was this more conspicuously true than in what came to be called the German Church Struggle.

It was the evolution of the international ecumenical movement in the 1920s and 1930s which made the relationship of Bell and Koechlin possible, indeed natural. They were men at large in the same world. The two first met at the great ecumenical World Conference in Stockholm in 1925. Here Bell, recently made Dean of Canterbury, was very much a figure in the foreground, not least as a primary author of the conference statement. Then a young pastor, Koechlin was there only as a substitute for a Swiss delegation but his services as a translator were soon in demand when the official interpreters proved inadequate.

The relationship of Bell and Koechlin, which is so fully documented by their letters, began in earnest in a meeting in London on 9 June 1933. As president of the executive committee of the Universal Christian Council for Life and Work, Bell now stood at the summit of the ecumenical movement. Following a request from Berlin, and after consulting with the joint secretary of Life and Work, Henry Louis Henriod, Koechlin had come from Basel with urgent news of the latest affairs in Germany. The seizure of power by the National Socialist Party (NSDAP) on 30 January had provoked a vivid, and rapidly intensifying, crisis across the German Protestant Church. Indeed, Germany was now a country being overtaken by a purposeful *Gleichschaltung* of its civil institutions by a state which established, within months, totalitarian claims. A long-developing plan to achieve the unity of Evangelical churches had now turned into a bid for power by a vigorously insurgent *Deutsche Christen* movement and a contest for a newly created position of *Reichsbischof*. Bell and Koechlin therefore met in the context of the first of many crises which would come to define what soon became known as the German Church Struggle.

This first meeting lasted two hours. It inaugurated an intensive collaboration which would prove to be profoundly influential. Both Bell and Koechlin were convinced that what happened in the German churches was no merely domestic affair but something that affected the universal church itself at a time when Protestants in all countries had come to meet, think and work together in what they rejoiced to think of as a new ecumenical age. The two men will have recognized, at once, what was at stake in this new relationship.

Alphons Koechlin

Alphons Koechlin was born on 6 January 1885 in Basel.[1] He would be the eldest of six siblings. His family had first come from Mulhouse in Alsace, and across 150 years members of the family filled leading positions in industry, politics and the army in nineteenth-century Basel. His father, Carl Koechlin (1856–1914), was an industrialist in the chemical factory of his uncle, Johann Rudolf Geigy, and he had been an active participant in the public life of the city. His mother, Elisabeth (born Iselin), died when Alphons was just eight years old. He became the first in the family to study theology and he did so at the universities of Lausanne, Basel, and Marburg. After he was ordained in the Cathedral of Basel in the autumn of 1908, he left Switzerland for more than a year; a stay in Paris was followed by another in Oxford and then a third in Edinburgh. The fruit of this time abroad was not only his confidence in the French and English languages but also a deepening knowledge of the thinking and life of the French and British churches, a knowledge which soon became the basis of his ecumenical work.

From 1910 to 1921 Koechlin served as pastor to the Protestant congregation of the little town of Stein on the Rhine in the canton of Schaffhausen. Here he became involved in the Blue Cross organization, then active in response to the problem of alcoholism, which was widespread across the community. When the cantonal church changed from being a state church to an independent one, Koechlin also worked as secretary of the new Church Council from 1915 to 1921. His theological position was essentially liberal, and while many of his peers soon revised their views in the tragic context of the Great War, Koechlin's earlier outlook appeared to be unshaken. In general, in these years he was less concerned with the problems of theology than with

---

[1] For the biography see Rudolf Lindner, 'Pfarrer Alphons Koechlin-Thurneysen', *Basler Stadtbuch* 86 (1966): pp. 26–33; Henri d'Espine, *Alphonse Koechlin. Pasteur et chef d'église, 1885–1965* (Genève: Labor et Fides, 1971); Andreas Lindt, *Einleitung in George Bell – Alphons Koechlin, Briefwechsel 1933–1954*, ed. Andreas Lindt (Zürich: EVZ, 1969), pp. 17–25; id., 'Alphons Koechlin', in *Der Reformation verpflichtet. Gestalten und Gestalter in Stadt und Landschaft Basel aus fünf Jahrhunderten*, ed. Kirchenamt der Evangelisch-reformierten Kirche Basel-Stadt (Basel: Merian, 1979), pp. 183–6; Immanuel Leuschner, 'Pfarrer Alphons Koechlin (1885–1965) – ein Mann der Oekumene und der Mission (UB Basel NL 37; VII, 2); Paul-Émile Dentan, 'Alphons Koechlin – "Schweigen können wir nicht"', in: id., *Nachgeben oder Widerstehen. Schweizer Protestanten gegen den Nazismus* (Zürich: EVZ, 2002), pp. 43–57, 147–55; Christoph Ramstein, 'Alphons Koechlin (1885–1965) – Schweizer Pionier der Ökumene', in *Aufbruch und Widerspruch. Schweizer Theologinnen und Theologen im 20. und 21. Jahrhundert*, ed. Angela Berlis, Stephan Leimgruber, and Martin Sallmann (Zürich: TVZ, 2019), pp. 380–92.

the tasks of his office in the church and with the concerns of the people at large.² He also married, on 4 June 1912, Emilie Thurneysen, who was the sister of the theologian Eduard Thurneysen, then pastor of Leutwil, a parish not far from Karl Barth, who was then busily at work in Safenwil. They would have two sons and two daughters. This marriage must have done something to cement Koechlin's place in the small but vigorous world of Swiss Protestantism.

In 1921 Basel called Koechlin back to fill the newly created position of preacher at St Martin's Church. This was not merely a city pastorate, for it was attached to the secretariat of the Church Council. Even so, the provision of the Sunday service at St. Martin's, with a sermon that was central to worship, was the most obvious public responsibility which Koechlin bore for some years to come. Koechlin was not a great pulpit orator and over time it was noted that the number of people attending the eight o'clock service dwindled. Nor did his theology alter under the growing influence of Barth's Dialectical Theology, even though he enjoyed a close friendship with his brother-in-law. In short, he remained an intermediary theologian; his thought very largely based on a spirituality which emphasized the place of personal trust in God.³ It was later that his work in missionary and ecumenical affairs would yield an eschatological perspective.

If he was not entirely at home in a congregational context, it was in his many administrative tasks that Koechlin got to know the various branches of the Basel church, their needs and possibilities, and in such a way he grew into a position of leadership. It would not have been difficult to predict that he might be elected by the local synod to be the president of the Church Council, and in 1933 this duly happened. By then he had also become the president of the city association of the YMCA and also the Swiss Association for Home Mission. In 1929, the Theological Faculty of the University of Heidelberg awarded him an honorary doctorate. Koechlin soon came to the attention of the Federation of Swiss Protestant Churches. In 1935 he was elected to the central board of the Federation and in 1941 to its presidency (a position which he held until 1954).

All of this might well have seemed unexceptional, but the parameters of conventional church life were changing. Koechlin's ecumenical commitment began in 1923 when he met John R. Mott (1865–1955) at the YMCA World Conference in Pörtschach in Austria. This great pioneer of the ecumenical movement opened his eyes to the global responsibility of the churches in the new age and brought him into the leadership of the YMCA World Federation; only three years later he would be elected its vice president.⁴ It was also in 1923 that Koechlin became a member of the committee of the Basel mission. By 1936 he would be its president, remaining in office until 1959. Meanwhile, Koechlin's commitment to Christian mission was also reflected in his teaching on mission and ecumenism at the university in Basel, where in 1941 he would be appointed an honorary lecturer. By the 1930s he was a regular participant in ecumenical conferences. It was in this context that in 1933 he became particularly drawn towards the new developments in Germany.

---

[2] See d'Espine, *Alphonse Koechlin* (see note 1), p. 17.
[3] See especially Ramstein, 'Alphons Koechlin' (see note 1), pp. 388–9.
[4] See Koechlin, 'Das missionarische Lebenswerk von Dr. John R. Mott' (1955), Basel UB, NL 37, III, 25: 'I learned a lot, if not everything, for my presidential posts'. Quoted by Ramstein, 'Alphons Koechlin', p. 384.

At their first meeting in June 1933 Bell recognized Koechlin's capabilities and saw that he might provide a vital link in his own search for reliable information, interpretation and guidance. Indeed, in this first hectic, and often bewildering, year of the 'church struggle' in Germany, the well-connected Koechlin became, almost at once, an important authority for the Bishop of Chichester.[5] Bell now gave Koechlin a new, and active, place in the counsels of the Life and Work movement at a crucial juncture. From its conference in Fanø, in Denmark, in August 1934 Koechlin regularly participated in the meetings of the executive committee. In 1937 he joined the committee which was set up to initiate the unification of the 'Life and Work' and 'Faith and Order' Movements, and to prepare for the two great conferences to be held that year in Oxford and Edinburgh. In the following years he would serve as a member of the 'Provisional Committee of the World Council of Churches (in process of formation)'. Between 1948 and 1954 he was a member of the Central Committee of the W.C.C.

Koechlin was constantly busy. Besides these ongoing ecumenical engagements myriad other activities remain conspicuous. Like Bell, Koechlin's ecumenism was invigorated by a profound humanitarianism, and he showed an alert sense of the dangers of political coercion and persecution. Their relationship represented not simply a meeting of minds but the mutual recognition of broader sympathies and affinities. Even so, they were not always entirely in tune: when they both attended a meeting of ecumenists convened by Bishop Berggrav to discuss a statement on peace negotiations at Apeldoorn in January 1940, Bell supported Berggrav's promotion of a negotiated settlement, while Koechlin was found among the sceptics.[6] During the war Koechlin chaired the World Council's Ecumenical Commission for the Chaplaincy Service to Prisoners of War; from 1941 to 1947 he headed Swiss Protestant Refugee Aid. As President of the Federation of Churches, he intervened several times with the Swiss Federal Council because of its unyielding refugee policy, especially when it asserted that the national borders be sealed to Jewish refugees in the summer of 1942. This made it possible for several hundred refugees to escape to Switzerland under the auspices of the CIMADE organization in France.[7] Meanwhile, Koechlin's important role in the rescue operation *Unternehmen Sieben* (Operation Seven) in 1941 offered further proof of the closeness of his German connections.[8] Here Hans von Dohnanyi, a brother-in-law of Dietrich Bonhoeffer and an implacable opponent of the Nazi regime, had collaborated with his employer, Admiral Wilhelm Canaris, the head of German Counter-Intelligence office, to rescue seven families by giving them papers to leave Germany for Switzerland, ostensibly as agents for operations in South America. It was Koechlin who obtained their visas while he collaborated with the tireless Charlotte Friedenthal in Berlin and with Karl Barth. The first of the party arrived in Basel on 5 September 1942. Thereafter the obstacles grew still greater, but the persevering

---

[5] See Gerhard Ringshausen, 'George Bell's Relations to the German Evangelical Church and the Problem of Information', *Kirchliche Zeitgeschichte / Contemporary Church History* 33 (2020): pp. 351–9.

[6] See W.A. Visser 't Hooft, *Memoirs* (London, 1973), pp. 116–20.

[7] Ibid., pp. 171–2. See too Marc Boegner, *The Long Road to Unity: Memories and Anticipations* (London, 1968), pp. 175–82.

[8] See Winfried Meyer, *Unternehmen Sieben. Eine Rettungsaktion für vom Holocaust Bedrohte aus dem Amt Ausland/Abwehr im Oberkommando der Wehrmacht* (Frankfurt/M.: Hain, 1993).

Koechlin overcame them, not least through further direct interventions with the highest Swiss authorities. The second group crossed the border on 30 September and were granted the right of asylum. In occupied France, meanwhile, Koechlin proved a steadfast ally of the vulnerable Saint Sergius Institute in Paris, for many years the sanctuary of many Russian Orthodox exiles from the Soviet state. He also presided over the Aid Organisation of the Protestant Churches of Switzerland, set up after the end of the war, from its foundation until 1954.

Bell was not alone in having a high regard for Koechlin's qualities. Across many years the French pastor and ecumenist Marc Boegner turned to him for 'wise counsel, based on a sure judgement'.[9] If Koechlin's relationship with Karl Barth was fruitful in the contexts of the *Kirchenkampf*, his collaboration with W. A. Visser 't Hooft proved to be no less creative during the war and, after 1945, in the years of reconstruction and ecumenical expansion. Later, Visser 't Hooft would write of him as 'among my most trusted counsellors'.[10]

George Bell, the German Church and the significance of Alphons Koechlin

When Bell and Koechlin met, Bell was of the two very much the senior figure in ecumenical affairs. The root of his own relationship with Germany lay in the Great War, a conflict in which he had lost two of his brothers. As Archbishop Davidson's chaplain he had overseen the awkward exchanges between Lambeth Palace and a number of German theologians who had in 1914 protested that their national cause was just, an opinion which Davidson had firmly repudiated. The early meetings of the Life and Work movement developed Bell's relationships with European church people in a number of important ways, and in this development the condition of German Protestantism had featured prominently. At the same time, Bell's place in inspiring and sustaining a succession of productive Anglo-German theological conferences between 1927 and 1930 was central. He came to know a number of German theologians at least adequately well and proved that he could show himself to be a credible and effective collaborator. In 1930 Bell had published a number of these papers in the Anglican journal *Theology* and then the English edition of an Anglo-German colloquium on the incarnation, *Mysterium Christi*, a volume which was matched by a German edition edited by the New Testament scholar, Adolf Deissmann.

Precious as these affinities and relationships were, Bell now needed a new source of information and guidance. Koechlin was perfectly placed to provide both. He perched on the border with Germany, by conviction and experience a European and by vocation a Christian internationalist who lived in a state which cared to cultivate cross-border exchanges. He was an experienced judge of churches and their affairs – a free citizen who lived safely in a conservative democracy who could communicate without fear or

---

[9] See Boegner, *The Long Road to Unity*, p. 63.
[10] See Visser 't Hooft, *Memoirs*, p. 365.

constraint. He was rooted in the world of the international Christian youth movements and the missionary societies too. Crucially, Koechlin was also fluent in German and English. All of this made him not only an important interpreter, mediator and source of wisdom for Bell but a superb ally. Even so, it should be acknowledged that Bell did not merely draw from Koechlin: he showed his own qualities in knowing how to make the most of his Swiss friend and how to recognize the authority of his views when so many other sources of advice, often partial, partisan or even dubious, were available to him. A contrast is not difficult to find. As chairman of the Archbishop of Canterbury's new Council on Foreign Relations, Bell's often-adversary in German matters, Bishop Headlam, invested in quite different correspondents – whom Bell appeared to keep at a distance – and accordingly achieved a quite different view of German affairs altogether.

Bell lacked a command of the German language, but this was only one of the elements necessary for an effective engagement with the crisis in the German churches. Unlike Headlam, who spoke and read German with some confidence, he had no illusions about his competence in judging the travails of another country. He took care and saw at once the need to create a solid, consistent body of advice and experience around himself. He learnt how to listen and be influenced. Perhaps still more to the point, what he did not possess in language he largely made up for in a rigorous, sympathetic understanding of souls. His German friends and allies knew how to value this. They looked on the bishop of Chichester with confidence and an admiration which often yielded affection. The correspondence of Bell and Koechlin presents these qualities in a unique fashion. Bell allowed himself to be led by a friend whose advice consistently rang true to him and whose voice became an important part of a consensus of ecumenical opinion which soon cohered in support of one vital element of the church struggle, the Confessing Church.

The German Church Struggle in an international perspective

The German Church Struggle, or *Kirchenkampf*, has inspired an immense interest among historians both inside Germany and outside.[11] The forces which provoked the crisis across the German Evangelical Church in 1933 were not new. The search for

---

[11] Over the years the research has led to an almost unmanageable number of publications. The following are considered standard works: Klaus Scholder, *The Churches and the Third Reich*. Vol. I: *Preliminary History and the Time of Illusions 1918-1934*; Vol. II: *The Year of Disillusionment: 1934 Barmen and Rome* (London: SCM Press, 1988); continued by Gerhard Besier, *Die Kirchen und das Dritte Reich. Spaltungen und Abwehrkämpfe 1933-1937* (Berlin: Propyläen, 2001). Kurt Meier, *Der evangelische Kirchenkampf. Gesamtdarstellung in drei Bänden*. Vol. I: *Der Kampf um das 'Reichskirche'* (Halle: Niemeyer, licence Göttingen: Vandenhoeck & Ruprecht, 1976); Vol. II: *Gescheiterte Neuordnungsversuche im Zeichen staatlicher 'Rechtshilfe'*, ibid., 1976; Vol. II: *Im Zeichen des zweiten Weltkrieges*, ibid. 1984. Besides special sourcebooks the most complete collection of sources is still Joachim Beckmann (ed.), *Kirchliches Jahrbuch für die Evangelische Kirche in Deutschland 1933-1944*, 2nd ed. (Gütersloh: Güterloher Verlagshaus, 1976). For State-Church Relations see John S. Conway, *The Nazi Persecution of the Churches 1933-45* (London: Weidenfeld and Nicolson, 1968); for a comprehensive collection of sources: *Dokumente zur Kirchenpolitik des Dritten Reiches*. Vol. I – 6/2 (Munich, 1971 – Gütersloh, 2017).

national church union had been making cautious progress for some years and the structures which oversaw such work were already in existence. The nationalist *Deutsche Christen* movement had been growing for some time, and the two movements which defined that strain had amalgamated in 1932. What had changed was the political context in which these currents collided. Many of those who now participated in the controversy were well-established names in the ecumenical scene: indeed, it is hard not to sense that much of the critical reaction which the controversial figure of Ludwig Müller now inspired owed something to the apprehension that he was a newcomer to the life of the churches, and one who lacked the conventional qualifications which those who led church affairs generally possessed. His principal claim, that he enjoyed the patronage of Hitler himself, simply made him all the more questionable. Equally, the *Deutsche Christen* themselves enjoyed the sense that they represented the power of a vigorous new force and now possessed a youthful ability to shake the old ecclesiastical oligarchies out of their offices. The arrival of the Hitler regime and the new mood of national unity galvanized the *Deutsche Christen*. They knew that their moment had come.

What followed was a contest between parties which vied for power in the darkening contexts of a new dictatorship. In Germany it was widely viewed as a dispute over the integrity of the Christian church and the purity of its faith, however, these things may be judged. Abroad the church struggle was seen as a contest between church and state, a confrontation made inevitable by the lengthening claims of a ruthless totalitarian power. This discrepancy between views created a good deal of awkwardness, not least because international opinion emphasized the very political realities which much German opinion preferred to avoid. More than this, the ensuing history of the German churches yielded a quality of complexity which was exceedingly difficult to follow, let alone interpret. The *Deutsche Christen* movement was one in which moderates were to be found in uncomfortable company with fanatics. Meanwhile, their opponents, first in the *Jungreformatoren* (Young Reformers' movement), then in the *Pfarrernotbund* of Martin Niemöller and his allies and then, by June 1934, the Confessing Church, professed theological principles which were largely obscure in the Anglophone world. Moreover, the Confessing pastors saw themselves as in no primary sense critics of the National Socialist state with which the *Deutsche Christen* sought to identify the Church. There were still other layers. The *Kirchenkampf* was conducted in the contexts of denominational identity (for the Lutherans and the Reformed Protestants were seldom in tune with each other and only in the Old Prussian Church were they united) and of regional churches (which proceeded on quite independent lines and with their own councils, synods and – in three Lutheran churches – bishops). At certain points these authorities were reconfigured by the victories, or defeats, of those who contended for power. At times they converged and at others broke apart again. It required some conviction and perseverance to maintain that essential issues of virtue and justice defined all of this. Bell was one of those who insisted that they did. Across the Protestant world the Confessing Church commanded the loyalty of most observers because it appeared to stand firm against the corruption of the Christian faith and its ecclesiastical order and because it was a persecuted church whose pastors experienced coercion and even prison.

It is tempting to place the *Kirchenkampf* in a category of its own and one barely connected with other dimensions which defined the National Socialist era, like the development of racial policy, the generation of state propaganda, the persecution of political critics and the changes in cultural or educational policy. In fact, these many themes interwove constantly. The *Kirchenkampf* revealed much about the nature of that state as it went about its work, reordering what it inherited, suppressing challenges or cultivating particular constituencies and alliances. It showed that Hitler himself could be both active and remote, how he might delegate, intervene directly when a certain advantage was to be gained, and remove himself from view almost altogether. In such circumstances the credulous thought him oblivious of the activities of his deputies, while only the convinced critics held him responsible for everything.

Historians have come to recognize the *Kirchenkampf* in three periods: from 1933 until the end of 1934 much was defined by the contest between the *Deutsche Christen* and a growing body of critics which soon coalesced in the form of the Confessing Church (*Bekennende Kirche*). The race for the new position of *Reichsbischof* placed in the foreground two figures: Ludwig Müller, the candidate of the *Deutsche Christen*, and Friedrich von Bodelschwingh, the pastor of Bethel, and nomination of the committee which had pursued church union. Although Müller enjoyed the active patronage of the state and capitalized on the insurgent qualities of his supporters, his victory in the contest was short-lived. An attempt to impose an Aryan Paragraph on the Church at large and a growing number of coercive measures which demanded conformity provoked a bitter response. Although like the *Deutsche Christen* the pastors of the Confessing movement never represented more than a minority within the churches at large, they were intellectually vigorous and tenacious too. In 1933 and 1934 agitation on their behalf broke out across the Protestant world and proved embarrassing to Hitler. In only two years the *Deutsche Christen* movement, never a unified whole, alienated many who were on its margins, fractured and went into a steep decline. By contrast, what became the Confessing Church achieved a viable solidity and coherence, winning admiration from many abroad who, like Bell, found that the activities of its members rang true to their own vision of Christian courage and their sense of what was now at stake in Germany. When this church solidified at Barmen in May 1934 and published a vivid confession of faith, international opinion was both moved and impressed.

Yet the minds of the Confessing pastors were not necessarily consistent on the role of the state in this dispute. They accused their opponents of importing politics into the life and doctrines of the church and they were firmly hostile when the state showed partiality to them. At the same time, they did look to Hitler himself to intervene. When Müller's star waned a second stage in the dispute emerged. Between July 1935 and February 1937 a new central committee was established under a minister of state, Hanns Kerrl, with a view to incorporating one regional church after another within a national whole. Kerrl was certainly a party man, but he persuaded many in the centre that he was, more than anything else, a bluff, practical figure who had no axe to grind, no explicit ideological agenda and no wish to impose. Perhaps as important was the figure of Wilhelm Zöllner, a trusted pastor and an ecumenist, who came out of retirement in February 1936 to chair the new Reich Church Committee under Kerrl. In Britain, Bishop Headlam could see nothing wrong in the new policy and he soon alleged that if anyone was now being unreasonable it was the pastors of the Confessing Church who remained resistant to it. Bell and Koechlin were not convinced by this: behind these committees could be seen an unrelenting determination to build a state church which incorporated a variety of ideological admissions and oversaw myriad ongoing depredations. To them it came as no surprise when Zoellner's central committee found its task impossible and disintegrated in the midst of official proscriptions and arrests.

What followed would be far more attritional: the resisting part of the Confessing Church, especially in the Old Prussian Church under the government of the *Deutsche Christen*, was steadily driven underground by the confiscation of funds, the closure of institutions and sporadic arrests and a far more explicit, sustained sense of threat. In this new period the arrest, trial and detention of Martin Niemöller, acquired an international notoriety, confirming the justice of the Confessing Church and the tyranny of the state in the eyes of foreign journalists, church people and observers at large. They responded with a loud campaign in his defence. By now, however, the National Socialist state had grown indifferent to critical opinion and had begun a tremendous acceleration of its foreign claims. Oversaw by the German Church Chancellery, under Friedrich Werner, in 1939 Kerrl handed over the leadership of the Reich Church to a Spiritual Council of Confidence. Its members were the Regional Bishop of Hannover August Marahrens, the *Deutsche Christen* Regional Bishop of Mecklenburg Walther Schultz and Vice-President of the Prussian Church Johannes Hymmen. From March 1940 these men were joined by Otto Weber, a representative of the Reformed Churches.

Of all this Bell and Koechlin were observers. But they did not pursue understanding for its own sake. It was a determination to play an active part in the *Kirchenkampf* which produced the need for information. This found a place within a vigorous coalition of international opinion much of which referred to the evolving patterns of the ecumenical movements, their committees and conferences, but a good deal of which emerged within the contexts of national political opinion and public life. Indeed, the dramas of German Christians were vivid in the moral imagination of many British people who read their newspapers, were alive to the world in which they lived and hardly knew of such bodies as *Life and Work* or *Faith and Order*. They saw an oppressive dictatorship that imprisoned its critics, persecuted Jews, harassed priests and pastors and vulnerable minorities at large. They were also encouraged to believe that while the National Socialist movement had overturned political opposition almost at once and provoked barely a flicker of resistance, it was above all in the churches that the stoutest refusal to bow the knee to Baal had occurred. All of this made figures like Bell and Koechlin a part of a far wider discourse, and one that included politicians and political institutions, trades unions and universities too. For how should any formal body which presented international connections now associate with their equivalents in Germany itself?

When war came in September 1939 the connection between German affairs and the world at large was abruptly severed. In March 1940 Koechlin could only confess to Bell that he now heard very little of the church in Germany. Bell saw that Christians in Germany were now to face a long, and bitter, night and so it proved to be. Many 'young brethren' of the Confessing Church were conscripted for military service; parishes were often maintained as well as possible by clergy wives. For these six harsh years what information emerged from Germany was sporadic and often haphazard. British debates about the war itself could look more and more remote to those who had once been allies on the continent. When Karl Barth was troubled to hear of Bell's speech on peace negotiations in the House of Lords in December 1939 it became the task of Koechlin to interpret Bell's views to him – not that Barth was in any degree convinced.[12] As a neutral country, Switzerland provided a precious channel between communities, and at the offices of the World Council of Churches in Process of Formation, Willem Visser 't Hooft was certainly busy, maintaining private (and secret) contacts. Bell would find himself a figure at large in the neutral states. Meanwhile, from December 1941 it was the Unification Work (*Einigungswerk*), overseen by the Regional Bishop of Württemberg, Theophil Wurm, that provided the basis for the foundation of the Evangelical Church in Germany. This crystallized after the war at the Church Conference in Treysa on 27–31 August 1945.

After the war

In April 1945, shortly before the German surrender, Koechlin travelled through liberated France to London for a meeting of the British Council of Churches. In Switzerland he was appointed president of a new body, 'Interchurch Aid'. One of the most important events that defined this period was the meeting of an ecumenical delegation, including both Bell and Koechlin, with German church leaders in Stuttgart in October 1945.[13] The declaration which proceeded from this gathering paved the way for participation by German Protestants in the post-war ecumenical movement.

The decision of the University of Basel to confer upon Bishop Bell an honorary doctorate in wartime was certainly a striking one. Koechlin's part in this is obscure – and it may well have occurred without him altogether – but he rejoiced warmly in it. Only after the war, and after the great ecumenical service in Geneva in February 1946 was it possible for Bell to visit Basel and receive it. Koechlin joined him for both of these occasions. Now, for the most part, their relationship no longer followed a principal purpose and it is significant that the immense crisis of post-war trans-continental migration and refuge, a phenomenon which overtook millions and which did draw Switzerland heavily into the foreground, provided no new context for a revival of an old alliance. The letters which Bell and Koechlin wrote to each other now relaxed into a state of retirement and a sporadic exchange of seasonal civilities. The two met for the last time at the second General Assembly of the World Council of Churches in Evanston in 1954. In the same year, at the age of seventy, Koechlin resigned from most of his various offices in the church, remaining only president of the Basel Mission until

---

[12] See Appendix 1.
[13] See Martin Greschat (ed.), *Die Schuld der Kirche. Dokumente und Reflexionen zur Stuttgarter Schulderklärung vom 18./19. Oktober 1945* (Munich: Chr. Kaiser, 1982); Gerhard Besier and Gerhard Sauter, *Wie Christen ihre Schuld bekennen. Die Stuttgarter Erklärung 1945* (Göttingen: Vandenhoeck & Ruprecht, 1985).

1959. Bell resigned as Bishop of Chichester at his seventy-fifth birthday on 4 February 1958 but he died in the same year, on 3 October.[14] Alphons Koechlin died on 8 May 1965, a few months after his eightieth birthday.

The historical importance of the letters

The Bell-Koechlin letters make a unique contribution to our understanding of the German *Kirchenkampf*. Above all, it can be seen how its many narratives emerged and interwove in the contexts of international opinion and involvement. The whole correspondence lasted almost two decades. The great weight of the relationship fell upon the period 1933 to 1939, and in this it achieved two peaks in intensity: between 1934 and 1935, when the leaders of the Protestant churches of western Europe and North America became direct participants in the turmoil in Germany, and then between 1937 and 1938, the time of the great Life and Work conference at Oxford and of Martin Niemöller's incarceration, trial and imprisonment. Yet across these seven years the letters maintain a remarkable consistency and coherence in attention and in discussion, and it is possible to trace many striking lines of development as they emerged and matured. We see both the strength and the fragility of the information that the two men sought to interpret; we observe the patterns of thought which moved beneath the surface of events and begin to see why certain courses of action occurred and why others were avoided. We also see clearly Koechlin's role in contributing to the drafting of the ecumenical statements which were issued. With the coming of war and the closing of borders, the correspondence ended almost at once, and almost entirely. When Bell and Koechlin met again it was in the context of post-war ecumenical encounters, a new age which saw the creation of the culmination of many hopes and labours in the creation of the World Council of Churches. Bell's elegiac, almost valedictory, return to Basel in 1946 brought a moving reunion, and of this their letters provide an eloquent testimony.

The two men certainly came to know each other well. What did Bell owe to Koechlin? First, a great deal of valuable information, for Koechlin was closer to the networks of discussion which directly emanated from the German church. Koechlin knew Barth almost as a neighbour, and in emphasizing Barth's significance sympathetically he certainly influenced Bell's own attitudes to a figure whose theological thought was often found to be an obstacle to Christians in Britain. He was able to help Bell to navigate a way through the complicated relationships which were at work in the heart of the ecumenical movement in Geneva, not least between the troubled Hans Schönfeld and the French ecumenist Henri-Louis Henriod. But Koechlin also provided Bell with a distinctive sense of emphasis. When the murders of June 1934 took place in Germany he was in no doubt as to what they exposed in the political state which now governed Germany, and because he saw this clearly, Bell saw it clearly too. Yet if Bell was often led by Koechlin it would also be true to say that they had reached comparable views of the German church struggle in their own way. Both saw the crisis as one expressing

---

[14] See Koechlin's obituary in *Kirchenblatt für die reformierte Schweiz* 114, 1958, pp. 326–8.

the inevitable consequence of a totalitarian state which sought to fashion everything in the image of its own power and ideology. This is to say that Bell would not have learnt so much from Koechlin if he had not first sensed their interpretive affinities. Ultimately, the two men came to know each other as allies in a vital cause for they laboured together in defence of Christian freedom and integrity in a menacing world of political coercion. It is in this context that their letters find their essential meaning and significance.

The presentation of the text

Editorial conventions

An excellent edition of the correspondence of Bell and Koechlin, translated into German, was published by Andreas Lindt in 1969. Lindt's book drew primarily from the Koechlin archive in Basel and also from the Bell collection in Lambeth Palace Library. This project predated the thorough organization of the Bell archive which took place under Melanie Barber at Lambeth Palace in the 1980s, and at least some of the material would seem to have been transferred to Basel. In particular, the letters which were written across the first half of 1938 did not return. In this edition we have worked from both collections, cross-referring as necessary. This has produced a quantity of new material which has developed, or altered, perspectives. Whereas the Koechlin set presents a clear and continuous sequence, at Lambeth the letters are dispersed across the volumes of papers dealing with German church affairs between 1933 and 1939, and elsewhere. Indeed, searching for the letters in the Bell archive is not always straightforward but the rewards are very real, for the volumes establish a vivid context for the relationship and they also establish myriad connections. While the Lambeth archive preserves many – but not all, evidently – of the enclosures which Koechlin sent to Chichester, it lacks, naturally, the handwritten letters which Bell occasionally sent to Koechlin.

In the present edition our editorial approach has been conservative throughout and, for the most part, only the most necessary minor alterations have been made to the text. Double inverted commas have been replaced by single inverted commas. Names of publications have been italicized. Minor typing mistakes have been rectified, and where stylistic infelicities have made the substance obscure (while Koechlin's English was excellent it could, at points, be awkward and unclear), the most minor adjustments have been made. Very occasionally indeed, where grammar or syntax has been obviously ill-considered, or a word has fallen awkwardly, a rearrangement has been made. Now and then modest changes have been made to paragraphing in order to ensure the flow of the text. German terms, often but not always rendered in inverted commas, have not been italicized but preserved in the form in which they have been written or typed. The term 'National Socialism', is often rendered 'national-socialism' by Koechlin. We have left this undisturbed, allowing for minor variations when they occur. The spelling of Basel/Basle has been standardized as Basel, while Hanover/Hannover has been standardized as Hannover and Uppsala/Upsala has been standardized as Uppsala.

While historians have long written of the 'Confessing Church', it was conventional in Britain during the *Kirchenkampf* to speak of the 'Confessional Church': this has been preserved. Koechlin often wrote to Bell as 'Lordbishop' or as 'Lord Bishop': there seems to be little point in preserving this difference and the latter has been consistently adopted. Very occasional simple mistakes in grammar (e.g. now and then Koechlin writes 'is' instead of 'are') are corrected. Furthermore, Koechlin often writes 'stays' where an English writer would prefer 'stands': we have decided to change this in order to achieve clarity. It may be acknowledged that the grammar and syntax of particular sentences by Koechlin will read awkwardly (to write in a second language can involve such questions quite as much as the choice of words), but we are sure that the reader will soon adjust to this. Now and then upper cases (e.g. Pastors) have been changed to lower cases (pastors). In quite a number of letters enclosed documents have fallen out of sequence or disappeared altogether from both archival collections. It is possible that individual documents will have found their way into further volumes of the Bell Papers which comprise gathered material from across the period. In such cases we have done what we reasonably can.

The chronological tables will provide the reader with detailed pictures of the twists and turns in what is an intricate narrative. This approach has allowed us to keep footnotes to a sensible level and often they provide biographical details, cross-references, necessary elaboration on a particular point or simply encouragement to look into further material.

The letters of George Bell and Alphons Koechlin, 1933–1954

1933

30 January	Adolf Hitler is appointed chancellor of a coalition government with Göring and Frick in the cabinet. Papen is vice-chancellor.
1 February	Dissolution of the *Reichstag*.
3–4 February	The Administrative Committee of Life and Work meets in Berlin. Bell is present and discusses the situation in the German churches with leaders there.
4 February	The presidential 'decree for the Protection of the German People' sets out new limits on the press and public assembly.
6 February	Archbishop Lang announces the appointment of the new Archbishop of Canterbury's Council on Foreign Relations under the chairmanship of Bishop Headlam of Gloucester at the Church Assembly.
27 February	The *Reichstag* fire.
28 February	The Hitler government assumes emergency powers by presidential decree.
March	Ecumenical study conference at Rengsdorf discusses 'basic theological principles' which may determine the churches' social teaching.
5 March	New elections to the *Reichstag*: the Nazi Party wins 288 seats making it the largest single party, but failing short of an overall majority.
5–7 March	A wave of *Gleichschaltung* across Germany co-ordinates the states of Hamburg, Hesse, Lübeck, Bremen, Baden, Saxony and Württemberg.
8 March	Frick, the Minister of the Interior, announces the creation of the first concentration camps.
13 March	The creation of the ministry for popular enlightenment and propaganda under Josef Goebbels.
21 March	The 'Day of Potsdam': 21 March 1933. Otto Dibelius preaches in the Potsdam Garrison Church at the opening of the new *Reichstag*. The 'Malicious Practices Law' prohibits criticism of the regime.
23 March	Hitler's government issues a declaration emphasizing the role of the churches for the preservation of the nationhood.

	The *Reichstag* passes the Enabling Law by 444 votes to 94 of the Social Democratic Party, for a first four-year term.
31 March	The first Law for the Co-ordination of the Federal States is passed.
1–3 April	Boycott of Jewish businesses across Germany.
3–5 April	Congress of the *Deutsche Christen* movement in Berlin calls for a unified *Reichskirche*, founded on the Führer principle and adopting an Aryan Paragraph.
7 April	Law for the Restoration of the Professional Civil Service and the Second Law for the Co-ordination of the Federal States.
23 April	Hermann Kapler, president of the German Church Federation, is authorized to arrange a new constitution for the Reich church. He will collaborate with the Lutheran bishop of Hannover Marahrens and the Reformed pastor of Elberfeld Hermann Hesse as the 'Three-men-Committee'.
25 April	Law against the 'Overcrowding' of German schools passed, limiting places for Jews to 1.5 per cent. Hitler appoints Ludwig Müller as his 'representative with full powers' to 'promote all efforts directed towards the creation of our German National Church'.
2 May	Abolition of free trades unions in Germany; the new German Labour Front under Robert Ley is established four days later.
4 May	The Three Men Committee meets in the Loccum monastery to produce an outline constitution for a united church; Ludwig Müller attends.
5–6 May	The Administrative Committee of Life and Work meets in London. Bell now expresses his concern about the German churches in a letter to Hermann Kapler.
10 May	Public book burning takes place in a number of German cities and towns.
20 May	Kapler's committee issues the 'Manifesto of Loccum'.
23 May	Ludwig Müller is appointed *Schirmherr* ('Protector') of the *Deutsche Christen* movement. He now becomes the movement's candidate for the new position of *Reichsbischof* of a new, unified church.
27 May	The Manifesto of Loccum is approved by the Church Federation. It nominates Friedrich von Bodelschwingh as its candidate for the position of *Reichsbischof*. With this an election campaign for the position begins.
June	In response to the unfolding dispute, Archbishop Lang, Bishop Bell and other church leaders in Britain prepare a public declaration on the 'religious liberty and constitutional rights of the Church'.
6 June	Hermann Kapler retires from church affairs.
14 June	*The Times* publishes a critical letter on the German churches by Bishop Bell.

24 June	Reichskultusminister Rust appoints August Jäger state commissar for church affairs in Prussia. Jäger appoints sub-commissars, in so doing depriving the church of administrative authority and assuming full administrative powers himself. Bodelschwingh retires. The Protestant Church of the Old Prussion Union is now supervised by the police. Pastors accused of hostility to the government are dismissed. This provokes an intervention by President Hindenburg, whom Hitler meets in East Prussia. Hitler now passes responsibility for church affairs to Frick. The state commissars are removed.
27 June	The bishops agree to Müller taking over the leadership of the Federation of Protestant Churches; that night he has the Church Federation office staffed by SS men.
28 June	Müller appoints himself chairman of the German Church Federation.
30 June	Hitler commissions Frick to negotiate on behalf of the Reich and with Müller to secure agreement between the groups on the new Reich Church Constitution. The party apparatus throws itself into the election campaign in support of Müller.
1 July	The Dean of Chichester A. S. Duncan-Jones flies to Berlin in search of information. He meets Hitler and is impressed.
2 July	A Day of Penitence and Prayer declared by the superintendents of the Prussian Church. The leader of the *Deutsche Christen*, Joachim Hossenfelder, converts this into a day of Praise and Thanksgiving to mark the intervention of the State.
4 July	The public declaration drafted by British church leaders is suspended after advice from German sources.
5 July	The Catholic Centre Party officially disbands.
6 July	Hitler announces the end of the 'national revolution'; Jäger transfers the right of church leadership to Müller, who proceeds to complete a new church constitution. The representatives of the regional churches accept this on 11 July and the Reich Cabinet, on 14 July, agrees to it.
7 July	Jäger transfers the right to the highest leadership of the Prussian Church to Müller.
8 July	The Concordat with the Holy Seat is signed; it is ratified on 20 July.
11 July	Beginning of the official campaign to elect representatives who will in turn appoint members of a synod to 'acclaim' a new *Reichsbischof*. The two candidates in the contest are Bodelschwingh and Müller.
14 July	All political parties in Germany are suppressed and a one-party state is announced. Jäger dismissed as state commissioner.

22 July	Hitler speaks a day before the election and declares his support for Müller.
23 July	The *Deutsche Christen* win the election with about 75 per cent of the seats in the new synod. There is an outcry and also claims of corruption.
29–30 July	Members of the German Faith Movement meet at Eisenach and ask for legal recognition of the movement.
4 August	Müller is appointed *Landesbischof* of Prussia by the senate of the Prussian Church. Elections now take place for provincial synods and their representatives to the general synod.
25 August	Müller outlines his view of a national church.
5 September	Evangelical Church Synod of Prussia meets. Müller is acclaimed as first bishop of Prussia. Future synods are abolished. The Führer principle is adopted and also an Aryan Paragraph for the office holders of the church. Critics face dismissal. A critical group, 'Gospel and Church', protests and walks out. Powers previously enjoyed by the general synod are now appropriated by a church senate. These include the power to revise the constitution of the church.
9–12 September	Life and Work conference at Novi Sad, Yugoslavia. The German church delegation is led by the new 'ecumenical bishop' Theodor Heckel. Heckel proves a querulous guest, not least for questioning the principles outlined by the 1925 conference in Stockholm. Bell, as chairman, manages to defuse the crisis but proposes that anxieties about antisemitism and the suppression of freedoms in Germany be recorded. He proposes to write to Müller and other German church leaders to express their concern. Heckel abstains from this motion.
11 September	The creation of the 'Pastors' Emergency League', or *Pfarrernotbund*.
12 September	The synods of the Regional Churches of Brunswick and Schleswig-Holstein endorse the Aryan Paragraph; on 16 September the Synod of the Church in Saxony. Three churches resist the tide: Hannover, Württemberg and Bavaria.
21 September	The first German national synod takes place at Wittenberg. The new Pastors' Emergency League affirms its opposition to the Aryan Paragraph. In this it is supported by the theological faculty at Marburg and other academics.
22 September	Creation of the Reich Chamber of Culture as a national organization of all cultural workers.
27 September	Müller is now adopted by the national synod at Wittenberg as *Reichsbischof*. He appoints a Spiritual Ministry to re-codify church law. A petition of protest, signed by 2,000 pastors, is distributed.
October	On behalf of Müller, the *Deutsche Christen* leader Joachim Hossenfelder and Professor Karl Fezer visit Britain as guests of Frank Buchman of the Oxford Groups movement.

20 October	The *Pfarrernotbund* is now overseen by a Council of Brethren. Not yet does it possess a unified structure.
24 October	Bishop Headlam publishes a letter, 'In German Eyes', in *The Times*. While Headlam views his letter as a model of detachment, it is seen by many as supportive of the Nazi state and provokes controversy.
13 November	Assembly of the *Deutsche Christen* movement at the Sportpalast in Berlin to mark the 450th anniversary of Luther's birth. Chaired by Hossenfelder it includes a provocative speech by Krause. A resolution demanding the dismissal of pastors opposing state religious policy is passed. A storm of criticism and many resignations follow. Müller dismisses Krause but there is now a growing sense that the movement is fracturing.
13 November	Bishop Bell's letter to Müller, agreed at Novi Sad, is published in the press.
16 November	The national synod suspends acts passed by the provincial synods and so suspends the application of the Aryan Paragraph.
19 November	Pastors of the *Pfarrernotbund* read from their pulpits a protest against the church government.
29 November	Hitler rejects direct state intervention, leaving Müller to force the resignations of Hossenfelder, Weber and Werner from the Reich Church cabinet.
30 November	Creation of the Gestapo.
1 December	Passing of the law to ensure the unity of party and state.
2 December	Müller creates a new Spiritual Ministry for the Church.
4 December	Müller forbids pastors to belong to any ecclesiastical groups.
8 December	Müller announces that the Aryan Paragraph has been suspended. Efforts to create a unified German Church will continue.
12 December	Bell writes to Müller requesting information on the state of the Christian Youth Movement.
15 December	Heckel writes to reassure Bell that the Sportpalast meeting did not represent the majority of views in the *Deutsche Christen* movement.
19 December	Müller passes authority over the Evangelical Youth Movement to Baldur von Schirach, leader of the Hitler Youth. Bishops Wurm of Bavaria and Meiser of Württemberg deliver an ultimatum that the acts of the Spiritual Ministry have no legal basis because it lacks a theological member stipulated by its own constitution.
21 December	Hossenfelder resigns from all church offices and from the leadership of the Deutsche Christen. He is succeeded by Christian Kinder.

J.H. Oldham[1] to Bell, 8 June 1933, Lambeth Palace Library, Bell Papers Vol. 4, fol. 73.

'Particularly glad to see Koechlin tomorrow suggest lunch Chichester Bishop'[2]

My dear Bishop,

Dr Koechlin, from Switzerland, is at present in London. I do not know whether you know him. I have as much confidence in his judgement as in that of any of the Christian leaders whom I know on the Continent. He has recent information regarding the present critical situation of the Church in Germany. I think that if you can spare the time you would be interested to meet him and have a talk. The only possible day on which he is free is Friday of this week and if it suited you he would be willing to come to Chichester. I am writing also to the Archbishop[3] who is at Canterbury and he might wish to see him. If the Archbishop is able to see him on Friday he might not be able to fit in visits to both Canterbury and Chichester. It is possible, however, that the Archbishop may not be free at such short notice and in that case Koechlin could come to Chichester. If you would like to see him and are free, perhaps you would let me have a wire tomorrow. If I do not hear from you I will assume that the plan is not convenient.

Yours very sincerely,

1 Joseph Houldsworth Oldham (1874–1969): Scottish layman, missionary leader and genius of ecumenical conferences and productive gatherings; secretary of the International Missionary Council, 1921--38; from 1912 editor of the *International Review of Missions*. In 1934 Oldham became the chairman of the research committee for Life and Work and, furthermore, of the research commission which prepared the Oxford Conference in 1937. He would go on to publish the influential *Christian News-Letter* and play a significant part in the early history of the World Council of Churches.
2 Added in Bell's hand.
3 Cosmo Gordon Lang, Archbishop of Canterbury, 1928–42. Lang was deeply concerned with the affairs of the German churches in the Third Reich and provided constant support for Bell in his interventions and enterprises. See Andrew Chandler, *British Christians and the Third Reich: Church, State and the Judgement of Nations* (Cambridge: Cambridge University Press, 2022).

Bell to Archbishop Lang, 10 June 1933, Lambeth Palace Library, Bell Papers Vol 4, fol. 77.

My dear Lord Archbishop,

I saw Dr Koechlin yesterday about whom J.H. Oldham had written. He told me the latest news of the German Church situation. He bore out in great detail what Dr Schönfeld[1] had said in the letter a copy of which your Grace has seen. He wanted some Churchmen in England to be informed of the situation so that they might watch developments. I asked him what he thought could be done in fact. He said that what would be a very great help indeed would be if your Grace were willing to make an official, but of course private, enquiry at the Foreign Office asking that the British Ambassador at Berlin[2] should be invited to report to the Foreign Office on the present position in the German Church, and particularly the agitation on the part of German Christians [i.e. *Deutsche Christen*] against the official Church leaders. Dr Koechlin thought that if such an enquiry were privately made, and the British Ambassador let Baron Neurath, the Foreign Secretary,[3] know that your Grace had enquired, it would show Hitler that a false step which would make the Church really a cog in a political machine would be really injurious to the reputation of the Church, and also the State, in the eyes of thoughtful people in England.

Yours affectionately and dutifully,

1. Hans Schönfeld (1900–54): German theologian and national economist. Since 1929 'scientific assistant' at the International Social Science Institute in Geneva, employed on behalf of the German Federation of Protestant Churches. After its transformation into the Study Department of the Ecumenical Council for Life and Work he became its director (1931–46). Schönfeld's relationship with Theodor Heckel caused doubts in the Confessing Church and also in churches abroad. The strain of his difficulties would exact a tragic toll.
2. In June 1933 Sir Horace Rumbold (1869–1941) retired from his role as ambassador to Berlin, to be replaced by Sir Eric Phipps (1875–1945). Phipps became ambassador to Paris in 1937.
3. Konstantin Freiherr von Neurath (1873–1956): Minister of Foreign Affairs 1932–8; replaced by Joachim von Ribbentrop in February 1938, Neurath became Reich Protector for Bohemia and Moravia 1939 to 1941. As a practicing Protestant he intervened in central government policy at certain points when crisis threatened to overtake the churches, citing the embarrassment caused to the foreign policy of the Reich in its relations with other countries. He also supported ecumenical protests against the Aryan Paragraph in order to influence the leadership of the Reich Church. See Boyens, *Kirchenkampf und Ökumene*, pp. 67, 109.

Koechlin to Bell, 14 June 1933, Basel, UB, NL 37, VI 1 (carbon), LPL Bell Papers Vol. 4, fol 95 (r. & v.).

Sir,

I am anxious to express to you once more my sincere gratitude for the very kind reception you have given to me Friday last.[1] I am holding the two hours I was privileged to spend with you in grateful memory.

The purpose of my visit was an extraordinary one. It was, as I quite feel, somewhat unusual to bring to you on my own initiative information and suggestions concerning the German church situation. I was and still am quite aware of the responsibility it meant to ask a leading personality of the church in England to take an action in so delicate a matter.

I would not have done anything if it had not been my firm conviction that the developments were of the utmost importance for the churches of Germany, for their oecumenical relations in the great church movements as well as in the mission field, and if I had not known that leading German personalities were anxious to hear some voices expressing the thought and anxiety of other churches.

Since I came home the situation has again developed. Dr. Kapler, as you will have read, has resigned, apparently under the pressure of the difficulties created by his opponents.[2] The thought of a popular election of the Bishop, which had been announced at the beginning of last week, has apparently been given up, as everyone seems to see that it would lead to quite an impossible situation. The efforts are tending towards some compromise between the national-socialist current and those holding for Dr. von Bodelschwingh.³

Though they on all parts declare to stand for a complete independence of the church, it remains thoroughly true that the political influences are prevailing far more than their adherents see or believe it. The situation is in principle as acute and critical to-day as I told you Friday last.

May I in closing tell you that one of my informations [sic] was not quite accurate. I told you that the vote for Bodelschwingh had been taken by 83 to 3 voices. In fact it was taken by 83 to 11, the three churches of Mecklenburg, Hamburg and Württemberg possessing together 11 voices, having voted against him.⁴ Please excuse that I have misled you in this question. When I got the information by a quite trustworthy man, I had expressively asked him if I could rely on the correctness of his saying. Returning home yesterday, I found the correct indication.

You will receive under separate cover as an expression of my gratitude the little report I had written some years ago on the Stockholm Conference.⁵ [It] may be that you find time to have a short look in it.

Will you kindly remember me to Mrs. Bell and believe me, Sir,

faithfully yours,

1   Bell and Koechlin had met on 9 June 1933.
2   Hermann Kapler (1867–1941): a lawyer in civil service, now at work in the consistory court in Berlin under the direction of the Upper Church Council, the central executive organ of the Protestant Church of the old Prussian Union (*Evangelischer Oberkirchenrat der Evangelischen Kirche der Altpreußischen Union*). In 1921 Kapler had become non-theological vice-president and, in 1925, president of the Upper Church Council and, as such, president of the German Protestant Church committee (*Deutscher Evangelische Kirchenausschuss*), the executive organ of the Federation of the German Protestant Churches (*Deutscher Evangelischer Kirchenbund*). An active ecumenist, in 1925 he had been the head of the German delegation at the Stockholm World Conference of the Churches. After the death of Nathan Söderblom in 1931 he became the head of the Universal Christian Council for Life and Work together with the Anglican Theodore Woods, Bishop of Winchester, and then, after Woods's death in 1932, with George Bell. In the spring of 1933 Kapler tried to meet the increasingly insistent demands for a renewal of the German Church by concessions and by drawing up a new constitution of the German Protestant Church. But when his candidate as Reichsbishop, Friedrich von Bodelschwingh, began to falter, Kapler resigned on 8 June 1933. See Carsten Nicolaisen, 'Kapler, Hermann', in *Religion in Geschichte und Gegenwart*, 4th ed., vol. 4 (Tübingen: Mohr Siebeck, 2001), col. 80.
3   Friedrich (familiarly named Fritz) von Bodelschwingh (1877–1946) had in 1910 followed his father as head of the Bethel Institution of the Inner Mission, the largest diaconal enterprise in Europe. In view of his reputation in German Protestant life, leading figures in the Young Reformation Movement (*Jungreformatorische Bewegung*) promoted him as their favoured candidate for the new position of Reichsbishop and he was elected on 27 June by the German Protestant Church Committee and the representatives of the regional churches. But the *Deutsche Christen* movement did not accept this election and Hitler refused to receive Bodelschwingh.
4   In fact, the three opposing churches had only eight voices: Württemberg 4, Mecklenburg-Schwerin 2, and Hamburg 2 voices. See Gerhard Ringshausen, 'George Bell's Relations to the German Evangelical Church and the Problem of Information', *Kirchliche Zeitgeschichte/ Contemporary Church History* 33 (2020): p. 354, n. 18.

5 See Alphons Koechlin, 'Die Weltkonferenz für Praktisches Christentum in Stockholm 19. bis 30. August 1925', in *Auftrag des Schweizerischen Evangelischen Kirchenbundes dargestellt* (Basel: Friedrich Reinhardt, 1926).

Bell to Koechlin, 14 June 1933, Basel, UB, NL 37, VI 2 (typewritten).

Private
Dear Dr. Koechlin,

It was a great gain and pleasure to have that good talk with you on Friday about the German Church. I thought much about it afterwards. Though I hesitated lest I should be causing embarrassment rather than helping, I decided to write to *The Times*. The letter ultimately sent, a copy of which from *The Times* of to-day I send herewith, was very much what I drafted when you were here, but better in composition. I most earnestly hope that I have not caused trouble – but the contrary. I shall be thankful for anything you can tell me of any reactions. I was moved to write by my confidence in yourself and your own strong feeling that a letter to *The Times* over my name at this particular juncture would do real good.

The Bishops of Gloucester[1] and Lichfield[2] wrote off as I suggested to Dr. von Bodelschwingh to wish him well. I have asked the Archbishop of Canterbury to approach the Foreign Office with a view to a report on the situation from the British Ambassador in Berlin.[3] His Grace has promised to consider my suggestion very carefully, but not unnaturally feels a considerable hesitation at taking any step, however slight, which even suggests intervention.

I shall be thankful for any news you can tell me as the days go by.
Once more with kindest regards,

Yours very sincerely,

1   Arthur Cayley Headlam (1862–1947), Bishop of Gloucester, 1923–45. Headlam was widely recognized as the outstanding ecumenical voice in the Church of England at this time. Formerly Professor of Dogmatic Theology at King's College London, 1903–16, then Regius Professor of Divinity at Oxford, 1918–23, he had given a particularly influential series of Bampton Lectures in 1920. In the same year he was a crucial figure in the innovative ecumenical discussions at the Lambeth Conference.
2   John Kempthorne (1864–1946), Bishop of Lichfield, 1913–37. He had previously been suffragan bishop of Hull, 1910–1913. He was an active member of the World Alliance for promoting friendship through the Churches.
3   The incoming ambassador to Berlin that month was Sir Eric Phipps (1875–1945), distinguished diplomat: envoy extraordinary and minister plenipotentiary to Austria, 1928–33; ambassador to Germany, 1933–7. He warned the British government with growing urgency against the aggressiveness of the National Socialist regime. Subsequently he was ambassador to France, 1937–9.

Enclosure: **Bell to the Editor of *The Times*, 12 June 1933, published 14 June 1933.**[1]

'POLITICAL CONFLICT'

Sir,– With your permission I should like to call attention to a crisis in the Evangelical Church of Germany which may have serious implications in both the political and religious fields.

In your issue of June 6 your Berlin Correspondent stated that 'the political conflict in the German Protestant Church became more marked than ever at Whitsuntide'. In ordinary circumstances it would be improper for an English Churchman to make any comment in a public way on such a situation. But the circumstances are not ordinary, and by the result of the present – please note the word – 'political conflict' in the German Church we, as well as members of many Churches in Europe and America, may be profoundly affected.

The situation at present is this. A strong national religious movement is now astir in Germany. It is partly expressed in the plan of uniting the different Evangelical Churches in a single Protestant Communion in the German State. This unification, with the full assent of Herr Hitler himself, was entrusted by the representatives of the German Churches to a committee of three – Dr. Kapler, the president of the Evangelical Church Federation, the Lutheran Bishop Marahrens,[2] and the Reformed Church leader, Pastor Hesse,[3] of Elberfeld.

The three plenipotentiaries had many tasks, but their most urgent was the nomination of a Reichsbischof, or Primate. They were in very close touch with the different trends of Christian opinion throughout Germany. At the end of their deliberations they unanimously recommended the appointment of Dr. F. Von Bodelschwingh. This nomination was significant. Dr. Von Bodelschwingh is very well known as a spiritual leader without any political attachment. He is the superintendent of the great Christian Social Institute, or mission, at Bethel, near Bielefeld, which his father founded at the end of the last century.[4] His work at this mission has brought him into touch with men of all political opinions. Here thousands of sick and epileptic people are cared for, and through it there travel tramps and unemployed men and lads from the ends of Germany. Dr. Von Bodelschwingh is not only a spiritual force and in touch with German scholarship, but a man of uncommon administrative ability. His nomination was announced in the week before Whit Sunday. It was widely welcomed and when put before the delegates of all the German Evangelical Churches who had been specially summoned to Berlin was endorsed by the overwhelming majority of 83 votes to three. So far all was well. Dr. Von Bodelschwingh was undeniably the choice of the Church and he immediately took up the duties of his office.

It is against this appointment by the votes of the Church that a political agitation has now begun. The promoters of the agitation are the body known as the 'German Christians'. This body consists entirely of members of the National Socialist Party, pledged to promote that party's political principles. Its leader is Pastor Mueller.[5] The object of the agitation is the overthrow of the Primate chosen by the Church and the putting in his place of Pastor Mueller as a Nazi Primate. It is an hour of great danger for the German Church, and it is significant that the 'German Christians' are being given the full use of the Nazi machinery, the radio, and the Press.

Conflict between Churchmen competing as rivals for election to the post of German Primate would in any event be a grave misfortune. But still graver, and much more damaging to the religious influence of the Church, would be the supersession, through political means, of the Primate whom the Church has chosen by the nominee of an all-powerful political party. Herr Hitler, in his official declaration of policy on becoming Chancellor, solemnly guaranteed the independence and constitutional rights of the

German Evangelical Church.⁶ It is the adhesion to this solemn guarantee which is of such vital importance to-day.

Yours faithfully,

1. This first letter to *The Times* on the German Church proved a nervous enterprise. Before sending it Bell had consulted his friend at the British Foreign Office, Alan Leeper. This makes clear to what extent Koechlin was the prime-mover in the proposal that Lang should approach the Foreign Office and that Bell himself should write to *The Times*: Indeed, Bell later told Hans Schönfeld (14 June 1933) that the letter was drafted in Koechlin's company: 'It is because you have told me of your full confidence in him and his ability to deal with the matter that I have trusted his recommendation.' The next day Bell admitted to Schönfeld that he had written the letter 'with considerable hesitation and on the strength of Dr Koechlin's strongly held view that such a letter would be a useful warning.' To Leeper Bell had written, 'I am ready to write such a letter but I do not want to do harm by it. Would it be considered interference on an Englishman's part with the German question?' (10 June.) Leeper promptly replied that he was 'personally entirely in favour' of such a letter: 'The risk of driving the Nazis to do the very thing you dislike must of course be faced. But I think the risk of their doing so if no one says anything here is probably considerably greater.' Leeper felt 'pretty sure' that the Foreign Office would not wish to offer official advice, but 'they would personally see no objection'. These views Leeper confirmed in a second note on Foreign Office paper, on 12 June. Bell dispatched these to Lambeth Palace so that Archbishop Lang could see them for himself. See Bell Papers, Vol. 4, fol. 78, 83 (r. & v) 84 (r.&v.), 94 and 98.
2. August Marahrens (1875-1950): the regional bishop of the Lutheran Church of Hannover (1925-47) was venerated in the pastorate as *pastor pastorum*. Marahrens was a leading member of the Lutheran World Convention (and from 1935 chairman of its Executive Committee) but his role during the Third Reich remains controversial. Actively (though cautiously) sympathetic to the Confessing Church, he was briefly deposed by the *Deutsche Christen* in December 1934. In 1939 he signed the Godesberg Declaration, which declared the Nazi world-view to be binding for the church too. In wartime his complexities deepened, and in 1943 he refused to support Bishop Wurm in signing a letter of protest against the persecution of the Jews. He would resign as bishop in 1947, to some extent because of the objections of the British occupying powers but also because German and international ecumenical opinion by then found him a compromised figure and a source of frustration.
3. Hermann Albert Hesse (1877-1957): Reformed pastor in Elberfeld and, since 1929, Director of Studies at the Reformed Seminary for Preachers and lecturer at the Elberfeld Theological School. With Marahrens and Kapler, Hesse was the co-author of the new 1933 Reich Church constitution; from 1934 to 1946 he was Moderator of the Reformed Confederation and a leading figure in the Confessing Church; in wartime he would be a firm critic of National Socialist policies and in 1943 he was arrested, detained and then imprisoned with his young son, the pastor Helmut Hesse, in Dachau. Helmut Hesse died there.
4. Friedrich von Bodelschwingh senior (1831-1910) had begun his work at Bethel in 1872.
5. Ludwig Müller (1883-1945): the military district pastor in Königsberg (East Prussia) was the only Protestant clergyman known to Hitler, who appointed him plenipotentiary

for questions of the Protestant Church on 25 April 1933. In this capacity he participated in the Three Men Committee on the reorganisation of the Evangelical Church. On 4 August 1933, the Old Prussian Church Senate, with a majority of German Christians, elected him president of the Higher Church Council with the title of bishop, and on 27 September 1933, he was elected Bishop of the Reich by the new National Synod. For Müller at large see Martin Schneider, *Reichsbischof Ludwig Müller. Eine Untersuchung zu Leben, Werk und Persönlichkeit* (Göttingen: Vandenhoeck & Ruprecht, 1993).

6   Hitler's government declaration, 23 March 1933.

Bell to Koechlin, 20 June 1933, Basel UB, NL 37, VI 3 (typewritten); LPL, Bell Papers, Vol. 4, fols. 217–18.

My dear Dr. Koechlin,

Many thanks for your letter of June 14th which crossed one from me to yourself. I am grateful, for what you say and also for the report about Stockholm[1] which you send me. I am delighted to have this.

The difference between 3 and 11, 'in the vote',[2] especially in the circumstances you describe of there being three Churches, is very slight, and I do not think material.

Perhaps, if it is not troubling you too much, you could give me a list of the Churches actually concerned in the Unification, including the Reformed Churches. I am very anxious to get any information from time to time.

I am rather afraid from what I hear that the Archbishop of Canterbury[3] feels that it would be rather too much interference for him to take the step which you and I talked over. Any further news that you can tell me will interest me greatly. *The Times* is now giving reports as to what is happening from time to time.

Yours sincerely,

1   See Koechlin to Bell, 14 June 1933, n. 5.
2   Ibid., n. 4.
3   On 19 June 1933 Lang's chaplain Alan Don wrote to Bell that the Foreign Secretary Sir John Simon had replied to his 'private and personal' letter that 'Here is no persecution as in the case of the Jew [*sic*] but one of internal ecclesiastical administration in which H.M. Government have no *locus standi* whatever and it seems to me that by displaying any direct interest in it we should merely be exposing ourselves to a rebuff.' Don added, 'His Grace is naturally abiding by his advice.' On 21 June 1933 Bell wrote to Leeper, 'I think both our Chiefs are unnecessarily cautious.' Bell Papers, Vol. 4, fols.103 and 107.

Koechlin to Bell, 27 June 1933, Basel UB, NL 37, VI 4 (carbon).

Dear Sir,

I am very thankful for your kind letter of June 20th. To answer your question concerning the different German churches, I am sending herewith the list I found in the handbook of the churches, edited 1930 by the International Christian Press Commission, Berlin-Steglitz, Beymestrasse 8.[1]

As you will have seen, the events have developed in a very dangerous way. Bodelschwingh stood as long as he was able to stand, though different church leaders and churches, having originally voted for him, had submitted themselves to the Nazi pressure and refused to give him their further support.[2] The 'German-Christians' dictated to all their members to stand against Bodelschwingh. They managed to refuse him the possibility of seeing Hitler and even Hindenburg and were able under the pretext that the church could not put order into the existing divisions, to get in Prussia a Kommissar for the church business. This Kommissar has put aside Kapler and the former church governing body. He has put aside Generalsuperintendent Schian[3] in Breslau, who dared to stand for Bodelschwingh and to speak openly against the German-Christians' convictions.

To illustrate the situation, I can tell you that all the social work of Professor Siegmund-Schultze[4] has at once been closed and that all his papers were searched through in the hope that he might be compromised by any foreign letter. He himself was a prisoner for some days, could get his liberty again, but on the advice of his doctor and his nearest friends has decided to leave the country like a refugee. He passed Basel Sunday last and will hardly be able to go back to Germany in the time to come. We are trying to help him to get out of Germany his wife and his children, hoping that they might get a permit to come over to Switzerland.

I know confidentially that Professor Karl Barth[5] in Bonn is facing the great possibility to be seized by the Nazis and that he has already taken all his measures necessary in such a case of urgency. However, he is decided to stay on in his post as long as he ever can for the sake of the church, especially of the reformed church of Western Prussia, of which he is the leading theological advisor. It will be relatively easy to help him if anything is happening, as he is still a Swiss citizen. Please do not make any official use of these facts. I mention them only to illustrate the situation.

If one asks how it is possible that so many most respectable and even leading church men of Germany are following the trend of thought of the German-Christians, one is facing the following facts:

1.) They see in the Hitler-movement the only possible solution, even the way of God having saved Germany from the danger of Bolshevism and having given back to the Germans the national feeling they had lost. They see in the awakening of the nation even a religious awakening after the time of Marxism and feel as church men obliged to throw their influence, the upbuilding forces and deep educational possibilities of the church into this great national rising movement. They think it necessary to go new ways, to risk a part of the church's existing formal life, to be trusted by the movement and to get the possibility of decisive influence on the leaders and on the people. They are afraid of reactionary political and economic forces standing behind the former church leaders and even behind Bodelschwingh. For these main reasons they are inclined to accept Wehrkreispfarrer Müller as bishop because he is fully trusted by Hitler and his movement, even though they know that as a religious and theological personality there can be no comparison between him and Bodelschwingh.

2.) A second very peculiar reason is that some of the theologians and church leaders feel the danger of racism swallowing the Christian principles and think the only way to overcome it is to stay in the midst of the nationalistic movement unfolding in that battlefield the flag of Christ. They do not seem to see how much the cause of Christ might be and is compromised by such an alliance and how impossible it is to overcome the nationalistic Satan by a nationalistic Balzebub who remains Balzebub even if he becomes [a] German-Christian nationalist.

Nevertheless there are signs of hope giving in the dark picture the possibility of confidence. I am meeting these very days at the convention of the Basel Mission men whose thoughts concerning all these questions might be very different from mine, but who very earnestly, even fervently, stand for the cause of mission, the cause of only propagation of the gospel of Christ. There you feel quite united in spite of all differences of view and judgement. You experience the reality of the fellowship in Christ, the living Christ, realizing in himself the unity of his Church.

I am glad to know that in your prayers and thoughts and with your sympathy you are following the situation and am thankful that you are giving me the possibility of sharing with you the concerns I feel we have in common.

With the expression of this deep gratitude, I am,
faithfully yours,
(To inform also Dr. William Adams Brown[6] I send him a copy of this letter.)

1 A commission established by the Life and Work Movement and chaired by August Hinderer (1877–1945), the head of the Protestant Press Association for Germany. This later became the Ecumenical Press Service.
2 August Jäger (1887–1949) was appointed state commissioner for the Evangelical Church of the Old Prussian Union, after Bodelschwingh stepped back from the contest to be Reichsbishop on 24 June. Jäger also became the ministerial director in the Prussian Ministry of Culture and head of the Church Department there. He was also an official administrator for Protestant church affairs in the Reich leadership of the Nationalist Socialist Party. On 19 April 1934, Reichsbishop Müller appointed him 'legal administrator' of the German Protestant Church: with this title, he functioned as a member of the Spiritual Ministry in the Reich Church Administration. But Jäger still ran into difficulties. The incorporation of the Württemberg and the Bavarian Regional Churches, in which he was instrumental, failed in the autumn of 1934. On 26 October 1934, he resigned from his positions. He would later play a ruthless part in the German occupation of Polish territories, earning particular notoriety for his persecution of the Catholic Church. In 1940 he was probably the decisive inspiration behind the 13-point programme of Gauleiter Greiser, which deprived the church of its status as a public corporation in the Warthegau, presaging a brutal reorganization across the German Reich.
3 Martin Schian (1869–1944): from 1911 professor of practical theology at Gießen University and from 1924 Generalsuperintendent (regional bishop in the Protestant

Church of the old Prussian Union) in Breslau (Silesia). On 24 June 1933 he was suspended from office, 'with immediate effect', by the first decree of the State Commissioner Jäger.

4   Friedrich Siegmund-Schultze (1885–1969): eminent German theologian, internationalist, pacifist and prodigious ecumenist, writer in social ethics. In 1914 he was a co-founder of the World Alliance for promoting International Friendship through the Churches and the pacifist International Fellowship of Reconciliation. From the beginning of the Third Reich, Siegmund-Schultze worked for an 'International Aid Committee for German (Protestant, Catholic and Mosaic) Emigrants of Jewish Descent'. On 23 June, he was forced to leave Germany. He and his family found a new home in Switzerland. See Heinz-Elmar Tenorth and others (eds), *Friedrich Siegmund-Schultze (1885–1969). Ein Leben für Kirche, Wissenschaft und soziale Arbeit* (Stuttgart: Kohlhammer, 2007).

5   Karl Barth (1886–1968): eminent and influential Swiss systematic theologian, whose landmark commentary on the Epistle to the Romans had been published in 1919 and revised in 1921; professor at Münster, 1925–30 and then Bonn, 1930–5. Barth was the leading theologian of the Confessing Church, especially as the main author of the Barmen Declaration (29–31 May 1934). He was not only brilliantly original but vastly productive, and over a long life he became a subject for scholarship in his own right. See, most recently, Christiane Tietz, *Karl Barth. A Life in Conflict* (Oxford: Oxford University Press, 2021).

6   William Adams Brown (1865–1943): American Presbyterian and leading ecumenist; a man much involved in Christian social service and settlement projects in New York where he was, until retirement in 1936, professor of systematic theology at Union Theological Seminary. Later he became general secretary of the Commission of the Churches established during the Second World War.

Bell to Koechlin, 1 July 1933, Basel UB, NL 37, VI 5 (typewritten).

'Private'

My dear Dr. Koechlin,

Very many thanks for your letter of June 27th and for the information which you give me concerning the different German Churches. I am very glad to have this.

I am deeply interested in what you say about the present situation. I saw Fräulein Lucas,[1] the Private Secretary of Siegmund Schultze, in London on Wednesday, twice. At that time she thought that he was a prisoner and not likely to be released from Germany. I am thankful that he is free at any rate.

This is a letter sent to you rather urgently to let you know that the Dean of Chichester, the Very Rev. A. S. Duncan-Jones, as Vice-President of the Church of England Council on Relations with Foreign Churches, left by air for Berlin this morning, and will reach Berlin this afternoon.[2] He has gone as an observer to report to the Archbishop of Canterbury and the Council on the situation. It was represented to the Archbishop that it was specially important that a responsible English Churchman should be in Berlin for tomorrow.

What you say about the trend of thought of the German Christians is very interesting, though it shows how serious and sad the situation is. To-day's news of Hindenburg's intervention[3] is a sign of great hope.

The Dean's address is:- Grand Hotel am Knie,
                        Berlin-Charlottenburg.
I shall be thankful for any further information.

During Thursday and Friday the question was being closely considered by the Archbishop of Canterbury, amongst others, as to the possibility and advisability of a declaration on the part of the British Churches, headed by the Archbishop, and of Life and Work and the World Alliance jointly, viz. two separate declarations following one another protesting against the attacks on the spiritual independence of the Church. I have written to Dr. Cadman[4] in U.S.A., and other enquiries about signatories are being made. But we are also – and this is the most important point – trying to find out, especially through Fräulein Lucas who has returned to Holland and is in touch with German Church leaders, whether such a declaration or protest would embarrass our friends in Germany, or whether it would help them. Much, no doubt, depends on what is said in such a declaration. I enclose a draft. The Dean of Chichester will return on Tuesday or Wednesday and we shall hear more from him. I should however be very thankful to know your own opinion in the matter, quite privately.

Yours sincerely

1. Gerda Lucas: In mid-June Siegmund-Schultze sent his co-worker in the Social Working Group Berlin-East to Holland to prepare for the opening of an aid centre for refugees from Germany. After the closure of the Ulmenhof children's home by the SA, he sent her to London, on 24 June, to inform church leaders there about the church situation in Germany.
2. Arthur Stuart Duncan-Jones (1879–1955): formerly a London priest, he became dean of Chichester in 1929, the year in which Bell became bishop there. He remained in this post until his death. Vigorously opinionated, he was deeply committed to the League of Nations, active in the Church Assembly and able to maintain a broad range of international and ecumenical commitments. He also spoke German confidently.
3. Hitler visited Reich President Paul von Hindenburg (1847–1934) on 29 June 1933 in Neudeck (East Prussia) Hindenburg used this opportunity to press Hitler at once to restore peace and order in the Protestant Church. One day later, 'as an evangelical Christian as well as the head of the Reich', he wrote to the chancellor of his serious concern about the church controversy: 'German Protestant Christians are deeply moved by these disputes and by the concern for the inner freedom of the Church. A continuation or aggravation of this state of affairs must result in grave harm to nation and fatherland.' This letter was published by all German newspapers, except the National Socialist *Völkischer Beobachter*.
4. Samuel Parkes Cadman (1864–1936): born and nurtured in Yorkshire Methodism, he soon moved to the United States, where he won an impressive reputation as a Methodist minister and then became, for thirty-five years, a Congregationalist minister in Brooklyn, New York. In these years he became well-known as a daily columnist for the *New York Herald Tribune*, a writer, broadcaster and ecumenist. He was a Christian firmly hostile to antisemitism.

Enclosure: **Draft, Basel UB, NL 37, VI 5 (typewritten).**

Draft.
In the name of the Christian communions which we represent we desire to make an earnest protest against attacks on the liberties and constitutional rights of the Churches in the German State which were guaranteed by Chancellor Hitler in Reichstag speech of March 23. German church members and leaders as loyal and patriotic German Citizens do not dispute authority of State in all purely state concerns. But in spiritual matters they have a spiritual allegiance. Such high-handed actions as those recently reported to have been taken by German government against spiritual independence and properly elected authorities of Church cause widespread distress in whole Christian world.

Koechlin to Bell, 3 July 1933, Basel UB, NL 37, VI 6 (carbon); LPL Vol. 4, fol. 145 (r. & v.).

Dear Sir,

I received this morning only the letter you sent me by air mail July 1st.

I can confirm [to] you that Siegmund-Schultze, Mrs. Siegmund-Schultze and four children, that is the whole family, anxious to leave Germany, are safe in Switzerland.

I am very thankful that The Most Rev. the Archbishop of Canterbury has sent an observer to Berlin, who will, I am certain, be able to bring to you the news I am getting relatively late.

As to a pronouncement to be made by Churches and Church Groups, I know from different German church leaders, that they hope we might outside of Germany find a word of protest and serious warning in view of the nearly incredible developments taking place presently. In a telegram of June 29th, printed in a leading Swiss Paper, I found the following note:

> An S.A. division occupied the building of the German evangelical Church Federation, the organization comprehending the whole Western protestantism, in which all the established churches are represented on an equal basis.[1] The leaders of Church Federation were dismissed and its members not allowed to enter the building. The protector of the German-Christians, the army-pastor Müller, referring to the full power received by Hitler, appointed himself to the directorship of the German evangelical Church Federation. He passed the businesses of the office to Admiral Meusel, a high navy-officer.[2] Müller himself takes the chairmanship of the Church Council, the powers of the Church Day and of the other organs.

In the draft you sent me, I miss, if I may be allowed to say so, a note sufficiently strong to be understood by the hard-headed Germans. I should like also to suggest a strong reference to the deepest foundation of all church organizations. I tried to put my thought in a certainly insufficient draft which you kindly will accept as the expression of my personal feeling. If you think that something of it might be useful for the public protest you have in view, you are of course at liberty to use my proposal as you think it wise.

I will gladly send you further information of importance, if ever possible, though I am leaving for a month's holiday next week. But you might always reach me through my Basel address, as I am not leaving Switzerland.

I am going tomorrow to Geneva and hope to see Professor Choisy[3] and Mr. Henriod.[4]

Faithfully yours,

1. On 28 June Müller occupied the premises of the Church Federal Office, accompanied by a detachment of the SA. This 'seizure of power' was followed by his first decree: 'The German Protestant Church is advised into a state of emergency; the absolutely necessary unity of people and church is in danger. This state of emergency requires extraordinary measures. In agreement with the State Commissioner for the Evangelical Church of Prussia, I therefore take over the leadership of the Federation of Protestant Churches for the sake of the Church and the Gospel, as authorised representative of the Reich Chancellor.' See Joachim Beckmann (ed.), *Kirchliches Jahrbuch für die Evangelische Kirche Deutschlands 1933-1944*, 2nd ed. (Gütersloh: Gütersloher Verlagshaus / Gerd Mohn, 1976), p. 24 (translation: Gerhard Ringshausen).
2. Ernst Meusel (1881–1933) had retired from active service as a naval officer on 30 September 1930 with a simultaneous promotion to the rank of rear admiral. He was one of Müller's closest collaborators in the summer of 1933.
3. Jacques Eugène Choisy (1866–1949): Professor of Church History at Geneva University (1909–39), pioneer of the ecumenical movement; actively involved in the founding of the Federation of Swiss Protestant Churches, whose Council he chaired from 1930 to 1941.
4. Henry Louis Henriod (1887–1970): conspicuous Swiss pastor and ecumenist; joint general secretary of the World Alliance for Promoting International Friendship through the Churches, 1932–8.

Enclosure: **Draft, Basel UB, NL 37, VI 6 (carbon).**

Draft.

In the name of the Christian communions which we represent, we desire to make an earnest protest against the present attacks on the religious liberty and the constitutional rights of the Churches in the German Empire, especially in Prussia. These liberties and rights are based on fundamental principles inherent in the Gospel of Jesus Christ and the character of the Church. They were guaranteed by the Chancellor Hitler in his programmatic speech before the representatives of the nation in the Reichstag, March 23rd 1933.

We are certain the German church members and leaders, to whatever fraction [sic] they might belong, as loyal and patriotic German citizens do not dispute authority of state in all purely state concerns. But in a spiritual matter they are bound by an allegiance to our Lord Jesus Christ, to deny it, even under extreme pressure of political and state forces, would mean to deny the only Lord of the Church. To refuse the duly instituted church leaders the possibilities of governing the organized Church in the realm of their indispensable constitutional rights and to monopolize by high-handed actions, as those recently reported, all church government in the hands of state officials, is creating a situation of great concern and distress for all Churches connected to the German evangelical Church in the fellowship of the spirit and in cooperation for God's kingdom all over the world.

Bell to Koechlin, 4 July 1933, Basel UB, NL 37, VI 7 (handwritten).

4 July 1933

[*Secretarial note*: Please call Dr Koechlin at Basel after 19.30 this evening.]

Dear Dr Koechlin,

Yours of 3rd inst. Just to hand (5 pm.) I am *most* grateful and value your draft which is a real improvement. I write hurriedly because what you say (July 3) of the German Church leaders' attitude to a protest from outside Germany is different from what Schönfeld said (29 June). He (and 'at present' Siegmund-Schultze) deprecate such protest – and also Dr Menn – as likely to hinder and embarrass. I suppose the question is what is really happening under Hindenburg's initiative? Any further light you can throw on expediency & helpfulness of a protest by Life and Work (and by Abp. Of Canterbury) when you have it will be welcome. I don't want to say or do what our German friends would dislike.

Yours sincerely,

Koechlin to Bell, 7 July 1933, Basel UB, NL 37, VI 8 (carbon).

Dear Sir,
I am confirming the telegram I sent to you just now:
'After consultation Schönfeld agree postponing action.' When your letter of July 4th arrived, I was absent from Basel. So I could not get in contact with Dr. Schönfeld before yesterday night. Having heard him, I see that [as] in fact the conference, due

to the intervention of Hindenburg[1] [is] taking place to-day, it would be unwise to publish an international protest, before one knows what will be the outcome of these decisive conferences. Dr. Schönfeld also had latest and rather encouraging news from the Rhineland, dealing with the attitude of the pastors Sunday last. In many parts of Germany the attitude of pastors seems to have been strong enough to let the German-Christians feel that they cannot go too far. My advice of last week was mainly based on news I had received indirectly from Karl Barth, who now might also be of a different opinion than he was, though he thinks it quite possible that from one day to the other his teaching might be not only interrupted, but entirely cut down.[2] From a private letter of one of his students I know that those holding a position against the German-Christians are afraid they might not even get the permissions to pass the examinations if they are following other theological lines than the 'official' ones.

I hope and pray that the whole situation might be led by God, who has ways we do not see, to a far better solution than we are inclined or able to think possible.

Faithfully yours,

1 See Bell to Koechlin, 1 July 1933, note 3.
2 This may be an echo of the prohibition of the Social Democratic Party, of which Barth had been a member, but Minister Rust himself explained to Barth that he had no intention of restricting his teaching activities. On 14–25 June Barth wrote his famous pamphlet 'Theologische Existenz heute!' (Theological Existence to-day!), a text which criticized not only the *Deutsche Christen* but also the Young Reformation Movement. He even sent a copy to Hitler, on 1 July. This pamphlet assured his readers that as a university professor he sought only 'to do theology and only theology'. Barth was in touch with Hesse, who called him to Berlin on 2 July to discuss the new constitution, but Hesse's attitude seemed to him too yielding to the cause of the *Deutsche Christen*.

Bell to Koechlin, 10 July 1933, Basel UB, NL 37, VI 9 (typewritten).

My dear Dr. Koechlin,

Very many thanks for your letter of July 7th. I quite understand. I am grateful for the trouble you have taken. The Dean of Chichester was in Berlin from July 1st to July 5th and saw Hitler.* He also saw many Church leaders including Müller. It was clear that anything in the nature of a protest from outside Germany would be embarrassing to our friends, so I am sure that we must do nothing for the moment.[1]

I am much interested in what you tell me about Karl Barth and his theological students. What an extraordinary situation! Do please keep me informed. I wonder very much what happened at the Friday conference with Frick.²

Yours sincerely,

*He was a little too easily impressed by Hitler's assurance, I think!

1 Material concerning this visit, written by Duncan-Jones himself, may be found in Andrew Chandler (ed.), *Brethren in Adversity: Bishop George Bell, the Church of England and the Crisis of German Protestantism, 1933-1939* (Woodbridge, 1997), pp. 47-8, 52-8.
2 Wilhelm Frick (1877–1946) member of the *Reichstag* 1924–45. On 23 January 1933 he was appointed Minister of State for the Interior and National Education in Thuringia (so becoming the first National Socialist minister in Germany). At this time Frick was one of the most influential Nazi politicians, but he was soon eclipsed. As early as March 1933 Frick had to cede the primary areas of his ministry to the new Reich Ministry for Popular Enlightenment and Propaganda, established for Joseph Goebbels. A year later, he lost further responsibilities to the new Reich Ministry for Science, Education and National Formation. In 1936 he lost authority over the German Police to Heinrich Himmler.

Bell to Koechlin, 27 September 1933, LPL, Bell Papers, fols. 217–18 (carbon).

My dear Dr. Koechlin,

It was a great pleasure to meet you in Basel, and my wife and I warmly appreciated all your kindness in guiding us to so many interesting places in Basel, and so hospitably entertaining us at your house.

I am sending by separate post a little book I wrote three or four years ago about the Church of England, as a memento of our visit.¹

I should be most grateful if you would from time to time let me know what happens in the German Church. I suppose the National Synod met yesterday in Berlin but *The Times* gives no report of the proceedings and one cannot be sure of getting reports in the English press regularly. I should be very grateful if you could let me know anything of a decisive character which the National Synod does, for example if the Non-Aryan paragraph is adopted by the National Synod² could you let me know, and send me the text of the paragraph and any Resolution if possible, and anything else of a vital character. We are having a Meeting of the Church of England Council on Foreign Relations shortly, and the question of the position in Germany is coming up. I have read Karl Barth's brochure with the keenest interest, and thank you very much for giving me a translation. I have also now got a translation of the Constitution of the German Church, and of Bishop Müller's letter accompanying it.

Are you, I wonder able to tell me what is the position in the Roman Church as to priests with a Jewish parent or grand-parent?[3] Have they been expelled or are they being protected in any way? Are their Church members, are their Church officers, given preferential treatment over Protestants?

I wonder whether you have any idea of the number of Protestant pastors involved, apart from the still greater number of Church members with Jewish blood? I am told by some Jewish friends here with whom I am in touch, as Secretaries of the German Refugees Hospitality Committee, that the investigation which is to be completed on September 30th will show over a quarter of a million persons of Jewish parentage or grand-parentage and the implication is that the majority of these are Christians by religion. I wonder if that really is an exaggeration?

If you felt able to write to me on the above points, and also to give me your own criticism of the things which seem to you most disastrous in the present development of the German Evangelical Church, and the ways in which it is betraying its precious trust, it would be an enormous help to us here.

Yours very sincerely,

1. This would appear to have been Bell's *A Brief Sketch of the Church of England* (London: SCM Press, 1930).
2. In view of the reactions of the foreign countries the Ministry for Foreign Affairs intervened on 22 September and the Non-Aryan paragraph was withdrawn.
3. The Non-Aryan question was only a problem in the Protestant Church where it was pressed by the *Deutsche Christen* Movement.

Koechlin to Bell, 30 September 1933, Basel UB, NL 37, VI 10 (carbon); LPL, Bell Papers, Vol. 4, fols. 220–22 (r and v).

Dear Sir,

Your very kind letter of September 27th reached me yesterday morning, just when Dr. Lilje, the general secretary,[1] and Dr. von Thadden, the President of the German Christian Student Movement,[2] met here in my house with Mr. Maury, the general secretary of the World's Student Christian Federation[3] to discuss with him the issues created by the new German situation. I took the opportunity of discussing the points you raised with these two men of truly oecumenical spirit, who both are very well informed of what happened and what is happening.

I cannot give you a clear report of the proceedings of the National Synod, but I think it is important to let you know the following facts:

The church elections of July 23rd are without any shadow of a doubt the result of strong political pressure, partly even terror of methods elsewhere not ever allowed in a regular political life and of the impossibility for the minority to express publicly its opinion and to answer untrue attacks. Lilje, whose words I am trying to translate, said that all these expressions are much too mild to give a true account of what has happened. He and Thadden affirmed that in districts where not 20% are German-Christians, this movement succeeded through nearly unbelievable tricks to get 90% of the mandates. The whole organisational structure of the church – that is the conviction I had to come to – is built up on untruth and the will to get the power at all costs. If you think that the National Synod has been nominated by the majority of the Synods of Prussia, Thüringen etc. so elected, you do not wonder that the German-Christians have got with a few exceptions all the votes. The day of the opening of the National Synod the official[s] of the German-Christians issued a public statement saying that Bishop Müller had reaffirmed its full loyalty to the German Christian movement and had expressed his firm purpose to fulfill his duties in closest confidence and accord with Hossenfelder, the leader of this movement. That means a complete submission of the first Reichsbishop to the will of the leaders of the German Christian movement.

In this movement an important development took place. The moderate elements who have had some influence have been put aside, f.i. Professor Fezer,[4] who had been member of the provisional ministry of the Bishop. Hossenfelder and with him the radical wing took his place. Of five members of this ministry, being the closest cooperating group of the Reichs Bishop, only Bishop Schöffel of Hamburg[5] is not [a] member of the German-Christians.

All signs point to the probability that during the next weeks and months the prominent pastors being not of this tendency will be sent to some lonely little parish in the woods and in the fields, without having an opportunity of expressing their thought in some periodical or other paper. A free expression of thought is no more possible in the German church. The religious youth movements are still in danger to see their existence questioned [sic].

As to the Christian Jews, Lilje has no certainty as to their number, but he believes it might be around 250,000. The pastors who lost their office for the reason of the Aryan paragraph are relatively few. But even lower church work like bible school teaching is closed to the Christians of half or even quarter Jewish origin. The race and not the baptism is the criterion necessary for admittance to any church work.

Lilje thinks that the state would not have asked the church to accept such consequences of its own attitude. The very sad fact is that this church movement of the German-Christians [acts] by its own will and thanks to its[,] in this and other points [,] antibiblical attitude has forced its attitude to become church law.

In the Roman-catholic Church there is no question of such an attitude. It is standing on its principles guaranteed by the Konkordat. The priests are free to teach in their churches old and young people whatever they like without the possibility of secular interference. The position of the Roman-catholic Church in Germany was never as strong as now and the position of the evangelical Church theologically and otherwise never so disturbed as now.

I am told that some protestant pastors have been in the camps of concentration and had to complain of physical ill treatment. There is no possibility of letting these things [be made] known to the Churches or the public. Officially they are simply denied.

As to the prospect for the future, the German-Christian movement having got all power in its hands will, if nothing unexpected happens, conform to its purpose and spiritual tendency – if this name can be anymore used – all protestant religious life.

As to the theological capacity of the new leaders, it will with all possible evidence prove to be insufficient for the very great task the new Church is pretending to fulfil, the missionary task amongst the masses of people to which they cannot always again repeat that the Church was always a fighting Church and that Luther was a German man, that the new Church is the people's Church. They will not have anything really substantial to give to the great needs of the people and the National-Socialists will not [in] the long run allow [them] to be commanded to go to church services. The impossibility of the theological attitude might be illustrated by the order of a Superintendent not to use in future any more the non-German words alleluiah and amen and by the order of a state officer to tell not any more in the schools the story of the sacrifice of Isaac, because it is not in accordance with the German conception of God. How the theological faculties will develop is not clear yet. The leading New Testament professor, K. L. Schmidt in Bonn,[6] has been set out of office. Many men with great academic ambitions but much less theological capacities are looking for a professorship.

So the new Church will hardly be equipped to face the great decisive intellectual theological issues ahead of it.

The group of the 'jungreformatorische Bewegung' is under these circumstances of the highest importance. It ought to be morally and otherwise helped as much as possible. Here we face an important task of the oecumenical movements. In accordance with Lilje, and I think with you also, [I think] that we ought to avoid an official break with the German Church but that we ought to let her know as clearly as ever possible that what is binding us to the German Church is this movement actually oppressed and partly persecuted. We have to point out this fact very clearly and to say that we decidedly disagree with the official attitude.

Here still lies a little hope because the German Church is most anxious not to lose the prestige of oecumenical relations. It is a question as well of church policy as of international state policy.

A week ago Professor Kohnstamm of Holland,[7] who has close contact with church minority circles along the German Rhine, was here and expressed very strongly the same opinion. We thought that first of all representatives of the different movements might go to their men in Germany and possibly through them to the leading men of the new Church, not to tell them agreeable things, but to tell them the truth as disagreeable as it might be to them. But of course we ought to agree [to] take the same attitude in the different movements and to reach possibly a united attitude.

I am going two weeks hence as Vice-President of Y.M.C.A. to Dr. Stange[8] for an unofficial, very personal and frank, discussion of all problems involved in the youth movement. But we will of course have to discuss the general oecumenical and German church questions. I do not think that I am going to Berlin to see other men. The situation is not ready for it. Such visits would have an official character before any of our official bodies would have had the opportunity of discussing things. I prefer to go for information and for maintaining contact. I gladly will send you afterwards a confidential report on what I was able to see and to hear. Before going to Germany I am meeting next week in Geneva Mr. Henriod and Dr. Schönfeld to discuss with them my plans which are not yet definitely fixed.

May I close in giving expression to my conviction that in a time to come sooner or later the present situation will have passed because the deepest spiritual needs still living will have found expression even under most unfortunate circumstances and that the power of the living Lord will raise men and voices and give them opportunity to overcome all hindrances being thrown now by the imperic Church itself in their way. We have to believe in this real Church of Germany, look forward to its future and go our oecumenical way in view of this our hope.

May I thank you once more for your very good letter and the book you so kindly have sent me. I am very glad to have it with your dedication and to read it. It will always remind me of your all too short stay in our city and our home. Mrs. Koechlin and myself were very glad indeed to have you here. Please remember us to Mrs. Bell and believe me

very faithfully yours,

1   Johannes (Hanns) Lilje (1899–1977): general secretary of the German Student Christian Movement, 1924–34; an ecumenically vigorous Lutheran he played a prominent part in the Confessing Church; during the war he was imprisoned and suffered abuse in the camps at Dachau and Buchenwald; in 1947 he became bishop of Hannover and then, in 1955, presiding bishop of the Lutheran Church in Germany. His memoirs were translated and widely read in Britain as *In the Valley of the Shadow* (London, 1950). See too Harry Oelke, *Hanns Lilje. Ein Lutheraner in der Weimarer Republik und im Kirchenkampf* (Stuttgart: Kohlhammer, 1999); Johannes Jürgen Siegmund, *Bischof Johannes Lilje, Abt zu Loccum. Eine Biographie, Nach Selbstzeugnissen, Schriften und Briefen und Zeitzeugenberichten* (Göttingen: Vandenhoeck & Ruprecht, 2003).

2   Reinhold von Thadden-Trieglaff (1891–1976): by background an international lawyer, he was a member of the Prussian General Synod from 1932 to 1944; he was at first co-chairman with Paul Humburg of the *Evangelischen Wochen* (Evangelical Weeks) programme, the first of which was held in Hannover in August 1935, but between January and August 1937 six of these Weeks were prohibited. A co-signatory of the Barmen Declaration, in 1934 he became deeply involved in the Confessing Church. After his release from a Soviet prisoner-of-war camp in 1945 he became the essential genius of the German Protestant Church Assembly (*Deutscher Evangelische Kirchentag*), the first meeting of which took place in Hannover in 1949. He was also prominent in international ecumenical work, particularly in the World Student Christian Federation (of which he was vice-president in 1937 and 1946) and the World Council of Churches.

3   Pierre Maury (1890–1956): French Protestant pastor and leading light in the international ecumenical movement. See Françoise Smyth-Florentin, *Pierre Maury: Prédicateur d'Evangile* (Paris: Labor et Fides, 2009). Joachim von Hossenfelder (1899–1976): the co-founder of the German Christians, he became Reich leader of the *Glaubensbewegung Deutsche Christen* in 1932. In the 'brown' synod of the Prussian Church in September 1933 he was elected bishop of Brandenburg. He visited Britain in October 1933 and was viewed there with some awkwardness, even

embarrassment. After the scandal of the *Sportpalast* rally he was forced to resign as leader of the *Deutsche Christen* movement and also from the National Spiritual Ministry.

4 Karl Fezer (1891–1960): professor of practical theology at the University of Tübingen (1930–59). A moderate member of the *Deutsche Christen* movement, Fezer had close contacts with Bishop Wurm. He was the author of a set of new guidelines for the *Deutsche Christen* in May 1933. He was a member of the interim leadership of the German Evangelical Church from July to September 1933. After seeking vainly to disconnect Müller from Hossenfelder, he resigned from the *Deutsche Christen* movement after the Sportpalast rally.

5 Simon Schöffel (1880–1959): bishop of Hamburg, 1933–4, 1946–54; head pastor of St Michael's Church in Hamburg, 1924–54. He was effectively deposed by radical *Deutsche Christen* forces on 1 March 1934 and followed by Franz Tüngel.

6 Karl Ludwig Schmidt (1891–1956): professor in New Testament studies at Bonn University, 1929–33; as a member of the Social Democratic Party, he was suspended in April and dismissed in September 1933 according to the requirements of the new Law on the Restoration of the Professional Civil Service and in light of his refusal to accept the Aryan Paragraph. In 1935 he moved to the University of Basel, holding the Chair in New Testament studies there until 1953.

7 Philipp Abraham Kohnstamm (1875–1951): eminent Dutch philosopher, scientist and public educationalist.

8 Erich Stange (1888–1972): international ecumenist and leading light in the German YMCA, Stange joined the National Socialist party in 1933. When the various individual associations merged to form the *Evangelisches Jugendwerk* (with *c.* 700,000 members) Stange became *Reichsführer* of the Protestant Youth of Germany in May 1933. He lost this position in December 1933 after protesting against the forced incorporation of Evangelical youth work within the *Hitler Jugend*. He was expelled from the party the following year. After 1945 Stange sought to re-establish his youth work but he was also productive in creating a Protestant telephone counselling centre. See Heiner Fandrich, *Carl Stange – Theologe und Wissenschaftsorganisator* (Gütersloh: Gütersloher Verlagshaus, 2022).

Bell to Koechlin, 4 October 1933, Basel UB, NL 37, VI 11 (typewritten).

My dear Pastor Koechlin,

Very many thanks for your deeply interesting letter and all the news it contains. It is a very great help. I wonder whether you could possibly secure a copy or a translation of the protest by the two thousand pastors at the National Synod which was mentioned in *The Times* the other day?[1]

I had the good fortune to see a young Westphalian Pastor, Gerhard Klose,[2] who came and spent the night here last week. He is a strong minority man, quite young, and lives in Bochum.

I send you herewith a copy of a letter published in *The Times* to-day. ᵃNo – it goes with my *Gazette* under separate cover.[a,3]

You did not actually say, by the way, that the Roman Catholic priests of non-Aryan parentage or grand-parentage are under no disabilities with regard to the exercise of their ministry. But I take it, in the general sense of what you say about the Roman Church, that they are as free to serve as priests as the Aryans[a]??[a]

My Wife sends her warmest regards to your Wife.

Yours very sincerely,

1   This formidable submission to the National Synod was delivered by Praeses Koch on 28 September. See Beckmann, *Kirchliches Jahrbuch*, pp. 35–6.
2   Gerhard Klose (1905–75): pastor in Wengern and, after the war, in Detmold; later a Superintendent in the Evangelical Church.
3   i.e. the Chichester *Diocesan Gazette*.

Enclosure:

Bell to the Editor of *The Times*, published 4 October 1933.
The Jewish Question

Sir,– Many will be grateful for your leading article of September 16 in which once again you point out that behind the Disarmament and all other international Conferences to-day lies the fundamental question, 'Is Europe capable of organizing itself on a common basis? Or must the nation continue to be a unit which isolates itself as much as it can from its fellows?' May I call your readers' attention to an international organization of the Churches which is very conscious of the need of this 'common basis' for the life of the nations, and illustrate its method by describing a meeting which it has just held?

The organization to which I refer is the Universal Christian Council for Life and Work (or Practical Christianity); and you kindly printed a letter from the writer about it a year ago. The Council is the continuation of the Stockholm Conference for Life and Work of 1925. It is composed of official representatives of nearly all the Christian Churches except the Church of Rome. It has as its object the application of Christian principles to international, national, and social life, in the belief 'that a Christian world order, *the* Christian world order, is ultimately the only one which, from any point of view, will work'; and for this purpose it enjoys the help of various commissions, theological and social, and has a permanent institute for study and research at 2, Rue de Montchoisy, Geneva.

This year the annual meeting took the form of a session of the Executive Committee at Novi Sad, Yugoslavia, where the members were the guests of the Orthodox Church. Among those attending were delegates from the Churches of Denmark, Sweden, England, Germany, France, Switzerland, Greece, Yugoslavia, Hungary, and the United States of America. Apart from the necessary administrative business it became quite clear that one of the chief problems for the Church in the different countries is the problem of Church and State. By this is not meant the question of establishment, though it may arise, but the problem of the place of the Church in the modern State, and the respective duties of a Christian to-day to the claims of the Church and the claims of the State. Where do the claims clash, or meet? Is it ever right for a citizen to disobey the State because of another allegiance which he may owe to the Church? In what, if any, departments has the State, or the Church, an absolute sovereignty?

One immediate issue of both religious and political significance occupied much of the Committee's time. It concerned the present position in Germany. And it is in dealing with it that I think that the method of the Universal Council is of special interest. On the one hand were the members of the German delegation. Three leading personalities of the new German Protestant Church, headed by Bishop Mueller, had announced their intention to be present. At the last moment they were prevented by the urgent task of preparation for the first National Synod of the new Church, now proceeding. But in their place they sent other delegates who brought a letter from the temporary governing body of the Church expressing its intention to continue cooperation. The German delegates rightly wished to give full information as to what was taking place in their country. On the other hand, many other delegates were gravely concerned at the suffering which the existing political system in Germany involved for Jews and those of Jewish origin, and the interference with liberty. Nor did they see how a Universal Christian Council could keep silent at such a moment. The debate, with adjournments, covered three separate days. It is not necessary to recount the various stages which led to the final result. But the point which I wish to make is that on the basis of the Christian principles set out at the Stockholm Conference in 1925 there was the frankest discussion, and through frankness came far clearer understanding with no breach of friendship, leading in the end to the following resolution: –

> The Executive Committee having received a letter from the temporary governing body of the German Protestant Church, expressing its intention to cooperate in the Oecumenical Movement, had a long discussion on the situation in Germany, in which many delegates took part. The delegates from the German Protestant Church gave an account of the general position, and of certain facts regarding the Church reorganization. The discussion was frank and friendly, and there were various differences of opinion. But grave anxieties were expressed in particular with regard to the severe action taken against persons of Jewish origin, and the serious restrictions placed upon freedom of thought and expression in Germany. After prolonged discussion the Executive Committee resolved to ask the Bishop of Chichester, as their Chairman and President of the Oecumenical Council, to write a letter to the temporary governing body in order to bring before the German Protestant Church the distress and anxieties which these disabilities caused to the members of the Committee and the Churches which they represented.

The Committee also decided to cooperate in the work of an international organization which is being formed in Holland for the relief of Christians of Jewish origin suffering through the action of the German Government.

During the next 12 months the various issues of the relations between the Church and the State of to-day will be further examined. An international study conference will be held in 1934, and it is hoped that preparatory conferences will take place in different countries on the following questions:

What is the nature of the authority of the State, and in what does its particular foundation consist, from the Christian point of view? Furthermore, where are the limitations of this authority of the State to be found in its relation to the individual, the world order, and the Church?

The Council itself will meet for its own discussions later, in the light of the results of these conferences. May I add that if there are any readers of this letter who would like to help the Council financially in the work it is undertaking in this and other ways I will gladly receive contributions and forward them to the proper quarter?

Yours faithfully

Koechlin's secretary to Bell, 12 October 1933: LPL, Bell Papers, Vol. 4, fols. 145–6.

Sir,
Dr Koechlin asks me to send you enclosed the protest of the two thousand pastors at the National Synod and to let you know that he has left for Germany today, going first to see Dr Stange in Kassel and then to attend the meeting of the *Deutscher Evangelischer Missionsausschuss* in Barmen. Dr Koechlin will not be back before October 21st.

Yours faithfully,

Enclosure: Draft
In the name of the Christian communions which we represent, we desire to make an earnest protest against the present attacks on the religious liberty and constitutional rights of the Churches in the German Empire, especially in Prussia. These liberties and rights are based on fundamental principles inherent in the Gospel of Jesus Christ and the character of the Church. They were guaranteed by the Chancellor Hitler in his programmatic speech before the representatives of the nation in the Reichstag, March 23rd 1933.

We are certain the German church members and leaders, to whatever fraction they might belong, as loyal and patriotic German citizens do not dispute the authority of State in all purely state concerns. But in a spiritual matter they are bound by an allegiance to our Lord Jesus Christ; to deny it, even under extreme pressure and political and state forces, would mean to deny the only Lord of the Church. To refuse the duly instituted church leaders the possibilities of governing the organized church in the realm of their indispensable constitutional rights and to monopolize by high-handed actions as those recently reported all church government in the hands of state officials, is creating a situation of great concern and distress for all churches connected to the German evangelical Church in the fellowship of the spirit and in cooperation for God's kingdom all over the world.

Bell to Koechlin, 25 October 1933, Basel UB, NL 37, VI 12 (typewritten).

My dear Dr. Koechlin,

I enclose for your private information a copy of a letter to Bishop Müller. It was written in accordance with the Resolution of Novi Sad.[1] I shall be interested to hear what reply it evokes. I am reserving the right to publish. Have you any views on this?

Bishop Hossenfelder was in England last week and I think he was rather busy with propaganda.[2] The Bishop of Gloucester, whose letter to *The Times* yesterday[3] was not very helpful on the general situation (though intended to be kind to Germany, missing the point) was persuaded by him. The Archbishop writes to me, after seeing the Bishop of Gloucester, to say that 'Bishop Hossenfelder definitely informed the Bishop of Gloucester the other day that the Aryan paragraph was to be withdrawn. Do you know whether this is the case or not?' I should be glad of an answer from you on this point. My own impression, for what it is worth, is that the Prussian Synod applies the paragraph and that that is the Synod which matters, while the National Synod did not in fact raise the question. That non-raising of the question was no doubt all to the good, but it does not alter facts by mere omission to legislate one way or another, does it?

I shall be deeply interested to hear how your own journey to Germany is faring.

Yours very sincerely
p.p. GEORGE CICESTR:
'S. Rowe'
Secretary.
(Dictated by the Bishop but signed for him in his absence.)

---

1 See Armin Boyens, *Kirchenkampf und Ökumene 1933-39* (Göttingen: Vandenhoeck & Ruprecht, 1969), pp. 59–66. Resolution of the Executive Committee of the Universal Christian Council for Life and Work at Novi Sad, September 9 to 12, 1933, p. 311. See too Henriod to Bell, 3 October 1933: 'In view of the really adequate information we have got since Novi Sad, I have a growing conviction that your letter to Bishop Müller, who is now the Reichbischof, should be very strong.' See Gerhard Besier (ed.), *'Intimately Associated for Many Years' George K. A. Bell's and Willem A. Visser 't Hooft's Common Life-Work in the Service of the Church Universal – Mirrored in their Correspondence* (Newcastle upon Tyne, 2015), p. 40.

2 The guests of Frank Buchman of the Oxford Group, Hossenfelder and Fezer were introduced to Archbishop Lang by a letter of commendation from Ludwig Müller. Lang merely acknowledged this and kept his distance. Hossenfelder did meet Bishop Headlam and his stay included a visit to Cambridge as the guest of Sir Edwyn Hoskyns.

3   *The Times*, 24 October 1933. This letter, with its reference to 'body-line bowling', was at once controversial and excited an angry reaction from critics of the Nazi regime. Bell himself wrote to Alan Don, Lang's chaplain, that it was 'just the sort of soft pedalling and white-washing which encourages the extreme Nazis to persevere with extreme measures'. Bell to Don, 25 October 1933, LPL, Lang Papers, Vol. 37, fol. 141.

Enclosure:
Bell to Ludwig Müller, 23 October 1933, Geneva, WCC Archives 420007/1 (carbon with some stylistic corrections and signature by Bell); Basel UB, NL 37, VI 3, nr. 20 (carbon and copy); LPL, Bell Papers, Vol. 4, fols. 252–6.

Right Reverend and dear Sir,

Last month at Novi Sad I had the pleasure of receiving the letter addressed by the Temporary Governing Body of the German Protestant Church on September 6th to the Executive Committee of the Oecumenical Council for Life and Work. I have no doubt that since our Committee met you have been fully informed by the delegates of your Church of the general course of the discussion, and of the Resolution finally adopted, a copy of which I enclose. As that resolution makes plain, I was asked as its Chairman by the Executive Committee to write to the Governing Body after our meeting, and to let its members know our thoughts on certain matters. It is therefore with a deep sense of responsibility that I address this letter to yourself as first German Reichsbischof.

I should like, first of all, to say with what profound sympathy I personally have watched the great awakening in the life of the German people, and the new hope, faith and enthusiasm, with which multitudes of your fellow-countrymen, not least the young, have been and are inspired; as well as the sense of release from Bolshevism and materialism with which their hearts and minds are filled. May I say also that I and my colleagues on the Oecumenical Council welcome the desire for a fuller life and the abundant signs of spiritual movement to which the new development of the German Church gives expression, and the wish of the Church to bring the gospel to the people in their language and their way? And I am very thankful for the desire to which you yourself gave utterance in your Message at Wittenberg on September 27th for a new comradeship of faith and sacrifice at home through the Church, and for a relationship of honest and true co-operation with the Protestant Churches of other nations, under the rule of the same eternal Lord.

I wish I need say no more. But there are other elements in the present situation which arouse very different feelings in my mind and the minds of fellow-Christians represented on the Oecumenical Council: and out of the friendship which has steadily grown between all our Churches and the German Church since the Stockholm Conference, I feel bound to let you know what those feelings are.

I write as a Churchman, and the spokesman of Churchmen from many Churches, to one who stands at the head of the German Evangelical Church. I am very conscious of the weakness in many particulars of the Church of England: and we are all conscious of various defects in our various Churches. How great nevertheless is our responsibility as Churchmen at the present time, and how urgent the call which comes to every one of us to be true to the precious trust of the Gospel which God has committed to His Church! It is just because I feel the vastness of the responsibility that I cannot, in honesty, refrain from indicating certain features that have emerged in the development of the new German Evangelical Church which are gravely disturbing to the Christian conscience. I refer especially to two things.

(1) The adoption of the Aryan paragraph by the Prussian Synod[1] and certain other Synods has come as a great shock to us and to innumerable other Christians. It is a great shock that Pastors and Church Officers and Church members should be deprived of their posts in the Church or made to feel outcasts or inferior Christians because they are Jews by birth or of Jewish descent. The shock is the more profound as the Church which thus makes race a determining factor in the status of the Christian is not a Church of little learning or immature, but one the scholarship and evangelical zeal which has been the admiration of Christendom. I am very glad that a large body of Professors of the New Testament in German Universities have made a public protest on this very point.[2]

(2) The further feature to which I am bound to refer is that which two thousand German Pastors set out so plainly in their declaration, presented at the National Synod at Wittenberg. It is enough to quote these sentences: –

> In critical and important meetings of the Synod the present majority of its members has refused the minority its fundamental right of giving advice and of free speech, even in regard to questions which touch upon the essential nature of the Church and its Commission. Church life has been kept by force for several months under the coercive control of a single group in the Church. It ought not to be that in denial of brotherly love, the Church of Jesus Christ should through the domination of force be made a Kingdom of this World.

Such suppression or forcible silencing of those holding views to which the controlling group objects is a great shock to other Churches, and to all Christians who stand for the free preaching of the Word of God and for the freedom of its preachers.

I have referred specially to two matters gravely disturbing to the Christian conscience. Is it not possible, seeing how great are the issues at stake, for you now finally to say, and by your action to secure, that such suppression and silencing of opponents on the one hand, and such discrimination against Church members of Jewish descent on the other hand, shall no more take place, while you are Reichsbischof, in the German Church?

Let me repeat, in conclusion, that I write with genuine appreciation of so much of what is now going forward in Germany, and that I long that Germany should hold without dispute its proper place of great leadership in the community of nations. But I felt obliged, just because I have this longing, and this admiration for Germany, to communicate my distress and anxiety, and that of my friends, with regard to particular items in the present situation. I have tried to do it in the spirit of the Oecumenical movement itself which stands for brotherly co-operation, with all frankness amongst the Brethren, who desire, whatever the nation to which they belong, to work and pray together for the reconciliation of the nations and the offering of a common witness to the peoples of the Universal Church and to the one saving Gospel of Christ.

With much respect,
I am
Yours very faithfully,

1 See 'Gesetz betreffend die Rechtsverhältnisse der Geistlichen und Kirchenbeamten', 6 September 1933, shortened in Beckmann, *Kirchliches Jahrbuch*, pp. 33–4.
2 The opinion 'Neues Testament und Rassenfrage', 23 September 1933, signed by 21 New Testament scholars, in: Kurt Dietrich Schmidt (ed.), *Die Bekenntnisse und grundsätzlichen Äußerungen zur Kirchenfrage des Jahres 1933* (Göttingen: Vandenhoeck & Ruprecht, 1935), pp. 178–82.

Koechlin to Bell, 28 October 1933, Basel UB, NL 37, VI 13 (carbon).

Dear Sir,

I wish to thank you most heartily for the copy of the letter you have written to Reichsbischof Müller. I am very thankful for the way you have chosen to bring before the leader of the German Church the concerns of the *Una Sancta* in view of the actual German Church situation, and at the same time the deep desire of a spiritual fellowship and union in Christ with our brothers in Germany. After the stern but very necessary criticism the new German Church leaders have had to hear and to accept, we have certainly, as you have done, [sought] to open the way for a positive spiritual help through personal brotherly relations and through intercession we have the privilege and duty to bring as an important element into the German situation.

As to your question about the Aryan paragraph, I can tell you from what I heard indirectly bei [from] Landesbischof Wurm in Stuttgart,[1] that Professor Fezer came back from England, the first time he went there without Bischof Hossenfelder, strongly impressed by the fact that the Aryan paragraph was the great scandal for the Churches and oecumenical movements and that the German Churches ought to get rid of it in the best way possible. It is quite possible, even probable, that Professor Fezer influenced Hossenfelder in this direction and that Hossenfelder, meeting English Church leaders, was convinced also.

Nothing has been done yet as far as I know. The Reichs-Constitution does not raise the Aryan question.[2] The Landeskirchen will have to act, which can be done very easily by an order of the Landesbischof who, with the consent of his ministry, has power to change law without consulting the Synods. It seems to me very possible, even probable, that before long this change might take place and will create a great relief inside and outside Germany.

You will be interested in this respect to hear that the German Mission Conference,[3] in which every missionary society was represented, voted unanimously that missions could not accept, neither abroad nor at home, the application of the Aryan paragraph. I will inform you as soon as I hear of any official declaration concerning this question.

Mr. Henriod mentioned to me the plan of a second visit of mine to Germany in relation with the journey of a representative of the Church of England. I had just a telephone [call] with Mr. Henriod, telling him that I could not at the present moment accept such a mission and that it seemed to me better to postpone such a journey of oecumenical personalities, at least until the German vote of November 12th had passed.[4] Personally I do not feel to have the right to call on the new Church leaders at the present moment. The position of the German Y.M.C.A. is actually such that an interference of the Vice-Chairman of the World's Alliance in Berlin is unnecessary and would even create harm.[5]

As to the missionary question I attended, as you know, the German Missionary Conference. I had full opportunity there of saying what I thought I had to say. The missionary forces were remarkably united in maintaining the liberty of missionary work and in refusing to be submitted to an undue organisational and spiritual Church pressure [sic]. Furthermore it was possible for me to have a long personal conversation with the member of the German-Christian Movement responsible for the missionary questions. In the realm of missionary work everything has been reached and done what seems to be necessary [sic]. I hear furthermore that Bischof Schoeffel of Hamburg, who in the Reichs Church ministry is responsible for missionary questions, is in agreement with the position taken by the Missionary Conference. It would be very bad policy, if in the capacity of member of the International Missionary Council I would try to go further. I feel certain that as well Dr. Mott[6] as Dr Oldham would not look favourably to my going to Germany now in a mission as it has been proposed to me by Henriod.

If you kindly allow me to express my opinion as to the advisability of the journey of an English representative to Germany, I feel that you ought to 'wait and see' what will be the reaction of your letter to Reichsbischof Mueller and of Hossenfelder's and Fezer's English visit. I know that the foreign minister von Neurath is strongly influencing the German Church leaders in the direction of oecumenical wishes and interests. If you think of the attitude of political Germany towards [the] League of Nations and international relationship[s], it is a remarkable fact, that the German Church is still anxious to do whatever seems possible to adapt itself to oecumenical relations and desires. Everything which could be interpreted as an undue pression [sic] or unnecessary interference could very easily spoil the atmosphere and weaken such intentions.

I hope to send you these very next days confidentially a report on my German journey.[8] May I already now mention one fact: I think you ought to maintain fully the position taken in your letter to Reichsbischof Mueller, namely not to declare yourself contented when the Aryan paragraph is withdrawn, as great as will be the relief if this happens. The domination of the Church by unworthy and politically minded Bishops, the spiritual suffering of many pastors not belonging to the German-Christian Movement still stands as an impossible fact. Confidence in the German Church and normal oecumenical relations, that is my conviction, are possible only if this scandal has come to an end. Even if the problem is a very delicate one, we are not allowed to welcome fully the governing German Church leaders in our spiritual and oecumenical fellowship, as long as they oppress unduly the great majority of the Church members and pastors standing on the truly oecumenical ground.

With hearty thanks for your confidence,

I am faithfully yours

1 Theophil Wurm (1868–1953): leading Protestant pastor who had a firm political profile before the advent of the Third Reich. From 1929 Wurm was church president of the Württemberg Regional Church; he was made *Landesbischof* in 1933 but was removed from office by Müller in September 1934. Wurm soon moved from an initial sympathy with the National Socialist movement to a critical position and an identification with the Confessing Church; this critical view yielded a number of opposition connections and initiatives until 1945. Widely admired by those who were hostile to the regime, he was one of the few to command the respect of a broad body of German pastors in the re-establishment of the Evangelical Church in 1945, not least playing a significant role in the Stuttgart conference of October 1945. See Jörg Thierfelder, 'Theophil Wurm', in *Profile des Luthertums. Biographien zum 20. Jahrhundert*, ed. Wolf-Dieter Hauschild (Göttingen: Vandenhoeck & Ruprecht, 1998), pp. 743–58.

2 After the foundation of the Pastors' Emergency League and the resolutions of the ecumenical conferences at Novi Sad and Sophia, this was finally a consequence of an intervention by the Ministry for Foreign Affairs on 22 September, one made with regard to the reaction of the Northern Lutheran churches.

3 The conferences of the German Evangelical Mission Federation and, at the same time, the German Evangelical Mission Board, held at Barmen on 18 to 20 October 1933, brought a reorganization of the fragmented federations. This produced the German Evangelical Mission Day, in which most German evangelical mission societies participated, and a new, more weighty, German Evangelical Mission Council.

4 On 12 November the election of the *Reichstag* was combined with a plebiscite about the withdrawal of Germany from the League of Nations.

5 This judgement was justified by the fact that Müller and Stange had successfully intervened with Schirach when he announced the dissolution of all youth associations at the beginning of October. But the question of incorporation determined the discussions in the Reich leadership, with Udo Smidt, *Reichswart* of the Bible Circles, in particular campaigning against incorporation. At this time other leaders were also in contact with the Pastors' Emergency League.

6 John Raleigh Mott (1865–1955): American Methodist layman, veteran missionary pioneer and international ecumenist; presiding officer at the 1910 World Missionary Conference at Edinburgh and chairman of the World's Student Christian Federation; at this time president of the World Committee of the YMCA. For Koechlin's admiration of Mott see Alphons Koechlin, *Dr. John R. Mott zu seinem 70 Geburtstag, in: Kirchenblatt für die reformierte* (Schweiz: 16 Mai, 1935), pp. 153–5.

7 See Koechlin's 'Report on a Journey in Germany, 12–20 October 1933' (German version), Basel UB, NL 37, VI 4,1.

Bell to Koechlin, 30 October 1933, Basel UB, NL 37, VI 14 (typewritten).

My dear Dr. Koechlin,

Very many thanks for your most kind letter and for the very interesting information which it contains. A young theological student from England has just published an article on the new régime in the monthly periodical *Theology*.[1] I have only just set eyes on it myself and have not read it when dictating this letter, but I will send the copy to you in case you have comments or criticisms.

I shall look forward with the greatest interest to receiving your confidential report. I will certainly maintain fully the position taken in my letter to Bishop Müller. I am under the impression that while the withdrawal of the Aryan paragraph is very important, it is the application of the principle underlying these restrictions that has to be so carefully watched, and that the fair treatment of the minority, or rather of the people disagreeing with the official Church government, is the vital thing.

I agree with what you say about 'Wait and See'. I am very much interested in what you tell me about the German Missionary Conference.

Yours sincerely,

---

1 This was Richard J. C. Gutteridge, a Cambridge student of Sir Edwyn Hoskyns who had spent the first months of 1933 studying with Gerhard Kittel in Tübingen. The article, 'German Protestantism and the Hitler Regime', was published in *Theology* 27, no. 161 (November 1933): pp. 243–64. It was widely judged to be too optimistic and even sympathetic to the German state. Gutteridge himself soon went on to become a friend and ally of Bell and, in later years, a significant historian of the Evangelical Church and the Jews. See his book *Open Thy Mouth for the Dumb. The German Evangelical Church and the Jews, 1879-1950* (Oxford: Basil Blackwell, 1976).

Koechlin to Bell, 1 November 1933, Basel UB, NL 37, VI 15 (carbon).

Dear Sir,

Included you receive my report, having, as you see, a very personal and confidential note.[1] I am sending other copies to Dr. Oldham, to Dr. Mott, to Mr. Gethman, General Secretary of the Y.M.C.A.[2] and to Mr. Henriod. Of course you are free to use it in a confidential way, if you think it to be in the interest of the cause.

Best thanks for the very kind letter I just received and with the content of which I fully agree.

Yours faithfully,

Enclosure:

1 See Koechlin to Bell, 28 October 1933, note 8.
2 Walter W. Gethman (1882–1938): American Christian internationalist; executive secretary to the World Committee for Literary Work at the YMCA office in Geneva, 1926–35.

Bell to Koechlin, 4 November 1933, Basel UB, NL 37, VI 16 (typewritten).

My dear Dr. Koechlin,

I am most grateful to you for your letter of November 1st and the confidential report of your journey in Germany. I shall read it with the keenest interest. It is very good of you to send it to me.

By separate post I am sending a copy of *Theology* with an article,[1] well-informed in certain parts but wanting in others, as it seems to me, especially knowledge of the Gospel and the Church Group.

We had a Meeting, as I expect Henriod will tell you, of the Administrative Committee of Life and Work and the World Alliance yesterday.[2] We discussed the question of a delegation to Germany and came to the conclusion that it would be better to do nothing at the present moment. As Lord Dickinson[3] pointed out, for a delegation of a weighty and representative character to go to Berlin and ask to be received, a rather special object and crisis is necessary, for a delegation could not be repeated with equal effect when there was something very urgent to present, and if the delegation were simply to urge the deletion of the Aryan paragraph, whichever way the answer went it would not be very satisfactory. As you point out, it is what happens afterwards if they consent that matters, and if they refuse it puts the delegation in an extremely awkward position. It was agreed that any individual members, like Adams Brown and Henriod himself, who had opportunities for going to Germany might informally express their anxiety. But generally speaking I thought we had better hold our hands for the present.

Yours ever,

1 Evidently, the article by Richard Gutteridge, mentioned in the earlier letter of 30 October 1933.
2 See Henriod to Bell, 29 September 1933, in: Besier, *Intimately Associated*, pp. 36–7.
3 Willoughby Dickinson, First Baron Dickinson (1859–1943): after a conspicuous career as a Liberal politician, particularly as a London councillor, he became a leading light in the World Alliance for International Friendship through the Churches, first as secretary-general and then as chairman of its international council. On these terms he was a regular correspondent with archbishops and bishops who sought to respond to international questions.

Oldham to Koechlin, 16 November 1933, Basel UB, NL 37, VI 17 (typewritten).

My dear Koechlin,

Thank you very much for your letter. I have had a long letter from Dr. Knak[1] in which he very fully and clearly explains the present situation. He is, on the whole, in favour of my paying a visit but quite rightly points out that in view of the uncertainties of the present situation any impressions I might gain would very probably be out of date in a few weeks. A letter has come from Schlunk[2] this morning in the same sense. It is evident from what Schlunk tells me that action in regard to the constitution of the German missionary societies will not take place for some weeks. Recent reports about the church situation in Germany in the English papers yesterday and to-day strongly confirm what Knak and Schlunk say about the struggle between the different forces in the German church. If I were to make a visit now anything that I might learn might have little or no applicability to the situation as it develops in the near future. The financial position of the International Missionary Council compels us to practice the strictest financial economy and if the cost of a visit to the Continent is to be incurred it ought to be at the most appropriate time. Schlunk's advice in his last letter is on the whole that a visit would probably be more fruitful if it were made after things had become more settled rather than now. In all the circumstances it seems to me clear that it would be better to postpone my visit.

I have always regarded myself as the servant of the missionary societies and feel this as strongly in regard to the societies on the Continent as with reference to those in Great Britain and America. The many and difficult problems which the German missionary societies are facing at the present time in regard to the future of their work makes a peculiarly strong appeal to me. I therefore am prepared to hold myself at their disposal and if and when they feel that a visit by me would serve a useful purpose I am ready to make it.

I am grateful to you for all the counsel and advice you have given me in the matter. I hope that we may continue to remain in touch with one another.

With warm regards,
I am,
Yours very sincerely,

1 Siegfried Knak (1875–1955): missiologist and, after 1921, director of the Berlin Mission, a position that he would hold until 1950.
2 Martin Schlunk (1874–1958): the director of the Norddeutsche Mission, was chairman of the German Protestant Mission Day and of the German Protestant Mission Board (1924–46).

Koechlin to Bell, 11 December 1933, Basel UB, NL 37, VI 18 (carbon).

Dear Lord Bishop,

Since I have last written to you, the situation in the German Church developed so rapidly that it was very difficult to have on it a clear judgement. I trusted you would have been regularly informed through different sources and mainly through your Geneva office, which had these last weeks more direct contact with Germany than I had the opportunity of having. So I did not undertake to write to you.

I am certain you will have felt a great relief in seeing thorough changes going on. I learned that Friday last Professor Fezer addressed a church gathering in Stuttgart of over a thousand pastors, reporting on his leaving the German-Christian Movement.[1] He stated that he could not anymore feel responsible for the doctrinal attitude of the German-Christians which he had in vain tried to influence in a decisive way.

Secondly he stated that the insincerity of Hossenfelder and others, not to use a stronger expression, became simply unbearable to him. He mentioned the fact that in his presence Hossenfelder had promised in England to Bishops of your Church that Reichsbischof Müller and himself would not allow the Aryan paragraph to stand, but that at the great Berlin assembly in the 'Sportpalast' of November 13th he declared officially that most certainly the life of the Church had to be exclusively Aryan and that no one would [take] care of any foreign opinion. This purely as an illustration. You might know that it was not possible for Müller to rebuild his church ministry with the names published, the men partly refusing to cooperate with him. Apparently the position of the Reichsbischof, who had with all his influence helped and backed the German-Christians and who had been elected by them, is becoming now quite impossible. One is beginning to discuss of [sic] the resignation of Müller, of [sic] a Church ministry of provisional character having the mandate to dissolve all synods and presbyteries elected in July and to push through new elections creating a new and true church situation and allowing to come [sic] to a fundamental change in the highest posts. The Government and even Hitler made strong declarations in the direction of no interference of State and national socialist party into the church developments.

You might also be interested in a statement I heard yesterday from Professor Karl Ludwig Schmidt in Bonn who had been dismissed and who had seen high Roman-catholic personalities who expressed their opinion that the evangelical churches with voices like that of Karl Barth and others and their fight for independence of church life were in a much better position than the Roman-catholic Church who in spite of the concordat had lost the possibility of open and free expression of their conviction concerning the life of the nation. May this impression be right or wrong, at any rate we have reason for deep gratitude in thinking of the courage of our friends in Germany. We may also be allowed to think that on the whole the oecumenical movements maintained a sound and wise attitude.

May I in closing mention for Mrs. Bell's and your private information a very personal matter, in which you had, when at our home, the great kindness of giving some advice. You allowed us to write to Mrs. Phillips in Seaford if she would be willing to take our daughter as a paying guest next summer. Mrs. Phillips wrote us a very kind letter and made [to] us very generous proposals, but friends of ours mentioned [to] us nearly at the same time a family in Woodbridge, offering, as we think, quite ideal possibilities of English family life. As Mrs. Phillips, who sent us a prospectus, is considering her home to be an educational home with quite a number of pensionnaires, you will understand that we preferred to make use of the other possibility. So our daughter will go to

Woodbridge in the family of Mrs. Henley which is also strongly recommended to us by the Rector of Woodbridge, Mr. Robert. B. Dand.

As you were so kind to interest yourself in the question and as possibly Mrs. Phillips will say a word to you, we wish you to know the reasons which have led us to follow another line.

With our best wishes for Xmas and New Year and the expression of our full gratitude for the kindness shown to us in the ending year, I am,

faithfully yours,

1 On 6 November 1933, Fezer left the circle of Müller's employees and his withdrawal from the *Deutsche Christen* followed, on 24. November, together with that of other formerly sympathetic professors of the theological faculty at Tübingen, Arthur Weiser, Hanns Rückert, and – finally – Gerhard Kittel.

Bell to Koechlin, 19 December 1933, Basel UB, NL 37, VI 20 (typewritten).

My dear Dr. Koechlin,

Very many thanks for your letter of December 11 which was most welcome. I have followed the developments in the German Church with the keenest interest, as you can imagine, and we have had a good deal of information in *The Times*. What specially interests me in your letter is the report of Professors Fezer's speech in Stuttgart. I know very well what Hossenfelder said to the bishop of Gloucester about the Aryan Paragraph, though to do him justice he did say that he himself regretted the cancellation which was bound to come. I imagine that Bishop Müller's position is indeed precarious.[1] I have had a letter from him myself in reply to my letter of October 23, and I send you a copy. He telegraphed yesterday to say that I might publish it. It will therefore probably appear in *The Times* tomorrow – certainly in *The Manchester Guardian*.

I am also very deeply interested in what you tell me about Karl Ludwig Schmidt and the attitude of high Roman Catholic authorities. That is extraordinarily interesting and encouraging.

Mrs. Bell and I are much interested in what you tell us about your daughter going to Woodbridge. I entirely appreciate your decision and hope that your daughter will be very happy there. It is obviously much more convenient for what you want. Would you ask Mrs. Koechlin to be sure and let Mrs. Bell know when your daughter arrives in England, and her address? We would very much like to have her to stay with us sometime when she comes.

With warmest good wishes for Christmas and the New Year from us both to you and Mrs. Koechlin and the family,

Yours sincerely,

1   Only with great difficulty was Müller able to assert himself in the dispute with Hossenfelder, while the party and the government refused to intervene, viewing it as a purely internal church matter. In the face of an ultimatum from Confessing pastors, Müller forced the clerical ministry to resign on 29 November, and on 20 December he demanded that Hossenfelder resign from all church offices. It was in order to regain Hitler's favour that Müller handed over the Protestant Youth Office to the Hitler Youth on 19 December 1933. This apparent betrayal raised the mood against him to a climax in the pastorate and the congregations.

Enclosure:
Müller to Bell, 8 December 1933, Basel UB, NL 37, VI 3, nr. 20 (copy, carbon).

Right Reverend Lord Bishop,
   In view of your far-reaching appreciation of the position of our people and our Church, it was with much gratitude that I received your friendly letter of October 23rd. The real issue for us to-day is a common defence of the Christian Churches against the powers of unbelief and irreligion. The two questions which you address to me also include problems which, in one way or another, concern the other Christian Churches of the world, and therefore demand a serious consideration in common.
   One thing I may certainly understand from your friendly letter – that you appreciate the specially great and responsible tasks which the German Evangelical Church has to discharge in relation to our people. You [?] can undertake these tasks all the more gladly when we are certain that the other Churches of the world realise that in this matter they not only have the same need but also possess the same grace and the same promise of our Lord Jesus Christ. You may be sure that, as you indicate in your second question, I will do all I can to reach a complete union of all the ecclesiastical and theological forces in the German Evangelical Church. The change in the spiritual ministry which has just been completed is very closely connected with this. I may similarly assure you that the subject of your first question has given rise here to serious theological consideration. You will have learnt already that the enactment of the well-known measure dealing with the officials of the different Churches, including the so-called Aryan paragraph, has just been stopped.
   We are concerned with such large questions that I may not say anything final. But it is my special wish that in the future we may find an opportunity for discussion together upon these questions which are too important to the Christian Church – the race problem, the State, and the international order.

With cordial greetings
I am
Yours very truly

Koechlin to Bell, 27 December 1933, Basel UB, NL 37, VI 21 (carbon).

Dear Lord Bishop,

May I send you the enclosed report on the journey I made last week to see the Reichsbishop and members of the church government in Berlin in connection with the developments of the evangelical youth question. Please consider the report to be a confidential one, as you did with my report of October last, but feel free to make of it the confidential use you think in the interest of the oecumenical movement.

I have received your very kind letter of December 19th and am anxious to express to you before the year is ending the feelings of my deep gratitude for all the kindness you have shown to me. I count it as a great privilege indeed to have been allowed to meet you summer last and since then to stay in constant contact with you. Feel certain that I will always have it at heart to serve in the limits of my possibilities the cause of the unity of the Church of Christ, to which you are giving so great a part of your work and which is owing to you and your leadership so widely its present development. May God himself lead his work through the dark days which seem still to be ahead of us.

With Mrs. Koechlin's and my own best wishes and greetings to Mrs. Bell and yourself, I am

Very cordially yours,

Enclosure: [1]

1   A Report on a journey to Berlin – Kassel, undertaken in connection with the inclusion of the German evangelical youth in the Hitler-Jugend (German version), 19–21 December 1933, Basel UB, NL 37, VI 4, 2.

Bell to Koechlin, 30 December 1933, Basel UB, NL 37, VI 22 (typewritten).

My dear Dr. Koechlin,

I am most grateful to you for your letter of the 27th December enclosing a confidential report of your journey to Berlin and Kassel. It is most kind of you to keep me so fully informed with regard to the critical situation in the German Church, and particularly with regard to the present crisis for Evangelical Youth. I have read your report with the deepest sympathy and appreciation. Miss Ruth Rouse,[1] on December 12th, when I was in London, told me of the rumour which she had received from Sweden about the absorption into the Hitler Youth. She did not know whether it was true, but she feared so. At her suggestion I wrote a letter to the Reichsbischof, a copy of which I enclose. I have had no reply. The position of the Reichsbischof must indeed be tragic. Your description of his own conception of his God-given task, even though isolated from all support, is very illuminating. I cannot suppose that he can continue much longer in his office. But supposing he falls, as you point out, the situation will still be very obscure, and very difficult, and there is much trouble ahead. I shall be only too grateful for any information you can give me as time goes on.

You are much too kind in what you say with regard to myself and my very poor efforts. It has been a very real privilege to have secured your friendship, and I cannot tell you what it means that you should be at the very heart of the international situation with constant access to those in the German Church.

With all warmest good wishes from myself and my Wife to you and Mrs. Koechlin,

Yours most sincerely,

1   Ruth Rouse (1872–1956): widely travelled international ecumenist; secretary of the World's Student Christian Federation, 1905–24; member of the executive committee of the YWCA, 1906–46, and education secretary of the Missionary Council of the Church of England's Church Assembly, 1925–39.

Enclosure:
Bell to Müller, 12 December 1933, Basel UB, NL VI, 3, nr. 22 (carbon)
Copy

Right Reverend and Dear Sir,

I have just been told of a report in the German newspapers that it is being planned at this very moment to incorporate the Christian youth organisation into the Hitler Jugend.

I hope you will forgive me if I ask whether such a statement is really true? I put the question because the report of the incorporation, involving the virtual suppression of distinctively Christian evangelical associations, has caused a good deal of anxiety among of those most deeply interested in the Christian youth organisation in England which have relations with similar organisations in Germany. And I should like, if possible, to be able to reassure them.

Yours very truly,

1934

4 January	Müller issues the 'Decree concerning the restoration of order in the German Protestant Church', drafted by Oberheid and Jäger, reinstating the Aryan Paragraph and including a 'gagging order' (*Maulkorberlass*) which at once becomes notorious. This forbids all rallies on church premises and all ministers to publicly criticize the church regime and its measures. References to the church struggle in sermons or publications are prohibited. Those who resist risk suspension and the withholding of one-third of their income.
7 January	A protest by pastors of the Pastors' Emergency League is read out from pulpits.
13 January	Reichsminister Rust extends the 4 January 'muzzling order' to the universities.
18 January	Bell writes again to Müller to criticize the new measures. A copy of the letter is also dispatched to President Hindenburg.
24 January	Archbishop Lang voices his anxiety about affairs in the German Church in Convocation.
25 January	Church representatives meet with Hitler in Berlin. Göring intervenes after a telephone conversation involving Niemöller is tapped. This is used with decisive effect against Niemöller. The bishops are dismayed.
27 January	Niemöller is formally suspended; he subsequently defends himself successfully in court. In Saxony the entire leadership of the *Pfarrernotbund* is briefly imprisoned. The bishops now fall in line behind Müller.
29 January	The administrative committee of Life and Work meets in Chichester and endorses Bell's letter of 18 January.
30 January	The Law for the Reconstruction of the Reich is passed.
1 February	Bell's letter of 18 January is published by the press and supplemented by a resolution by the administrative committee.
8 February	Bell meets Heckel, Krummacher and Wahl in London.
19 February	Synod of the Provincial Church of the Rhineland.
1 March	From now Müller's powers as Prussian regional bishop are transferred to the Reich Church, making Prussia only a centrally directed territory of a wider whole.
16 March	The Gestapo dissolves the synod of the Westphalian Church, removing Präses Koch; an alternative Westphalian Synod is established with Koch in charge and presiding over a new Council of Brethren.
March	Bishops Wurm and Meiser meet Hitler, revoking the declarations made on 27 January. Synod of the Provincial Church of Berlin-Brandenburg.

5 April	Synod at Dortmund establishes the constitutional church of Westphalia, a 'Confessional' Church led by Praeses Koch.
11 April	Bishop Meiser invites Confessing pastors to Nuremberg for consultations. They form an action committee under Koch which will prepare for a new synod.
12 April	Müller appoints August Jäger as lawyer on the Spiritual Ministry with the new title of *Rechtswalter* to 'consolidate and expand the external order of the German Protestant Church'.
13 April	A capitulation: Müller annuls the orders of 4 January.
19 April	Jäger is appointed legal member of the Spiritual Ministry and head of the church chancery. This is widely seen as ominous. Müller now moves to incorporate more churches into the *Reichskirche*.
22 April	The Confession Day of Ulm. Leaders of the Confessing movement in the churches under German Christian rule and the bishops of Bavaria, Württemberg, and Hannover declare that they now represent the constitutional 'Evangelical Church of Germany'.
23 April	*Deutsche Christen* leaders come to Berlin to meet with Jäger who now seeks to press ahead with unification.
26 April	Ernst Ludwig Dietrich, a *Deutsche Christen* leader proposed by Jäger, is installed as a regional bishop of Nassau-Hesse.
May	In Britain, Bell and J. H. Oldham prepare a new public intervention with the support of Archbishop Lang.
2 May	The committee of Confessing pastors at Nuremberg appoints Karl Barth, Hans Asmussen and Thomas Breit to draft a theological statement for the forthcoming synod which will be held at Barmen.
10 May	Bell issues an Ascension Day message to the churches declaring concern for the Evangelical Church in Germany.
16 May	*The Times* publishes a letter by Archbishop Lang protesting vigorously against the defamation of the Jewish people by the National Socialist paper *Der Stürmer*.
29–31 May	Synod of the Confessing pastors at Barmen. This is attended by representatives of nineteen regional churches. A statement, largely drafted by Karl Barth, is agreed and a Council of Brethren is created.
7 June	Both houses of Convocation debate the German Church crisis, passing motions prepared by Bell and Duncan-Jones.
17 June	Former Chancellor Franz von Papen criticizes Hitler in a speech at Marburg.
22 June	A controversial Second Report of the Archbishop of Canterbury's Council on Foreign Relations is submitted to Church Assembly.
30 June	The 'Night of the Long Knives' removes the SA as a threat to Hitler's authority and sees the murder of other critics, including the leader of Catholic Action, Erich Klausener.

18 July	Jäger and Müller meet Hitler. By now 22 out of the 28 *Landeskirchen* are part of the Reichskirche.
1 August	The offices of president and chancellor of Germany are combined.
2 August	Death of President von Hindenburg. Now the Reichswehr swears an oath of personal loyalty to Hitler.
9 August	The second national church synod takes place in Berlin. Müller assumes greater powers from the synod and orders that pastors and church officials now take a new oath of allegiance to the German Evangelical Church. The churches of Hannover, Württemberg and Bavaria will now be incorporated into the new *Reichskirche*.
19 August	Hitler proclaims himself Führer and Reich Chancellor.
24 August	The Council of Life and Work meets at Fanø. In a private session Heckel is cross-examined on the coercive measures taken against Confessing pastors. News is leaked to the *New York Times*. Heckel is now joined by a new representative from Germany, Birnbaum, a National Socialist party man. A number of resolutions on German affairs are still passed, one expressing 'grave anxiety' that 'vital principles of Christian liberty should be endangered or compromised at the present time in the life of the German Evangelical Church'. With this conference Bell's chairmanship of the council ends.
September	Müller now orders the dismissal of Aryan pastors who are married to non-Aryan women.
2 September	Müller refutes the declarations passed at Fanø.
September	Bishops Wurm and Meiser resist incorporation into the *Reichskirche* and receive strong popular support.
19 September	Müller addresses a gathering at Hannover and affirms Hitler's wish to preserve the rights of the Church.
23 September	Müller's inauguration as Reichsbishop in the Cathedrale of Berlin without oecumenical participants.
27 September	Beginning of the attempt to bring the Württembergian Church into line with the *Reichskirche* law 'on the amendment of the constitution'.
October	Bell and Oldham continue to build international support for their new intervention. It will now become a co-ordinated, public *demarchement* by the heads of the protestant churches of England, Sweden, Norway, Denmark, Finland, France, Switzerland and Holland.
11 October	*Gleichschaltung* of the Bavarian Church by Jäger leads to massive protests in the following days.
19–20 October	The Confessing pastors meet at Dahlem. In accordance with ecclesiastical emergency law, a Council of Brethren is formed and also an executive inner council.

26 October	An important victory: Jäger resigns. Müller now appoints a council of bishops to replace him. Bell and Lang regard this is a vindication of their threat to the German embassy to issue a major protest.
28 October	Jäger's acts in Bavaria are ruled illegal by the court there.
30 October	The three Lutheran bishops meet Hitler who declares that he washes his hands of the dispute.
6–7 November	Minister of the Interior, Frick, prohibits the discussion of church questions in the press or in other publications.
8 November	The Confessing Church demonstrates against Müller in Berlin.
18 November	Müller refuses to stand down.
20 November	Now on the defensive, Müller repeals his own law of enforcement.
22 November	Leaders of the Confessing Church form a 'Provisional Church Council'.
25 November	Müller is reduced to rescinding all orders given since January.
26 November	Karl Barth is suspended from his chair at Bonn for refusing to take the oath of loyalty.
21 December	Barth is dismissed by a disciplinary court.
December	Frick reissues his decrees of November.

Bell to Koechlin, 10 January 1934, Basel UB, NL 37, VI 23 (typewritten) LPL, Bell Papers, Vol. 5, fol 100.

My dear Pastor Koechlin,

I have been asked to write an article of 5000 words on the German Church for a very influential English quarterly called *The Round Table*.[1] I enclose the letter which put the request to me, so that you may see exactly what lies behind it. Mr. Geoffrey Dawson who is mentioned in the letter, is the Editor of *The Times* and he works in the closest touch with *The Round Table*.[2] That paper's articles are all of them anonymous. The paper deals with political and imperial questions from an independent point of view, and has a very wide circulation amongst political people and others in all parts of the British Empire. The fact that it should want an article on the German Church is very significant and very important. I wrote in reply to the Editor that I could not myself write such an article in the time at my disposal for I am overwhelmed with business. But I offered to help him in getting an article written by one who speaks with authority and could do the article needed with independence, sound judgement and accuracy. I cannot think of anybody who would write such an article more appropriately than yourself.[3] Will it be possible, do you think, for you to do it, and to be able to send it in by the end of January? You see that a fee of just under £15. is offered, and the article would, as I say, be anonymous.

I do very much hope that it may be possible for you to do it. It is, you will understand, hardly to be expected that a German Pastor, on whichever side of the conflict his sympathies may be, should feel free to write such an article. His authorship might leak out and prove very embarrassing for him hereafter.

With all warmest regards
Yours very sincerely,

1. *The Round Table: The Commonwealth Journal of International Affairs*: a journal first published in 1910 to present informed opinion and discussion to interested private readers. At this time it provided a forum for such eminences as Lionel Curtis, Philip Kerr and Sir Alfred Zimmern, all of whom were very much a part of Bell's intellectual world.
2. Geoffrey Dawson (1874–1944), *Times* journalist and, in 1912–1919 and between 1923–1941, editor of that newspaper. Dawson was an admiring friend of many senior politicians, also a member of the Anglo-German Fellowship and, later, a leading supporter of the policy of Appeasement.
3. At first Bell had asked Dietrich Bonhoeffer to consider writing the article, but he turned the invitation down. See Bethge, *Dietrich Bonhoeffer* (Gütersloh: Christian Kaiser Verlag, 2005), pp. 420–1.

Koechlin to Bell, 15 January 1934, Basel UB, NL 37, VI 24 (carbon).

Dear Lord Bishop,

Returning Saturday last from a few days rest in the mountains, I found your very kind letter concerning the article on the German Protestant Church for *The Round Table*.

As you think I might render to the readers of *The Round Table* and to the cause of the German Protestant Church the service which is asked for, I am willing to accept your offer and to send to you the article for the end of the month.

You may be sure that I am trying to do my best to meet the situation, to give with the help of different friends an information [sic] as accurate as possible and to submit my English style to some expert counsellor.

As to the actual German situation, I had news from a Y.M.C.A. World's Committee secretary,[1] who spent some days last week in Germany. He was encouraged to see the good fighting spirit of a still growing number of pastors and of the different evangelical youth movements. Hitler seems to be much disappointed in regard to his evangelical followers. To a member of the Swiss Parliament, who saw him last week, he expressively said that he did not wish to interfere in any way in the Church questions.[2] But I am afraid he does not realize that the totalitarian character of his national-socialist ideology is getting at the root of evangelical church life.

A question the evangelical youth leaders have much at heart is the rehabilitation of Dr. Stange who constantly is attacked in national-socialist papers because he stood against the will of the Leader in the youth question. The Church officials evidently do not try to stand against such attacks. So he is obliged to stand in second line. The leader in the actual fight of the evangelical youth is Pastor Riethmüller, head of the Y.W.C.A.[3]

In the next number of the *World's Youth*, quarterly of the World's Alliance of Y.M.C.A., we say a word in Dr. Stange's favour. May I submit to you the question, if you could in some way say or write a word to help him in pointing to the services he has rendered to the Movement of 'Life and Work'? I know, Stange's attitude these last months does not make it easy for us to stand wholeheartedly to [with] him. But I think it is important for our oecumenical movements as for the German Church, not to allow his personality to become impossible in German public and church-life.

Thanking you for your confidence and your kindness,

I am,
Very cordially,
yours

---

1 American Christian youth leader and general secretary of the YWCA, 1920–1935.
2 According to Lindt, *Briefwechsel*, p. 103, this was probably Dr. Albert Oeri, editor-in-chief of the *Basler Nachrichten*, who was received by Hitler on 10 January 1934.
3 Otto Riethmüller (1889–1938): director of the Burckhardt House of the German Evangelical Reich Association of German Women in Berlin-Dahlem. He was a strong opponent of the integration of the Evangelical Youth into the Hitler Youth. In 1935 he was appointed chairman of the youth chamber of the Confessing Church.

Bell to the Editor of The Times, 16 January 1934, published 17 January 1934.[1]

The German Church. Meeting with the Chancellor

Sir,– The eyes of Christendom at this moment are on the German Church. To-morrow the Reich-Primate, Bishop Müller, is to meet the Chancellor.[2] And the question to which the answer is so anxiously awaited is this. Is force to be invoked, against the constitution of the German Church, to determine issues in which the spiritual nature of the Church and the Gospel are at stake? Is the State to intervene, against the solemn promises of Herr Hitler himself, in a fundamentally religious dispute?

There is no doubt of the loyalty of the dissenting Bishops, or of the 6,000 pastors and their supporters, to the German Reich. There is no taking sides for or against a political party. Indeed, practically the whole body of Churchmen opposed to Bishop Müller are supporters of the Nazi regime. Their stand is for the Gospel and the Church – spiritual principles and spiritual facts – and they declare that these cannot be dragooned into a 'German Christian' system.

The German Church crisis may not be dismissed as a purely German concern, for anything which weakens the spiritual nature of the Church loosens the ties with the Christian Churches abroad which, as Bishop Müller said, it is his task to preserve. Bishop Müller has himself appealed to the Churches abroad in his Open Letter of September 1:–

> The German Protestant Church, founded upon the Gospel, feels itself a limb of the 'One Holy Catholic Christian Church'. It is our earnest hope that the mutual esteem and spiritual unity with the Christian Churches abroad will ever be strengthened and lead to a constantly increasing mutual service;

and again,

> The German Protestant Church consciously takes its stand with the Christian Churches abroad under the banner of the Gospel.

There is no doubt that the Churches abroad, Orthodox, Anglican, Lutheran, Reformed, represented on the Universal Christian Council for Life and Work, desire the closest cooperation with the German Church. But they have already expressed their grave anxieties to the Reichsbischof about the suppression and silencing of opponents. It had been hoped, as a result of Bishop Müller's reply to the letter expressing these anxieties, that the coercion would cease. The restoration of coercive methods, or the use of superior force now, would be a wrong to the Christian conscience and a wrong to the Gospel and to the whole Christian Church.

Yours faithfully

---

1 At Bonhoeffer's suggestion, a day later Bell wrote to Müller and to Reich President von Hindenburg; see Bethge, *Dietrich Bonhoeffer*, p. 421.
2 The meeting was postponed at short notice to 25 January.

Bell to Koechlin, 18 January 1934, LPL, Bell Papers, Vol. 5, fol. 114.

My dear Dr Koechlin,

I am very grateful for your letter last night and for the telegram in which you so kindly accept my invitation to write an article on the German Church for *The Round Table*. It is an immense satisfaction to me, and I am profoundly thankful. I think it possible that Mr Dove, the Editor, may write direct to you, in which case he will give you the necessary instructions as to sending your MS to him, probably, rather than to me. It is a great relief that you are able to do it. I have complete confidence in the wisdom with which you will handle the matter, and the accuracy of your interpretation, and shall be deeply interested in seeing what you say.

I sent you yesterday, before getting your telegram, a copy of my letter to *The Times*. Hitler has not yet seen Bishop Müller, but my letter will do no harm for that. I have felt it right (you may say that I am a rash man, but I hope not) to write a further letter to Bishop Müller myself, a copy of which I enclose.[1] I think this bringing of the oecumenical movement into the situation is very necessary, and that Bishop Müller's own repeated emphasis on his desire for co-operation with other Christian Churches shows itself a ground for our expressing what we feel.

I note what you say about Stange. It is possible that he will be in Chichester for the Administrative Committee of Life and Work, January 26–29. It is difficult to know quite where I can put in a word for him, but I will remember what you say and seek an opportunity.

Yours most sincerely,

1   Not preserved.

Koechlin to Bell, 8 February 1934, Basel UB, NL 37, VI 25 (carbon).

Dear Lord Bishop,

Enclosed I am sending you the article for *The Round Table*.

Another copy has left yesterday for the Editor's office, so that you might keep this one. To say no wrong things, I have shown the article to Dr. Thurneysen, Pastor at the Cathedral,[1] my and Karl Barth's close friend. He is in complete agreement with everything.

If however you should have this impression that something had better not be said or would not meet with the needs of the readers of *The Round Table*, please write to Mr. Dove to change it. In doing so, you will render me a service. At any rate I am giving you full power to do what you think necessary.

The situation in German is very dark indeed. I have certainty that Hitler obliged the Bishops to accept furthermore [for the future] the Reichsbischof Müller. The wording of the official announcement of that fact was not shown to the Bishops and was not a true expression of the real situation.[2] At any rate the Bishops consider the actual state of things to be only an 'Armistice'.

In spite of such a conception, large circles in Germany do not agree with the attitude of the Bishops. On the other hand Reichsbischof Müller is establishing once more his power, backed by Oberheid, a very clever, but not all too scrupulous boy[3] and by Goering's state police. Every day news reach[es] me of Pastors being put out of office or imprisoned. Yesterday Oberkirchenrat Zentgraf of Hesse,[4] who had been proposed to become Reichschurch-Minister, received here by phone the news of his deposition when present for meeting of the Basel Mission. Asmussen[5] and Knuth in Altona,[6] prominent leaders, are out of office since two days. In Dresden Arndt von Kirchenbach, youth leader and Pastor at the Dome,[7] as well as the Superintendent Hahn,[8] whose brother had been shot by the Bolshevists in Dorpat, are in prison. It might be necessary to come before long to new action. In the meantime the publication of your letter dated January 18th has everywhere been considered as a very important and effective testimony of Christian oecumenical unity.

With kindest regards,
Yours very sincerely

Enclosure:[9]

1. Eduard Thurneysen (1888–1974): Swiss theologian, friend, ally and collaborator of Karl Barth. Between 1927 and 1959 he was a pastor at Basel Minster, and after 1941 he became associate professor of practical theology at the university there.
2. A reference to the statement issued following the meeting with Hitler of 25 January.
3. Heinrich Oberheid (1895–1977): *Deutsche Christen* bishop of Köln-Aachen; assistant to Ludwig Müller since the end of 1933 and, from March 1934, his effective chief-of-staff. Oberheid was an active member of the SA and dressed in their uniform at *Deutsche Christen* events. His influence in the church soon waned and he was pushed to the margins of influence. Later he served as a captain in the *Wehrmacht*. After the war his future lay in the employment of a Düsseldorf steel company.
4. Rudolf Zentgraf (1884–1958): superintendent of the Province of Rheinhessen in Mainz and *Oberkirchenrat* in Darmstadt; after removal from office as superintendent in connection with the organisation of the newly formed Regional Church of Nassau-Hessen in 1934 he became pastor of the little village of Bingenheim. From 1935 to 1937 Zentraf was chairman of the Landskirchenausschuss (regional Church Committee), which, after the *de facto* removal of Bishop Dietrich from office in 1935, led the Regional Church of Nassau-Hessen.
5. Hans Asmussen (1898–1968): Lutheran pastor and theologian; co-author of the Altona Declaration of 1932 and leading figure in the Barmen synod of 1934. Active in the foreground of the church struggle, he was arrested in May 1941 with the examining board of the Old Prussian Council of Brethren. During the war he experienced prison and, when free, maintained contact with the resistance leader, Carl Goerdeler. After the war Asmussen participated in the conferences at Treysa and Stuttgart but his influence began to wane. From 1949 to 1955 he was provost of Kiel.

6 Wilhelm Knuth (1905–1974): friend and ally of Asmussen and pastor of the Altona community, 1932–4; pastor of Düneberg in Schleswig-Holstein, 1934–9; actively involved in the church struggle and also in the Evangelical Weeks programme. Imprisoned by Soviet forces at the end of the war, he only returned to Germany in 1950, becoming provost of Flensburg, 1954–70.
7 Arndt Friedrich von Kirchbach (1885–1963): student pastor and cathedral preacher at the Sophien Church in Dresden. As a leading member of the Pastors' Emergency League and participant in the Barmen Synod, he was briefly imprisoned several times and was granted leave of absence from his office in the autumn of 1934. But he continued to work and in 1936 he was transferred to Freiberg Cathedral as pastor and superintendent, representing his church in the Lutheran Council. Only a year later he was removed from office again. A chaplain in the *Wehrmacht*, he was taken prisoner by American troops at the end of the war; the remainder of his career was spent in appointments at Freiberg and Goslar and he died a year after retiring from the latter.
8 Hugo Hahn (1886–1957): an active figure in the Confessing Church, in 1934 he was the superintendent of Dresden-Land. He was removed from office and in 1937 retired by the *Deutsche Christen* government of the Lutheran Church of Saxony. After 1939 he became a church administrator in Stuttgart and after the war, bishop of the Regional Church of Saxony, 1947–53.
9 This now appears to be missing.

Koechlin to Bell. 13 February 1934, LPL, Bell Papers, Vol. 5, fol. 180 (r and v).

Dear Lord Bishop,

Yesterday Miss van Asch van Wyck, the President of the World's Alliance of Y.W.C.A. passed through Basel on her way from Geneva back to Holland. She developed a plan more or less agreed upon in Geneva by the representatives of the different oecumenical Movements including Dr Schönfeld, who had just returned from Germany. The feeling was that the Church developments in Germany asked for a very close contact as well with personalities as with the situation. Very quick decisive changes might arise, asking for energetic action on our part. Staying outside the frontiers one could not see clearly what was going on. They thought it would be useful, even necessary[,] to send an observer to Germany, staying there, gathering information, getting contact with leading personalities, able to write regularly to Geneva and if urgent to come back and report directly.

Our Geneva friends did not think of an official personality, but of an inofficial [sic] one whom we could fully trust and who could judge the situation from our oecumenical point of view.

I felt from the very first moment very hesitating in view of such a plan and am even more hesitating today. I do not see the personality able to render such a service. I do not see how she could fulfil the very difficult task without being observed, maybe by the State-Police. I see a risk for our German friends, for our oecumenical Movements and also for such a personality in the constant secret mission accomplished in our name.

On the other hand I have the impression that we get outside Germany enough news to see clear. In special moments Dr Schönfeld or another man could go out and have direct contact with our friends in Germany, bringing back the complement of other news we had already received. An action of oecumenical circles can only take place, as I see it, on the ground of solid knowledge and long views. Personal impressions of one moment or another could be very much misleading.

But of course I agreed to bring before you this plan and am quite ready to look at it from another side and to submit to other views than mine, if that will appear to be the way to meet best the situation. Dr Schönfeld will bring before you what is most on his heart, so that you will see both sides in giving us your advice.

I should be most grateful if you would kindly let me know what is your thought in this most important matter.

Very cordially yours,

Bell to Koechlin, 13 February 1934, Basel UB, NL 37, VI 26 (typewritten).

My dear Dr. Koechlin,

Very many thanks for your letter and for the article for *The Round Table*. Before it came I had seen the orginal with the Editor of *The Round Table*. He has gone over the article, shortening it in certain ways and bringing out some points more clearly in the English. He has asked me to look through the article from the point of view seeing whether a little more could not be added so as to inform a forgetful public as to some 'more' of the main facts, and I am going through the article carefully with this view. I think that a little more history (not more philosophy but more facts) might be included, and I hope you will not mind if a few points of this factual kind are inserted. The article is most useful and will be a great help to the public.[1]

You may have seen in *The Times* that Dr. Heckel[2] and other representatives of the German Evangelical Church came to see me in London on Friday.[3] What they wanted was to persuade me that the situation was much more complicated than I thought, and could not be understood except from within; and to extract a promise from me that I would not write more letters or make more statements, say for another six months, while the 'pacification' went forward! They brought me a special confidential message from the Reichbishop to the effect that the Aryan paragraph was not to be enforced and that all the Bishops had agreed to this. Dr. Heckel said he would put this in writing in a letter to me for me to use. I said however I could not use it unless it was a very positive and substantial statement – not a mere general pious hope. They were very anxious to have the note of their interview communicated to the Press, and suggested a form of words to the effect that it was the *task* of the oecumenical movement to have brotherly theological discussions – the implication, I suppose, being that it must not deal with burning issues in a practical or public way. I could not agree to this, but I thought that no harm would be done in the announcement that they had seen me and that we agreed to promote steps for frank and brotherly discussion of various problems before the Churches. At the same time (and we had a discussion in two parts, lasting two hours each) I went over the points with regard to the use of force, which I said disturbed members of the other Churches so greatly. I wrote the points out and gave the paper to Dr. Heckel. I enclose [for] you a copy of the paper. You will see that they are put with a certain bluntness. Obviously Dr. Heckel and Co. are most anxious to keep in touch with the oecumenical movement, and do not want to lose their contact. But I am afraid that a breaking point may come unless there is a change in policy. I wish your letter with the article had come before I saw them, and that I had known of the visits of the police to pastors' houses reported in Saturday's *Times*. I am however now writing to Dr. Heckel calling his very serious attention to these incidents, and reminding him of the danger to relations with other Churches which such a policy creates.[4] They told me that a Reich Minister for dealing with the relations with the Evangelical Church was in all probability to be appointed. I said that I viewed this prospect with a good deal of alarm, and pressed the dangerous character of such an appointment upon them: for in the present circumstances of the Evangelical Church, such an appointment would seem to carry far more in the way of control with it than happens in the case of other Churches, even though those Churches, like our own, are Established.

I hear to-day, privately that there is a very important Meeting taking place in Hannover, of leaders of the Pastors' Emergency League, to consider future policy and whether they are to work for separation and so forth.[5] It is a very anxious moment indeed. Any news that you hear will be most gratefully received.

Yours ever,

1   N.N., 'The Church in the Third Reich', in *The Round Table*, March 1934, pp. 319–33.
2   Theodor Heckel (1894–1967): he was appointed head of the Evangelical Church's foreign relations department in 1928; the *Reichsbischof* gave him the title Bishop on 21 February 1934; by character a nationalist who was supportive of the National Socialist state (and of the Aryan Paragraph), he was viewed sceptically by international ecumenists, and by Bell himself; during the war Heckel became responsible for internees and prisoners of war, work for which he was widely praised; in 1950 he became dean of Munich, a position which he held until 1964; in 1961 he had also become a member of the Bavarian Senate. See Rolf-Ulrich Kunze, *Theodor Heckel 1894–1967. Eine Biographie* (Stuttgart: Kohlhammer, 1997).
3   9 February 1934; see Bethge, *Dietrich Bonhoeffer*, pp. 406–7. Heckel was accompanied by the theologian Friedrich-Wilhelm Krummacher and, from his own office, the lawyer and chief consistorial councillor Hans Wahl.
4   See also Bell's letter to Heckel, 10 February 1934, reproduced in Boyens, *Kirchenkampf und Ökumene*, p. 317 f.
5   This information about the meeting of the Council of Brethren of the Pastors' Emergency League was provided by Bonhoeffer.

***First Enclosure*: Informal Notes, 9 February 1934, Basel UB, NL 37, VI 26 (carbon).**

INFORMAL NOTES
(handed to Dr. Heckel, 9 February 1934)

1. The prohibition of opposition to actions or decrees objectionable on spiritual grounds.
2. The power taken by Reichbishop to abolish posts, enact or suspend decrees, at his simple unfettered discretion.
3. The use of the police to help the suppression of opponents.
4. The dismissal of pastors because of their opposition to a German Christian policy.
5. The putting of State considerations above religious considerations, and especially above the principle of the freedom of the Gospel.
6. The grave danger of the Church being used as the instrument of the National Socialist Party; and being absorbed by the State.

***Second Enclosure*: Statement: The German Church, 10 February 1934, Basel UB, NL 37, VI 26 (carbon).**

THE GERMAN CHURCH
The Bishop of Chichester on Friday received representatives of the German Evangelical Church in London. In connexion with the correspondence which has passed during the past month between the Reichsbishop and the Bishop of Chichester as President of the Universal Christian Council for Life and Work, it was agreed to promote a common study in a frank and brotherly spirit of various problems now before the Churches, including the investigation of the religious and theological principles involved, under the auspices of the Universal Christian Council.

***Third Enclosure*: Bell to Heckel, 13 February 1934, Basel UB, NL 37, VI 27 (typewritten).**

Copy
Dear Dr. Heckel,
At our conference on Friday, it was agreed to take steps to promote discussion in a frank and brotherly spirit of various problems before the Churches, including the religious and theological principles involved, under the auspices of the Universal Christian Council. In the course of our discussion I handed you a paper headed 'Informal Notes' and containing six points. Amongst these points were: -

'The use of the police to help the suppression of opponents'
'The dismissal of pastors because of their opposition to the German Christian policy.'

I desire to ask you, as immediately arising out of our discussion and the notice in the Press, to assist me in the investigation of the problems, caused by the use of the police against pastors, and the dismissal of pastors in the number of instances, which have arisen only in the last few days.

Since we met I am sorry to say that news has reached me which adds greatly to my anxiety on the subject of coercion, following on my letter to you of Saturday.

(1) At an informal reception after Bishop Peter's investiture at Magdeburg on February 4th,[1] much satisfaction prevailed because, in the words of the Berlin Correspondent:– 'The conflict was felt to have been satisfactorily settled for the Reich Primate and the German Christians: "everything has been cleared up and the Leader is standing by us."' Reference is also made to Bishop Peter's reference to the Potempa murder in 1932[2] when Bishop Peter is reported to have said that the Leader must be followed all the way 'even to Potempa'.

(2) In *The Times* of February 10, the following appears: -

> Munich, Feb. 9
> 'The Karlsruhe secret police state that a series of raids have been made on the residences of Protestant clergymen in various parts of Baden. A list of members of the Pastors' Emergency League is stated to have been confiscated.'

(3) On February 7, Oberkirchenrat Zentgraf of Hesse, who has been proposed to become Reichschurch-Minister, received the news of his deposition by telephone when present at Basel at a meeting of the Basel Mission.
(4) Two prominent leaders, Asmussen and Knuth in Altona, were deposed last week.
(5) Pastor Arndt von Kirchbach of Dresden and Superintendent Hahn have been sent to prison.
(6) Pastor Beckmann[3] and other leaders of the Rhine Pastors' Fraternity[4] have been suspended.

There are other questions, indicating other dangers, such as that of which you told me in the probable appointment of a State Minister for the German Evangelical Church, to which I referred in our talk and indicated in the informal notes which I handed to you.

When writing to the Reichsbishop I was obliged to refer to the possibility of the strongest protests from the Christian Churches abroad if the methods of coercion, to which I referred in the letter, continued, and still sterner methods were employed.

I cannot disguise from you the fact that however reluctant one may be personally to voice such a protest, silence may be impossible if the policy which we fear, and of which we have such ominous warning, takes shape. I think it only right to tell you this, as I express the most earnest hope that nothing further may be done in the way of imprisoning members of the Pastors' Emergency League or dismissing them from their posts because of their opposition on theological grounds to very important elements in the policy of the Reichbishop.

Yours ever sincerely,

1. Friedrich Peter (1892–1960): 1932 co-founder of the *Deutsche Christen*; in August 1933 *Oberkonsistorialrat* in the leading council of the Evangelical Church of the Old Prussian Union and by October bishop of the Provincial Church in Saxony. In the face of strong opposition, he was recalled in July 1936 and transferred to Berlin Cathedral. Here, however, he was unable to perform any official acts because of the objections of the Cathedral Church Council.
2. In the upper Silesian village of Potempa on 10 August 1932 five SA men murdered a Polish communist, at home and in the presence of his mother and brother. The day before the Papen government had introduced the death penalty for politically motivated murders. After the five were sentenced to the death penalty, Hitler sent them a supportive telegram. In the face of increasing pressure from the National Socialists, Reich President Hindenburg commuted the death penalty to life imprisonment on 2 September 1932. Once in power, the National Socialists announced an amnesty for the murderers of Potempa and for other 'champions of the national uprising'. They were released on 23 March 1933.
3. Joachim Beckmann (1901–87): pastor in Düsseldorf 1933–48, founder of the Rhenish Pastors' Brotherhood in July 1933 and leading member of the Confessing Church. In February 1934 he was temporarily removed from office and, in the following years, he suffered several disciplinary measures, including being taken into protective custody.
4. After the victory of the *Deutsche Christen* in the church elections of 23 July 1933 the path towards the creation of what became the Confessing Church soon grew, with the formation of circles of pastors and parishioners who devoted themselves not only to practical congregational work but also to framing a theological justification for their opposition. Already, on 19 July, Beckmann had begun to gather pastors who were faithful to the Confession of the Rhenish Pastors' Brotherhood (*Rheinische Pfarrerbruderschaft*).

Fourth Enclosure: Bell to Schönfeld, 17 February 1934, Basel UB, NL 37, VI 28 (carbon).

Copy
My dear Schönfeld,

I have thought over very carefully the proposal for the appointment of an Observer representing the international Christian organisations, who shall reside in and travel about Germany. I cannot help thinking that there is a good deal of difficulty about the proposal. The situation is, as you say, fluid from week to week, and I suppose also different in different parts of Germany. If we had a net-work of Observers (though that would be open to serious objections on various other grounds) we could presumably rely on getting satisfactory information over the whole area. But I do not see quite who is to be the one Observer for the whole of Germany and always be on the spot at the right time. Moreover I cannot help thinking that as things are, in one way or another we do contrive to get pretty accurate information, through our existing contacts. You know a good deal, Dr. Koechlin knows a good deal, and news comes in fresh. Moreover supposing the German Church authorities got to know that we had appointed an

Observer, I think the situation might be very awkward for the Observer, and we might be fairly asked what new developments led us to send a sort of spy – for that is how it might be regarded by them, even though unfairly. There is also the difficulty, supposing he were living in Germany, of getting his news out of Germany by letter, if conditions became very stringent.

I quite realize that it is not always possible for a travelling Secretary to go to Germany at the precise moment when wanted, but I myself think that the various difficulties in the way of the Observer proposal are very much greater. So I do not feel inclined to commend it myself.

Yours ever,

Koechlin to Bell, 23 February 1934, Basel UB, NL 37, VI 29 (carbon).

Dear Lord Bishop,

A rather busy week with missionary lectures in Strasbourg has prevented me from answering earlier your very kind letter of February 13th. May I express to you my warmest gratitude for the trouble you have taken to improve my article for *The Round Table*. I fully agree with the addition of certain historical facts. I had not sufficiently in mind that the readers of *The Round Table* had not been, as it is the case in European countries, in the position of following the different stages of the development. Furthermore the letter of the Editor addressed to you in January led me to think that the fundamental problems involved were in his view of first importance.

I feel also very certain that all other changes you might have been led to make will contribute to more clearness and effectiveness of my article. My only regret is, that my lacking of thorough competence has loaded your all too busy time with additional work.

I was also very glad to read your letter addressed to Dr. Schönfeld February 17th. The more I think of it, the more I am convinced that it would have been unwise to send an observer to Germany. Dr. Visser 't Hooft's[1] report, you might have received, is confirming this view. The psychology of our German friends living outside Germany is somewhat lacking in balance and sometimes in judgement. Going to Germany they are perplexed in finding an unexpected situation, the beginning and further development of which they are not able to go through with their fellow-countrymen. Being outside Germany, they are constantly fearing to miss important opportunities of help. Germans inside Germany and foreigners outside the frontiers are in a much easier psychological position to take longer views and maintain an attitude of more objective calmness.

Of course we have to do our best to follow as closely and with as much sympathy and understanding as possible the situation. I feel a special duty of doing whatever I can in this respect in as close a contact with yourself and with Geneva as possible. Miss van Asch van Wyck[2] is in Berlin at present, staying at the Burckhardt-House, the headquarters of German Y.W.C.A. She promised to send information soon after her return to Holland.

As you might know, we look forward to having in London from March 18th to 20th, together with Dr. John R. Mott, an Officers Committee of the World Alliance of Y.M.C.A. I wonder if Stange, who is member of it, will be present or if after his last London experience he does not feel free to come. I have written to him to know his plans. If he does not come, I think of making my way to London through Kassel, Barmen and Düsseldorf, to bring to our Committee an account as accurate as possible on the German Y.M.C.A. and Church situation. I prefer at the present moment to avoid Berlin, because I have no desire whatever to call on Dr. Heckel, newly created Bishop, or on the Reichs-Youth Pastor Zahn,[3] before the relation of Evangelical Youth to German Church and State is much more clear to me than it is to-day.

So I might possibly be able to bring to you also fresh information. At any rate I would most appreciate the privilege of seeing you at that time and would be very glad to make my plans in view of a possible short visit in Chichester, unless you would happen to be in London during those days. It would be easier for me to look forward to meeting you before our Officers Committee, say Friday, March 16th, but I could if necessary arrange to see you Wednesday 21st. Would you kindly let me know in time if you see any possibility of receiving me even for as short a time as might be necessary to share our views.

The visit you had from Dr. Heckel was most interesting to me and I am very glad indeed that you took the attitude indicated in your letter. Personally I have no great confidence in Heckel's character. Dr. Thurneysen, who knows him for many years, feels the same. His new appointment does not seem very clear. His main task will certainly be the supervision of German Evangelical Churches abroad. And it seems as if he would have to be also the head of the 'Foreign Office' of the German Reichskirche.

Hoping to see you before very long, I am

Very cordially yours,

1 Willem Visser 't Hooft (1900–85): a protégé of J.R. Mott, he rose through the Student Christian Movement and became the centre of the emerging WCC in Geneva, serving as its effective general secretary from 1938. After the Second World War he became the essential presiding presence over the organization in the peak period of its history. He remained a close ally and frequent correspondent of Bell.
2 Cornelia Maria van Asch van Wyck (1890–1971), Dutch youth leader and president of the World's Alliance of the YWCA.
3 Karl Friedrich Zahn (1900–1943): a pastor, he replaced Erich Stange as Reich Youth leader on 29 December 1933 with the task of superintending the incorporation of Evangelical youth organizations within the Hitler Youth movement – against the resistance of the Evangelical Youth Work itself and the leaders of the associations.

Bell to Koechlin, 27 February 1934, LPL, Bell Papers, Vol. 5, fol 220.

My dear Dr Koechlin,

Very many thanks for your letter. It is most interesting. I write hurriedly to say how glad I am you are coming to London. Friday, March 16th, would suit me very well. I am not, I fear, likely to be in Town until March 19th when I have Committees all afternoon, and all day Tuesday and most of Wednesday. I could make two proposals – either could you come to lunch with me at the Athenaeum Club, Pall Mall, at 1 o'clock on Monday, March 19th? My meeting is at 2.30. If you could come before 1 all the better. Or perhaps what would give us more time would be if you could come down to Chichester for lunch at 1 o'clock on Friday, March 16th, and we could have two or three hours that afternoon together.

Yours sincerely,

Koechlin to Bell, 7 March 1934, Basel UB, NL 37, VI 30 (carbon).

Dear Lord Bishop,
Your very kind letter of February 27th has reached me just when I had to leave Thursday for a short trip to Kassel, where I had [on] Friday morning a long conversation with Dr. Stange, getting up to date information in view of the Youth Work.[1] Wednesday, February 28th we had considered in Geneva together with Miss van Asch van Wyck, the President of the World's Alliance of Y.W.C.A., the opportunity of a new call on the Reichsbishop in view of the new critical stage the youth question had reached. We did not however follow this plan.

As you will have read, the Reichschurch-Ministry[2] has, after I have left Dr. Stange, dissolved the whole independent Y.M.C.A. work, going far beyond the contract signed with Baldur von Schirach[3] in December. The constitutional basis for such a solution seems to be completely lacking. I am expecting new information before leaving Wednesday next for England.

As you will be kind enough to receive me in Chichester, I shall be very glad to have lunch with you on Friday, March 16th 1 o'clock and to stay with you in the afternoon as long as it will seem desirable. Possibly I am arriving already at 10.46 a.m. for some sight-seeing. Last year I regretted very much that I could not even visit the Cathedral. On Monday and Tuesday we have meetings going over luncheon time, so that it would hardly be possible for me to see you at the Athenaeum Club.

If the arrangement for any reason would have to be changed in view of other plans of yours, a note will reach me here until Wednesday evening and on Thursday evening at the Red Triangle Hotel, 26, Bedford Place, London W.C..

The situation in Germany seems to become worse every day. But I do not think I need to give you to-day detailed information, looking forward to the opportunity of seeing you before long.

Very cordially,
yours

1 See Koechlin, 'Besprechung mit den Herren D. Stange und Lüst', 2 March 1934, Basel UB, NL 37, VI 4,4. On 2 March 1934 Reichsbishop Müller had enacted the law 'Betreffend die Jugendarbeit der Deutschen Evangelischen Kirche', stating that, according to the incorporation agreement, church youth work would now be limited

only to the preaching of the word. On 3 March the incorporation was officially shut down and the association formally extinguished. Youth work for boys and girls under eighteen years could now only be carried out in the form of parish youth work.
2   i.e. the Spiritual Ministry of the *Reichskirche*.
3   Baldur von Schirach (1907–74): National Socialist Reich Youth Leader since 1931 and, at this time, a privileged member of Hitler's inner circle. During the war he became *Gauleiter* and *Reichsstatthalter* of Vienna, responsible for overseeing the deportation of the 65,000 Jews living in the city to the death camps in Poland. He was found guilty of crimes against humanity at Nuremberg and served twenty years in prison.

Bell to Koechlin, 10 March 1934, Basel UB, NL 37, VI 31 (typewritten).

'Private'

My dear Dr. Koechlin,

Just a line to thank you for your letter, and to say how much I look forward to meeting you on Friday. As a matter of fact I want to be in London myself on Friday. I am in Eastbourne on the Thursday night, and it would be more convenient for me to come back to Chichester via London. I suggest therefore that instead of your coming to Chichester for luncheon, and having our talk there, you should meet me at 1:30 p.m. at the Athenaeum Club. We could have plenty of time at and after luncheon for a talk. I shall not be in a hurry.

I am much interested in what you tell me about the Youth Movement and the Reichsbishop, and there are various things in which I want your advice.

(1) This is very confidential. The Archbishop of Canterbury is taking soundings as to the possibility of having a conference of Church leaders from Europe, just before Whitsunday, in London. He is in touch with the Patriarch of Constantinople and the Archbishop of Uppsala on the matter, and I have been assisting in some of the preliminary enquiries. I should like you to turn this matter over in your mind. The object of the Conference is religious, with a view to considering and praying together, and issuing a common Christian message. But there is a great difficulty as to what is to be done about the German Church. I need say no more.
(2) I am very much wondering what steps ought to be taken now by the Oecumenical Movement in the present position of the German Church – whether the time has come for a possible joint visit to Berlin.[1]

Yours very sincerely,

1   With support of the Swedish chaplain in Berlin, Pastor Forell and a number of German Churchmen, Schönfeld had suggested that, 'as the best way of influencing the present situation, Archbishop Eidem and I should have a confidential discussion with Hitler without any communication to the Press in foreign countries'. Quoted by Bell to Pastor Karlström, 23 March 1934, cited in Boyens, *Kirchenkampf und Ökumene*, pp. 323–5; here p. 323. Hitler proved unavailing when he met Eidem on 2 May.

Koechlin to Bell, 26 March 1934, Basel UB, NL 37, VI 32 (carbon).

Dear Lord Bishop,

After having returned home by way of Geneva from London Thursday evening, I am anxious to thank you most heartily for the time and hospitality you have given me in London last week. It was of greatest value for me to be allowed to discuss with you the German problem. I felt extremely sorry that in view of the very important personal questions we had to deal with [with] Dr. Mott at the same hour, it proved to be impossible for me to accompany Mr. Guillon[1] to the interview you had fixed with him. Your card speaking of a still other interview of 9.30. a.m. at Lambeth Palace, has reached me at Bedford Place. I hope that there was no misunderstanding and that you did not wait for me, as in fact Mr. Guillon had not told me anything of such another possibility to meet you.

The Officers Committee of the World's Alliance Y.M.C.A., after having heard my report, has discussed the German situation and has very generously trusted me in giving me full power to follow the situation very closely and to take action if that proved to be necessary. It asked me however, of course in fullest agreement with my own thought, to stay in the closest contact with the other oecumenical Movements and to act as far as ever possible not without having taken counsel with you.

In Geneva we decided last Thursday, when Dr. Schönfeld was present, to ask one of our secretaries, Dr. Joachim Müller,[2] to go out to Germany, to study the Y.M.C.A. situation there, to meet as far as possible other leading people and to report on the situation. He has left Geneva yesterday. You will hear of this report soon after his return.

The news coming from Germany are [sic] bad. It becomes evident that the Church Government aims at the complete destruction of the independent Youth Organisations.[3] Dr. Karow[4] resigned as Bishop of Berlin for reason of conscience. You might have read that the Provincial Synod of Westphalen, the only one with a German-Christian minority, met a week ago.[5] The German-Christians refused to be present and had asked that the Synod should not meet. When nevertheless the majority met, the secret State Police, very probably on the instigations of Oberheid,[6] dissolved the Synod. At once the Synod constituted itself as a free Synod and great assemblies, attended by 20–30,000 people, were held to stand for the freedom of the Gospel. Amongst those attending this meeting was Pastor von Bodelschwingh.

Though the action of the Reichs Church Government, mainly directed by Oberheld, is becoming more dangerous, on the other hand, signs that the opposition is becoming stronger again, not only in circles of Pastors, but mainly in the parishes, are evident. Our attitude toward the official Church Government has certainly to encourage and not to discourage this opposition.

With kindest regards,
I am cordially yours

1   Charles Guillon (1884–1965): French theologian, active in the ecumenical movement, member of the office of the World Alliance of YMCA at Geneva 1927–48.
2   Joachim Müller (1891–1966): German theologian, member of the office of the World Alliance of YMCA at Geneva 1927–36.
3   See Koechlin to Bell, 7 March 1934, note 1.
4   Emil Karow (1871–1954): in 1928 Karow became *Generalsuperintendent* of the city of Berlin; he was forced from this position by Jäger on 28 June 1933 but then appointed regional bishop of Berlin that September 1933 by the synod of the church of the Old Prussian Union. The Anglican bishop of Fulham and North and Central Europe, Staunton Batty, met Karow in December 1933 and found him 'a convinced Nazi and a German Christian, but not a sympathizer with the extreme section'. See Andrew Chandler, *Brethren in Adversity*, p. 73.
5   On 16 March 1934.
6   It is more likely that this was influenced by Bishop Adler.

Koechlin (via Secretary R. Preiswerk) to Bell, 19 April 1934, Basel UB, NL 37, VI 2 (unpaginated) (typewritten); NL 37, VI 33 (carbon).

Sir,

At Dr. Koechlin's request I am herewith sending you in English translation the copy of a letter to Dr. Schönfeld, containing the latest news on the events which took place in Württemberg between April 12th and 15th.

May I add for your information that Dr. Koechlin left this afternoon for a short holiday. He will be back by Thursday next.

Believe me, Sir,

Yours faithfully

Enclosure:
Koechlin to Schönfeld, 19 April 1934, Basel UB, NL 37, VI 2 (unpaginated)
Copy

Dear Dr. Schönfeld,

Having sent yesterday to Dr. Keller,[1] with whom I had a telephone conversation, the latest news on the events in Württemberg, I am anxious that you should also be fully informed.

Last year the Württemberg Church Synod representing only a small majority of German Christians, its Executive consisted of four German Christians and 3 Non-German Christians. So Landesbishop Wurm was given full power and his budget was accepted. This year the four-headed German Christian majority of the Executive decided unofficially to accept the budget provided that certain changes in the personnel of the high Consistory (Oberkirchenrat) be effected, having in view to assure the majority to the German Christians. Wurm refused, pointing to the fact that the majority of the Synod would not fail to accept the budget. As a matter of fact the majority was on his side; there were some members of the Synod, who formerly belonged to the German Christians, but who had left them. To hinder the approbation of the Synod, the Executive was called together, refused the budget and declared[,] under protest of the minority, that the Church Government was in the impossibility of normal functioning and of calling together the Synod.

The President of the Executive then suggested to the State Governor Murr to call the Reichsbishop to Württemberg for intervention. Murr acted. The Reichsbishop telephoned to Wurm, asking him to call together the Executive of the Synod, which was to meet in the presence of the Reichsbishop without the members of the high Consistory. Wurm opposed to the declaration that the Church Government was in the impossibility of normal functioning, refused to call together the Executive and to attend such a meeting. In spite of Wurm's protest the meeting was called together, though by means which cannot be called legal.

The minority refusing to attend the meeting, the State Governor made use of the State Official law and gave to two members of the minority, a high Councillor and a Professor, the official order to attend the meeting. The third member did not appear. Professor V. protested against this proceeding and retired. The second one was annoyed until he left. At last the rump parliament, in the presence of the Reichsbishop and the absence of Wurm, decided to accept the budget and declared that the normal functioning of the Church Government was re-established.

In the evening, Jäger, who had accompanied the Reichsbishop to Württemberg, telephoned to Wurm that he would like to see him and asked him to resign for the reason that his political situation proved to be unbearable as he did not belong to the national-socialist party. Wurm refused to resign, pointing to the fact that he had the Church as well as the majority of the Synod on his side. After three hours of unprofitable conference, Jäger produced the latest number of the Reichs Church laws, already printed, in which there was stated that by a decree of the Reichsbishop the Württemberg Synod was not to meet and would be called together by the Reichsbishop himself for June 11th.

Müller and Wurm had not met. When Jäger saw Wurm, a radio communication had already gone out, stating that the Reichsbishop had come to Württemberg, encouraging all the parties and thus re-establishing the Church peace.[2]

This untrue communication then went through the press. Wurm asked for rectification, which was refused to him. Two days later, Sunday April 15th, Wurm was preaching in the crowded Stiftskirche. At the end of the sermon, amongst different notices he read out the radio communication and protested against the untrue statement of the events. Cries of shame against the Reichs Church and the German Christian Church government were heard, but at once stopped by the spontaneous singing of the hymn 'Aus tiefer Not schei ich zu Dir', in which all the people joined.

The whole event is a question of illegal, false and violent interference, in which the State has been taking part and which is an insult of the whole amnesty legislation. What will be the consequences in Southern Germany cannot be foreseen yet. But there is no doubt whatever that the latest phase of the Reichs Church Government is again brutal violence and that the so-called amnesty legislation – as Pastor Forell wrote to Professor Runestam[3] to Paris – is only an insincere attempt to legitimise the violence being practiced.

In addition to these communications I can tell you of another very significant fact. Professor Köberle[4] when meeting Professor Fezer, asked him why he had agreed to become a member of the Commission on the training of the rising theological generation. Fezer replied that he had had no notion of his election whatever and that he had only heard of it through the papers; he had written to Berlin at once, protesting against his name being misused and his being elected without having been asked. He never got an answer from Berlin.

I am sending a copy of this letter to Dr. Joachim Müller and to Dr. Oldham. He might like to have these news [sic] in hands when conferring with the Bishop of Chichester.

With kindest regards,
yours very sincerely

1   Adolf Keller (1872–1962): Swiss reformed theologian and pioneer and driving force of the Ecumenical Movement. He left the church ministry in 1923 under the influence of C. G. Jung, but he served as secretary of the Federation of Swiss Protestant Churches until 1941. As second general secretary of Life and Work, he was head of the International Social Science Institute founded in 1926.
2   The degree 'zum Schutz der Volksgemeinschaft' (9 July 1934) prohibited any discussion of the church controversies in public assembly rooms and in the press.
3   Arvid Runestam (1887–1962): Lutheran pastor and leading theologian of the Swedish Luther Renaissance, married to Söderblom's daughter Lucie. From 1938 to 1957 he was professor of systematic theology at Uppsala University and bishop of the diocese of Karlstad.
4   Adolf Köberle (1898–1990): Lutheran theologian and professor of systematic theology at Basel University (1930-9) and Tübingen University (1939–66).

Bell to Koechlin, 23 April 1934, Basel UB, NL 37, VI 34 (typewritten).

Private

My dear Koechlin,

Very many thanks for sending me the copy of your letter of April 19th to Dr. Schönfeld about the Württemberg Church Synod. It is most important and most interesting. I have seen Dr. Müller's letter of April 7th to Mr. Chamberlain and have been in touch with Mr. Chamberlain.[1] As a result I have written to the 'German' Ambassador to ask for an interview on the general Church question and incidentally the Church Youth question.[2] I have asked him whether he can see me next Monday. My object in seeing him will be to give him information as to what people in this country and other countries interested in the Churches think of the present Church regime and the difficulties which it creates for friendly relations. I need not say that I should be more than grateful for any statement of points to be brought forward in such an interview.

Mr. Chamberlain is writing to-day to you or Müller or Willis³ on the Youth question and I am to see Chamberlain on Thursday. But it is on the situation generally that I should so much welcome your help.

Yours very sincerely,
p.p. GEORGE CICESTR:

(Dictated but not signed by the
Bishop owing to his absence)

1 F.J. Chamberlain (1879–1958): general secretary of the National Committee England, Ireland, and Wales of YMCA, 1930–8.
2 Leopold von Hoesch (1881–1936): German diplomat and ambassador to London from November 1932 to his early death. Increasingly critical of events in Germany, he was much admired by British politicians and church leaders and those who sought to protest against the policies of the National Socialist state. One of them, Amy Buller, wrote of him affectionately in her later book, *Darkness over Germany* (London, 1943). See Hoesch's Report of Bell's visit, 30 April 1934, in: Boyens, *Kirchenkampf und Ökumene*, pp. 328–9.
3 Frank Willis (1890–1974): General Secretary of the National Committee England, Ireland, and Wales of YMCA, 1939–55; member of the Executive Committee of the World Alliance of YMCA. See Clyde Binfield, "An Artisan of Christian Unity": Sir Frank Willis, Rome and the YMCA', R.N. Swanson (ed.), *Unity and Diversity in the Church: Studies in Church History* 32 (1996): pp. 489–505.

Koechlin to Bell, 28 April 1934, Basel UB, NL 37, VI 35 (carbon).

Dear Lord Bishop,

I was most interested in receiving your letter of April 23rd.

As to the recent developments in Germany, you will have heard that the official representatives of the opposition all over Germany and of the official Churches of Württemberg and Bavaria have met in Ulm for a great manifestation. Bishop Wurm of Württemberg preached and the Bishop Meiser of Bavaria¹ read a very strong manifest[o], which sounds like a declaration of war against the present Reichsbishop and the Reichs Church Government.²

You will have read also that a Court of Law of Prussia has declared illegal the decrees and church laws issued by the Reichsbishop on his own and only authority these last three months, so that the suspensions of Pastors enforced by the Reichsbishop seem also to be illegal.³

Evidently this last fact very strongly influenced the so-called amnesty decree.⁴ [It] may be that it also led to the rather favourable agreement with a group of big interdenominational city Y.M.C.As in Germany, about which Dr. Müller has written to you more fully.⁵ On the other hand pronouncements of Göring and Jäger are sounding very unfavourable. I read these days in the *Frankfurter Zeitung* that in an interview Göring had said that he would prove his power to any church people bringing any unrest into State Unity. 'I am not afraid even of Church Leaders, they may be evangelical or catholic.'

According to yesterday's Basel paper, Jäger has stated to a representative of the 'United Press', that he would use the full power of law against any pastor who would not accept the peace proposal of the Reichsbishop. He dealt [with] those pastors as political reactionaries and compared the present fight of the Reichsbishop with the fight Hitler had fought up to his victory.

It is very difficult indeed to foresee the result of this fight between State power and spiritual power. What may be the way God is leading his Church in Germany, we certainly do not know.

I am sorry that owing to an absence for some days of rest my letter is coming too late to help you in any way in your visit to the German Ambassador. I am very glad you made this important step and hope very much indeed that it may be of strong consequences.

With kindest regards,
Yours very sincerely,

1. Hans Meiser (1881–1956); Regional Bishop of the Evangelical Lutheran Church of Bavaria, 1933–55; in October 1934 he fell foul of August Jäger but he was prepared to accept much of the new political order too and his overall record has often been regarded as a mixed one. According to his Lutheran position he was a leading figure in the union of Lutheran churches in Germany.
2. See the Ulm Declaration, 22 April 1934, in: Beckmann, *Kirchliches Jahrbuch*, pp. 65–6.
3. See *Junge Kirche 2*, 1934, pp. 333–4.
4. See the 'Church Law of the Spiritual Ministry of the German Reichschurch for the Pacification of the Church Situation', 13 April 1934, reproduced in Beckmann, *Kirchliches Jahrbuch*, p. 63. This law was only intended to provide short-term relief, not a change of course. Only a week later Müller appointed Jäger as *Rechtswalter* of the German Evangelical Church.
5. Hermann Göring (1893–1946): leading politician of the National Socialist régime, and a fierce opponent of the Confessing Church. In August 1932, he was elected president of the *Reichstag*. On the day of the seizure of power, Adolf Hitler appointed him Reich Minister without portfolio, Reich Commissioner for Air Transport – from 5 May Reich Minister of Aviation – and Reich Commissioner for the Prussian Ministry of the Interior. More significantly, on 11 April 1933, Göring also became prime minister of Prussia. From October 1936, as commissioner for the Four-Year Plan, he oversaw the rearmament of the *Wehrmacht* in preparation for a war of aggression. After the quick end of the Western campaign in 1940, Hitler appointed Göring *Reichsmarschall*. During the war, despite an accumulation of offices and titles, he lost key powers to rival Nazi functionaries, especially because of the defeat in the Battle of Britain and the beginning of the devastating bombing of Reich territory by the Allies.

Bell to Koechlin, 2 May 1934, Basel UB, NL 37, VI 36 (typewritten).

My dear Dr. Keochlin,

I send you by express and air mail a draft letter to members of the Oecumenical Council.[1] I should be most grateful if you would tell me how it strikes you. I think myself it is too long. I hope it is properly balanced. Any points which you think might be better expressed or omitted or added will be most thankfully received. I should naturally be grateful for the earliest possible reply.

You will note a guarded reference to the Ulm Declaration at the end of the second paragraph.

You will be glad to know that I had over an hour with the German Ambassador on Monday, and had most fruitful discussion with him. I really think that a very definite impression with regard to the anxiety of other churches was made upon him – especially as I was able to give a definite and, for him, rather alarming piece of evidence. Your letter did come in time. Thank you for it.

Yours ever,
p.p. GEORGE CICESTR.
(Dictated but not signed by the
Bishop owing to his absence)

1   Bell also sent this draft letter to Bonhoeffer, Oldham and Schönfeld; see Hans Goedeking, Martin Heimbucher and Hans Walter Schleicher (eds), *Dietrich Bonhoeffer, London 1933–1935*, (*Dietrich Bonhoeffer Werke* 13) (Gütersloh: Christian Kaiser Verlag, 1994), p. 132, note 2.

Enclosure: **To the representatives of the Churches on the Oecumenical Council, NL 37, VI 36 (typewritten).**

PRIVATE AND CONFIDENTIAL DRAFT
TO THE REPRESENTATIVES OF THE CHURCHES
ON THE OECUMENICAL COUNCIL.
FROM THE PRESIDENT.

I have been urged from many quarters[1] to issue some statement to fellow members of the Universal Christian Council for Life and Work upon the present position in the German Evangelical Church, especially as it affects other Churches represented on the Universal Christian Council for Life and Work.

The situation is, beyond doubt, full of anxiety. To estimate it aright we have to remember the fact that a revolution has taken place in the German State, and that as a necessary result the German Evangelical Church was bound to be faced with new tasks and many new problems requiring time for their full solution. The friendship of our Churches with the German Evangelical Church is strong, and in many cases of long standing. Any action therefore on either side which would diminish that friendship would cause deep regret. We welcome the public assurance of the Reichsbishop last September that 'the German Evangelical Church will continue to take the liveliest interest in the oecumenical Churches', and that it was his wish and task 'to preserve our ties with the Christian churches abroad',[2] and we welcome any steps that can be taken both to preserve those ties and to make them more powerful.

We are nevertheless compelled to admit that the present situation is being followed by members of the Christian Churches abroad not only with great interest, but with a deepening concern. Among the matters which have caused concern are the assumption by the Reichsbishop in the name of the principal leadership of autocratic powers unqualified by constitutional or traditional restraints which are without precedent in the history of the Church and which seem to be incompatible with the Christian principle of seeking in brotherly fellowship to receive the guidance of the Holy Spirit; the taking of disciplinary measures against ministers of the Gospel on account of their loyalty to what they believe to be Christian truth; and the introduction of racial distinctions in the universal fellowship of the Christian Church.

With such grounds for anxiety we cannot wonder that voices should be raised solemnly declaring before the whole Christian world that the confession of the German Evangelical Church is in danger.[3]

I am nevertheless most anxious that the members of our Council should avoid any immature or one-sided judgement. Great issues are at stake. The developments in Germany are bound up with fundamental questions relating to the nature of the Church, its witness, its freedom and its relation to the secular power, which have deep significance not only for the Church in Germany but for the Christian Church throughout the world. The present situation with its perplexities and difficulties seems to be a call to the Churches to endeavor through consultation and conference to arrive at a common mind[4] on the implications of their faith in relation to the dominant tendencies in modern thought and society, and in particular to the growing demands of the modern state.[5] At the end of August the Universal Council will be meeting in Denmark. A Committee has prepared the way for its work by a report shortly to be published on 'The Church, the State, and the World Order', which met under the Council auspices last month in Paris. The principal item on the Council's Agenda will be the problems raised so conspicuously by the situation in Germany. I do not suggest that the use of coercion in spiritual matters, or the introduction of racial distinctions in the Church, are open questions. I hope that our anxieties with regard to both these questions of principle will have been completely allayed by the time of our Meeting. But 'The Church and the State and the World Order' offers a very large and very important field for the frankest discussions, and I trust that as a result we shall all receive light on various problems, that our anxieties may be lessened if not removed, and that the ties which bind us to the German Evangelical Church, the causes for misunderstanding having been by then removed, will[6] be made stronger and firmer.

1   It was not least Bonhoeffer who urged Bell to take a stand on the church struggle on behalf of the ecumenical movement; see Bonhoeffer to Bell, 14 March and 25 April 1934 in *Bonhoeffer, London, 1933-1935*, pp. 111, 122, 126.
2   Quotations from a translation of the letter sent by Müller to the Churches of the Ecumenical Movement, 25 August 1933. The letter was presented to the Executive Committee of the Universal Christian Council for Life and Work at its meeting at Novi Sad, 9–12 September 1933. For the German original see Boyens, *Kirchenkampf und Ökumene*, pp. 309–11; here p. 311.
3   See Bell to Bonhoeffer, 2 May 1934, in: *Bonhoeffer, London 1933–1935*, p. 132.
4   Here Koechlin has marked one line with a black line in pen; see his letter of 5 May 1934.
5   Ditto.
6   Here, from 'our anxieties' to 'removed', Koechlin has added a further black line.

Koechlin to Bell, 5 May 1934, Basel UB, NL 37, VI 37 f. (carbon).

Dear Lord Bishop,

I received your letter of May 2nd yesterday in Geneva but was not in the possibility of giving quiet thought to it before coming home yesterday night. If you very kindly allow, I should like to suggest to you two considerations:

In our continental Churches there is some unbelief in the result[s] of conferences and consultations in general. The crisis of the League of Nations as well as the difficulties to find the real methods of oecumenical work, strengthened by the theological attitude f[or]. i[nstance]. of Karl Barth and many of his friends, lead to such a criticism. For this reason I should like to see the main emphasis in the second part of page 2 laid on the fact, which is certainly in your mind, that the actual perplexities present a call to the Churches first of all to prayer and very earnest theological work, which of course has to lead to a common consideration of the problems in view of the necessity to get as far as possible a common mind in regard to these common world problems.

The second consideration is that if you express our strong wish to be in as close a relationship as possible with the German Church, the impression ought to be avoided in Germany and in German quarters, as if this certainly dominant thought could be trusted by the official Church Government as being for them a guarantee in view of whatever future developments might be chosen inside Germany.

I am very glad indeed that you were able to have such an important interview with the German Ambassador in London. I am convinced it will sooner or later prove to be very effective.

Wednesday last I met in Karlsruhe Mr. Lüst, the representative of Stange in the Y.M.C.A., and Mr. Herde[1] of the interparochial Y.M.C.A. of Bremen. They told me that the Reichsbishop would leave Berlin 'to take some rest' and that this leave had to be considered as the end of his bishopship [*sic*]. The wish was, they told me, to come to a change in a way as quiet as possible. They seem to have this information from trustworthy sources, but I was not able yet to get any confirmation of it. Certainly the decision of the Prussian Court, which very probably will be followed by a second even more serious sentence these next weeks, and the events in Württemberg[2] have definitely weakened his position. It seems to have been decided in the Church Ministry to suspend Bishop Wurm and Bishop Meiser and all those having taken part at the demonstration in Ulm, but that on the one hand the attitude of the people of Württemberg and Bavaria and on the other hand international considerations brought forward very strongly by the Foreign Minister, have prevented this measure to be taken. In Württemberg faithful members of the national-socialist party, seeing the harm done to the party by these Church events, very evidently exercised some influence in Berlin in favour of Wurm and against the Church Ministry.

You will be interested to know that the Reichsstatthalter of Württemberg[3] went as far as to give to the post service the order not to forward any letter of the Württemberg Church Government. At once an independent bicycle and motor-car service was organized all over the country to render possible the functioning of the Church communication.

I got also most interesting news on the arrangement between the Church Government and the interparochial Y.M.C.A.s of Germany. Dr. Goebbels, Minister of propaganda,[4] had been informed that the Japanese Y.M.C.A.s, having in hands all the preparations for the Olympic games of 1936 in Japan, were in correspondence with the German Y.M.C.A.s about this matter. A high official of this Ministry, formerly member of the Bremen Y.M.C.A., had brought to the attention of Goebbels the importance of all these relations, so that the Ministry called a meeting of representatives of the Y.M.C.A.s with Dr. Heckel and Youth-Pastor Zahn. When the latter two did not come themselves, but sent Dr. Wahl as a representative, the Ministry sent to the Church Government so strong a letter, that Oberheid himself took the matter in hands and agreed to the arrangement in spite of the opposition of Heckel, who wished to have all oecumenical relationship[s] in his own hands. At a conference in the Church Government, Mr. Herde gave to the member of the Church Government the history of the first century of the Y.M.C.A. and pointed out the importance of this interparochial work in the big cities.

Oberheid and Youth-Pastor Zahn confessed that they never had thought of the possibility of doing such interparochial work (!) and agreed that such a work had its great importance and its right to independent existence. That shows in what an incompetent and purely theoretical way these men are dealing with vital existing forces entrusted to their care.

Now the further existence of these Y.M.C.A.s is solemnly guaranteed by Church and State, the centenary of the Bremen Y.M.C.A. will be celebrated the first Sunday of September. It is hoped to have a strong attendance from all parts of Germany and from outside Germany. The World's Committee of Y.M.C.A. is willing to help to bring to Bremen representative delegations of other national Alliances, provided that the whole program is on a sound oecumenical basis and not used for any Nazi propaganda. We hope that it will prove possible to render not only to Bremen but to the whole Y.M.C.A. Movement and to the Church of Germany an important service in bringing to them the clear message of the unity of the Church of Christ, essential for any national Church.

It would be most important for me to have on this delicate question any thought and advice you would wish to give to me. I am most anxious that all our proceedings and doings are in the great line taken by the oecumenical Movements towards the situation of Germany.

With my very best regards I am,
Very cordially yours,

1   Georg Herde, since the end of 1934 general secretary of the Working Group of the German YMCA; died 1952.
2   After the radio reported a church emergency in Württemberg on 14 April 1934, Wurm declared the next day that he would not yield to this pressure. This was followed by a plethora of expressions of loyalty and accelerated the developments that culminated in the Ulm Confession Day on 22 April.
3   Wilhelm Murr (1888–1945): from 1928 *Gauleiter* in Württemberg-Hohenzollern; in 1933 *Staatspräsident* and then *Reichsstatthalter* in Württemberg
4   Joseph Goebbels (1897–1945): *Gauleiter* of Berlin from 1926 and Reich Propaganda Leader of the NSDAP from 1930; Reich Minister for Popular Enlightenment and Propaganda and President of the Reich Chamber of Culture, 1933–45.

Bell to Koechlin, 9 May 1934, Basel UB, NL 37, VI 40 (handwritten).

My dear Koechlin.

I am very grateful for your letter. It was a great help in in the final drafting of my Message, as you will see – esp[ecially] at the conclusion. It is to be published in England and abroad on *Saturday*.

Thank you also very much for all the other facts in your letter.

On Mondays Goering's sister-in-law (a Swede) Countess Wilamowitz Moellendorff[1] came to Chichester to see me. She knows Goering extremely [?] well–and knows Hitler. My talk was, I think, vy. useful, and I made some points which she took away with her. She was a friend of Söderblom.[2]

Yours ever,

1   Fanny Gräfin Wilamowitz-Möllendorff, née Freiin von Fock, (1882–1956): sister of Carin Göring (1888–1931), Hermann Göring's first wife.
2   Nathan Söderblom (1866–1931): from 1914 to his death, Archbishop of Uppsala and Primate of the Lutheran Church in Sweden; initiator and leader of the ecumenical Life and Work movement, the roots of which lay in the World Conference, over which he presided in Stockholm in 1925. In 1930 he was awarded the Nobel Peace Prize. Söderblom was a fundamental influence on Bell who, like Koechlin, attended the 1925 conference and drafted its Report.

Enclosure:
Bell's Message to the Representatives of Life and Work, 10 May 1934.[1]

A Message

Regarding the German Evangelical Church to the Representatives of the Churches on the Universal Christian Council for Life and Work from the Bishop of Chichester (President).

I have been urged from many quarters to issue some statement to my fellow members of the Universal Christian Council for Life and Work upon the present position in the German Evangelical Church, especially as it affects other Churches represented on the Universal Christian Council for Life and Work.

The situation is, beyond doubt, full of anxiety. To estimate it aright we have to remember the fact that a revolution has taken place in the German State, and that as a necessary result the German Evangelical Church was bound to be faced with new tasks and many new problems requiring time for their full solution. It is none the less true that the present position is being watched by members of the Christian Churches abroad not only with great interest, but with a deepening concern. The chief cause of anxiety is the assumption by the Reichsbishop in the name of leadership of autocratic powers unqualified by constitutional or traditional restraints which are without precedent in the history of the Church. The exercise of these autocratic powers by the Church Government appears incompatible with the Christian principle of seeking in brotherly fellowship to receive the guidance of the Holy Spirit. It has had disastrous results on the internal unity of the Church; and the disciplinary measures which have been taken by the Church government against Ministers of the Gospel on account of their loyalty to the fundamental principles of Christian truth, have made a painful impression on Christian opinion abroad, already disturbed by the introduction of racial distinctions in the universal fellowship of the Christian Church. No wonder that voices should be raised in Germany itself making a solemn pronouncement before the whole Christian world on the dangers to which the spiritual life of the Evangelical Church is exposed.

There are indeed other problems which the German Evangelical Church is facing, which are the common concern of the whole of Christendom. These are such fundamental questions as those respecting the nature of the Church, its witness, its freedom and its relation to the secular power. At the end of August the Universal Council will be meeting in Denmark. The Agenda of the Council will inevitable include a consideration of the religious issues raised by the present situation in the German Evangelical Church. It will also have to consider the wider questions which affect the life of all Churches in Christendom. A Committee met last month in Paris to prepare for its work, and its report will shortly be published entitled, 'The Church, the State, and the World Order'. I hope that this meeting will assist the Churches in their friendship with each other, and 'also' in their task of reaching a common mind on the implications of their faith in relation to the dominant tendencies in modern thought and society, and in particular to the growing demands of the modern State.

The times are critical. Something beyond conferences and consultations is required. We need as never before to turn our thoughts and spirit to God. More earnest efforts must be made in our theological study. Above all more humble and fervent prayer must be offered to our Father in Heaven. May He, Who alone can lighten our darkness, give us grace! May He, Who knows our weakness and our blindness, through a new outpouring of the Spirit enable the whole Church to bear its witness to its Lord with courage and faith!

Ascensiontide 1934

1 Minutes of the Universal Christian Council of Life and Work, Fanø, Denmark, Geneva 1964, pp. 65–6; reprinted in: Bonhoeffer, *London 1933–1935*, pp. 137–9.

Mason to Koechlin, 10 June 1934, Basel UB, NL 37, VI 39 (handwritten).

Dear Dr. Koechlin,

The Bishop of Chichester desires me to send you the enclosed cuttings from the *Times* of Friday, June 8th. One is a report of a resolution which the Bishop moved in the Upper House of Canterbury Convocation on Thursday, and which was adopted unanimously by the Bishops of the Province of Canterbury. The other is a leading article on this discussion in Convocation.

The Bishop hopes that you will not think that he was too strong in what he said!

Yours sincerely
Lancelot Mason, Chaplain

First Enclosure: **Convocation of Canterbury: German Church Struggle, from *The Times*, 8 June 1934.**

'Faith imperilled'

Both Houses of the Convocation of Canterbury ended their sittings yesterday at the Church House, Westminster.

The Archbishop of Canterbury (Dr. Lang) presided over the Upper House.

The Bishop of Chichester (Dr. Bell) called attention to the present position in the German Evangelical Church, and moved the following resolution:–

This House while unwilling to intervene in questions relating to the organization of another Church with whom the Church of England desires to have friendly relation, is convinced that the present struggle which, in its essence, is concerned not merely with organization but with the actual substance of the Christian faith, is one in which all Christians have an interest. It calls attention to the warnings given in the recent declaration of the Confessional Synod of the German Evangelical Church at Barmen against certain tendencies regarding revelation, race, and the State by which the Christian faith is imperilled.

He said that the Church crisis was not a petty squabble on secondary matters between Churchmen of different schools, or a struggle about organization, but about the substance of the Christian religion. It could be fought out only by the opposition within the Church itself, but if the cause of the opposition were lost its defeat would be a blow to the whole Church. He had no political motive in sounding this note of anxiety. He recognized the enthusiasm which the National-Socialist revolution had aroused in Germany and the great good it had done in restoring national vitality and in improving national morals. But two forces were fighting for the soul of Germany, the forces of Christianity and the forces of paganism. It was on the arena of this great conflict that the special struggle within the Evangelical Church itself was being fought out.

'Rival to Christianity'
He spoke of the doctrine of the totalitarian State, which claimed to regulate every department of human life, and the introduction of a new Nordic or Germanic religion, which was being set up as a rival to Christianity. It was just because a large body of German pastors saw that the very life of Christianity was involved that they organized an opposition, claiming that the primary allegiance of Christian people was to Christ and not to the State, that the mission of the Church was not political, and that the converted and baptized Jew was a brother in Christ. He lamented the use of coercion by the Church Government with a view to the suppression of opposition and criticism, and, most significant of all, the carrying into the government of the Church of the leadership principle, through which a practical dictatorship was created which disposed of the free consent of the Church members. If the opposition were suppressed, that suppression would carry with it, whether wished or not, the perversion of the Christian faith in the German Evangelical Church, and thus reduce that Church to something which other Churches, however reluctantly, would have to cease to regard as fully Christian. Whatever might be the effect with regard to other countries, if Great Britain once believed that Germany had in fact repudiated the Christian religion, the whole attitude of English people towards Germany would be one of grave doubt, or even alienation.

He called attention to the recent meeting of the Synod at Barmen, which placed the whole opposition on a firmer basis, and welcomed the declaration, which the Synod adopted, as quoted in *The Times* of June 4. The challenge which it contained could not be gainsaid. It set out in unmistakable terms the universal character of the Christian Church, God's claim on the whole of human life, and the inadmissibility of the claim on the part of the State, divine though its task was within its own sphere, to become the single and total regulator of human life, and thus also fulfil the vocation of the Church.

The Bishop of Oxford (Dr. Strong)[1] seconded.

Archbishop's Warning

The Archbishop of Canterbury said the issue was one of very wide significance. He recognized fully the responsibility of that House pronouncing any opinion upon what might seem to be internal matters of another Church in another nation, but the limits here went far beyond the confines of the German nation. He had the very greatest sympathy with the immense, undoubted, and, on the whole, beneficent awakening which had come to Germany and German life in every aspect, in the remarkable revolution associated with the name of Herr Hitler. He had every sympathy with the desire that, at the time of this great national unity and awakening, the Christian forces should be engaged in assisting that unification of German life they could not but recognize. However, there had been currents of thought and opinion let loose on German life which were in their essence contradictory to all they meant by Christianity. If those opinions prevailed and captured the whole Christian Church in Germany, it was no exaggeration to say that it would mean the surrender of German Christianity to something hardly distinguishable from paganism. Against those forces there was now introduced in the most complete and organized form the Confessional Synod which had met at Barmen. That Synod had given expression, in language with which they might not agree, to a spirit which was very fundamental to Christianity itself. It was in that connexion that they ventured to make their appeal. On their side there was no sort of wish to have any break with the Evangelical Church in Germany. On the contrary, they were living in a time when there had been very real relationships - religious, social, and intellectual - with German Protestants. They would be very sorry if there was any schism in the Church in Germany.

The resolution was carried unanimously. [. . .]

The Lower House adopted the following motion:-

> That this Lower House observes the serious religious situation which has arisen in Germany, and expresses its concern at the possibility that doctrines of race and nation may be imposed in such a way as to imperil religious freedom and impair the substance of Christianity.

1   Thomas Strong (1861–1944): Bishop of Oxford, 1920–37. Like Bell, Strong was very much a product of Christ Church, Oxford, where he had been Dean, 1901–20.

Second Enclosure: The German Church, from *The Times*, 8 June 1934.

The anxious interest with which developments in the German Church are being watched in other Churches was shown in signal fashion yesterday, when the two Houses of Convocation adopted the extremely unusual course of passing Resolutions on a foreign event. It was emphasized by the Archbishop of Canterbury and recorded in the Resolution of the Upper House that there was no desire or intention to interfere in what might seem to be the internal affairs of another Church. But both he and the Bishop of Chichester, who moved the Resolution, insisted that the issue was one which could not possibly be regarded as exclusively relating to Germany. In its essence it clearly concerns the actual substance of the Christian faith in which all Christians have an interest. And there can, in the opinion of the Upper House, be no compromise on the principle that the primary spiritual allegiance of a Christian is to Christ and not to the State, and that no earthly leader can be a new Messiah. All the members of the Upper House who spoke were careful to point out that there was no political motive whatever behind their action. The Archbishop indeed expressed the greatest sympathy with the 'immense and beneficent awakening' that had come to Germany through Herr Hitler, whose revolution, as the Bishop of Chichester recognized, had done great good in restoring national vitality and improving national morals. But the National-Socialist revolution had been marred by excesses of action, thought, and opinion, which were contrary to all that was meant by Christianity. Starting with motives of which most were in themselves excellent, the Nazi movement had carried the exaltation of the State to such a point that in some of its aspects a struggle seemed to be going on between the forces of Christianity and the forces of paganism. The soul of Germany is being torn between them. Suppression of free thought may easily carry with it the perversion of the Christian faith; and it cannot be denied that there is some danger, as the Resolution in the Lower House phrased it, that 'doctrines of race and nation may be imposed in such a way as to impair the substance of Christianity.' In other words the two Houses of Convocation have been moved to this unprecedented action by the fear that other Churches may hardly be able to continue to regard the German Evangelical Church as fully Christian.

The struggle within the German Church arose as a perhaps inevitable counterpart of the struggle outside it. When the National-Socialists seized power they applied methods of terrorism to their political opponents which drove them out of the country or underground, and which superficially has by now given the State the appearance of unanimity. The Nazi leaders were eager that the same process of *Gleichschaltung* should be applied to the Evangelical Church–that it should be unified, nationalized, and given leadership. The demand was not wholly unreasonable. The German Church was but loosely organized. In the German Empire there had been no Established Church, but only a series of autonomous Lutheran and Reformed Churches in the various States. They formed, it is true, a German Evangelical Federation; but each individual Church was closely tied to his own State. Their expenses were paid by the State. The separate Princes were *summi episcopi*. When the Princes disappeared in the Revolution of 1918 some new authority had to be set in their place, and some of the Churches restored the office of Bishop. Then came the Revolution of 1933; and not only the Princes but the separate organization of the States themselves were swept away. The particularist institutions, which Bismarck himself had not attempted to suppress, were subordinated to one central authority. The leadership principle was personified in Herr Hitler, who controls every side of the nation's life–political, economic, and cultural. There was quite naturally a parallel movement, by no means unwelcome to many Churchmen, which aimed at building up a strong central authority under the direction of a Reichsbishop. Unfortunately a group of pastors determined to try to carry the National-Socialist ideal into every detail of Church life and to identify Christian belief with National-Socialist ideology. They applied the Aryan race theory to the *personnel* of the Church, and in some prominent instances preached the old German sagas instead of the Old Testament. They sought to abolish the Crucifix, and more recently they have been placing a portrait of Herr Hitler on the altar. The German Christians, as these extremists were called, rushed the general Church election with the help of the party machinery and established a sympathizer with their movement, Dr. Müller, as first Reichsbishop. He has made spasmodic attempts to blend conciliatory gestures with his totalitarian tendencies; but the leadership principle has had nothing like the same success in the clerical as it had in the political life of Germany. There is an unexpected strong vain of democracy in the German Church, and its congregations cling most tenaciously to their tradition of self-government. The movement in opposition to Reichsbishop Müller is built up on the system of the Councils of Brethren who are elected by their congregations, and all of whose members are equal. Decisions there, almost alone in Germany to-day, are taken after friendly deliberation among all; and appointments are made from below, not from above. The chosen leaders of the opposition came out into the open at the recent Synod held at Barmen. There a Declaration was adopted, to which special attention was drawn yesterday by the Bishop of Chichester in his resolution and his speech. The Declaration of this Free Synod set out in unmistakable terms the universal character of the Christian Church and denied the claim of the State to become the single and total regulator of human life; and many of the beliefs which the new Church authorities of the German State are trying to instil were condemned as heresies. In particular the heresy was refuted that the Church has the right 'to surrender its organization to the vagaries of temporarily prevailing philosophical or political convictions'. These 'Free Reich Synod' opponents of the Reichsbishop are beginning to build up an independent Church. In the meantime Dr. Müller is still trying to organize a Constitutional Church for the whole of Germany. The Archbishop of Canterbury said yesterday that he hoped a schism would be avoided; but a compromise satisfactory to both sides seems to be becoming more difficult. The chief hope of finding it resides in Herr Hitler, who is known to desire intensely the unity of the Church, and who seems to realize that in that sphere at least persuasion and conviction alone can make men agree to work together.

Koechlin to Bell, 5 July 1934, Basel UB, NL 37, VI 41 (carbon).

Dear Lord Bishop,
I have still to thank you for your having sent me very kindly the two extracts of the *Times* of June 8th concerning the convocation of Canterbury and the German Church. I was most interested in reading the official attitude taken by the Anglican Church. In the light of the developments of the last weeks I do not think at all that the expressions used by yourself and by the Archbishop of Canterbury are in any way too strong. As they stand, they might be of a real help to those fighting for the liberty of the true Church of Christ.

If I have not written to you these last weeks,[1] it was because I did not hear of any important event which did not become public through the *Times* and other papers. You might however be interested in two events.

Some weeks ago the Reichs-Youth-Pastor Zahn came to see me here in Basel, evidently to create some personal contact. He asked to speak in public, a plan which we did not feel free to accept. He spoke however in a private circle, some fifty people being present. Personally a charming, well educated man, he made it evidently clear that the present official Church Leaders did not accept any Church life and Government being not national-socialist in form and even in spirit. He proved to be of a fatal ignorance concerning education of youth and even real possibilities of church youth work. I hardly ever saw such a tragedy of a man unfit for his task, placed into a responsibility of highest importance. I was able to have a long and brotherly conversation with him and am glad to think that in spite of greatest differences of view a link of personal fellowship is created which might prove to be useful in future.

The second event I wish to bring before you is the convocation of the Basel Mission of last week, where many of the Brethren of Southern Germany came to meet with us here in Basel. Two days before that the German Evangelical Mission Council had met in Bethel near Bielefeld, the city of Pastor von Bodelschwingh's great work. They had come unanimously to an understanding according to which in principle the Mission declared to be the work of the whole Church, but the declaration states quite firmly that the foundation of [the] Mission is in agreement with the basis of the Barmen declaration of May.[2]

The Home Base of our Basel Mission agreed to this declaration. Our German Brethren unanimously refused to accept the present German Church Government's rule on missionary questions. All statements made in connection with the German Church policy were very clear in refusing to accept any renouncement on Church Government of Württemberg, Baden and other countries concerned. I do not think Reichsbishop Müller and Mr. Jäger will take the risk of achieving their end with state force.

The consequences of the so-called second revolution of June 30th [3] on Church questions cannot be seen yet. According to latest news the backgrounds of these terrible events have nothing whatever to do with the Church problems. For this reason it might be hoped that the Church of the opposition will not have to suffer more than before.

May I be allowed to tell you that I am intending to come to England about July[4] 16th to see my daughter in Suffolk and to stay 2 or 3 days in London before going to the IMC[5] in Salisbury the 21st of July and then directly to the Plenary Meeting of the YMCA in Oxford July 25th. With the close of the latter meeting I think of coming directly home [on] the 31st to have holidays with my family in the Engadin.[6] If for any reason you should wish to see me, I would do my best to make it possible. I do not however think that I can bring to you any important facts you do not know already. I wish however to tell you that I am at your disposal if you think it might be useful to see me. I do not need telling you that it is always a great privilege and pleasure for me to see you and to be of any service to you.

Very cordially yours,

1. For Koechlin's position see too his paper 'Die Stellung der Christen gegenüber den neuesten Strömungen in Staat und Volkstum', presented to the Stadtmission Basel, 18 June 1934, Basel UB, NL 37, II 16.
2. 'Kundgebung des Deutschen Evangelischen Missionsrates zur Kirchenfrage', in *Die Bekenntnisse des Jahres 1934*, ed. Kurt Dietrich Schmidt (Göttingen: Vandenhoeck & Ruprecht, 1935), pp. 105-6.
3. i.e. The Night of the Long Knives (the so called "Röhm-Plot"), 30 June-2 July 1934.
4. Erroneously typed as June.
5. i.e. International Missionary Council.
6. A popular holiday region in the southern parts of the Swiss Alps.

Bell to Koechlin, 7 July 1934, Basel UB, NL 37, VI 43 (typewritten).

Private.

My dear Dr. Koechlin,

I should be very grateful for your views on the desirability of my inviting representatives of the Confessional Synod of the German Evangelical Church which met at Barmen to the Meeting of the Universal Christian Council for Life and Work in Denmark next month.[1] I have put the case as I see it in a letter to Bishop Ammundsen[2] of which I enclose a copy. Your views would be most valuable on this point.

Where is your daughter staying? My wife and I would like to see her if it is at all possible. I heard on Monday that she was already in England, for by a strange chance I saw your nephew, Dietrich Burckhardt, at a little village near Rye where he is staying in a clergyman's house where I was lunching.

Are you, by any chance, coming to Denmark yourself?

Yours sincerely,
p.p. GEORGE CICESTR:
(Dictated but not signed by the
Bishop owing to his absence)

1. The biennial meeting of the Universal Christian Council for Life and Work took place on the Isle of Fanö on the West Coast of Denmark, 24-30 August 1934. See the reports of Koechlin in the *Basler Nachrichten* of 5 September 1934 and of Bell in Chichester Diocesan Gazette 15, 1934, pp. 409-11, and also his article 'A Warning from Fano' in *The Times* of 7 September 1934 – two days before the youth conference of Life and Work and the World Alliance for International Friendship through the Churches began.
2. Valdemar Ammundsen (1875-1936): Danish pastor, theologian, ecumenist and first bishop of Haderslev, 1922-36; a firm ally of the Confessing Church.

Enclosure:
Bell to Bishop Ammundsen, 7 July 1934, Basel UB, NL 37, VI 42 (carbon).

Copy
Private.
My dear Bishop,

It has been suggested to me that I should invite representatives of the Confessional Synod of the German Evangelical Church which met at Barmen to send representatives to the Denmark Meeting of Life and Work. The point made is that the Confessional Synod is in fact a Church, whether or no[t] one admits its claim to be the legal Evangelical Church of Germany – a claim that is very strongly supported on legal and constitutional grounds by learned German lawyers. I am given to understand (by Bonhoeffer,[1] with whom I have discussed the matter) that if an invitation were to be presented to Praeses Koch[2] it would be welcome, and that representatives would undoubtedly be sent. I admit that I should like to send an invitation. In ordinary circumstances it rests with the Churches in the countries concerned to agree amongst themselves as to their respective quotas in their national delegation. But clearly one cannot expect Bishop Heckel to negotiate with Praeses Koch as to the proportion in this case. I do not at all know whether Bishop Heckel is in fact coming, or how far the German Evangelical Church will be represented. I think one wants to do anything within reason to give encouragement to the Confessional Synod.

I am writing to Schönfeld in the same way as I am writing to you. I should be most grateful if you would give me the help of your very wise advice, and if you could let me have an answer during this coming week it would be particularly welcome.[3]

The present situation in Germany generally adds an urgency to the whole question.

Yours ever,
p.p. GEORGE CICESTR:
(Dictated but not signed by the
Bishop owing to his absence)

---

1 Dietrich Bonhoeffer (1906–45): theologian, at this time pastor to the German congregation at Sydenham; active in the German church struggle he, and other members of his family, later became active in resistance against the National Socialist State; he was killed in the last days of the war; a close friend of Bell, after 1945 his reputation grew in Germany and across the English-speaking world as one of the most significant, and distinctive, theologians of the century.

2 Karl Koch (1876–1951): pastor in Bad Oeynhausen (1916–49), superintendent of the Church district Vlotho (1927–48); from 1927 Praeses of the Synod of the Westphalian Provincial Church. After its closure by the Gestapo on 16 March 1934 this was constituted as Westphalian Confessing Synod under the Council of Brethren with Koch as chairman.

3 See Ammundsen to Bell, 11 July 1934, partly quoted by Bethge, *Dietrich Bonhoeffer*, pp. 439–40.

Koechlin to Bell, 10 July 1934, Basel UB, NL 37, VI 44 (carbon).

Dear Lord Bishop,

I am very much obliged to you for your very kind lines of July 7th. In the meantime you will have received my letter dated July 5th.

I am answering first your very important question concerning the attendance of representatives of the Confessional Synod at the Denmark Meeting of Life and Work.

As far as I see, The National Free Synod, which met in Barmen May 29th to 31st (see new book of Adolf Keller: *Religion and the European Mind*, page 198 ff)[1] and attended as well by Reformed as by Lutherans, can in no way be considered as an independent Church constitutionally instituted. It is a free Synod constituted by representative men, claiming still to be members of the official Church.

The Free *Reformed* Synod assembled at Barmen January 4th 1934 (see Keller 178 ff) has more or less developed to be an independent and more or less legally constituted Church. If representatives of one of these two Synods should be invited, I feel that it ought to be representatives of the National Synod which met in Barmen May 29th to 31st, which cannot be considered as representative for a duly constituted Church.

Nevertheless the local character of the Synods does not seem to be under the present circumstances of decisive importance. Looking at the general Church situation in Germany and at the attitude taken by the Life and Work movement and by yourself as its President, I think Praeses Koch ought to be invited as a representative of his group. The real Church of Germany would not be duly represented only by the Berlin Church Government. But for constitutional reasons I think Praeses Koch could only be invited as a guest.

Such an invitation addressed to him would be of great support for the Free Synod, especially in view of the new decree of Dr. Frick.[2]

The only uncertainty I am feeling in this respect is grounded on the possibility of strong resolutions which could be proposed and voted against the present state of Church affairs in Germany. If you think of leading the Conference in such a direction and if you foresee delicate discussions on the German question, it would become difficult and even compromising for the representatives of the Free Synod to be present and to influence by their presence the attitude of the Oecumenical Council. On the other hand it seems very difficult for the Oecumenical Council to deal with all these questions without being helped by the representatives of both sides. After all I feel that the best way is to invite Praeses Koch, to submit to him the situation as you see it and to leave it to him to decide whether or not he wishes to accept.

As to the more innocent question of my daughter's stay in England, her address at present and probably until the beginning of October is c/o Mrs. V. E. Henley, Leigh House, Woodbridge, Suffolk. From October to December I hope to make it possible to have her in some settlement work in London. I am trying to settle this question with my daughter in London. It is most kind of Mrs. Bell and yourself to think of seeing her. I had the impression that she had first to improve her English and to be quiet in Suffolk, otherwise I would certainly have made use of your permission to tell you of her stay. If you kindly allow, I am sending you a word after having seen my daughter next week.

My nephew is very happy in Rye and was, as my sister told me, very pleased to meet you.

It is possible that I am coming as a representative of the Swiss Church Federation to Fanö, as Professor Choisy is unfortunately for reasons of health prevented from making the journey.[3] The matter will be decided these very next days.

With kindest regards,
Yours very sincerely,

1   Adolf Keller, *Religion and the European Mind* (London: Lutterworth Press, 1934).
2   The degree 'zum Schutz der Volksgemeinschaft' (9 July 1934) forbade any discussion of the church controversy in public assembly rooms and press organs.
3   At this Koechlin would represent the Swiss churches with the ecumenical internationalist, Adolf Keller, another close ally of Bell.

Koechlin to Bell, 14 July 1934, Basel UB, NL 37, VI 45 (carbon).

Dear Lord Bishop,

I am just receiving from [a] most trustworthy source the enclosed very important facts concerning the German Church situation. You might use them as you think it wise. I am leaving to-morrow night for London, but was anxious to send these news [*sic*] at once to you.

With my very best regards,
Yours very sincerely

Enclosure:
LPL Bell Papers, Vol. 6, fols. 89–91.

Basel, 14 July 1934.

1. *General situation*. Much more critical, the Reichs-Church using everywhere methods of force. Dr. Frick's law results in a control of the whole evangelical press by the Reichs-Church. New Church law gives to the Reichsbishop power to exclude from the National Synod everyone who is not German-Christian. At the Committee for Church Constitution (Verfassungsausschuss) held in Erfurt, no leader of the opposition present. Of a great number of theologians only Professor Hirsch and Meyer present.[1]
2. *Württemberg*. Wurm's position strong. Pastors united on his side as well as the Free Communities. Some of the latter have left the German-Christian front. The same is true for the faculty of Tübingen. All decided not to deal with the Reichsbishop before withdrawal of his measures of urgency of April and his return to constitutional ground. Württemberg Church Government decided to go to the last for the sake of the Gospel.

3. *Baden*. Bishop Kühlewein,[2] having given way to the Reichsbishop and governmental pressure, the Church has been unified with the Reichs-Church by decision of an enlarged Church Government. This Church Government dissolved the Provincial Synod, elected by the people[,] and nominated a new Synod. Members of the Church Government being not German-Christians, will probably withdraw from office.
4. *Hessen-Kassel*. A German-Christian is elected as Bishop in an unconstitutional way. The police took possession of the house of Church Government. Dr. Merzyn,[3] former head of the Hessen-Kassel Church, left with his staff Kassel for Marburg and governing the confessing communities from the exile. Force measures against many pastors seem imminent.
5. *Hessen-Nassau*. The head of the confessing community, Ritter,[4] in 'Schutzhaft'. Bishop Dietrich[5] forbidding every 'political activities' [*sic*] meaning the brotherhood of confessing pastors. The police asked by Church Government to proceed against confessing pastors. Especially violent situation in Waldeck, where the Dean has received orders to leave the town with his family.[6]
6. *Saxony*. Inhibition of any assemblies and devotional exercises of the confessing Church, even if held in private houses.
7. *Westfalen*. The President of the Government (Regierungs-präsident) asked his subordinates (Landräte) to interfere in the Church struggle, allowing them to make use of state power against pastors and members of presbyteries of the confessing Church. Threat to take hold of Church collect[ions]s of confessing pastors. Different pastors imprisoned, not allowed to see wife and children for weeks.
8. *Prussia*. Especially difficult situation, front of confessing Church growing and beginning to institute seminaries and examinations of its own. The Hitler Youth dispersing a Church assembly f[or]. i[nstance]. in Potsdam with the words murderers '(Aasgeier) of the German Nation.' Strong influence of the Hauer Movement amongst radicalised youth.
9. *Hannover*. 'Staatskommissar' imminent. Opposition developing to become independent confessing Church. Bishop Marahrens still hesitant.
10. *Bavaria*. Lutheran Convent for whole Germany will be constituted in Würzburg these days to support the confessing front of Barmen.

1   The Committee for the Church Constitution met on 6/7 July and continued on 27 July. The majority was *Deutsche Christen*, including the professors Emanuel Hirsch (Göttingen), Erich Seeberg (Berlin) and Wolf Meyer-Erlach (Jena).
    Emanuel Hirsch (1888–1972): Protestant theologian, from 1921 professor of church history and from 1936 to 1945 of systematic theology at Göttingen University. During the Third Reich he was the most influential theologian of the *Deutsche Christen* Erich Seeberg (1888–1945): Protestant theologian, from 1927 professor of church history at Berlin University; he became a follower of Karl Holl. In 1933 he was Dean of the Theological Faculty. He was a vigorous member of the *Deutsche Christen* and the NSDAP.
    Wolf Meyer, from 1935 Meyer-Erlach (1891–1982): Protestant theologian. From 1922 he acted as propaganda speaker of the NSDAP. Without academic degrees

and against the will of the faculty, he became professor of practical theology at Jena University in November 1933. Against the *votum* of the teaching staff, he was rector of the university 1935-7. In line with his antisemitism he declared his collaboration with the Eisenach *Institut* zur Erforschung und Beseitigung des jüdischen Einflusses auf das deutsche kirchliche Leben in 1939.

2   Julius Kühlewein (1873-1948): minister, regional bishop. Since 1924 as Prelate the spiritual head of the United Evangelical-Protestant Regional Church of Baden and regional bishop between 1933 and 1945. In April 1933 he welcomed the seizure of power by the National Socialists and thereafter cultivated supportive relations with the National Socialist church government. Even so, by 1937 he joined the ninety-six church leaders in protesting against of the ideas and influence of Alfred Rosenberg.

3   Gerhard Merzyn (1877-1945): minister. Until 1933 the president of the regional church office (*Landeskirchenamt*) of the Protestant Church in Hesse-Kassel. On 12 September 1933 the Regional Church Assembly (*Landeskirchentag*) established a provisional church government. The candidate for the new regional bishop was Merzyn, supported by both the *Pfarrernotbund* and the *Deutschen Christen*, but he did not receive the necessary approval of the Prussian government. On 29 June, a state church convention without a quorum elected Karl Theys as bishop. On the orders of Jäger, the *Deutsche Christen* church president of the Church of Hannover, Johannes Richter as a commissioner of the Reich church government, broke the passive resistance of the provisional church government by driving them out of office with the help of the police. On 13 July he declared the decisions of 29 June legal.

4   Probably Karl Bernhard Ritter, a student pastor in Marburg and a leading light in the Confessing Church of Hesse-Kassel.

5   Ernst Ludwig Dietrich (1897-1974): bishop in the newly-formed regional church of Nassau-Hessen 1934-45, member of the National Socialist Party, but not of the *Deutsche Christen*. He began to lose authority with the establishment of the Regional Church Council on 5 November 1935 and his role ended when the Council was replaced by a Regional Church Committee on 15 January 1936. After the resignation of this committee, on 28 July 1937, the leadership of the church practically gave up under the president of the regional church, Paul Kipper. By now Dietrich simply served as parish administrator at Wiesbaden. In 1937 he began to distance himself from National Socialism altogether.

6   After a degree of the Reichschurch the Regional Church of Hesse-Kassel merged with the Regional Church of Waldeck on 12 June 1934 to become the Protestant Church of Kurhessen-Waldeck.

Bell to Koechlin, 19 July 1934, Basel UB, NL 37, VI 47 (carbon).

My dear Dr. Koechlin

Ever so many thanks for your letters of July 5th, 10th and 14th, the latter enclosing the latest facts on the German Church situation. I am very glad indeed to have these. I have seen Bishop Nuelson[1] who has just come to London, Hotel Russell, Russell Square, from a long stay in Germany. He gave a most distressing account of the German Church situation. It might be worth your while seeing him if he is still at the Hotel Russell. I think he goes to Edinburgh to-day (perhaps you are going too?) for the Central Relief Meeting[2] which will be attended I gather by Bishop Heckel amongst others.

I tried to get in touch with you in London on Monday and Tuesday, thinking you might be at the Red Triangle Club[3] where you have stayed before. But you cannot have been there and very likely went to Suffolk. I should like to have seen you if you had been available. I send this letter to Salisbury. Westman[4] is staying with me on his way to Salisbury. I do not think there is much chance of our meeting if you are going straight from Salisbury to Oxford. If it did so happen that you could spend the night of Tuesday, July 24th, here – you can get a train direct from Salisbury to Chichester – it would be very nice indeed to see you. But I think you are probably very heavily engaged at Salisbury and such an arrangement would be impossible. If something were to happen during the next few days, as Bonhoeffer, whom I saw on Tuesday, thought extremely likely, i.e. a decisive move either by the Church government or the State, showing its hand, I would get into touch with you at Salisbury and see if we could arrange a Meeting. It is most kind of you to be so ready to help. I am so very delighted that you are coming to Fanø.

What you told me about the National Free Synod and the Free Reformed Synod cleared up matters very decidedly, and I am very glad you pointed out the possible embarrassment for Praeses Koch or his colleagues. Bishop Ammundsen and Schönfeld both wrote that they thought it would be useful to invite Praeses Koch as a guest and an expert. I have accordingly sent him a letter on these lines. I enclose a spare copy which is not very legible, but will show you what I said if you can decipher it. Please destroy on reading. I will let you know what answer I get.

Yours very sincerely,

---

1 John L. Nuelsen (1867–1946): German-American Bishop of the Methodist Episcopal Church and the Methodist Church, elected in 1908, responsible for Central Europe from 1912, but from 1920 only for the Zürich Area. He retired in 1940. In the ecumenical field he stressed that the small Christian communities were also important.
2 The Central Bureau of Relief in Geneva, overseen by Adolf Keller.
3 The Red Triangle Club was the London home of the YMCA on Greengate Street, Plaistow. An immense structure, it was built in 1921 as a memorial to those who had died in the Great War.
4 Knut B. Westman (1881–1967): professor of missionary and East Asian religious history at Uppsala University since 1930; leading light in the Swedish Student Christian Movement; formerly a missionary in China.

***Enclosure*: Bell to Karl Koch, 18 July 1934, Basel, UB, NL 37, VI 46.**[1]

UNIVERSAL CHRISTIAN COUNCIL FOR LIFE AND WORK
Ökumenischer Rat für Praktisches Christentum
Conseil oecumnénique du Christianisme pratique

Right Reverend and Dear Sir,

The Universal Christian Council for Life and Work is holding its Meeting at Fanø, in Denmark, from August 23 to August 30. It is expected that the Meeting will be one of grave importance. On the Saturday the Council will engage in a discussion on the recent Message which I sent as a President to the representatives of the Churches on the Universal Christian Council at Ascensiontide. On the Monday and the Tuesday the same theme for discussion will be 'The Church and the Modern Conception of the State' and also 'The Church and the World Order'.

I write as President, after consultation with Bishop Ammundsen and some others, to invite you to attend the Meeting of the Council and to bring a colleague with you; or if you are for any reason unable to attend yourself, to send two representatives. If it happened to be convenient for Dr. Bodelschwingh to be one of such representatives his presence would be very valuable.' I invite you 'and your colleagues or representatives as guests and as authoritative spokesmen in a very difficult situation from whose information and advice the Universal Christian Council would be certain to derive much benefit.

I am well aware that you may yourself perceive difficulties which you will no doubt carefully consider as this invitation reaches you. The Universal Council will be obliged to hold a discussion, and in all probability to express an opinion, on the German Church situation. It will be very difficult for the Council to deal with the questions raised without the assistance of spokesmen representing different 'positions' and points of view. I also appreciate the fact however that attendance may have its embarrassment 'for those who take a different view from that of the Church government'. I would only say that you are able to come 'or to send representatives' you 'and your colleague' would be most welcome.

With most respect and sympathy,
I am
Yours very faithfully,

1 The letter, with official letterhead, was revised several times by Bell; the version sent to Koch may be found in Boyens, *Kirchenkampf und Ökumene*, p. 330, here drawn from the archives of the Evangelical Church in Westphalia.

Bell to Koechlin, 15 August 1934, Basel UB, NL 37, VI 48 (carbon).

My dear Dr. Koechlin,

I have had a very important communication from Bishop Ammundsen who saw Dr. Koch and others on August 10. I think it very unlikely that Dr. Koch and his friends will be allowed to come to Fanø,[1] but that Bonhoeffer will.[2] Dr. Koch asks whether I could see him at Oeynhausen before going to Fanø. This is very difficult for me and you will see what I have said to Henriod. But I should like your personal view as to whether you think that I could do real good by seeing Dr. Koch before Fanø. Is it not better to see him afterwards? If it is a matter of life and death of course I would go, but I find it very difficult to see quite clearly what is the best course, leaving out considerations of any actual personal difficulty as far as tickets for this voyage are concerned. Can I learn so much more by a personal conversation that it would be good to go? If you hold a decided view that I should go, telegraph the one word 'Go' and I shall understand, for I have the greatest confidence in your judgement.

Yours very sincerely,

1. Two decisions hindered Koch's coming to Fanø. At first, Koch's report to the Foreign Office and Heckel's influence meant that only the delegation of the German Protestant Church was allowed to travel (see the documents published in Boyens, *Kirchenkampf und Ökumene*, pp. 330–1, 333–337). Furthermore, the Council of Brethren of the Confessing Church had decided that no individual from the Confessing Church could attend unless delegates from the Confessing Church were invited as such.
2. Bonhoeffer came not as delegate from the Confessing Church to Fanø but as a participant in the youth conference as youth secretary together with some of his students. On 30 August he and Koch were added as 'consultative and coopted members' to the Ecumenical Council for Life and Work.

Enclosure: Bell to Henry-Louis Henriod, 15 August 1934, Basel UB, NL 37, VI 47 (carbon).

Copy

My dear Henriod,

I have received Bishop Ammundsen's report of his interview with Dr. Koch. It is very important. I have just heard on the telephone that Bonhoeffer is at Esbjerg[1] now and he is to see Ammundsen tomorrow and I am telling him that it is so difficult for me to start in the time to see Dr. Koch at Oeynhausen before Fanø that unless there are overwhelming reasons why I should, I shall not do so, and that I am not at all sure that a visit after Fanø with the results of the Council would not be more profitable. But I do think that it would be of very great value that you and Dr. Koechlin should go to Oeynhausen if you possibly can. I gather that it is only about a hundred miles from Esbjerg. What do you yourself think? I would gladly make a contribution to pay for the difference in travelling expenses for you both.

I am sending a copy of this letter to Dr. Koechlin.

Yours ever,

1. A Danish harbour town just across from Fanø.

Bell to Koechlin, 1 October 1934, Basel UB, NL 37, VI 49 (typewritten).

My dear Dr. Koechlin,

I returned home from holiday on Friday. As you can imagine, after Fanø I was really tired, and am thankful that my holiday had already been arranged to follow the Council Meetings instead of preceding them. I spent most of a day in the difficult task of preparing my article for *The Times* for they wanted it as soon as possible. I wrote this at Lund, before going on to Dalecarlia.[1] But I had most refreshing holiday in Sweden then, and had the opportunity of very full talks with the Archbishop of Uppsala[2] ten days ago. He, you may like to know, was not in favour of a delegation at the present moment as he thought it would certainly achieve nothing, though it might be used by the Church Government as an indication of friendliness. He thought it would be much wiser and much more profitable if from time to time leading members of the council happened to pay visits to Berlin and to drop in on the Church Government officials and express their anxieties and difficulties. If a more or less steady stream of anxieties, at intervals of a month or six weeks, expressed by personal visits, friendly but critical, could be kept up, the total effect might be very valuable. I agree.

I am really writing however to tell you that last Wednesday, at the request of Praeses Koch, I passed through Germany on my way home and had six hours' conference with Praeses Koch and other members of the Confessional Synod. Incidentally I explained why I had not read his letter to the Council. I think that they understood the reason, and they certainly never intended to claim that their Praesidium was the governing body of the true German Evangelical Church but simply a committee of management to carry on in between Meetings of the Confessional Synod, which of course is the authoritative body from their point of view. We had a most illuminating talk and I was much impressed by the earnestness, statesmanship and courage of Praeses Koch and his friends. It is a great thing to have got into personal contact and to know the kind of men who are leading the Confessional Synod.

One particular request they made. The nomination of Praeses Koch to the Council has caused much objection in the German Church Government.[3] But the Church Government is consoling itself with the thought that it is a paper action as the Council will not meet for two years and much may happen before then. Hence the importance, says Praeses Koch, of making the connection between himself and the Council real, and to give evidence of it from time to time. I assured him that the Council wanted to make the fellowship a very real thing. When he asked me therefore whether I thought a member of the Council could come officially as a representative of the Council to the next Meeting of the Confessional Synod, which they might have to call in the fairly near future should a crisis arise, I said that I should certainly hope that this could be arranged. I did not make [a] promise and he understood this. But I said that I was sure that it would be the wish of the Council that steps should be taken to bring this about, and he was very much cheered by this and said 'Schön'. They all seemed pleased.

I think that I ought not myself to go, at any rate just yet, as I am President. It would be too strong a step unless some quite new calamity takes place, apart from the question of my not speaking German. I am writing therefore to ask whether you, than whom none could be better, could hold yourself free to attend the next Meeting of the

Confessional Synod. It would be an enormous encouragement to me personally to feel that I could count on you as the person representing the Council, for I have the greatest confidence in your wisdom and your ability to say the right thing. May I ask you to do this? Of course your expenses will be paid.

Yours very sincerely,

1   An hotel in Tallberg, Sweden.
2   Erling Eidem (1880–1972): archbishop of Uppsala, 1931–50; New Testament scholar; a leading ecumenist and figure in the Lutheran World Federation.
3   Already at the meeting in Fanø, Heckel had protested against Koch's co-optation; see Boyens, *Kirchenkampf und Ökumene*, Vol. 1, p. 339.

Koechlin to Bell, 3 October 1934, Basel UB, NL 37, VI 50 (carbon).

My dear Lord Bishop,

Your very kind and important letter of October 1st is just coming in. Dr. Schönfeld, returning from Germany, has brought to me [on] Saturday night very important and perplexing news concerning the critical church developments. Dr. Oldham will have give[n] to you similar information. I hope to be able to write more fully before long on these questions, giving you some personal impressions I had being present at the centenary of the Bremen YMCA three weeks ago.[1]

With these short lines I wish to thank you very heartily for the great confidence you are placing in me, and to tell you once more how deeply I appreciate to be related to you in such a way.

In view of your call I feel very deeply that one has no right to refuse certain services one is asked to render for a great cause in a critical time. As far as I am personally concerned, I would be ready though I am fully aware of the great responsibilities involved.

I feel however obliged to give closer consideration to certain aspects involved, before I can give you a definite answer. First I do not feel entitled to accept to be, even for a short time, liaison officer between the Oecumenical Council and the Confessional Synod, if Professor Choisy, who is the President of the Swiss Church Federation, does not fully agree. I am writing him to-day and hope to get his answer before long.

I have secondly to consider if such a mandate is not in opposition with my Vice-Chairmanship of the World's Alliance of YMCA and of the Basel Mission. As the Mission as well as the German YMCA Movement are standing in one line with the Confessional Synod, I do not see on this point any serious difficulties, but I need some quiet thinking and some confidential consultations before being quite clear.

And thirdly I am somewhat hesitant, because I am not [a] regular, fully entitled member of the Oecumenical Council. My regular status is that of a substitute member of the official Swiss delegation consisting of Professor Keller and Professor Choisy. In this capacity I took in Fanø, but only for that meeting, the place and rights of Professor Choisy, who was unable to attend.

I wonder if under those circumstances I am entitled to be entrusted with the important official mandate to represent the Oecumenical Council at the next meeting of the Confessional Synod. I am very anxious that you might give fullest consideration to this aspect of the question, because I am inclined to think that in writing your letter you were not aware of the fact of my not being a regular member of the Oecumenical Council. The action you are proposing and with which I am in complete agreement, is so important that even very formal questions have their full weight. May I ask you therefore to 'rethink the mission' you thought of entrusting to me and to feel at full liberty to come back to your decision if you think it necessary.

Yours very sincerely,

1   The responsible leaders of the Bremen centenary celebration on 10 September were able to justify such a large-scale international event to the authorities by emphasizing the international significance of the YMCA; and they secured financial support from the state, on the grounds that it was a demonstration of religious freedom. See Manfred Priepke, *Die evangelische Jugend im Dritten Reich 1933-1936* (Hannover: Norddt. Verl.-Anstalt Goedel, 1960), p. 139; Koechlin, 'Hundertjähriges Jubiläum des CVJM Bremen, 9 September 1934', Basel, UB, NL 37, III 15a, 15b.

Bell to Koechlin, 8 October 1934, Basel UB, NL 37, VI 51 (typewritten).

My dear Koechlin,

Very many thanks for your kind letter of October 3. I shall be much interested to hear further about your impressions derived at the Bremen Centenary.

But I write especially to say how greatly I appreciate the very responsive and friendly way in which you reply to my request. I thoroughly appreciate the need of your giving closer consideration to the various aspects of that request which you indicate in 'firstly' and 'secondly'. But after reflection I feel that you need have no hesitations with regard to the point of your status on the oecumenical council. I think there are two things to be borne in mind – the first thing is that it is vital that the representative of the oecumenical council at the Meeting of the Confessional Synod should be one who was in all the throes of the Meeting at Fanø, because it is of very great importance that our representative should be one who can speak from intimate acquaintance with all that went on there. This qualification you possess to a peculiar degree. But there is this further point that at Fanø the Continental Section elected you as its Secretary, in succession to Dr. Stange. In that capacity you are a full member of the Executive Committee to which 'the Secretaries of the Sections' definitely belong. You are thus, without any doubt, a member of the Council till the Council meets again, and you will be expected to come as Secretary of the Continental Sections, i.e. not 'necessarily' as a Swiss delegate, to the Meeting of the Executive Committee next year. There is thus a rather special qualification from the formal point of view for your attending the Meeting of the Confessional Synod.

So I hope very much you may see your way to saying 'Yes' after considering the other points. I quite appreciate in particular what you say about Professor Choisy. I hope he would be agreeable.

Yours very sincerely,

Koechlin to Bell, 9 October 1934, Basel UB, NL 37, VI 52 (carbon).

My dear Lord Bishop,

The answer of Professor Choisy to the letter I had addressed to him October 3rd is just coming in. The delay is due to his being away from Geneva for a short holiday. He does not see any difficulty from the Swiss point of view in my attending as a delegate of the Oecumenical Council the next Confessional Synod in Germany. He is kind enough to underline the fact that I might be considered as his permanent representative in the Oecumenical Council. He does not see the possibility of attending furthermore the meetings. It is only the fact of his being President of the Swiss Church Federation which makes him desire to have his name on the list of the regular members of the Council.

As to my connections to the Basel Mission and the World's Committee of YMCA, I came to the conclusion that there is no difficulty either. The Basel Mission is fully on the side of the Bekenntniskirche. The leading members of the Board, whom I consulted confidentially, were strongly encouraging me to be at your disposal. As to the YMCA, the German Movement has lately taken so clearly a position in favour of the Confessional Movement, that I do not fear anything from this side.

You might be interested to know that I have seen, shortly after having received your letter, Karl Barth and you will, I hope, not mind my having consulted him. He was very strongly in favour of a delegation of the Oecumenical Council coming to the next Synod and encouraged me very much to accept your offer. The only thought in his mind was, that it might be very advisable to send not only a reformed, but also and even in first line a Lutheran representative. He thought of a man like Bishop Aulen.[1] I think this to be a very wise suggestion. If you think of sending only one representative, I have no doubt whatever that it ought to be a Lutheran. I am even wondering if it would not be wise to send in second line a duly representative man of the Anglican Church. Such a delegation might be more impressive as well for the Church as for the Government circles. Please feel at any rate quite free to give up your plan of sending me to the Synod, if you think another solution in the better interest of course.

If however you think of sending me in spite of these suggestions, I would be very much obliged to you if you would give me as clearly as possible your view as to what I have to do and to say and not to do and not to say.

Looking forward to your further news, I am,

yours very sincerely,

1   Gustav Aulen (1879–1977): bishop of Strängnäs, 1933–52; eminent Swedish theologian who won an international audience, particularly for his book *Christus Victor* (1930), which had appeared in an English edition in 1931.

Koechlin to Bell, 11 October 1934, Basel UB, NL 37, VI 53 (carbon).

My dear Lord Bishop,

I have to thank you for your letter of October 8th and to confirm our conversation by phone of yesterday night.

As to your letter, may I state the fact that I have not been elected secretary of the continental section in succession of Dr. Stange. Dr. Stange has been officially re-elected and I have only been appointed to take his place if for reasons of general German or personal developments it would prove impossible for Stange to maintain his post. I accepted this appointment, because Bishop Ammundsen wished strongly that such a provision was made, but as long as Stange is holding the office, there can be no question of my secretaryship and, as far as I see, of my being a member of the administrative or executive Committee. I can only, if you think my position established enough, be considered a member of the Oecumenical Council.

Your telephone [call] of yesterday night mentioned a telegram you had received from Germany, stating that 'the Church situation was reaching its climax, the State using more and more its power against Church opposition and that you were strongly urged to send a representation of the Oecumenical Council to the next Confessional Synod'.[1] You asked me to be such a representative and gave me power to act in your name according [to] circumstances. I accepted this mandate, being fully aware of the responsibility involved and decided to limit my action to what the resolution of Fanø is stating in connection with the Confessional Synod.

May I explicitly repeat what I said in my last letter of October 9th, that I will be thankful for any further advice you will be kind enough to give me. It is equally true that you might feel free to change your appointment if in view of arising emergencies you should think [it] wiser to send a more representative delegation or altogether another personality.

I telephoned this morning to Henriod, because I think it to be essential to be with him in as close a contact as possible. He told me of his proposal to you, to call a meeting of the administrative Committee to London or Paris for October 20th. I expressed the thought that it might be better to postpone such a meeting until you can discuss the report on the Confessional Synod.[2] It would indeed be difficult to lay down a plan of action, before this certainly very important meeting of the Synod has taken place.

The situation in Württemberg actually is such, that I am afraid the Synod will have to take very decisive steps, which the Oecumenical Council certainly ought to know before deciding on his [sic] further actions. I don't think Henriod is right in assuming that the break with Rome and the legal constitution of a new Church is coming before January. Different signs seem to prove that the German Government will not take irreparable steps before the vote in the Saar has taken place, though the German situation in the Saar is becoming more and more dangerous and might lead the German Government to desperate actions.[3]

As Praeses Koch has told Henriod and, not more than three days ago, Visser 't Hooft, they think of holding the Synod the 31st of October. I do not think they will change the date unless some alarming calamity might arise. I am trying to get in direct contact with Praeses Koch, asking him to give me in time the necessary information.

If, as Henriod told me, the Synod should be held in Berlin, I wonder if I should not call on Heckel. It would be rather difficult to ignore him in Berlin itself. May I ask you for advice in this matter?

You mentioned your willingness to come to the Synod yourself if absolutely necessary, but expressed the opinion that this could only be a very last step of the Oecumenical Council. I am of your opinion and think that for the moment you ought not to come yourself but reserve the weight of your personal presence for a last, really decisive action. If however I should come to another conviction, I of course would let you know.

In Württemberg Bishop Wurm is prisoner in his own house. He might be led to prison before long. In some villages the S.A. refused to take steps against the pastors and when the S.A. of the city came out in the country, the whole population obliged it by a menacing attitude to withdraw. The situation is becoming more and more impossible and dangerous. In Bavaria the Berlin Church Government evidently does not dare for the moment to go ahead.

To inform Henriod, I am sending him a copy of this letter.

With kindest regards I am,
Cordially yours,

P.S. You gave me power yesterday to ask Henriod to accompany me to the Confessional Synod. I might come to the conclusion to have him with me. For the moment I am inclined to think that he would be in a rather awkward situation, holding in his capacity as general-secretary the second place in the delegation. It would of course be quite otherwise if prominent men like Bishop Ammundsen or Bishop Aulen would be heading the delegation. In such a case his being in the second place, would be quite natural. For this reason I do not for the moment mention your proposal to Henriod.

1. The situation was provoked when August Jäger attempted to use the decree of 3 September to incorporate the churches of Württemberg and Bavaria into the Reichschurch. A letter from the Presidential Chancellery on 11 September, on behalf of the 'Führer', declared that Meiser's and Wurm's objections to the integration were 'not justified'. But the pastors and congregations supported their bishops through church services and demonstrations of sympathy. On 14 September, Wurm and a number of church councillors were given leave of absence; from 4 October, they were under house arrest. In Bavaria, on 11 October, Jäger declared Meiser and the *Oberkirchenräte* and *Kreisdekane* deposed. On 12 October, Meiser was placed under house arrest by the Bavarian political police. However, acknowledging the force of foreign opinion, on 26 October, Hitler invited the two deposed bishops and Marahrens to a discussion of the church situation. This followed on 30 October. In consequence, the Reich Ministry of the Interior restored their freedom.
2. The second Reichs-Confession-Synode at Dahlem was planned for 30–31 October, but because of the dramatic developments in the Church in Bavaria this took place on 19–20 October.
3. The voting in the Saar area on 13 January 1935 was certainly prepared by intensive propaganda, but it was not followed by desperate actions.

Bell to Koechlin, 11 October 1934, Basel UB, NL 37, VI 54 (typewritten).

My dear Dr. Koechlin,

I am very grateful for your letter of the 9th inst. received to-day, and I am most thankful that you can attend the Confessional Synod. This is just a preliminary acknowledgment. I am seeing Dr. Oldham to-night and if I can persuade him to go with you I will.[1] I have also written to Bishop Aulen to press him if he can possibly come. I think if you and Bishop Aulen and Oldham were to go it would be a very powerful combination. In any event I want you to go, and I will let you know, after talking it over with Oldham, what sort of points are to be kept in view. And I think Henriod might well go as well, as Praeses Koch has pressed him to come personally. I have also written to Archbishop Eidem to tell him what is happening and to ask him to do his best, if Bishop Aulen is too heavily occupied to permit of his coming, to try and get Professor Runestam[2] to come.

Henriod suggests that the principle of the Watching Group should be maintained with regard to continuous study of and contact with what is happening in Germany. This means that a chosen representative of our own should be present. Henriod suggests, and I whole-heartedly agree, that it would be of enormous value if we could have you as our key man, to keep us informed. *I should be most thankful if we could regard you as our Watcher.*[3]

Yours very sincerely,

1 Oldham wrote a long and thorough letter to Koechlin on 12 October 1934. See Bell Papers, Vol. 6, fols. 223–8 (r and v).
2 Arvid Runestam (1887–1962), Professor of Theological Ethics at Uppsala University and later bishop of Karlstad (1938–57).
3 Underscored, apparently by Koechlin.

Bell to Koechlin, 13 October 1934, Basel UB, NL 37, VI 56 (handwritten), Basel UB, NL 37, VI 57 (typewritten).

Very private.

My dear Dr. Koechlin,
Many thanks for yours. I will write more fully about the 'mission' next week.
'Meantime let me say briefly'

(1) You are anyhow a member of the Council – so that is all right.
(2) I am most anxious that you should (as Oldham suggests) be collecting *facts*, which could if need be, be used in a next [?] universal Church statement, should the extremity arrive.
(3) And please *watch* and study and keep closest possible contacts with the situation!
(4) I rather think *you* should come to the Admin. Cttee Oct. 25–27 here. Henriod has explained why *before* the Synod.

(5) I enclose copy of Oldham's [telegram] to Cavert U.S.A.[1] – as to *possibility* as last resort of worldwide action!
(6) I saw the Archbishop of Canterbury yesterday – he is very sympathetic and knows all I am doing.
(7) I saw Prince Bismarck[2] at the German Embassy in London yesterday, and made a strong impression on him of the[3] gravity of crisis.

Forgive haste, yours ever

1. Samuel McCrea Cavert (1888–1976): American Presbyterian minister and influential ecumenist; General Secretary of the National Council of Churches, 1921–54.
2. Prince Otto Christian von Bismarck (1897–1975): grandson of the former Chancellor of the Reich, he entered the Foreign Service in 1927 and worked at the German Embassy in London from 1928 to 1937.
3. 'of the' only in the handwritten letter; in the typewritten letter there is one lacuna.

Enclosure:
Oldham to Cavert, no date, Basel UB, NL 37, VI 58 (carbon).

'Very Confidential'

CAVERT CONFIDENTIAL STOP GRAVITY OF GERMAN CHURCH SITUATION INCREASING STOP EVENTUALITY MAY ARISE WHEN ONLY MEANS OF AVERTING DISASTER WILL BE TO INFORM GERMAN GOVERNMENT PRIVATELY THROUGH EMBASSIES IN DIFFERENT COUNTRIES THAT IF ATTEMPT MADE TO DESTROY CONFESSIONAL SYNOD REPRESENTING EVANGELICAL CHRISTIANITY CHURCHES WILL BE COMPELLED TO TAKE MOST EFFECTIVE MEASURES TO SUBMIT FACTS TO THEIR WHOLE CONSTITUENCIES STOP RESULT WILL BE THAT CIRCLES NATURALLY MOST FRIENDLY TO GERMAN PEOPLE WILL BE ROUSED TO INDIGNATION STOP TIME A VITAL ELEMENT STOP AVOID ALL PUBLICITY AND DELAY ACTION UNTIL RECEIPT OF LETTER OR FURTHER CABLEGRAM BUT TAKE VERY CONFIDENTIAL STEPS TO PREPARE FOR PROMPT VIGOROUS ACTION IF REQUIRED STOP SIMULTANEOUS ACTION IN ALL COUNTRIES DESIRABLE STOP BISHOP OF CHICESTER CONSULTING COLLEAGUES PERSONALLY APPROVES THIS CABLEGRAM.

OLDHAM.

Bell to Koechlin, 15 October 1934, Basel UB, NL 37, VI 58 (handwritten).

My dear Dr. Koechlin,
I enclose a copy of my reply to a question brought to me to-day personally by Pastor Hildebrandt[1] from Praeses Koch. I think that you will agree with it. I have sent a copy

to Henriod and asked him to keep in touch with you. Please note the final paragraph of the letter. I think it very important that you should come to Chichester if you possibly can for the Administrative Committee, as a guest. And I very much want you if this is also possible to see Koch on your way to Chichester. If you cannot see Koch, then I am asking Henriod to do so. I feel that we ought to have the latest from him before we meet.

Yours sincerely

P.S. Koch also sent a message asking *us* to investigate the Church situation in Bavaria and Wurttemberg. Can you do anything about it?

1   Franz Hildebrandt (1909–85): German Lutheran theologian and, since his days as a student in Berlin in 1929, Bonhoeffer's close friend. Ordained on 18 June 1933 in Berlin, he resigned from his pastorate in September in protest against the introduction of the Aryan Paragraph in the Church as his mother was of Jewish origin. After three months at Bonhoeffer's pastorate in London, he returned to Berlin at Niemöller's request and worked for the *Pfarrernotbund*. Shortly after Niemöller's arrest, Hildebrandt was also arrested in 1937, but was released with the help of friends. Hildebrandt migrated to Great Britain in September 1937, becoming a curate to Julius Rieger in London. From 1939 to 1946 he served as pastor to a refugee congregation at Cambridge. In 1944–6 he was district secretary of the British and Foreign Bible Society. He later became an eminent Methodist. See Holger Roggelin, *Franz Hildebrandt. Ein lutherischer Dissenter im Kirchenkampf und Exil* (Göttingen: Vandenhoeck & Ruprecht, 1999); Amos S. Cresswell and Maxwell G. Tow, *Dr. Franz Hildebrandt. Mr. Valiant-for-Truth* (Leominster: Gracewing, 2000).

Enclosure:
Bell to Koch, 15 October 1934, Basel UB, NL 37, VI 55 (carbon).

Copy
Private and Confidential
My dear Praeses Koch,
At the very first moment, nearly three weeks ago,[1] when you asked whether it would be possible for a member of the Oecumenical Council to be present at the next Meeting of the Confessional Synod, I raised the question in my own mind whether it would be right for me, as President, to attend myself; and I have already discussed the possibility with others. I have the feeling, and I find that this is definitely shared by other wise counsellors whose sympathy with the Confessional Synod is beyond all doubt, that, as I am at present advised, it would not be the most helpful thing that I could do for me to come to Berlin to attend this Meeting.

My reason is that while other members of the Oecumenical Council may most usefully attend, if the President of the Council comes now, there is nobody left in reserve for further action at what may even be a more crucial stage; and also that other action of a private kind is being taken by myself, and a public step of the nature which your messenger invites me to take, at this juncture, would I fear destroy the chance of useful results from this private course.

You will I am sure agree if the Oecumenical Council is to be of the greatest service in a crisis which concerns the whole Christian Church, we must conserve our strength and see that it is used to the greatest possible effect at the really vital moment for affecting decision.

I have summoned the Administrative Committee of the Oecumenical Council to an emergency Meeting at Chichester next week (October 25–27) so as to precede the meeting of the Confessional Synod. The situation may be clearer then and more light may have come as to the wisest and most effective way of helping in these tragic days. I hope that it may be possible for one of the members of the Administrative Committee to see you, or another prominent leader, so as to have your latest wishes and news before we confer at Chichester.

May God guard you and guide you!
Precibus oecumenicis conjuncti sumus.[2]
Yours very sincerely,

P.S. Pastor Koechlin of Basel has promised to attend the Confessional Synod, at my request, and I have also asked, and am hoping to secure the presence of, a prominent Lutheran from Sweden.

1   See Bell to Koechlin, 1 October 1934.
2   We are linked together by ecumenical prayers.

Koechlin: Telephone Bishop of Chichester, Wednesday, 17. Oktober 1934, 21.30 Hours, Basel UB, NL 37, VI 58 (typewritten).

Thanks for telegram. The Archbishop of Canterbury saw the German Ambassador in London on Tuesday, 16th and had a long conversation with him about the great anxiety the people in England have. He hoped there would be a great alteration within a week. Otherwise it would be impossible to resist a strong expression of opinion by the Church Leaders and Free Church Leaders in England. The Archbishop wants to communicate with the non-Roman Church Leaders in America and Scandinavia in view of a concerted expression of opinion. The lines on which an alteration could be made are to relieve Dr. Jäger of his office, to have the proceedings in Bavaria and other places with a declaration that they were open to reconsideration, that Bishop Müller also should be suspended and that full opportunity should be given to Meiser, Wurm and Koch to state their cause to Hitler. The Archbishop is very strong. I (the Bishop of Chichester) saw Prince Bismarck last week, and told him how disturbing the news were [sic]. The strong reaction of the Archbishop followed my smaller reaction. I was in correspondence with the Archbishop of Uppsala, Leiper[1] and Boegner.[2] I will be in Chichester until Monday and afterwards at Lambeth Palace till Thursday morning.

1   Henry Smith Leiper (1891-1975): American Presbyterian missionary, from 1930 executive secretary of the American section of the Universal Christian Council for Life and Work and also executive of the Commission of Relations with Churches Abroad of the Federal Council of Churches of Christ in America. From 1938 to 1952 associate general secretary of the WCC (in Process of Formation). After two journeys through Germany in 1933 and 1934 he supported the Confessing Church and was considered a special expert on the situation in Germany. See William J. Schmidt and Edward Ouellete, *What Kind of a Man? The Life of Henry Smith Leiper* (New York: Friendship Press, 1986).

2   Marc Boegner (1881-1970): French Reformed theologian, personally influenced by John Mott, he was active in the World Student Christian Federation, chairman of the French section 1923-35. He was President of the Protestant Confederation of France 1929-61, and chairman of the National Council of the Reformed Church of France 1938-50. After 1939, he became one of the vice-presidents of the WCC (in Process of Formation) and, in 1948-54, one of the presidents of the WCC. In wartime, he was a notable member of the French Resistance and played a courageous role under German occupation rescuing Jews.

Koechlin to Bell, 17 October 1934, Basel UB, NL 37, VI 60 (carbon).

My dear Lord Bishop,
   I have telegraphed to you this morning the following words:

Convocation by phone confessional Synod Berlin-Dahlem Friday 19th leaving Basel Thursday afternoon Berlin address Swiss Legation.

Yesterday night at 11 o'clock a phone came directly from Oeynhausen by someone who did not mention his name. He told me in the name of Praeses Koch, that they had got your letter telling them I was coming to the Confessional Synod. For reason of shortness of time they were obliged to use the phone to tell me that the 'Confessional Synod of the German Evangelical Church' would take place this Friday 19th in Berlin-Dahlem, opening with a church service in the St. Annenkirche. I was asked to get into touch after my arrival with Pastor Jacobi.[1] Furthermore I was asked to tell you of these news, asking you to let Oeynhausen know, if you would come yourself or not. I told them that you had written to me that you were unable to attend and he asked me to come in your name, probably together with a delegate of Swedish nationality.
   This morning I telephoned with Henriod, who had received a cable from Pastor Runestam telling him that Bishop Rodhe[2] would come to Chichester and go afterwards to Barmen. He has cabled Bishop Rhode at once about the change of date and the exact place of the meeting. No doubt Pastor Forell of the Swedish Church in Berlin,[3] who knows much more than the State Police, will look after him. I will be taking counsel with Bishop Rhode on every point of our common action. Henriod asked me if I thought he ought to accompany me. Having given some thought to this question before, I answered him I thought it was better to reserve his influence for a later possibility. To have Bishop Rodhe and myself would fulfil the purpose and if Bishop

Rodhe could not come, it would not be quite normal to have two Swiss Reformed as the official delegates of the Oecumenical Council. Henriod fully agreed with this point of view. I am meeting him to-morrow at the Oecumenical Committee of the Swiss Church Federation and am glad to have this possibility of discussing with him very fully our mandate.

My train is leaving to-morrow night. [It] may be that some instruction you thought of sending me will reach me before my departure. Otherwise I might find them in Berlin, where the Swiss Minister[4] knows of my arrival and will hand to me your letter if you have sent one to his address.

The Synod, if not interrupted and ended by State interference, will probably last until Saturday afternoon. I think of coming back to Basel via Munich to see some people there. From Württemberg I have a very full account of the facts, so that I ought to be able to bring to Chichester a pretty complete report.

May I thank you for your letter of October 13th as well as that of October 11th. I have not answered earlier because you had written a third letter would reach me in the course of this week.

It might be enough to tell you that I have very much in mind what you are saying and that, as things are standing, I prefer going into details and single facts when coming to the meeting of the Administrative Committee.

I feel it to be a duty to accept your invitation and am looking forward with great pleasure to seeing you at Chichester Thursday next, October 25th. You will receive earlier news if emergencies are arising.

I am very grateful to know that your thoughts and prayers will accompany me.

With kindest regards I am
cordially yours

P.S. This letter was dictated but not signed, when you phoned yesterday night. I am leaving in an hour, having seen Henriod this morning. Bishop Rhode telegraphed that he could not be in Berlin to-morrow. Henriod was quite clear that he ought not to go now, but possibly after the Administrative Committee. So I am going alone – and not alone!

---

1   Gerhard Jacobi (1891–1971): Lutheran pastor, since 1930 pastor of the Kaiser Wilhelm Gedächtniskirche in central Berlin; a leading light in the Young Reformation group and an active member of the Confessing Church, he was effective president of the Confessing Church in Berlin until 1939. After the war he became, in 1946, general superintendent of the Evangelical Church in West Berlin and from 1954 Evangelical Lutheran bishop of Oldenburg, retiring in 1967.
2   Edvard Magnus Rodhe (1878–1954), Swedish Lutheran theologian, professor of practical theology at Lund University, bishop of the Diocese of Lund, 1925–48.
3   Birger Forell (1893–1958): Swedish pastor who served the Swedish church in Berlin between 1929 and 1942; he was actively involved in refugee work and it is believed that he was repatriated to Sweden after pressure from the German state; in 1944 he

was invited by Bell to work for German prisoners-of-war in Britain, a task which culminated in the establishment of educational programmes, not least at Norton Camp; in the following year he created the Committee for Christian Post-War Aid. See Klaus Loscher, *Studium und Alltag hinter Stacheldraht, Birger Forells Beitrag zum theologisch-pädagogischen Lehrbetrieb im Norton Camp, England (1945-1948)* (Neukirchen-Vluyn: Neukirchener, 1997); also Harald von Koenigswald, *Birger Forell: Leben und Wirken in den Jahren 1933-1958* (Witten and Berlin: Eckart Verlag, 1962).

4 Probably the Swiss diplomat Paul Dinichert (1878-1954), ambassador at Berlin 1932-8.

Bell to Koechlin, 17 October 1934, Basel UB, NL 37, VI 59 (handwritten).

My dear Dr Koechlin,

I shall think of and pray for you in these anxious days, and trust guidance may be given, and a true way may be found through these trials. My warmest greetings to Praeses Koch and other friends. I shall be at home till Monday morning – then at Lambeth Palace to the Thursday morning. Looking forward much to seeing you again.

Yours ever,
George Cicestr.

Bell to Koechlin, 19 October 1934, Basel UB, NL 37, VI 61 (handwritten).

My dear Koechlin,

After a communication from Oldham by telephone this morning I felt it right to telegraph to you – and enclose rather fuller expression of sentiments in compressed telegram. Of course only meant for your private guidance. I remember and pray for you.

Yours ever,
George Cicestr.

Bell to Koechlin, 19 October 1934, Basel UB, NL 37, VI 62 (telegram).

Pastor Koechlin Schweitzer Botschaft Berlin

Private suggest emphasising contrary to policy of council to take sides in internal controversy in a church or particular theological position but quite different issue arises when Christian group prevented from [exercising] Christian conscience this draws sympathy of whole oecumenical movement. Bell

Bell to Koechlin, 19 October 1934, Basel UB, NL 37, VI 63 (handwritten)

Private suggest your emphasising that it is contrary to the policy of the Universal Council to take side with any party in internal controversy in a church, or to identify itself with any particular theological position but it is a quite different issue when any group of Christians is prevented forcibly from obeying the dictates of their Christian conscience and it is because this liberty is denied to the Confessional Synod that the sympathies of the whole Ecumenical Movement represented by the Universal Council are so strongly drawn to the Confessional Synod and are bound to find emphatic expression. Bell.

Koechlin to Bell, 22 October 1934, Basel UB, NL 37, VI 64 (carbon).

My dear Lord Bishop,
 I am just returning from Berlin and Munich. You will have understood that I did not write from Berlin, the more as Mr. Gregg[1] told me that he was writing to you. This letter also can only be a very brief note to let you know that as far as the mission, with which you had entrusted me, is concerned, I hope that I moved in the line which had to be taken. I had to speak a short word right at the beginning of the proceedings,[2] before I had received your telegram, as Praeses Koch was anxious to have the presence of a representative of the Oecumenical Council stated from the start. I had just read the first draft of the statement which finally has been unanimously adopted. It was so far reaching, that I could not but be very cautious. So I simply explained the meaning of the Fanø Resolution, the indebtedness of all Churches to the German Church since the time of the Reformation and our wish to share in the spiritual fight and experience through which the German Church was led by God, so that we might have [a] part also in the blessings God was giving to the Evangelical Church in Germany. I mentioned especially the imprisonment of the Bishops of Bavaria and Württemberg, including all pastors and Church members suffering in any way with them, and asked for the Confessional Synod the peace of God surpassing all understanding so that even in their fight and trial and decision they might be rooted in that peace of God.
 Yesterday I spent the whole day in Munich, seeing the leading men and taking part in the service held in the garden of Bishop Meiser, who was allowed to speak some words from the balcony and to give to the community the blessing.[3]
 The situation in Berlin and Bavaria is as acute as possible. To-day you could not get foreign papers in Germany. Deputations representing tens of thousands of peasants of Bavaria, are in Munich to-day to press on the Government circles. I hope Jaeger will be dismissed [in] these very days[4] and that Müller will not have the possibility of swearing his oath to the State to-morrow as was provided.[5]
 I am leaving again to-morrow night and hope to be in London, Kingsley Hotel, Bloomsbury Street, Wednesday 4th, coming then to Chichester with the morning train of Thursday.

Let me closing saying that I was most encouraged knowing that your thoughts and prayers were with me.

With kindest regards,
yours very sincerely

1   Probably Roland Herbert Cragg (1882–1951): chaplain to St George's Church and to the Berlin embassy; his regular bulletins to Bishop Headlam and to the Archbishop of Canterbury's Council on Foreign Relations played an important part in informing senior figures in the Church of England of developments in the German churches.
2   See Koechlin's welcoming address in Wilhelm Niemöller, *Die zweite Bekenntnissynode der Deutschen Evangelischen Kirche zu Dahlem* (AGK 3), (Göttingen: Vandenhoeck & Ruprecht, 1958), pp. 198–9.
3   On 11 October Jäger came to Munich with the order to dismiss the entire Bavarian church leadership, and on 12 October Bishop Meiser was arrested by the Gestapo in his official residence, but after fourteen days, the Reichschurch capitulated and allowed the previous church leadership to resume its official duties.
4   Jäger actually announced his resignation from his church and state offices on 26 October.
5   The official conclusion and state recognition of the integration work was announced at a state reception of the Reich Bishop and all Protestant bishops as well as all members of the Spiritual Ministry by Hitler with the swearing-in of Müller. The cancellation was for diplomatic reasons due to Hoesch's report on Bell's intervention. Instead of the state reception came Jäger's resignation.

Koechlin to Bell, 30 October 1934, Basel UB, NL 37, VI 65 (carbon).

My dear Lord Bishop,

I safely arrived home yesterday morning and have, as carefully as possible with the help of others, tried to translate as accurately as ever possible the important document of the Confessional Synod.[1] You had asked me to do it for you in Chichester, but the task to reach a translation in which the wording as well as the interpretation of the German document was quite accurate, was too difficult to be fulfilled in a short time and alone. [It] may be that the document, as I am sending it to you, is not written in a perfect English, but at any rate you may rely on the fact that it is giving to you the real meaning of the original.

Yesterday night I heard that Bishop Wurm has been set free and went directly to Berlin.[2] Under those circumstances I think that the sending of an official delegate of the Oecumenical Council to Bavaria and Württemberg has become unnecessary. The situation in Berlin, as seen from here, is not clear at all. Evidently Hitler does not like to abandon the Reichsbishop, who has been his follower since 1926. The theory that the early follower[s] of the Nazi party have a first right to hold offices in spite of more or less evident insufficiency, has still a great weight with Hitler and the party. The resignation of Dr. Jäger is not clear either. His relations to the Church Government are not ending and in the Council of Bishops you find the name of his closest followers, especially the name of Bishop Dietrich, of whom it is known that he became Bishop because he had married Jäger after two divorces, what other Pastors had refused to do. The Confessional Synod is staying firm in asking [for] the complete dismissal of Reichsbishop Müller and Dr. Jäger. Hitler seems to look for a compromise and to avoid the clear decision which sooner or later becomes inevitable. On the Church and on the political side many men are busy in helping him to find such a compromise and to avoid the clear-cut issue.

From outside we cannot, as I see it, stand behind the position taken by the Archbishop of Canterbury. I cannot help feeling that it would be very difficult and even dangerous to go to Berlin in this atmosphere of compromise. It is evident that those looking for a compromise will try everything to have a leading foreign visitor on their side.

The latest news: Wurm, still prisoner, was asked by Hitler to come at once to Berlin. He answered to be unable, because guarded by police. Then Hitler gave [the] order himself to give him free [sic].

You might be interested also to know that the German Mission Council, assembled last week, has voted [on] a resolution stating very clearly that it is standing behind the Confessional Synod.

And now may I thank you and Mrs. Bell once more most heartily for the very kind reception you gave us last week. I remember with greatest gratitude the two days of common thinking in the atmosphere of your episcopal home and your study and I shall not forget how generous you have been in giving me your sympathy and confidence. I feel very much encouraged by it not only in my oecumenical work, but also in the work God has entrusted to me in my home city and home country.

Enclosed [is] a reproduction of the photograph of the Confessional Synod, reproduced in a Basel paper.

With kindest regards,
yours very sincerely,

1 The Message of the second Confessional Synod is reproduced in Beckmann, *Kirchliches Jahrbuch*, p. 82; but for complete documentation see Niemöller, *Die zweite Bekenntnissynode*.
2 Wurm and Meiser were set free on 26 October on Hitler's orders.

Bell to Koechlin, 1 November 1934, Basel UB, NL 37, VI 66 (typewritten).

My dear Koechlin,

Ever so many thanks for your most valuable letter of the 30th October, and for your great kindness in translating the Message of the Confessional Synod, which is most admirably clear. It is a very great help to have the text so accurately put into English. May I thank you too for all the very great help that you have given during these many months, and especially in these last weeks. I think the Universal Council and the German Evangelical Church owe you a great debt, and I personally am deeply grateful. It is a very real satisfaction to me that we should be in such close contact and friendship on such a matter at such a time.

The situation develops with somewhat startling rapidity. *The Times* to-day suggests that the State will not only declare itself but prove strictly neutral. At the same time it looks as though this neutrality does not remove the National Church idea by any means from the sphere of practical politics, and the steadfastness and vitality as well as courage of the Confessional Synod and their friends, will be tested in new ways. However that eventuality is rather in the future, and we must be profoundly thankful for the present measure of independence which has been secured for the Evangelical Church, and the freedom won by the Confessional Synod. I shall naturally be very anxious to hear from you any further light you get on the developments. I entirely agree that it would be very difficult and even dangerous for an outsider to go to Berlin at the present juncture. The situation is too complicated, and a word or a deed might prove most embarrassing.

Thank you too very much for the photograph of the Confessional Synod.

Yours very sincerely,

Koechlin to Bell, 9 November 1934, Basel UB, NL 37, VI 67 (carbon).

My dear Lord Bishop,

Many thanks for your very kind letter of November 1st. I am just receiving some fresh news which might interest you. For two or three days the Bishops Meiser, Wurm and Marahrens seemed inclined to agree to a solution including Dr. Kinder.[1] The leaders of the Confessional Synod had great anxieties in this respect, as they thought any compromise with the rotten system of the German Christians impossible. Dr. Kinder has also tried to get an agreement with Praeses Koch and Karl Barth, saying that the State would withdraw any legal and financial help, if peace would not be reached. Praeses Koch simply said that the Pastors of the Confessional Synod knew by experience what that meant and were not afraid of it. After all the three Bishops Wurm, Meiser and Marahrens came to an agreement with the Confessional Synod according to which Praeses Koch, in a very unselfish and fine way, offered to give his place to Dr. Breit of Munich,[2] the man [in the] confidence of Meiser. Some claims of the Bishops, being not of doctrinal importance, were also agreed to. On the other hand the Bishops gave up their plan of a purely Lutheran Reichs-Church headed by a Reichsbishop Marahrens or Bodelschwingh. The new Church, according to the plan agreed to, will have a less episcopal and a more synodal character. This settlement is of course not overbridging the gulf between the common front of the South-German Bishops and the Confessional Synod on the one side and of the Reichsbishop and the German Christians on the other side.

As to the position of Hitler, I think we ought to be clear that his words and acts cannot be fully trusted. He allowed Jäger to disappear, because he could not do otherwise. He refuses to ask Müller to leave and will certainly not give up the plan of some kind of national-socialist community of some religious character, including Protestants and Catholics. His closest followers have not done it either. The whole plan might be postponed and be pursued by other ways and means, as has been the case these last few months.

We hardly can do more from outside than we have done until now. The moment for another common official or unofficial action might come again, but I think that for the present we do better in avoiding to use our weapons so often as to become ineffective.

With kindest regards,
Yours very sincerely

1   Christian Kinder (1897–1972): German lawyer, in 1933 plenipotentiary of State Commissioner Jäger in Schleswig Holstein and legal vice-president of the Regional Church Office in Kiel. In 1936 he became provisional president, being permanently appointed in 1938. After the Sportpalast scandal Kinder succeeded Hossenfelder as *Reichsleiter* of the Faith Movement (later named Reich-Movement) of the Deutsche Christen.
2   Thomas Breit (1880–1966): Lutheran pastor and senior church councillor in Munich. As a member of the executive committee for the Confessing Church in October 1934, Breit was appointed a member of the Provisional Church Government of the Evangelical Church on 22 November 1934. Later retiring in 1945, his future lay in the work of the Martin Luther Federation while he also served as a member of the Bavarian senate.

Bell to Koechlin, 12 November 1934, Basel UB, NL 37, VI 68 (typewritten).

My dear Koechlin,

Very many thanks for your most interesting letter of November 9th. I am exceedingly glad to know the latest news and that it is of the character described. Koch is a very fine man.

I enclose a note of my interview with von Ribbentrop which I should like you to read: but would you mind sending it back when you have read it?[1]

Yours ever,

'Your daughter comes on Saturday – I am glad to say.'

1   Joachim Ribbentrop, from 1925 von Ribbentrop (1893–1946): Hitler's foreign policy advisor and, from 1934, 'Foreign Policy Advisor and Commissioner of the Reich Government for Disarmament Affairs'. In 1935 he was appointed 'Ambassador Extraordinary and Plenipotentiary of the German Reich' in London, succeeding Leopold von Hoesch. On 4 February 1938 he succeeded Neurath as Reich Foreign Minister. For Bell's note on his meeting with Ribbentrop on 6 November see Chandler, *Brethren in Adversity*, pp. 89–92.

Koechlin to Bell, 13 November 1934, Basel UB, NL 37, VI 69 (carbon).

My dear Lord Bishop,

The latest news from Germany is strengthening the impression that the situation is far from being clear. If what Dr. Kinder has said November 5th to Dr. Koch and Professor Karl Barth, when he tried to come to an agreement with them, is true, the Reichsbishop will not resign, because Hitler will refuse his place to anyone else. It seems as if Müller had received orders to stay at his place.

It seems also that Hitler himself had given his agreement to the proceedings of Dr. Jäger in Württemberg and Bavaria. Under the pressure from inside and outside he had unwillingly enough been obliged to agree to the resignation of Jäger and to a change of policy in Bavaria. In his conversation with the Bishops Meiser and Wurm however he lacked so much in clearness that in spite of court and official State decisions a band of party S.A. is allowed to prevent Bishop Wurm to enter his offices. The Reichsbishop who formally reinstituted Bishop Meiser in his post, did not [do] the same for Bishop Wurm. The attitude of Hitler included evidently only a change of tactics with the strategic aim of the national-socialist Church policy being still the same. It is expected that no legal help whatever will be given to the Confessional Synod, the hope being that the financial difficulties will weaken to inefficiency the Church opposition, the legal and financial help still given to the official Church and the changes to be operated in the theological faculties changing the situation more and more in favour of national-socialism.

Nevertheless the Confessional Synod is hopeful, working as hard as ever possible to build up the spiritual life and strength of the congregations throughout the country.

With kindest regards,
yours very sincerely

Koechlin to Bell, 15 November 1934, Basel UB, NL 37, VI 70 (carbon).

My dear Lord Bishop,

I have been very interested indeed in reading your notes on the conversation you had with Herr von Ribbentrop, though one has not the impression that the man has a deeper understanding of what Church and Church life mean. He is certainly in a position to throw some light on different aspects of the situation, not easy to understand for those standing far away from national-socialist leadership. From what Mr. Ribbentrop said, it seems quite evident that the position of the Reichsbishop might last some weeks or even months longer.

This morning I saw Pastor Riethmüller, the Leader of the German Young Women's Christian Association, who told me that Praeses Koch and his colleagues had their headquarters in their house, Berlin-Dahlem, and that he had been asked to organise the whole evangelical Youth Work, Y.M.C.A., Y.W.C.A. etc. in the new framework of the Confessional Church. The latter is hoping that some time might be given to it to build up, starting with each individual congregation and parish, a strong Church life, able to resist new attacks and sufferings coming maybe not only from the official Reichs Church Government, but even from State Government. Riethmüller, certainly one of the strong men in the Confessional Church, with a very clear vision of spiritual as well as of other realities, who had just some weeks of rest in Lugano, is most perplexed in realizing the nearly desperate international situation of Germany. Being inside Germany, he had not been in a position of seeing things as they are. He told me of the depths of demonic forces revealed [by] June 30th and certainly not cleared up [sic]. He stressed the fact that it was hardly impossible [possible] to influence Hitler himself, who has no idea whatever about the spiritual reality of a Church. He counted even with the possibility that the Church and in first line the Confessional Church, driven more and more in opposition to official ideology and official policy, would be in some vague or direct way declared to be the cause of unsuccess and be the object some day of a new 30th of June, no one having in circumstances of such critical days real control over the forces of evil. At any rate, the Confessional Synod is convinced of the growing seriousness of the situation into which it might be led.

On the other side it seems evident that the *Reichswehr* is developing its forces so as to be able to control the situation inside Germany at any critical moment and that some day, may be not very far away, it will take in [its] hands, if not directly so indirectly, the destiny of the country. The *Reichswehr* is not interfering for the moment with other plans of Hitler, because Hitler is giving to it what it likes. It is however waiting for its hour.

Military Government is certainly not ideal, looked at from the point of view of the Church. New dangers might be expected then, but certainly the army, as has been proved through different incidents, will not allow Church oppression and Church persecution to go on. It would probably give the way free [sic] to new men, waiting to undo some of the biggest mistakes of the present Government resulting from the national-socialist philosophy of life.

These indications do not pretend to throw light on the future. Nevertheless they gave me some help to visualize some possibilities on which one feels unable to express any judgement.

Riethmüller said that it would be an invaluable service to help them inside Germany to see things as they are and to express to them our anxieties in view of their own attitude, behaviour and policy. He is seeing, very clearly, how difficult it is for them to judge and to avoid mistakes bringing irreparable harm on the Church of Christ in Germany. I promised him that all of us in the oecumenical Movements do our very best to stay united with them and to share with them with full sincerity our thoughts, our hopes and our anxieties and that you especially were fully aware of the great responsibility of the Churches outside Germany towards our Brethren in a situation full of perplexities.

I received a letter of my daughter Elizabeth this morning. She is looking forward with greatest pleasure to be allowed to stay for the week-end at Chichester. May I express in the name of Mrs. Koechlin and myself to Mrs. Bell and to yourself our deep gratitude for the kindness you are showing to Elizabeth. Will you give her best greetings if she is already in your house when this letter is coming in.

Very cordially yours,

Enclosure.[1]

1 This has not been traced in either collection.

Koechlin to Bell, 26 November 1934, Basel UB, NL 37, VI 71 (carbon).

My dear Lord Bishop,
    Through Professor Karl Barth I received last Saturday news which seem[s] to me to be symptomatic and even important. In the Council and the Bruderrat of the Confessional Synod decisive decisions have taken place these last two weeks with the result that Karl Barth, Pastor Hesse of Elberfeld, Pastor Immer of Elberfeld,[2] three Reformed members of the Bruderrat, Pastor Asmussen, the Lutheran member and Pastor Niemöller[3] of Berlin-Dahlem, of the Prussian Church, have left the Bruderrat and the Council of the Church.[4] They still remain members of the Confessional Synod. The reason seems to be the following:
    After the rights of the Churches of Bavaria, Württemberg, Baden and Hannover have been restored, the Bishops of these Churches wished to build up again the German Evangelical Church life on its former constitutional basis and not on the Emergency Constitution of the Confessional Synod. Their case is that the need for such an Emergency Constitution is not any more[,] given the old true constitutional basis being restored.
    Back of this argument [sic] seems to be the other main argument that the Lutheran Bishops wish to build up a truly Lutheran Reichs-Church, allowing the Reformed and the 'United Church' to have so to say at an annex of the great Lutheran cathedral two chapels of their own. The thought of Barth, Niemöller, Asmussen, Hesse and Immer was to give in the new Church having three branches in principle the same right to the three branches. After some resistance Praeses Koch and also Pastor Humburg of Elberfeld[5] gave way to the pressure coming from the South and from large parts of Prussia. Pastor Bodelschwingh did his utmost to win Barth and his friends for this new plan, without success!
    On the other hand you know that the Reichsbishop, converted by the national-socialist Professor Nowack, a man of law,[6] agreed to revoke one of his unlawful actions after the other, leading back the Reichs-Church to a more and more constitutional life. The constitutional development seems bound to come back to its normal basis.
    As to the purely confessional basis of the new Church, the strong opposition between the theological leaders of the Confessional Synod and the episcopal leaders of the different German Churches is breaking up, the constitutional question being of course involved in the confessional one.
    No one can of course see how things under these circumstances may develop. It is of course impossible for the Oecumenical Council to take in this matter any position. As I look personally at the matter, Barth and his friends were convinced that the new Church ought to be built after what has happened without compromise on the new confessional basis. In the depth of their heart[s] they might be very sorry that the reconstruction of the old constitutional basis, whose breaking down was so much

deplored, is unexpectedly made possible again. They see in this solution a solution of compromises which might become dangerous in view of the great fight against national-socialist ideology still in front of the Church. You know Barth, Asmussen, Niemöller never have been men of compromise and never will be. Maybe they are according to their character more leaders of opposition than leaders of the governing majority. Some of the leading Churchmen might not be all too sorry to see them leave the governing Church Council. Please take this impression as a purely personal one. I wished however to share it with you in a confidential way.

Elizabeth wrote us an enthusiastic letter on her weekend stay in Chichester. She enjoyed the days spent in your Palace thoroughly and will remain most grateful for the kindness Mrs. Bell and yourself have shown to her. Mrs. Koechlin and myself are joining her in the expression of our gratitude to you.

With kindest regards,
very cordially yours,

1 Karl Immanuel Immer (1888–1944): Reformed pastor in Elberfeld and leading figure in the Confessing Church; he was arrested in 1937 and suffered a serious stroke under detention; from this he never recovered, dying after a third stroke in June 1944.

2 Martin Niemöller (1892–1984): arguably the leading personality and organizer of the Confessing Church. As the pastor of the community of Berlin-Dahlem in May 1933 he was one of the founders of the Young Reformation Movement, standing alongside Friedrich von Bodelschwingh. In view of the introduction of the Aryan paragraph in the Old Prussian Church, Niemöller called for the founding of the Pastors' Emergency League (*Pfarrernotbund*) in September 1933. He contended for the freedom of the Church and the purity of its doctrine and preaching, although Niemöller himself was not free of antisemitism. After the *Pfarrernotbund* and other sympathetic groups of pastors and church members combined to create the Confessing Church at the synod in Barmen. In this Niemöller became a leading voice. As a nationalist he had voted for the National Socialist Party in March 1933, and only in his last sermons before his arrest, on 1 July 1937, did he turn against the regime and Hitler himself. Even so, the National Socialists consistently regarded him as a dangerous opponent. After a trial which attracted international attention, and the passing of only a minor sentence, Hitler declared him a 'personal prisoner of the Führer' and had him transferred to Sachsenhausen concentration camp for solitary confinement. In July 1941 he was transferred to Dachau. In April 1945, he was transported to South Tyrol, together with about 160 special prisoners, and freed by US Army troops on 4 May.

3 They declared their decision to leave on 20 November. On 22 November the Brotherhood Council of the German Evangelical Church and the bishops Marahrens, Meiser, and Wurm decided to establish a provisional church government. Marahrens became chairman, Breit joined as a Lutheran member, Humburg as representative of the Reformed and Koch as a representative of the United Churches. *Reichsgerichtsrat* Flor was appointed as a legal member but was permanently represented by Eberhard Fiedler. The composition was in accordance with the Reich Church Constitution of 11 July 1933. Marahrens' chairmanship soon became problematic, not least because he offered no guarantee for the implementation of the Dahlem resolutions, something for which Immer insistently pressed.

4   Paul Humburg (1878–1945): Reformed pastor in Elberfeld, leading light in the German YMCA and in the Confessing Church in the Rhineland. Between 1934 and 1936 he was a member of the national Provisional Government of the Evangelical Church. He retired in 1943.
5   Erwin Nowack (1899–1967): lawyer and honorary professor at Halle University; member of the National Synod; from September 1933 to June 1934 he was president of the Provincial Synod of the Church Province of Saxony. He became president of the second Senate of the Court of Honour for Lawyers, vice-president of the Reich Bar Association and a member of the Nazi Academy for German Law. Later he was one of the two defence lawyers of Otto Remer in the controversial trial of 1952.

Bell to Koechlin, 29 November 1934, Basel UB, NL 37, VI 72 (typewritten).

'Private'
My dear Koechlin,

Very many thanks for your letter of November 26th with its exceedingly important news from Professor Karl Barth. I am very sorry to hear of the departure from the Bruderrat and the Council of Karl Barth and the others you name. It is very difficult to form a judgement of value about such things from outside. At the same time, from my impressions of Praeses Koch and Asmussen in my talk at Hamburg, I am bound to say I feel that the statesmanship and the constructive ability are much more with Koch than, for example, with Asmussen, fine type of man as the latter is.

I am not quite certain about the meaning of the third paragraph on the second page of your letter, about the breaking up of the opposition between the theological leaders of the Confessional Synod and the episcopal leaders of the different German Churches. But I suppose that with the reconstruction of the Reich Church and the Lutheran basis with the Reformed and the United Church as two chapels at an annex of the great Lutheran Cathedral, the problems of the confession and the constitution together dissolve.

I understand the danger of compromise, especially in view of the fight against National Socialist ideology. At the same time one has to remember the great mass of people, and to try to keep the strong Church idea and the connection of the Church with the people as strong as we conscientiously can keep it.

It was a real joy to have Elizabeth with us. She was a delightful guest and we all found her most happy and admirable in every way.

Yours sincerely,

Koechlin to Bell, 1 December 1934, Basel UB, NL 37, VI 73 (carbon).

My dear Lord Bishop,

I have written to you November 26th about the changes taking place in the Confessional Synod. May I add to-day that, as far as I have heard, Asmussen has joined again the 'Council of the German Evangelical Church' instituted by the Confessional Synod. As far as I can gather, the situation is not clear yet: the Reichsbishop surrounded again by unexpected legality, trying to strengthen the constitutional basis of his position, but not trusted because of his past doings and of his all too great willingness to follow the lead of national-socialist policy; the Bishops of Bavaria, Württemberg, Hannover maintaining their independent position, refusing to join the Reichsbishop in his new programme and still in some distance from the Confessional Synod; the Confessional Synod itself trying to find its way under the completely new circumstances, the State taking certainly a more impartial attitude towards all Church parties and underlining more than it did its friendly attitude towards Christianity. According to latest news the Hauer/Rosenbergs tendency[1] f[or] i[nstance] has been forbidden to be all-powerful in the Hitler Youth.

But the main purpose of this letter is to tell you about Karl Barth. You know that in his capacity of a University Professor, holding an official State position, he was asked to take the oath every State official has to take: 'to be faithful and obedient to the Leader Adolf Hitler in all things'. He refused to accept this oath in such a form. Returning from Switzerland where he had spent his summer holidays about seven weeks ago, he spoke about it with the University authorities of Bonn. Since then he had not heard of the matter. Several hundred students came to Bonn to hear him. The lectures were going on and he thought that possibly, as in other points, the State would not touch his position, until the other day the Minister of Cult[ure],[2] Rust,[3] suspended him in his functions. Such a measure is certainly not astonishing. The students thought of demonstrating in favour of Barth in front of his house, but he asked them to avoid every manifestation. He was asked to give account of his position to representatives of the Minister of Cult[ure] and declared that he was ready to accept the oath if he was allowed to add to the words quoted above the sentence: 'as far as, being an evangelical Christian, God is allowing me to do so'. (*sofern ich es als evangelischer Christ vor meinem Gott verantworten kann*). Barth had accepted the old constitutional oath. He would have accepted a new oath limited by very clear constitutional guarantees but he could not sell himself, body and soul, to a man able to dispose of every member of the nation as he liked to do without any limitations brought to his dealings and to his will. He refused to accept for himself the totalitarian claim of a single man, but he is fully accepting the obedience to the State according to chapter 13 of Saint Paul's epistle to the Romans.[4]

The Official conversation between Barth and the State officials seems to have been quite friendly. They asked him to solve the difficulty in giving his resignation. He refused to do so, declaring his readiness to meet their claim as far as ever he could, in accepting the oath with the limit just indicated. The official report has gone from Bonn to Berlin and the final decision rests now in Berlin.

The question arises, if from outside something could be done. There are two aspects of the question: On the one side it is important that the German State officials know of the interest the outside world is taking not mainly in Barth's personality, but in the great Church principle involved. *Is a State really not allowing a professor of theology to stay in his office if the foundation of his theological evangelical teaching does not allow him to accept the oath of obedience to Hitler without the limitation implied by the faithfulness to the Gospel?* In the view of Barth – and I think he is fully right – the implications of the Gospel and not an individual conscience are involved.

On the other hand pamphlets are already published in Germany, saying that Barth is calling his influential foreign friends to his rescue. The purpose of such a publication is very evident. We have to be very careful in what we do.

I was yesterday in Geneva and saw Schönfeld. He told me that Dr. Leiper had cabled to Professor Keller to telegraph to Berlin in the name of the Federal Council of the Churches of Christ in America. Keller, being now in Vienna, has cabled from there to Neurath and Frick. Schönfeld wondered if the Oecumenical Council ought to do something. I confess that I do not know what to answer. I do not think a very strong action would be appropriate, but I think that possibly you could through Prince Bismarck or Mr. von Ribbentrop act in a more personal way. At any rate I was anxious to bring the matter before you. I am writing a short word to the German Minister in Bern, von Weizsäcker,[5] with whom I have spoken more than once in an unofficial way of the whole matter.

[It] may be that the State, who [sic] more than once wished to get rid of Barth, is feeling that the Confessional Church and mainly the Lutheran branch of it are not behind Barth, [and] is even somewhat frightened by his influence. Bishop Marahrens has said in Bavaria: 'Are you aware that Karl Barth is the great danger for the German Evangelical Church?' and another influential Lutheran personality said that 'Karl Barth is submerging Germany with Calvinism.' Such feelings are certainly known in the Ministry of Cult[ure] and if the tendencies of Church and State are going towards a great German Lutheran Church, the step taken against Barth might have to be judged in the light of such a policy. Lutheranism always has been inclined to follow the State lines since the time when Luther has created the Princes to be the Bishops of the Church [i.e. given to princes the authority of bishops]. The Reformed Churches have more distanciated [sic] themselves from full State allegiance. For this reason a Lutheran State Church is judged by the Government to be more reliable than a Church built up according to conceptions as Barth is proclaiming them.

May I add that Schönfeld is in complete agreement with the view I am taking in the matter.

With kindest regards,
yours very sincerely,

1   That is, the tendency of the new German Faith Movement which was at this time establishing itself under the leadership of the Indologist Jakob Wilhelm Hauer (1881–1962).
2   The position of a Minister of Culture is unknown in Switzerland; Koechlin followed the example of Württemberg where the title *Kultminister* was used instead of *Kultusminister*.
3   Bernhard Rust (1883–1945): Gauleiter of Southern Hannover and Brunswick; in 1933, provisional Prussian Minister of Culture and in 1934, with the formation of the Reich Ministry of Science, Education and National Education, Reich Minister. Rust soon found that he had little influence in the chaos of office politics and had to cede more and more responsibilities to competing organizations.
4   That is, 'The powers that be are ordained of God . . .'
5   Ernst von Weizsäcker (1882–1951): from September 1933 to May 1936 German ambassador in Bern; subsequently head of the Political Department. 1938–43. Secretary of State, subsequently ambassador to the Holy See. Tried for complicity in the deportations of Jews from France, he was sentenced to seven years in prison but released in October 1950. Weizsäcker remained a figure whose record of neutrality and tacit support for resistance circles attracted both defenders and critics.

Bell to Koechlin, 3 December 1934, Basel UB, NL 37, VI 74 (typewritten).

My dear Koechlin,

Very many thanks for your letter of December 1st about Karl Barth. You raise a very important and difficult problem. I am consulting Oldham about it and will write to you again.

In the meantime would you give me a little advice about a proposal that has been suggested to me – viz. that a group of English Church leaders should go over to Germany to meet some German Church leaders – not about the Church conflict in any way but about peace and friendship between the nations? The man who has made the proposal is a man in the City who I think would be able to arrange all the necessary finances.[1] It is, of course, the sort of proposal which commends itself to the layman who reads the newspapers, and is not a great philosopher, but it is nonetheless on that account a proposal worth thinking of, for the newspapers do make an impression on their readers, and it does seem to me possible that a group of Church leaders going over to Germany to talk about the spiritual foundations of peace might really do good at this juncture. The date that would seem to me possible would be the beginning of February. I know that one must be very careful about the Church conflict and the present obscurity in that situation, and also the delicacy of the Saar situation.[2] I mention the beginning of February because I could not myself go before then, but possibly January would be better, and perhaps it would also be better for me not to go, owing to my connection with the Church question. Tell me how it strikes you.

That I am most deeply interested in what your earlier letters tell me, I need hardly tell you.

Yours ever,

1 This initiative, and its sponsors, remains obscure.
2 In view of the coming Saar plebiscite of 13 January 1935.

Koechlin to Bell, 5 December 1934, Basel UB, NL 37, VI 75 (carbon).

My dear Lord Bishop,

Best thanks for your letter of December 3rd which reached me yesterday night. I have to confess my reaction to the proposal that English Church Leaders might go over to Germany to discuss there with German Church Leaders the spiritual foundation of peace, to be a distinctly negative one. I quite understand a layman's thought going in such a direction under the impression of the latest political debate in the House of Commons,[1] but I think the Church under the present circumstances has to stand on its own ground and concentrate its efforts to the most important task for which it alone is responsible. The Church question of Germany is far from being settled. We don't know at which moment the influence and action of the Church of England and of yourself as Leader of the Oecumenical Council has again to throw its full weight into the struggle. By no means this weight ought to be weakened now by a diversion into political fields. Such a weakening would, as I see it, be unavoidable, because at once it would be said in Germany in all parts that in all their actions the foreign Churches were dominated by general pacific humanitarian tendencies, so terribly discredited in the mind of Germans by the Versailles Treaty and the League of Nations, and not by the deepest Church issues. Possibly it would even be said that the action of the Church has proved by such a step to serve more or less some political aims I would at any rate ask you most earnestly to stay personally outside such a step.

It has furthermore to be born in mind, that at the present moment it would be very difficult to find the right Church Leaders of Germany to talk with. What group, what mixed composition of representatives of different groups would it be? Who would decide and choose it? I wonder also if the German Church Leaders, discussing with the English visitors political issues – you cannot, I think, discuss to-day the spiritual foundations of peace without being involved in political discussion – would not be led into considerable difficulties with their own Government. Thinking of the actually so dangerous tension between State and Church in Germany, I am reluctant to see the Church drawn into new difficulties and dangers. I remember how frightened our friends in Germany always are to be said to use their foreign relations against the interests of the German Nation.

On the whole my distinct impression is that the Churches outside Germany in the actual historical moment serve peace best in helping the German Church to maintain its independence on spiritual grounds, which means to build up in the German Nation a stronghold of peace having the deepest and strongest possible roots. The task is important and [it is] difficult enough to concentrate on it all our influence and strength.

As to Karl Barth, no further news. I was quite aware of the delicacy of my proposal and did not of course think of any official step. I only thought of some personal word following your confidential conversations. You might be interested to know that I have written such a word to the German Minister in Bern, von Weiszäcker, without even suggesting to him to send my letter to Berlin. In thanking me, he underlined the fact how important it was for him to know how the principle involved is seen by me and that with my permission he should like to let it be known in Berlin. I am of course giving my consent to it. The fact that no definite decision has been taken yet, seems to indicate that the Government is somewhat hesitant and that some personal voices – official pressure would, I think, be unwise – might do some good. But I quite see that for you such a step is much more delicate and difficult than for me.

With kindest regards
very cordially yours,

---

1 A reference to the House of Commons debate on the King's Speech, which took place across 23, 26, 27 and 28 November 1934. This emphasized the demands of national security in the face of German rearmament.

Koechlin to Bell, 12 December 1934, Basel UB, NL 37, VI 76 (carbon).

My dear Lord Bishop,

Dr. Hanns Lilje, the leader of the German Christian Student Movement and editor of the *Junge Kirche*,[1] had spent some days in Geneva and came yesterday, returning to Germany, to see me here in Basel.

He has been asked to become the first secretary of the actual provisional Marahrens Church Government. What he told me, is of extreme gravity. All signs in Germany seem to point to the fact that after the Saar plebiscite a very strong fight of national-socialism against oppositional circles of any kind might be expected, the Church opposition being not only included, but even in a very special evidence.

The general discontent of large circles of party and population evidently needs some outlet. The Government cannot prevent it, has even to create it, taking care of course that its own position is safeguarded. To direct the discontent towards Church opposition circles seems to be part of the general policy.

Dr. Lilje pointed to the very dangerous atmosphere and situation created by the fact that all round in Germany officially as well as unofficially it is said that important decisions and events will take place as soon as the question of the Saar is settled. The general impression is that the Government is for the moment reserving every action in the interest of the Saar victory. Himmler the leader of the S.S.[2] has a special bureau on Church questions and seems to have a list of the most important and dangerous oppositional Church leaders. Lilje saw an order of a District-Leader of the German-Christian Church party, stating that after January 13th an action of the Government against [the] opposition might be expected and asking to take note of personalities against which [sic] decisive action would have to take place. Even speeches of Ministers are moving in such lines. Goebbels again and again is mentioning in his speeches, made known by radio, the political dangers involved in the church opposition. Frick the other day said in a speech listened to by some 20,000 people the words I am including.

What the second, third and fourth rank leaders of political S.A. and S.S. organisations might think, say and plan, cannot be but strongly influenced by these highly authoritative utterances of Ministers.

I know that Bishop Wurm these very last days, assembling his leading pastors, told them that in his view they would have to pass during the next weeks the most dangerous time of the Church conflict and their life.

Lilje seemed to think that very grave danger was imminent and asked me, as he did in Geneva with Henriod and Schönfeld, if we could not help avoiding it by speaking to the representatives of Germany in England and elsewhere and if we could not try to get in time an official assurance from state authority, that the Government would not allow such a thing to happen.

If something can be done, I think the place to do it can only be London. I venture even to suggest, if you could not approach your own Government and ask if it could not tell in some way the German Government what would be the alarming consequences for Germany if a new 30th of June would happen and be used to get rid of the Church opposition. The reason why I am thinking of such a possibility is the recent speech of Mr. Baldwin in the House of Commons,[3] which seemed at any rate to me to indicate the willingness of Great Britain to help under certain conditions Germany in its difficulties. The settlement of the Saar business in Rome and Geneva, which Mr. Baldwin, when speaking, must have known, strengthens my impression. Would not a friendly, but clear advertisement coming from Downing Street possibly be of greatest importance and effectively help in avoiding a situation of extreme gravity?

I asked Dr. Lilje, if he thought it advisable to have someone going now to Germany and trying to get further information. He did not think it necessary and even advisable at the present moment, but asked my permission to telegraph whenever the leaders of the Confessional Church would like to get into direct touch with us. Following his desire, I promised him to come if ever possible as soon as a telegram would reach me. I promised him also, as I did to Pastor Riethmüller, that someone would come to see them if we felt it to be necessary for any reason. I of course would not act without taking counsel with Mr. Henriod and Dr. Schönfeld. I am also sending a copy of this letter to Mr. Henriod to share with him my whole thought after having phoned with him this morning.

With kindest regards,
very cordially yours,

P.S. I hear that an official resolution voted by the German-Christian majority of the Hessen-Kassel Provincial Synod is threatening the Pastors of the Confessional Church, that they will find their punishment when after the 13th of January the State will crush every political and other opposition. The wording of this resolution unfortunately is not in my hands.

Enclosure.[4]

1 *Junge Kirche* was a quarterly periodical of the Young Reformation Movement. The journal was founded by the publisher Günther Ruprecht in 1933. Openly supportive of the Confessing Church and often confiscated, it ran until 1941 and was revived in 1949.
2 Heinrich Himmler (1900–45): From 1929 Reich leader of the SS. At this time he was moving firmly into the foreground of national politics in the aftermath of the Night of the Long Knives. Himmler's Security Service became the sole Security Service of the National Socialist party. Himmler was known to be explicitly anti-Christian.
3 See the speech by Baldwin in the House of Commons, HC Deb., Vol. 295, cols. 872–5 (28 November 1934). Baldwin emphasized the difficulty of working with a new dictatorship in the pursuit of international peace. Stanley Baldwin (1867–1947): British conservative politician, prime minister 1922–3, 1924–9, and 1935–7.
4 This now appears to be missing.

Henriod to Bell, 13 December 1934, Basel UB, NL 37, VI 77 (carbon).

My dear Bishop,

Two days ago we had in Geneva a visit from Dr. Hans Lilje, who has become the right hand of Bishop Marahrens, with the appointment of Chancellor of the Confessional

Synod Church administration. His report to a small group of us in Geneva was very serious. Among other things, we urged that the Churches outside Germany, and especially the Oecumenical Movement, should contemplate very definite steps before January 13. He recommended especially that whenever possible approaches should be made to high officials of the National Socialist Party or representatives of the Government on missions in other countries. He mentioned that Herr Hess,[1] who was to-day to be in France, would be one of the most important men to speak to. I therefore telephoned to M. Boegner, giving him an extract of our conversation prepared by Dr. Schönfeld, and he promised that if Herr Hess did not postpone his visit, as indicated in the Press, he would be glad to see him. I also arranged that on his way back to Berlin Dr. Lilje should have a conversation with Dr. Koechlin. This took place on Tuesday night and yesterday morning I had a long conversation with Dr. Koechlin over the telephone. He fully agreed with me that the situation is such that further steps are required, and he was going to write to you.

What we understood from Dr. Lilje to be the causes of greater dangers are: 1) the German Government is taking steps to make it impossible for the Confessional Synod to have any meetings and to reduce as much as possible the number of services held by Confessional Synod pastors, under the pretext that disturbances occur at such meetings, the cause of which is interruption from German Christians and others. Since the *Junge Kirche* has been suspended, (and the latest news is that "die Junge Kirche" is again allowed, but for how long?) there is at present no effective way for the Confessional Synod to make its point of view known, with a view to defending itself against the wildest type of accusations. If both the press and the holding of meetings are closed to them, their very existence is threatened.

(2) From the beginning, the Confessional Synod has had, within the Government, friends, or at least people who understood their position and did not regard them as traitors to the country. These people are Neurath, Frick and Schwerin,[2] and they are in a more difficult position than they were. They are regarded as reactionary by the National Socialists, and they are compelled to silence, or at least to a withholding of their support of the Confessional Synod, threatened as they are with expulsion from the Government, possibly after January 13.

(3) Reich Bishop Müller's position, which was shaken after the holding of the Confessional Synod in Berlin and made critical by the statement of the National Socialist lawyer who declared that all Müller's decrees were illegal, is now strengthened legally by the fact that he has simply abolished all decrees issued since January 4 and has returned to the conditions prevailing on January 3.[3] This means, among other things, that Bishop Hossenfelder and others are again in power. Therefore, together with the German Christians and with the help of the authorities and the effective measures of the secret police, he is in a stronger position, although the vast majority of the Churches and Church members and pastors are against him.

(4) The Radio, articles in the press and elsewhere, spoke some time ago of a black list, on which are a number of names of people who might, after January 13, have the same fate as those who disappeared on June 30. I took this at first as doubtful, and in any case as information needing careful confirmation. Dr. Lilje, who is a very well balanced man and who knows the whole situation intimately, told us without any

hesitation that the menace was very real and that the names of Koch, Niemöller and many others were on such a list, and that further enquiries are being quietly made by the police and the German Christians with a view to making such a list that will kill any possible action on the part of the Confessional Synod some time after January 13. Such people would be declared traitors to the state, either on the grounds of having Bolshevist leanings or of being dangerous reactionaries. Lilje says that if we wait until some drastic action is taken by the Government, probably soon after January 13, it will be too late. Among the influences which had made the Confessional Synod possible, Lilje gave as the first the approaches made to embassies in London, Washington and elsewhere. He pleaded for a renewal of such action, but thought that it might be the best to postpone it till a week or ten days before January 13. But as I have said above, he thought that in the meantime no effort should be spared to get in touch, if at all possible, with the men who do not care for the Church, such as those whose unique interest is *real Politik*, but who for this purpose have to keep in mind the humour and unity of Germany, and to whom one could stress that in violating consciences and in acting crudely against those Christians in Germany who cannot accept the laws of Reich Bishop Müller, treating them as traitors to the country in the same way as was done on June 30, they would greatly risk endangering the moral reputation of Germany in other lands, and would thus create for Germany serious economic and political difficulties. Lilje stressed that it would be necessary not only to obtain oral declarations, but if possible to get such people to agree to statements that these rumours and news are ill founded, and that the Government will never resort to such action. There may be some such high officials in London whom it would be worthwhile approaching. The point of Lilje's advice against acting at once with the Embassies is that for weeks and weeks Neurath has been the man who again and again has had to bring before the Government questions raised through his ambassadors, while the main power and the main responsibility for a change rests with the heads of the party. We also agreed with Lilje that if he and Praeses Koch and others felt that Koechlin or somebody else should go to Germany, he would let us know at once, but that we would not move without receiving such an invitation. Koechlin and I absolutely agree on this point. Lilje felt that if the Universal Christian Council declared in definite terms that it repudiated its association with Reich Bishop Müller, it would probably be the greatest service that could rendered to the Christian Church in Germany. I explained to him the reasons why we did not feel it advisable to do this, and that we could not be a kind of court on ecclesiastical matters. Yet the question is worth reconsidering when our Administrative Committee meets. Unfortunately we shall meet a fortnight after January 13. Therefore it rests with you and those whom you think it advisable to consult to take such steps as may bring relief in a situation which has never been so critical as it is now, I would appreciate it if you would let me have your opinion. We are exchanging with Koechlin any information we receive.

Yours sincerely,
(signed) HENRY LOUIS HENRIOD

Extrait du Journal de Geneve, 13 December 1934

Goering parlant á la presse mondials mardi soir, sur l'écrasement du communisme. 'C'est par les mesures prises pour combattre le danger communiste, a dit l'orateur, que l'on reconnaître, les méthodes du national-socialisme qui, à tous les points de vue, est l'opposé du communisme. Le Gouvernement allemand revendique toute liberté dans l'application des moyens qu'il juge appropriés et il ne peut tenir aucun compte des recommandations étrangères.'[4]

1 Rudolf Hess (1894–1987): Deputy-Führer of the National Socialist party since April 1933. Bell and Hess met for the first time in Germany in September 1935. The meeting appeared to give Bell some hope of leverage but, if that is indeed so, he soon lost faith in the connection.
2 Johann Ludwig von Krosigk, since 1925 Graf Schwerin von Krosigk (1887–1977): Minister of Finance 1932–45.
3 See his ordinance of 20 November 1934, in: Beckmann, *Kirchliches Jahrbuch*, pp. 86–7.
4 Thus Göring, talking to the world press on the destruction of communism: 'It is through the measures taken to combat the communist threat that we recognize the methods of National Socialism, which is in every respect the opposite of communism. The German government claims complete freedom in doing whatever it considers appropriate and it can take no account of foreign recommendations.'

Bell to Koechlin, 15 December 1934, Basel UB, NL 37, VI 78 (handwritten).

My dear Koechlin,

Very many thanks for your very important letter of December 12. I had a letter from Oldham to-day communicating similar information from Schönfeld. I am considering the whole matter very seriously, and am in touch with the Archbishop of Canterbury. I will write again next week.

Yours sincerely

Koechlin to Bell, 21 December 1934, Basel UB, NL 37, VI 79 (carbon).

My dear Lord Bishop,

Receiving this letter, you will have heard that Karl Barth has been dismissed. He telephoned yesterday night with his friend Thurneysen and told him briefly that the proceedings of the disciplinary court (*Disziplinargericht*) had taken place yesterday in Cologne. The accusation was built up on the fact that Karl Barth refused to swear the oath to the Leader Adolf Hitler as prescribed for every State official. The sentence Karl Barth wished to put in and which I have quoted to you in a former letter, was declared to be unacceptable. The oath could only be a total oath to the Leader, who better than anyone else in Germany knew if what he asked the State officials to do, was in agreement with God's command or not. The State official, putting his case, mentioned especially that as well [as this] the utterances of the Reformed Church as of the Marahrens Church Council, stating that every evangelical Christian would swear the oath under the mental reservation put expressively forward by Karl Barth, was an unacceptable interpretation and could not stand.

Following the official act of accusation, the Court dismissed Karl Barth as University Professor and granted him for 6 months half of the amount he would have been entitled to receive as retirement pension. As Karl Barth has only been official State Professor for 9 Years, this amount comes to a very small sum.

Evidently Karl Barth is still allowed to stay in Germany. If it will be possible for him to remain there in connection with some institution of the Confessional Church, has to be seen. I hope that he and his family won't be the object of ill-doings. Being not any more a State official, he has lost his German citizenship and is only [a] Swiss citizen. I know that the Swiss Government is doing everything possible to give him protection. But one has to count [i.e. reckon] with irresponsible acts of Nazi students or other people.

The other day, when a picture of Karl Barth was exhibited in the window of a bookshop, the owner was asked to take it off at once if he did not wish to have his window broken and the picture taken away from outside.

What seems to be the most important feature is the officially accepted statement of the totalitarian character of the Hitler oath, excluding explicitly the interpretation all other theological professors and Christian State officials had thought to be entitled to accept when swearing the oath. Their situation does not become easier by the decision of the disciplinary court of Cologne! In fact the judgement is proving that Karl Barth had seen clear[ly] in the whole matter.

I trust this letter will reach you before Xmas. May I send Mrs. Bell and yourself once more my heartiest wishes for the coming days. Mrs. Koechlin is joining me with Elizabeth who came home safely this morning with very happy memories and full of gratitude for all those who had contributed to make her England stay a real event in her life.

With kindest regards, yours very sincerely

Bell to Koechlin, 29 December 1934, Basel UB, NL 37, VI 80 (typewritten).

My dear Koechlin,

Very many thanks for your letter of December 21st telling me the facts about the dismissal of Karl Barth. I have seen a statement in one of the papers that Karl Barth has since been offered a Professorship in Basel and has accepted it. Is this so? Of course I appreciate the seriousness of the dismissal and the circumstances in which it is made.

The whole position inside the German Church at the moment seems more obscure than ever. *The Times* to-day leads one to anticipate rather more difficult conditions when negotiations are resumed next week, and also the intensification of the conflict between Christianity and paganism. I have not heard anything from Germany for a little while. I wrote to Koch about a fortnight ago sending my letter through Cragg who wrote acknowledging it from Berlin on December 19. But my letter was simply to tell Koch of the proposal which had been made for a visit from this country of English Church leaders, and to ask him what he thought about it and explain that of course there would be no following up of the proposal unless it was welcome to him. Bonhoeffer was in Berlin for a fortnight at the end of November and beginning of December. I saw him on his return, but he had not any very special news, except signs of a good deal of unsettlement generally.[1] Incidentally he gave me the most curious information that quite recently – that is I think last month – the order had gone out that no member of Hitler's bodyguard must be attached to any Church, while simultaneously another order had gone out that every member of the *Reichswehr* must be a member of a Christian Church. I need not say that I shall be thankful for any news that comes your way.

I hope you have had a very happy Christmas and will have a very happy New Year.

Yours sincerely,

1   The exact date is unclear, but Bonhoeffer had probably met Bell on 1 or 2 December 1934.

1935

11 January	Hitler meets Müller.
13 January	Saar plebiscite: the region is returned to Germany.
February	The *Deutsche Christen* move against Müller.
27 February	Hitler and Müller meet again. They discuss a suggestion that a member of the Reich cabinet be appointed *Minister in evangelicis*.
March	Over 700 pastors in Prussia are arrested and briefly detained.
11 March	A new law establishes departments for church finances in Prussia.
16 March	Conscription is introduced in Germany and the disarmament clauses of the Versailles Treaty are rejected.
17 March	Pulpit declaration against idolatry in Prussia; nearly 500 pastors and vicars arrested
28 March	Pastor Grossmann in Berlin is sent to the concentration camp at Dachau.
April	State grants to the church are withheld in Baden.
10 April	The Provisional Church Government makes an appeal to Hitler.
26 April	A rally of the German Faith Movement takes place at the *Sportpalast* in Berlin.
27 April	Pastors in Wuppertal send a telegram of protest to Hitler voicing their concern about the growth of paganism.
14 May	Rudolf Hess speaks of the church dispute in a visit to Stockholm.
3 June	*The Times* publishes a new letter by Bell deploring the 'internal war' being waged against Christianity in Germany.
4–6 June	The third Reich Confessing synod meets in Augsburg.
5 June	Archbishop Lang expresses his concern about the German church at the Church Assembly.
26 June	The German government transfers legal disputes in the church from the courts to a new bureau, the *Beschlussstelle in kirchlichen Rechtsangelegenheiten* in the Ministry of the Interior.
16 July	A new Reich Ministry for Church Affairs under Hanns Kerrl is announced.
16 July	Interior minister Frick prohibits registrars from permitting 'mixed' marriages.
22 July	Frick announces to the state governments that the administration of church affairs will now be transferred to Kerrl's ministry.
24 July	Hitler appoints Ribbentrop ambassador to London.
4 August	Kerrl assumes responsibility for the *Beschlussstelle in kirchlichen Rechtsangelegenheiten*.
18–25 August	The executive committee of Life and Work meets at Chamby-sur-Montreux in Switzerland.
21 August	Kerrl meets Müller and other churchmen sympathetic to the *Deutsche Christen*.

23 August	Kerrl meets leaders of the Confessing Church and tells them that he will not tolerate further disputes in the church.
26–30 August	The first Evangelical Week takes place in Hannover.
September	Bell visits Germany.
15 September	Two new laws resolved by 7th party congress at Nuremberg define and legalize discrimination against Jews and 'non-Aryans': the Reich Citizenship Law and the Law for the Protection of German Blood and German Honour.
24 September	The Prussian Confessing Synod meets in Berlin and rejects the work of the new bureau and the attacks on Jewish Christians. The publication of the Law for the Safeguarding of the German Evangelical Church.
14 October	The Reich's Church Committee is created. It is chaired by Wilhelm Zöllner. The Confessing Synod refuses to recognize it.
28 October	The propaganda ministry imposes censorship before publication on church publications.
1 November	Two Confessing Church colleges are prohibited by the police.
4 November	Kerrl announces a relaxation of restrictions on the church press.
9 November	Resurrection celebration of the NSDAP at the Feldherrnhalle
14 November	The first supplementary decree to the Reich Citizenship Law dismisses Jews from public service.
20 November	The fourth report of the Archbishop of Canterbury's Council on Foreign Relations is submitted to the Church Assembly. Bell moves a motion on the persecution of the Jews in Germany and Bishop Henson speaks powerfully in support of it.
28 November	The trust funds of the Confessing Church are confiscated. Kerrl threatens the dissolution of the movement.
2 December	Kerrl assumes dictatorial powers over the church by abolishing executive or administrative functions by church organizations.
4 December	The Berlin-Brandenburg Confessing synod protests against Kerrl's act of 2 December. Niemöller is prohibited from public speaking.
6 December	Bishop Marahrens of Hannover pledges his support for Kerrl.

Koechlin to Bell, 7 January 1935, Basel UB, NL 37, VI 81 (carbon).

My dear Lord Bishop

Best thanks for your letter of December 29th.

As to Karl Barth, I saw a very detailed letter he has written during the Xmas days to his friend Thurneysen. It confirmed that the Disciplinary Court at Cologne had taken the view according to which the national-socialist state had to ask from any man holding an official position an unlimited allegiance to National-Socialism, personified in Adolf Hitler. The interpretation of the oath, given by the Confessional Church, was declared to be inacceptable [sic] and incompatible with the conceptions underlying National-Socialism. It is a noteworthy little incident that the President of the Court asked the attorney-general if he was quite certain that the Minister Rust agreed fully with his views! Karl Barth does not know yet if he will appeal to a higher Court. Before doing it, he is waiting to have in [his] hands the written judgement which he will probably not get before some weeks [have passed]. The leaders of the Confessional Church press him to appeal. He does not feel inclined to do it, because it seems evident to him, that no other judgement can be expected and because the dealings of the Court in Cologne had been very courteous.

Karl Barth is evidently looking for his future. He feels morally obliged to stay in Germany and to help the German Church as long as possible, but only if the Confessional Church can make him a sound offer in a confessional seminary or elsewhere. If that is not the case, he will see his way to leave Germany. You know of the offer made to him to go to Geneva and to help in the building up of the oecumenical seminary. On the other hand the government of Basel, whose citizen Karl Barth is, has offered him in principle a position at the theological faculty of the University and has asked him to come personally as soon as possible, so that an agreement could be reached. The[se] things have not gone further for the moment. Karl Barth will consider the two possibilities most seriously. The one in Basel would enable him to go on in a quiet way with this main theological work, the writing of his systematic theology. Geneva would enable him to have possibly wider influence into the Latin and Anglo-Saxon world. He seems to be a little afraid in thinking that the quiet work of thinking could be hindered by the restlessness of a possibly ungood [sic] internationalism.[1]

As to the general situation in Germany, I have nothing new to tell you. The atmosphere is still that of expectancy, of unsettlement and of anxiety.

I hope you too have had a good Xmas and a good beginning of the New Year. We have had very happy days and are beginning work again with new courage.

With my best regards I am

cordially yours,

---

1 For a thorough narrative see Eberhard Busch, *Karl Barth: His Life from Letters and Autobiographical Texts* (London: Wm Eerdmans, 1976), pp. 256–7.

Koechlin to Bell, 15 January 1935, Basel UB, NL 37, VI 82 (carbon).

My dear Lord Bishop,

A word to tell you that I saw Saturday last Karl Barth, who came for a fortnight's holiday to Switzerland. He has strongly been asked by the *Reichsbruderrat* of the Confessional Synod to appeal to a higher Court against the judgement of the Cologne Disciplinary Court. He is decided to do so, but has to wait until the written judgement of December 22nd is in his hands. Before the higher Court will have pronounced its judgement, Karl Barth cannot of course take any definite decision about his future. Nevertheless he is thinking of it most seriously. Two possibilities are taking the first place in his thoughts:

First the offer of the Reformed Churches of the Rhineland to take the lead of the Reformed theological Seminary in Elberfeld and to develop it. That would give him a possibility of teaching in Germany, allowing him to continue his theological systematic work and give him the possibility of staying in Germany still helping the Church, as he is strongly urged to do, in the maybe decisive part of its struggle. Karl Barth, even being not a German, is strongly feeling that unless decisive reasons are obliging him to do so, he is not allowed to leave the German Church now. But on the other hand of course he is not certain at all if the German State will allow him to stay in Germany in any capacity.

The second very serious offer is that of the University of Basel. All the bodies concerned have in a remarkable unanimity offered him a situation at our University. He could do here his quiet work of thinking as well as his work of teaching. As far as I could gather, Karl Barth seems to prefer the Basel possibility to the possibility of Geneva. But he does not seem to feel free yet to leave Germany and his brethren of the Confessional Synod, especially because he is strongly impressed by the difficulties ahead of the German Church.

A representative group of pastors and laymen of Basel met with Karl Barth to tell him how unanimous was the desire to have him here, but [we – deleted] did not feel allowed to press him for acceptance of the call, if his conscience commanded him to stand firm at the more dangerous and uncertain post in Germany.

As to the Church situation in Germany, Karl Barth confirmed that Bishop Marahrens and those around him wished not at all costs, but if ever possible, to come to an agreement with the State and Dr. Kinder. Niemöller, Barth[,] as well as a very quiet man having been the main helper of Dr. Kapler and staying since July 1933 away from every conflict,[1] have the impression that an agreement could only be reached on the basis of a compromise, which would leave the most important issue dangerously unsolved. They do not think time has come to give in[to] the hands of the State the Church organisation, which presently would have in some ways to leave the only strong basis of the freedom of the Gospel.

Now the Saar question is solved,[2] the vague uncertainty of the situation might give way to a rapid clearing of the whole situation. Karl Barth and the *Oberkirchenrat* Henselmann,[3] whom I have just mentioned, confirmed that day after day already now the aspect of the situation was changing and that what seemed to be true one evening was questioned again next morning under some uncontrollable influence. The President Koch of Eastern Prussia, member of the Prussian Synod,[4] seems to play a very influential role in the present negotiations. Even acting personally he has evidently State and party in some ways behind him.[5]

May I add that I am coming to London according to present plans Tuesday, January 29th 3 p.m., intending to stay at Kingsley Hotel, Hart Street, to attend the 30th and 31st at the YMCA building, Great Russell Street, the Officers Committee of the World's Alliance of YMCA.

Knowing of it, Henriod has asked me if I could not attend at least partly the Administrative Committee of the Oecumenical Council and if I could not beforehand go to Berlin to bring to you the most recent information. After some thinking I came to the result that it would not be wise to attend under present circumstances your Committee. The situation is not calling for my presence as it did in October. I also do not see the need and wisdom of my going now to Germany to see some people and to bring to you the latest news, which already might have grown old when I will have arrived in London. Furthermore Stange, being the leader of the YMCA Movement and attending as well your as my Committee [sic], I would in my capacity as Vice-President of the World's Alliance feel embarrassed to go to Germany just before our Officers Committee is meeting and is expecting to hear from *him* on the German YMCA situation so closely connected with the whole Church problem.[6]

I feel certain you will understand the position I am taking and approve of it. Nevertheless I am anxious to tell you that if the situation should be changing until January 27th and if you should feel my passing through Berlin to be urgent, I would try my best to be at your disposal. I do not need to say that I should be very glad to have the opportunity of seeing you during my stay in London. It would however be difficult to meet you the 30th or 31st as I have to preside [over] the meeting and as we need all our time to do the necessary work before I have to leave London again the evening of the 31st at 4 o'clock. I cannot stay longer, but I could possibly, though with some difficulty, come to London a little earlier. At any rate I can be at your disposal Tuesday after 4 p.m.

With kindest regards,
Yours very sincerely,

---

1   This refers to Bodelschwingh.
2   At the plebiscite in the Saar area on 13 January 1935 90.7 per cent of those voting declared their allegiance to Germany.
3   Peter Henselmann (1883–?): *Oberkirchenrat*, later pastor in Lugano (Switzerland).
4   Erich Koch (1896–1986): *Gauleiter* of the NSDAP in East Prussia from 1928 to 1945. Later, from 1941 to 1945, he was head of the civil administration in the occupied district of Bialystok and *Reichskommissar* of the Reichskommissariat Ukraine from 1941 to 1944. Extradited to Poland in 1950 by the British military government in Germany, he was sentenced to death there in 1959. The sentence was commuted to life imprisonment a year later.
5   Koch's plan to pacify the church was only one of several unsuccessful attempts to achieve peace in mid-December 1934 and was rejected by Hitler.
6   See also Koechlin's report: 'Relationship of the World's Alliance of YMCA to the German national YMCA Movement in 1933 and 1934'; Basel, UB, NL 37, VI 4,3.

Bell to Koechlin, 21 January 1935, Basel UB, NL 37, VI 83 (handwritten).

My dear Koechlin,
   Many thanks for your letter. I agree with you about non-attendance at the Administrative Cttee of Life & Work. But I should greatly like an opportunity of speech with you.
   Our meetings last all day Jan. 28 & 29: yours all day Jan. 30 (when I am out of London and very busy) & and Jan. 31 when I am also working in my diocese.
   I think it would hardly be fair to urge you to come earlier – as I don't know what our own programme or timetable will be. It ought to be possible to get a talk with you on Tu. Jan. 29 at 4 or soon after. So I will drop a line to the Kingsley Hotel suggesting an hour, or await your arrival.
   I agree too that you are not going *now* to Berlin. And I am *much* interested in your news of Barth.

Yours ever

Koechlin to Bell, 22 March 1935, Basel UB, NL 37, VI 84 (carbon).

My dear Lord Bishop,
   I have not written to you these last weeks because I was not in a position to give to you facts you could not read in the *Times* or hear from other sources. Even on what has happened these very last days I cannot give you clear light. It is very difficult to judge accurately the actual German situation. The left wing of the National Socialist party including the tendencies of Rosenberg,[1] seem in general to gain ground. The whole Rosenberg propaganda amongst youth is causing more and more anxiety and alarm. The ordinance of Rust given to the professors of the theological faculties are pointing also in this direction.[2] You will have heard that Karl Barth is not any more allowed to speak in any meeting in Germany. Not long ago I heard from [a] trustworthy source that the S.A. and S.S. circles had prepared in January in Munich an attack against [the] Church and Church officials, but that the *Reichswehr*, having alarmed some troops, succeeded in taking this measure to make impossible the realization of that plan. The attack against the 400 pastors of March 17th,[3] initiated by Mr. Stuckart,[4] a friend of the all too well-known Dr. Jäger, has probably been [at]tempted because the *Reichswehr* was during these days all too busy in other directions. If really Ludendorff[5] and Göring[6] are to be the decisive factors in the new army and if Blomberg,[7] who always backed powerfully the Confessional Church, is becoming a personality of third rank in the army, the position of the Church will in a double sense be weakened.
   Until now the army was strongly against favouring the so-called third confession[8] and counterbalanced in the State action, in a very efficient way, the extreme tendencies of S.A. and S.S. The army did not allow the third confession to penetrate into its ranks and did not even allow officers and soldiers to leave the Christian Church. Ludendorff and especially his very hysteric and active wife,[9] being strong exponents of the new

German paganism, all that might change. The 17th of March might already have been a first sign of such tendencies.

Others still hope that the army will maintain its previous line in spite of Ludendorff and gain influence because the S.A. evidently will in future not have any more the important position it had. They think that the action of Dr. Stuckart was a last desperate attempt to crush the Church opposition and that this attempt failed. In stating these different views, I of course realise that in the last analysis the position of an army cannot be decisive in Church matters.

Another light is falling on what has happened if one considers it from the angle of the international situation. The possibility of influencing Germany from outside in Church questions seems not any more to be the same. Evidently some German circles think and hope that f[or]. i[nstance]. English interest is too much absorbed by the military and diplomatic developments to give great importance to Church developments. They might think also that Germany had to hurt England so strongly, that the new Church attacks could not add very much to the existing tensions. Under those circumstances the risk could be taken. At any rate the voice of von Neurath seems not any more to have the same weight it had even some weeks ago.

In pointing to such possibilities, I am not certain at all if they do correspond to real facts. In writing to you, I am somewhat thinking aloud, without being able to reach clear conclusions.

You might be interested that next week Dr. Hesse of Elberfeld, the Moderator of the Rhineland Reformed Church, has called to Siegen a Free Reformed Synod of [the] whole [of] Germany. He has kindly invited me to come, but as I have to attend the Synod of our Basel Church Wednesday next, I cannot go. Dr. Keller or Dr. Choisy, who also have received invitations, might be in a position to accept.

As to Karl Barth's remaining in Germany, the final court decision, which most certainly will be negative, as Gogarten[10] has already been called to take his position in Bonn, has not yet been reached. But it has been agreed with him, that as soon as the German judgement will have been announced, the official call of the Basel University to him will be published and that he will accept at once.

Please kindly remember me to Mrs. Bell and believe me very cordially yours,

---

1   Alfred Rosenberg (1893–1946): politician and leading ideologist of the National Socialist Party. A member of the party since 1920, from 1923 to 1938 he was the editor of the Party newspaper *Der Völkische Beobachter*. After various antisemitic and racialist writings he published his fiercely controversial book, *The Myth of the Twentieth Century* (*Der Mythus des 20. Jahrhunderts*) in 1930, becoming in the same year a member of the *Reichstag*. In 1933 he was appointed head of the Foreign Office of the Party, but he enjoyed little success there and in 1934 Hitler appointed him Commissioner of the Führer for the Supervision of the entire spiritual and ideological training and education of the NSDAP. In 1941 he became Commissioner for the central handling of issues relating to the Eastern European region. Tried at Nuremberg after the war he was sentenced to death.

2   Decree of the Reich and Prussian Minister for Science, Education and National Formation to the Theological Faculties, 28 February 1935, in Carsten Nicolaisen

(ed.), *Dokumente zur Kirchenpolitik des Dritten Reiches*, Vol. II: 1934/35 (München: Christian Kaiser Verlag, 1975), pp. 271-2.

3   The planned reading from the pulpit of the statement of the second Confessional Synod of the Old Prussian Union against the New Paganism (to be found in Beckmann, *Kirchliches Jahrbuch*, pp. 90-2) was prohibited on 9 March by the Minister of the Interior, Frick. On 16 March all pastors had to declare in writing that they would not read the Message in public; if they did so they would face house arrest or be taken into protective custody. The number of pastors arrested or placed under house arrest is unknown but would appear to fall between 400 to 715. On 19 March Frick changed his approach, releasing the arrested pastors but now taking the responsible leaders of the synod into protective custody. This new order was rescinded after Praeses Koch prohibited the reading of the statement. After further discussion in the Reich Ministry of the Interior, the Council of Brethren of the Church of the Old Prussian Union lifted the ban on the condition of publishing a new preamble: 'The word is directed only against the new paganism and wants to warn of the danger threatening the people and the state.' See Nicolaisen, *Dokumente*, pp. 273-7.

4   Wilhelm Stuckart (1902-53): lawyer; from May 1933 as ministerial director in the Prussian Ministry of Culture he was decisive for the implementation of the Law on the Restoration of the Professional Civil Service; from 1934 he was State Secretary in the new Reich Ministry of Science, Education and National Education. Temporarily retired on 13 November 1934, in the following March he was appointed to the Reich Ministry of the Interior. As head of 'Department I – Constitution and Legislation', Stuckart was responsible for the anti-Jewish laws, and especially the Nuremberg Laws of September 1935. Later he participated in the Wannsee Conference in January 1942.

5   Erich Ludendorff (1865-1930): German general of the Great War, military theorist and nationalist politician; an early supporter of Hitler he became a vigorous polemicist against Christianity in the company of his second wife, Mathilde von Kemnitz.

6   In May 1933 Göring, a highly decorated fighter pilot of the Great War, had been appointed Reich Minister of Aviation. In May 1935, he was given the supreme command of the newly founded Luftwaffe, at the same time being renamed *General der Flieger*.

7   Werner von Blomberg (1878-1946): member of the German general staff; Hindenburg appointed him Reich Defence Minister in 1933. In 1935 he became commander-in-chief of the *Wehrmacht* but was pushed aside after a plot by Göring in January 1938. During his farewell visit, he proposed Adolf Hitler as the new commander-in-chief of the *Wehrmacht*.

8   'The third confession': i.e. those who had left the churches, especially for the German Faith Movement. This category became official by a decree of the Reich Ministry of the Interior on 26 November 1936, introducing the term '*gottgläubig*' instead of the designations 'dissenter' or 'non-denominational' on registration and personnel forms. While the *Luftwaffe* had no military chaplains, in the army they worked under Field Bishop Franz Dohrmann. All of them avoided any direct entanglement in the church struggle. Inasmuch as Dohrmann certainly had sympathies for the Confessing Church, neo-pagan pastors were unwelcome.

9   Mathilde Ludendorff, née von Kemnitz (1877-1956): a psychiatrist, supporter of *Völkisch* paganism and writer of esoteric mystical works, usually antisemitic and anti-Christian in character.

10 Friedrich Gogarten (1887-1967): Lutheran dialectical theologian. In 1922 he founded the journal of the dialectical theologians, *Zwischen den Zeiten*, together with Karl Barth. In 1929 they parted ways and by 1933 he was a member of the *Deutsche Christen*

movement. By then he had held the Chair in systematic theology at Breslau University for two years. In the summer semester of 1935 Gogarten had to stand in for Karl Barth, who had been dismissed from the ministry, in Bonn. He was then appointed professor of systematic theology in Göttingen.

Bell to Koechlin, 25 March 1935, Basel UB, NL 37, VI 85 (typewritten).

My dear Koechlin,

It was a special help to get your letter just at this time. I have just had a letter from Forell and Winterhager[1] telling me that the National Synod of the Confessional Communities is to be held in Augsburg on April 3 and 4, and that Praeses Koch wants me to go.[2] It appears that Praeses Koch has to put the matter before Bishop Marahrens who is considering the question of inviting one or two members of the Universal Council or other Churches. Would you be free to go if the need arose? It is very difficult indeed for me to get away, but the matter may be so urgent at this very juncture that I ought to put other things aside in order to go, and I am inclined to say that I would go if I were officially invited.

Yours ever,

1   Jürgen Wilhelm Winterhager (1907–89): Lutheran pastor, fellow-student of Dietrich Bonhoeffer in Berlin who, like Bonhoeffer, had served the German congregations in London, 1933–4. Based in Berlin and close to Otto Dibelius, he remained active in international ecumenical conferences and circles after the war, contributing to the promotion in Germany of the new World Council of Churches.
2   See Birger Forell and Jürgen Wilhelm Winterhager to Bell, 16 March 1935, Basel UB, NL 37, VI 3, nr. 32.

Koechlin to Bell, 27 March 1935, Basel UB, NL 37, VI 86 (carbon).

My dear Lord Bishop,

Your very kind lines of March 25th are just coming in. I am very glad indeed to hear that you hope to make it possible to attend yourself the certainly most important Synod meeting of the Confessional Church, April 3rd and 4th. I think at the present juncture, when it is evidently clear that the Church Government of the Reichsbishop has become under every aspect impossible, when the struggle of the great Confessional Church against the new paganism has officially been taken up and when the provisional Reichs-Church Government of Bishop Marahrens has the official backing of more than 80% of the German Evangelical Church and has at least begun to have [an] official relationship with Government circles, the moment has come when you personally without any risk can and ought if ever possible to attend the Synod.

As to the attendance of other members of the Oecumenical Council, I would suggest to get this time[.] if possible[,] another personality than your representative at Dahlem.¹ I think of a representative of the Swedish Church and maybe Professor, who is in some ways representing the American Churches also. You will remember that Dr. Leiper asked in Fanø that he might be one of the representatives of the delegation we at a certain moment thought of sending under your leadership to Berlin.

If however for very special reasons you should wish to have me with you at the Synod, I would do my best to make it possible. As far as I can see just know, I would be able to manage it without great difficulties. If you kindly would let me know as soon as possible your decision, I would be most grateful.

With kindest regards,
yours very sincerely,

1   Despite his early doubts, Koechlin did represent Bell and the Ecumenical Council at the second Reich Confession Synod.

Koechlin to Bell, 29 March 1935, Basel UB, NL 37, VI 87 (carbon).

My dear Lord Bishop,

A friend of mine, who had on special invitation attended the Reformed Free Synod at Siegen, held March 26th to 28th, came to see me yesterday night directly after his return. You might be interested to hear that he found the attitude against the whole Hitler regime very striking. Pastors and lay representatives of city- and country-parishes distrust more and more the governmental attitude towards neo-paganism, towards Reichsbishop Müller and towards protestant as well as catholic Churches. The dislike of the regime seems to make great progress. As well in regard to the inner policy as in regard to the foreign policy greatest anxieties have been expressed.

A telegram, sent to Hitler, protested against his attitude favouring neo-paganism and the constant governmental interferences hindering the normal development of Church life. The proposal, to add to this protest a declaration of loyalty, was expressively rejected because the Synod did not wish to weaken the effect of the protest.

The Synod voted its thanks to Praeses Koch and the Prussian Church for their very firm attitude against neo-paganism.¹ On the other side great reserves [sic] were felt in regard to the attitude of Bishop Marahrens and his high Lutheran policy² all too anxious to maintain even under present circumstances the unity of Church and State. The Synod finally decided to create a theological faculty of its own, independent from State and University.³

The general impression of the members of the Synod seems to have been that the real great fight against paganistic national-socialist ideology, more and more backed by State and Party, is coming nearer and nearer and that the fight against German-Christians was only a relatively easy beginning of far more decisive events ahead of the German Evangelical Church. My friend was much impressed by the willingness to throw into this decisive fight the full and last weight of the life of the Church and its members.

It was also yesterday that I saw a document of private character the content of which I am allowed to bring to your knowledge. It is revealing a quite different attitude towards the present circumstances and events. A man holding an important position in Berlin and personally very near to the events[4] is stating in his letter that Praeses Koch and his friends (Niemöller, Asmussen etc.) had issued their declaration against neo-paganism without having told Bishop Marahrens anything about it.[5] He thinks that the reading of such a document on the Sunday, when the whole Nation was thinking of the warriors of 1914 to 1918, was most unfortunate. The tension between Praeses Koch and the Reichs-Brotherhood of the Pastors on the one side and Bishop Marahrens seems to have been particularly strong these very last weeks in connection with this document and also in connection with general policy. The position of the Reichsbishop is declared in this letter to be very desperate and the hope of the man I am speaking of, who is [a] member of the Party, is evidently, that with Bishop Marahrens having the real lead, a solution between State and Church might be found, provided, however, [that] Praeses Koch, Karl Barth, Niemöller, Asmussen etc. could be put out of the picture. The writer of the letter is still highly enthusiastic about Hitler and his policy, confident even in view of his attitude towards the Church and enthusiastic especially in view of the great military events of these last weeks.[6] It is most instructive though not very hopeful to compare the two tendencies of this letter and of the Reformed Synod being both inside the great confessional movement, fighting both the Reichsbishop and the German-Christian Movement.

A picturesque detail mentioned to me from [a] third side is that Göring had asked Niemöller to bless his second marriage April 11th, but that on an intervention of Goebbels Hitler had not allowed such a thing to happen![7]

May I finally say that I have asked my friend if he had heard something about the larger Confessional Synod to be held at Augsburg next week. He said that nothing at all had been said about it, neither privately nor in the official discussions. In the case that the Synod should be postponed until after Easter, I am anxious to tell you, that I would in no case be in a position to attend between Friday, April 26th to Sunday, May 5th, as I have to go in my capacity of Vice-Chairman of the World's Alliance of Y.M.C.A. during these days to Vienna and Hungary.[8]

Very cordially yours,

1 See Koechlin to Bell, 22 March 1935, note 2.
2 Marahrens was a staunch opponent of the Union and saw in the Confessing Church the danger of a united Church of Germany. He found that the Barmen Declaration contradicted his confessional principles, arguing instead for a Lutheran Church of Germany, achieved through the unification of the Lutheran regional churches on the basis of the Lutheran Covenant (*Lutherischer Pakt*) on 12 February 1935.

3   In view of Karl Barth's dismissal in Bonn and the role of *Deutsche Christen* members as professors at the state theological faculties, efforts were now being made across the Confessing Church to found new Church Colleges of Reformation Theology in Wuppertal-Elberfeld and Berlin-Dahlem. Both existed by August 1935 but were soon closed by the Gestapo. Thereafter they continued underground. A third college, in Barmen, found shelter in the Elberfeld Theological School until it too was closed in December 1936.
4   See Koechlin to Bell, 22 March 1935, note 2.
5   This refers to the statement against the new paganism issued by the Confession Synod of the Evangelical Church of the Old Prussian Union (4–5 March 1935). See Koechlin to Bell, 1 April 1935.
6   The new law to rebuild the *Wehrmacht* (16 March 1935) reintroduced compulsory military service.
7   This was only a rumour. Göring's wedding with Emmy Sonnemann was celebrated by Reichsbishop Müller.
8   See Koechlin, 'Report on a journey to Hungary and Vienna, 26 April–3 May 1935' (German version), Basel UB, NL 37, III 16.

Bell to Koechlin, 29 March 1935, Basel UB, NL 37, VI 88 (typewritten).

My dear Koechlin,
   Very many thanks for your letter of the 27th inst. What you say about the importance of the Synod meeting on April 3rd and 4th carries the greatest weight with me. But I have not received any invitation to be present, so in any case I cannot go without an invitation. Forell 'and' Winterhager simply wrote this warning *via* Sweden that the Synod was arranged for that date, and that Koch was taking up the possibility of an invitation to me and to the Archbishop of Uppsala with Bishop Marahrens. It is very likely that Bishop Marahrens may feel that they had better keep to themselves at the moment, and *not* ask for what he may feel a possibly embarrassing foreign attendance.
   I shall keep in touch with the Archbishop of Uppsala, who is staying only twelve miles away from Chichester; and please keep yourself free if possible in case it should be a good thing to go. But of course I have some rather important work here which I shall have to abandon at a considerable cost of time, but as I say the real fact is that no invitation has reached me yet, and I don't at all want to ask for one or to suggest that you or anybody else should indicate that none has come. For I don't want to go unless it is an absolute duty and a very strong and urgent wish is expressed.
                                                                              Yours ever,

P.S. I hear from Cragg (date March 27) that the Synod is that of the *Bekenntnis* Church, and not yet a National Synod. And Cragg and Kramm both deprecate any attendance.

Koechlin to Bell, 1 April 1935, Basel UB, NL 37, VI 89 (carbon).

My dear Lord Bishop,

I thank you most heartily for your air mail letter received yesterday morning. Reverend Cragg might of course have in Berlin an insight into the situation inducing him to 'deprecate your attendance' to the Confessional Synod. I could also imagine that the far-reaching general responsibilities in regard to world peace, entrusted at this highly critical moment to the English Nation and its Government, might lead the responsible leaders of England to look unfavourably to your personal mingling with the internal German political situation.[1] From the point of view of the Confessional Church of Germany however I would regret if the invaluable help of your personal presence at the Confessional Synod could not be given to it, provided of course that the Reichs-Church Government urgently feels the desirability of your attendance.

You might be interested in the following news I received yesterday through Dr. Hartenstein, Director of the Basel Mission,[2] from Dr. Lilje, still the right hand of Bishop Marahrens, [who has] decided to stay there and refusing finally the general-secretaryship of the World's Student Christian Federation:

1. The German Christians are becoming more and more weak. Their theological leader, Pastor Christiansen is in prison because involved in a bad money business of the League for 'Mother and Child'.[3]
2. The Reichsbishop has been badly received by Hitler February 28th. The Chancellor did not hide his discontent that Müller had not succeeded in reaching any result in the affairs entrusted to him. Müller in response pledged that he had no executive power, asked Hitler to be *summus episcopus* of the Evangelical Church and to nominate a Minister *in evangelicis* with full power for all questions of legislation, jurisdiction and finance, leaving to the Reichsbishop only the spiritual leadership. Hitler refused the first offer, being catholic. The question of the Minister in evangelicis is not answered yet.
3. The Government of Bishop Marahrens is in daily close contact with State officials. The Reichsminister of Justice, Gürtner (catholic)[4] is helping to reach a favourable settlement. A memorandum of Bishop Marahrens is asking for opportunity of a year's time to build up an independent Church organization with power to put aside personalities like the Reichsbishop and his followers.
4. The document against new paganism has been issued by Praeses Koch without the knowledge of Bishop Marahrens, but Bishop Marahrens was afterwards backing the document and Praeses Koch, especially in protesting most energetically against the State interference by which 800 (eight hundred!) Pastors had been for a day or two put into prison.[5]

    This State interference is due as it seems to Dr. Frick being at that moment under the influence of Dr. Jaeger's friend Stuckert. The agitation in the population, the congregations assembling hundreds and thousands of faithful Christians at the doors of the prisons, singing hymns, was such, that even Goebbels, furious that the *Bekenntnis* Church had got the possibility of such reaction and strengthening of its life, insisted to give [or: make] free all these pastors at once.

Of the six Pastors of Hessen, who had lately been put to [or: in] prison, three are in the concentration camp of Dachau, all too famous for ill-treatment of its prisoners. Grave anxiety is felt in regard to these faithful servants of the church.

5. Praeses Koch had after all these events such a breakdown, that he had to go for complete rest to a sanatorium.
6. Actually the State is considering the fight of the Confessional Church as a political one, because the national-socialist ideology is attacked in its foundation. That makes at present the situation particularly dangerous, the whole extreme wing of the Party [being] most anxious to destroy a Church being a strong-hold of anti-national-socialist philosophy.

The Confessional Synod is expected to be held at the latest next week 1) to take [a] most energetic position against the new paganism of German faith and 2) to claim for the freedom of the Church and the Gospel.

With kindest regards,
yours very sincerely,

P.S. In case you should wish me to attend the Confessional Synod, I am at your disposal except April 26th to May 5th.

---

1 A reference to negotiations which would lead to the Anglo-German naval agreement of June 1935.
2 Karl Hartenstein (1894–1952): from 1926–39 director of the Basel Mission and member of the German Evangelical Mission Council. As an authorised representative of the Basel Mission (German branch), he did his best to secure the assets of the mission society in Stuttgart from 1939 onwards.
3 Nikolaus Christiansen (1891–1973): from 1926 to 1933 consistory councillor of the Evangelical Church of Schleswig and Holstein in Kiel; from 1933 to 1935 'spiritual' vice-president of the German Protestant Church in Berlin, retiring in 1935; finally he was a pastor in Büsum from 1936 to 1956.
4 Franz Gürtner (1881–1941): appointed Reichsminister of Justice under the Papen administration in June 1932 he continued in that position under the new Hitler government, joining the National Socialist party only in 1937. Advised by Hans von Dohnanyi, the brother-in-law of Dietrich Bonhoeffer, he attempted to guarantee the independence and rule of law, protesting against abuses and murders by the SA in concentration camps. Such efforts were mostly ineffective and at the same time he signed a succession of National Socialist acts laws or decrees. After 1935 his political influence waned.
5 On the number see Koechlin to Bell, 22 March 1935, note 2.

Bell to Koechlin, 3 April 1935, Basel UB, NL 37, VI 90 (typewritten).

My dear Koechlin

Very many thanks for your letter. It is most interesting and the news of great importance. I saw the Archbishop of Uppsala on Saturday and discussed the possibility of going to Augsburg with him, supposing an invitation came. He was pretty clear that the time had not yet come for such an official act as the presence of a Swedish or an English Bishop. He thought that the situation was still fluid. However no invitation has in fact reached me. Pastor Forell has always been inclined to anticipate events, and I think that he must have been too prophetic this time. But from what you say a Synod of an important kind must be near at hand, whether at Augsburg or elsewhere. I note what you say about your own possibilities and impossibilities.

Now by some curious chance I have been asked to write an article of [a] thousand words for Easter in the *Berliner Tageblatt*,[1] and I am to choose any subject I like. I have decided to accept. I have got to get the MS. into the London Editors' hands by April 15. I am approached because [of] the general interest in religion in Germany. I am obviously expected to deal with Christianity. My task will require careful accomplishment because I am a foreigner who is given the courtesy of a well-known German newspaper. How much one can say is the question, and whether to speak about the reasons for the interest in the Church struggle on the part of the Church outside Germany, and exactly how, is the problem. I shall be more than grateful for any reflections you like to send me, and the sooner the better, as they occur to you.

                                                              Yours ever,

1 The *Berliner Tageblatt und Handels-Zeitung* often asked foreign authors to contribute to the commemoration of significant events such as Christian feast days. The newspaper was a high-circulation national daily from 1872 to 1939 and it had become well-known for its left-liberal orientation in the Weimar Republic. For cultural and political reasons, Goebbels ensured its continued publication under Paul Scheffer as the new main editor until his retirement at the end of 1936. Scheffer sought to preserve the paper's independence, but finally gave up in frustration and left Germany at the end of that year.

Koechlin to Bell, 6 April 1935, Basel UB, NL 37, VI 91 (carbon).

My dear Lord Bishop,

Best thanks for your air mail letter of April 3rd. May I give you very briefly my thought on your Easter article for the *Berliner Tageblatt*. As far as I know, the *Berliner Tageblatt* is still considered to be a paper of a relatively oppositional character representing the tendencies held up in former times by Stresemann[1] and his followers. You might be interested to know that, because it makes the task even more delicate.

Nevertheless I am very glad that the opportunity to write such an article has been offered to you and that you have decided to accept it. I wonder if you could not simply write an article on the Christian meaning of Easter, combining it with the Christian meaning of Good Friday. As your article will be published Saturday, April 20th, it seems quite natural that you speak of the Cross and the Resurrection, grace of God and victory over death and sin as the fundamental basis of Christianity and every Christian Church. And you could certainly write it in such a way, that without even mentioning the new paganism and national-socialist ideology, it is becoming quite evident that the Christian Church is distinctly separated from such tendencies and has to fight them. Speaking of these facts as the foundations of the Church universal, the deepest unity with the Confessing German Church and the Churches outside Germany, will become evident. Such an article, standing on purely religious ground, could not, as it seems to me, be considered as a mingling into internal questions of policy and Church policy. I think that apart from your position and the days of Good Friday and Easter, an article written for the Easter-day ought not, even in actual Germany, deal with controversial questions of Church policy.

In saying that, I am judging from my own experience with such articles [as] I had to write in local Basel papers. I know that the readers of these papers are looking to hear and read even in the article of a political paper the word entrusted to the Church in regard to the special day, and not ideas the writer might have on some questions of actuality. That of course does not hinder that a [sic] Christian Easter message of the Church, being the real message of God, can become very actual for the time and the day in which it is written.

I have not got further news on what is happening in Germany, except that a member of the Confessional Synod, [a] Pastor in Frankfurt, passing through Basel these days, told me of their anxieties concerning the three pastors of Hessen being in the concentration camp. In the papers I have read[,] and you might have read also, that the possibility of a *minister in evangelicis* seems to be considered very seriously by the State.

With kindest regards
yours very sincerely

---

1   Gustav Stresemann (1878–1929): pre-eminent national-liberal politician (of the national-liberal German People's Party) and statesman of the Weimar Republic; briefly Chancellor in 1923 but then foreign minister until his early death. Because of his efforts to reach an understanding with the victorious powers of the Great War, he received the Nobel Peace Prize in 1926 together with his French counterpart Aristide Briand.

Koechlin to Bell, 12 April 1935, Basel UB, NL 37, VI 92 (carbon).

My dear Lord Bishop,

A pastor's letter, dated Leipzig April 9th, came these days with quite alarming news. It is confirming that three Pastors of Hessen are in the concentration camp of Dachau, because they would not acknowledge Bishop Dietrich. From March 26th to April 3rd they were brought together with criminals from prison to prison and badly treated. The President of the Police of Leipzig, evidently on some instigation[,] ordered that no one was allowed in the Church service[s] to include in the prayers an intercession for these Pastors. He did not allow either [any pastor] to read any word against [the] new paganism. The Pastors Lewek of St. Nicolai and Meder of St. Thomae nevertheless read the declaration[,] the wording of which had not been opposed by the Ministers of the Reich and of Saxony.[1] Nevertheless the two Pastors were put into prison and are treated like other prisoners. Lewek was griev[ous]ly wounded during the war and is partly paralyzed. His wife is expecting these days her 7th child. Pastor Walther, who had not read the paper, but tried to help his colleagues in influencing the President of the Police[2] in their favour, has also been put into prison, in prisoner's clothes, his hair cut. The governmental Ministers declared that all these prisoners had to be given free[dom] at once, but the matter has become a question of prestige and the President of the Police, backed by the Reichsstatthalter,[3] is not even allowing a normal procedure to take place. The wives are not even allowed to approach the Police Administration and that after the 9th day of imprisonment! Last Sunday every intercession for the prisoners was explicitly forbidden.

All the three Pastors have Confirmation[s] in their parishes. The parents were asking for liberation of the Pastors. They were told that national-socialism led by Hitler did not need any religious act like that. The endeavor [sic] of these parents was called to be sedition. All these Pastors and also the writer of the letter, a Pastor himself, are convinced and loyal to the duties of the State and obedient to the Government in all secular matters.

Bishop Marahrens was expected to speak in Leipzig April 8th, but was prevented from doing so. The assembly of four thousand people waited for him in vain.

I do not really know what to do but to intercede. All action through political channels seems at the present moment condemned to complete inefficacy. I wonder if the time might not come before long for strong declarations from the pulpits in all Churches around Germany. I wonder also if a very strong letter to Reichsbishop Müller, pointing to these impossible procedures going on with his tacit and open agreement, could not be written to let him know how the Christian Churches think of the real persecution going on and of a Church Government claiming officiality and patronising, even stimulating[,] such imprisonments.

I am not clear myself what best could be done. I just give you the thought which under the sudden impression of the letter received is coming to me, thankful to be allowed to share with you my anxiety and to leave it to you what following you might think best to give to these my suggestions.

Very cordially,
yours

---

1 The Confessional Community of the Lutheran Church of Saxony had now ordered that the statement made by the Provisional Church Government against the new paganism on 31 March be read out in public, combining it with intercessions for the Pastors of Nassau-Hessen who were now in the concentration camp Dachau. Although the message was to be read in the version that had been legitimised in the Old Prussian

Church, the pastors were still obliged to make a statement to the police that they would desist; refusal led to several punishments ranging from the imposition of house arrest to imprisonment in the concentration camp at Sachsenburg. The three Leipzig pastors, Lic. Georg Walter, Oskar Meder, and Ernst Lewek, were arrested on 31 March; twenty others were taken into custody between 16 April and 13 May. All were released on 4 June 1935 by order of the Reich Minister of the Interior. In this Frick was evidently responding to an intervention by the Archbishop of Canterbury and also manoeuvring in view of the Anglo-German naval agreement. See Lang to Bell, 3 March 1935, LPL, Lang Papers, Vol. 319, fol. 119.

2   Oskar Knofe (1888–1978): president of police of Leipzig 1933–7. After the invasion of Poland, Knofe was entrusted with the leadership of the police in the military district of Posen. He would be responsible for many war crimes against Poles and Jews.

3   Appointed in the course of the *Gleichschaltung der Länder*, *Reichstatthalter* were governors and permanent representatives of the Reich government, responsible for, among other things, appointing and dismissing the chairman of the state government. In Saxony *Gauleiter* Martin Mutschmann (1879–1947), a confidant of Hitler and an active advocate of National Socialist ideology, went on to become one of the most powerful state politicians in the Third Reich.

Bell to Koechlin, 17 April 1935, Basel UB, NL 37, VI 93 (typewritten).

My dear Koechlin,

Very many thanks for your two letters. The first letter about the article in the *Berliner Tageblatt* was most useful and I have acted upon it. The article is a religious article and if I get a spare copy sent me I will send it along to you.

I saw Bonhoeffer on Monday in London. He was on his way to Berlin. He is now, I think, giving up his Pastorate in London and will certainly be away for six months at least, possibly for good.[1] He told me that the situation in the German Evangelical Church was critical but at the same time he did not think that very drastic measures were going to be taken immediately. He thought rather that the Government policy was to let things drift a little, and especially to see how far the lay people supported the Pastors when such oppression and persecution as you described in your letter of April 12 was attempted. In other words they wanted, without committing themselves too far, to see how much the people would stand. He is to keep me in touch with what is happening, and Pastor Rieger in Blackheath[2] will be a very useful link. I sent a line to Praeses Koch through Bonhoeffer assuring him of my sympathy and my desire to help in case of need. I think that Bonhoeffer believes that a need may arise in the not distant future when an appeal might have to be made to the Oecumenical Church. I have talked the matter over, and keep talking the matter over, with the Archbishop of Uppsala who is spending Holy Week, with his wife and daughter, in my house. I have showed him your letter.

Before I got your letter, having seen similar news in *The Times*, I wrote a personal strong protest to Herr von Ribbentrop, telling him that if it really was desired to maintain Evangelical Christianity, it must be recognised that a Confessional Synod, from the point of view of the Churches outside, was the only instrument, and that an attack on that, or the suppression of that, would be interpreted as an attack upon Evangelical Christianity.[3] I took as my starting point the attacks on the Pastors and their imprisonment, and sent him a cutting from the *Christian World*,[4] to show how strongly Church people from different Churches in this country felt on the matter.

Yours ever,

1 Bonhoeffer left London on 15 April to take over the leadership of the seminary of the Confessing Church in Pomerania, initially in the Zingsthof near the Baltic coast but from 24 June in Finkenwalde. Bonhoeffer took this letter along to Berlin; there is a copy in the Staatsbibliothek in Berlin: Handschriftenabteilung; Nachl. 299 (Dietrich Bonhoeffer); signature: Nachl. 299, A 42,3 (10).
2 Julius Rieger (1901–84): German pastor serving the London German congregation at St George's church, he was a firm friend and ally of Dietrich Bonhoeffer and of other pastors who now made their way from Germany to Britain; on numerous occasions he was an important advisor to Bell. Interned during the war he remained in Britain until 1953, when he became Superintendent of Berlin-Schöneberg.
3 See Ronald C. D. Jasper, *George Bell. Bishop of Chichester* (London: Oxford University Press, 1967), p. 204.
4 *The Christian World*: influential evangelical periodical founded by the publisher James Clarke in 1857. In 1914 it sold 100,000 copies a week but by this time was something of a declining force.

Bell to Koechlin, 22 May 1935, Basel UB, NL 37, VI 94 (typewritten).

My dear Dr. Koechlin,

We had a Meeting of the Administrative Committee of Life and Work in Paris last week at which Dr. Oldham gave a full report of his visits only a few days before to Berlin and Hannover. I had been ready before the Meeting, as I had let some friends know, to go with Bishop Ammundsen to Düsseldorf in order to see some of the leaders of the Confessional Synod privately if that were considered useful. Oldham however, after talking it over with Praeses Koch and others, reported at Paris that it was not desirable in the interests of the Confessional Synod leaders who might be exposed to danger. Nevertheless on Saturday night, just after my return from Paris, Bonhoeffer rang up, having flown over from Berlin to see me, at the special request of Koch.[1] Praeses Koch said that he was sorry that I had not come to Düsseldorf and he had advised against my coming, for it would have been useful, but he realised what had happened.[2] He wanted me to write a letter for the Meeting of the Confessional Synod to-day and tomorrow.[3] He also wanted me to be ready to come at the shortest possible notice if there were a very grave necessity. I am of course ready to go if such a grave necessity arose. The reason I am writing to you is this. I should be of little use by myself owing to my ignorance of German. Supposing – which Heaven forbid – that such a necessity arose, would it be possible for you to meet me in Berlin? I could telephone to you from here to ask whether you could come if the day were to arrive. This letter however can state the situation more easily than a telephone call. I expect what it would mean would be that I should, if the necessity arose, fly to Berlin and ask you to meet me at some convenient place in Berlin, say at the Grand Hotel am Knie.[4]

With all best wishes,
Yours ever

1 Bonhoeffer flew to London on 18 May. It was later that he got a copy of this letter, now in Staatsbibliothek zu Berlin. Handschriftenabteilung; signature: Nachl. 299 (Dietrich Bonhoeffer), A 42,3 (11), Blatt 12.
2 On 11 May the Gestapo appeared for the first time in the offices of the Council of Brethren in Dahlem.
3 On 22/23 May representatives of the 'destroyed Churches' met at the little villages Gohfeld and Bergkirchen near Oeynhausen and discussed the situation preparing the Confession Synod. One week later, at Marahrens' invitation, the 'church leaders who are friends of ours', i.e. the Lutheran bishops, met in Würzburg.
4 The prestigious hotel on the Unter der Linden, much favoured by international visitors and used by A. S. Duncan-Jones on his earlier visit to Berlin.

Koechlin to Bell, 24 May 1935, Basel UB, NL 37, VI 95 (carbon).

My dear Lord Bishop,
Your letter of May 22nd reached me this morning. I am anxious to answer it at once, the more as I had thought these days to let you know what I have very recently heard on the German situation.

Karl Barth is these days in Switzerland. The final decision of the State Court concerning his official situation in Germany will be taken June 14th. Unfortunately one or two very striking utterances of his concerning the rearmament to some official Basel people have been quoted in a Swiss political paper and sent to the Reichsbishop and have come to the knowledge of the leaders of the Confessional Synod and the Bishops of Hannover, Bavaria and Württemberg.[1] The Bishops consider that they cannot deal any more in the Confessional Church with a man of the political opinions of Karl Barth and even men like Koch and Immer are doubting that it will be possible for them to maintain the cooperation with Barth. Barth even said that the Bishops did not accept to come to the Confessional Synod [sic] as long as he was holding an office in it and that this very attitude was one of the reasons for the new postponement of the Confessional Synod these last days.

You might know that Karl Barth is strongly opposed to the Church Government of Bishop Marahrens and to the attitude it is taking towards the State.

On the other hand I heard this morning through Director Hartenstein of our Basel Mission, who has met last Sunday Bishop Wurm and Oberkirchenrat Breit of

Bavaria, that Bishop Marahrens backed by Bishop Meiser and Bishop Wurm, was again in consultation with the Reichsminister Frick and that the negotiations seem to be hopeful. Under such circumstances the Bishops thought that the holding of the Confessional Synod would be unwise and urged Praeses Koch to postpone it. They evidently wished that the two tendencies, both very strong in the Confessional Synod, should not break out at this very moment, the one attitude, more Lutheran, backing the Bishops, the other under the influence of Barth represented by the brotherhood of Pastors.

That does not mean that the two tendencies of the Confessional Synod are hopelessly in opposition to one another. The good result of the consultation of the Bishops and the heads of the Brotherhood, held in Leipzig beginning of April, is still standing.[2]

Nevertheless I am in great doubt if in your position you ought to accept a one-sided call coming from Koch and Bonhoeffer, who is very near to Karl Barth, to come to Germany, if Bishop Marahrens is not very clearly backing such an invitation. You know that personally I am inclined to think that the very critical attitude of Barth, Koch, Niemöller and the Brotherhood towards the State is the better line than the tendency of Bishop Marahrens to come to some compromise with the State. I realize however that the Oecumenical Council cannot be [the] judge in such a question and that you would be in a very awkward situation if it would be said that your coming had in any way handicapped the negotiations of Bishop Marahrens with Dr. Frick, even more if Bishop Marahrens would have the impression that Praeses Koch and his followers had used your coming to strengthen their own position.

The changes in the attitude of Dr. Koch, who first asked you to come, who then agreed with your not coming and then again urged you to come in sending Bonhoeffer to London, does not seem to indicate an attitude and policy clear and convincing enough to allow you to trust it absolutely and go to Berlin.

My advice therefore would be once more to hold back your journey to Berlin. If of course the State would interfere very strongly and annihilate the hopes of Bishop Marahrens, then the situation would be radically changed and a common agreement of Bishops and Brotherhood of Pastors to invite you to come, would be possible. Then the moment to accept the invitation might have come.

Taking such a view, I am somewhat embarrassed to offer you in any case my assistance in Berlin. I most certainly will be at your disposal in the case of [a] very serious emergency and I will do my very best to be, of course in a very personal capacity, at your disposal if you see a necessity of going to Berlin before the situation has cleared, trusting in the wisdom of your judgement. May I however mention to you that the dates of June 5th, 11th and 12th are booked by the Synod of our Basel Church and the Assembly of the Swiss Church Federation, both of which I have to attend in any case.

Hoping that my letter is to you of some help and sending you my very best thoughts and wishes, I am,

Yours very sincerely

1   In a conversation in Basel about his possible appointment, Barth had also been asked about Swiss national defence. In reply, he remarked that 'he was in favour of a strong defence of the northern border'. This statement was exploited by Reich Bishop Müller in his attack on Barth on 10 May. On 15 May, Bishop Meiser barred Barth from attending the third Reich Confession Synod in Augsburg, even though he had been invited on behalf of Praeses Koch two days earlier.
2   On 10 April representatives of the Reich Council of Brethren, the Council of the Lutheran Churches and the Provisional Church Government met at Leipzig. In an 'Appeal to the Leader' they rejected the concept of a state-church-system (*Staatskirchentum*) which subordinated the Church to a secular state.

Koechlin to Bell, 27 May 1935, Basel UB, NL 37, VI 96 (carbon).

My dear Lord Bishop,
You will have received my letter of May 24th. This morning I hear that yesterday the Brotherhood of Pastors of the district of Baden has met. [An] official communication made there stated that Bishop Meiser has met with Praeses Koch and that they succeeded to overcome the difficulties mentioned in my last letter, difficulties which certainly have been of real gravity.

Bishop Meiser had not agreed with the holding of the Confessional Synod last week, because he thought [himself] to be in a position to believe that Hitler would in his great speech of Tuesday evening, May 21st, say an authoritative word on the Church situation.[1] Evidently the negotiations between the Lutheran Bishops and Dr. Frick had led him to think in this direction. Now this word had not been said. Praeses Koch and Bishop Meiser agreed to hold the meetings of the Confessional Synod next week, probably towards the end of it, in a place, which will be communicated at the last moment by telegram. The word to be said at this Confessional Synod will be directed to the Church communities, but its content will state that the situation of the Church which has been created by the State and party officials, has become unbearable. The propagation of the new-paganism is becoming more and more powerful and more and more backed by the actual regime.

I do not of course know if the Oecumenical Council will be asked to be represented at this Synod. If it would be the case, I think the invitation ought to be accepted and if it would be possible for you to go, it would certainly be a good thing, provided the two parties stay united until the Synod and give you the necessary guarantee that the united statement will be possible.

May I add that if you should think it desirable to have me with you at the Synod or to give me any mandate, I would accept it, provided that I had not to leave Basel before Wednesday, June 5th, in the evening. I am bound during the 5th to be here at our Basel Synod as President of the Basel Church Council.

With kindest regards,

yours very sincerely

1   Hitler's speech was devoted to international affairs and did not mention questions of the Church; see Max Domarus, *Hitler. Reden und Proklamationen 1932-1945*, vol. I/2 (Munich: Würzburg, 1965), pp. 505–14.

Bell to Koechlin, 31 May 1935, Basel UB, NL 37, VI 97 (typewritten).

Private and Confidential

My dear Koechlin,

Very many thanks for your two letters. Since receiving them I have seen both Pastor Forell and a quite unexpected messenger from Berlin, Dr. Michael,[1] who had come over especially from Koch and has been in conference with Oldham and myself. It is clear that the full Synod is to meet on Tuesday and Wednesday. It is also clear that the situation is very grave. But they want to be by themselves and though, as Michael says, it would be easier for them to have the help of foreign Churchmen, they feel that it is their own task and they do not want representatives of foreign Churches to attend. So the question of my going or suggesting that you should go is, at any rate at this stage, off.

The Archbishop of Canterbury is fully informed of all that we have heard, and if I hear more I will tell you. I shall be at Lambeth Palace from Tuesday to Friday next.

Yours ever,

1 Horst Michael: historian, member of the Council of Brethren of Berlin-Brandenburg. See Bell on Conversation with Dr. Michael, 29 May 1935, LPL, Bell Papers 13, fols. 187–91. For the assessment of Michael see Oldham to Lang, 6 September 1935, LPL, Lang Papers 319, fols. 165–70.

Koechlin to Bell, 22 June 1935, Basel UB, NL 37, VI 99 (carbon).

My dear Lord Bishop,

May I be allowed to send you a report I have written on my recent visit in Hungary and Austria. Though I went there in my capacity of Vice-Chairman of the World's Alliance, I was far too much interested in the general and Church situation to neglect this whole aspect of the national life. What I have written about it in my report, might, as I hope, be of some interest to you.

As to the German Church situation, I have hardly anything to tell you that you don't know by other sources. The friendly attitude the Government has taken recently towards the Confessional Synod, is certainly largely due to your and other British intervention. The desire of the German Government, to come to an agreement with England and to avoid everything which could create difficulties in British feelings, has, as I feel, also helped enormously.[1] It has to be hoped that now the main agreement is reached, the Government might not change again its church policy. I am not without some anxiety in this respect.

Karl Barth, whom I saw longly last week, [sic] did not expect at all the favourable sentence of the Berlin Court.[2] He is of course willing to be faithful to the new possibilities open to him in Germany. He went to Berlin and is hoping to see the Minister of Cult [sic], Dr. Rust, and to clear with him his whole situation.[3] The call, our Basel University was ready to address to him, has not been made public under the new circumstances.

With kindest regards,
Yours very cordially,

Enclosure.[1]

1   On 18 June 1935, the German-British Naval negotiations came to a conclusion. Contrary to the Treaty of Versailles, the new treaty sanctioned German rearmament at sea within certain limits.
2   On 14 June 1935, the Higher Administrative Court in Berlin overturned the judgement of 20 December 1934 due to formal errors. While the other charges were dropped, Barth received a reduction in salary of one-fifth for a period of one year. He was deeply disappointed that even though the Confessing Church had urged him to appeal he had received no further support from it.
3   On 21 June 1935, Rust retired Barth according to the Law for the Restoration of the Professional Civil Service.
4   This now appears to be missing.

Bell to Koechlin, 19 July 1935, Basel UB, NL 37, VI 98 (typewritten).

My dear Koechlin,
   I must apologize for never having, I think, written to thank you for your most interesting letter and report of your visit in Hungary and Austria, sent on June 22nd.
   I have heard little new about the German Church. I do most earnestly hope that the German government will not again change its Church policy. I wonder whether I shall see you at Chamby?[1]

                                                                    Yours sincerely,

1   From 18 to 25 August 1935, the Universal Council of the World Alliance for International Friendship through the Churches met in Chamby near Montreux. The conference confirmed the resolutions of Fanø and began to prepare for the 1937 World Conference in Oxford. A representation of the *Reichskirche*, under Heckel, went to Chamby. Because of this the Confessing Church declined the invitation. See Koechlin's dossier 'Oekumenische Konferenz in Chamby-Montreux 1936', Basel UB, NL 37, I 3.

Bell to Koechlin, 21 October 1935, Basel UB, NL 37, VI 100 (typewritten).

My dear Koechlin,
   We have not corresponded for some time and I write in haste now. I was in Germany last month.[1] I had a very useful talk for an hour with Rudolph Hess, and I have been in correspondence with him since.[2] He wants, it seemed to me, to have a reasonable and happy solution of the Church question, and I have put in the form of a Memorandum what I believe the fundamental issue to be. He has acknowledged this Memorandum with much gratitude. Praeses Koch knew that I was seeing him, and approved, Praeses Koch also asked me to see Ribbentrop and Kerrl[3] if I could in Berlin. I did so and had nearly two hours with Kerrl, and a most friendly conversation. I reported all these

conversations not only to Lilje at leisure but also to Bishop Marahrens on whom I called at Hannover on my way back to England on September 21st. The fundamental issue as I stated it both to Kerrl and to Hess may be stated as follows. Does the National Socialist Government intend and wish to bring the Church under the hammer of the State and make it a State department from all practical points of view, or does it wish to give the Church a life and a place of its own, free to preach its Gospel and to live according to its faith? Most emphatically the answer from each was that there was no desire for a State Church or for a Church under the hammer of the State, but every desire for a Church able and free to live its own life.

Now I have just had a message from Berlin brought to me from Kerrl to the effect that a Joint Committee has been appointed on which Zoellner serves and others who represent both German Christians and the Confessional Church, i.e. not purely a Committee of neutrals but lacking, not unnaturally, the well-known leaders on both sides. The way in which this Joint Committee has been interpreted in our English papers is, in Kerrl's judgement and Ribbentrop's, unfair. I am told that the statement which was issued on Friday in the form of an appeal to the German Evangelical Church and signed by all the members of the Joint Committee, was approved by Marahrens and that Marahrens was present when it was drafted. Further, Kerrl had nothing whatever to do with the drafting of the statement, but was most happy when he saw its complete text.[4] My informant tells me that Pastor von Bodelschwingh is working sympathetically with Kerrl,[5] and[,] he believes[,] approves of the joint statement, but he is to verify this statement and let me know on Wednesday in London at Lambeth Palace where I shall be.

Now it is suggested that a reserved statement from somebody in England welcoming this step towards a solution should be made now. It is further said that if this step is a genuine step, as they believe, and it is disregarded or ignored, it is very discouraging to the National Socialist Government. It is also suggested that what would really be useful would be a statement intimating one's awareness of the new move but at the same time leaving it quite open to the writer - say myself - to criticise later developments if they are not in accordance with the spirit of this document.

I know one has to be very careful, so I do not wish to do anything rash. At the same time I want to be reasonably encouraging, as I feel sure you will appreciate. Kerrl and Hess, to whom for personal reasons I am in a position to write at any time now, have shown their goodwill and have been very reasonable in their conversations with me personally, and I believe that the fact that I have taken a little trouble to understand them has been a help in the present situation. So you will understand that there is something to be said for a bare recognition of their efforts if I can be satisfied that the efforts are genuine and that Marahrens and Co. would feel sympathetic to a short letter, say from myself, in *The Times*.

Let me know what you think, and the sooner the better. I can be reached at Lambeth Palace till Thursday night by air mail - otherwise Chichester.

Yours ever,
p.p. GEORGE CHICESTR.
(Dictated by the Bishop of Chicester but not
signed owing to absence.)

1 Bell's visit to Germany took place in September 1935; he visited Rudolf Hess on 20 September, Lilje on 21 September, Marahrens on 23 September and Kerrl on 28 September.
2 Bell's account of this meeting may be found in Chandler, *Brethren in Adversity*, pp. 97-8. See too Peter Raina (ed.), *Bishop George Bell: House of Lords speeches and correspondence with Rudolf Hess* (Bern: Peter Lang, 2009), pp. 185-219.
3 Hanns Kerrl (1887-1941): member of the Nationalist Socialist Party since 1923, Prussian minister of justice 1933-4, subsequently Reich Minister without portfolio. On 16 July 1935 he was appointed Reich Minister for Church Affairs. After Müller's defeat Kerrl's policy of church committees signified a new phase of confrontation with the Confessing Church. From February 1937 Kerrl, who was frequently ill, lost direct access to Hitler, and church questions fell into the hands of Hitler's Secretary of State, Hermann Muhs.
4 The *Aufruf des Reichskirchenausschusses und des Landeskirchenausschusses für die Evangelische Kirche der altpreußischen Union* (Appeal of the Reichs Church Committee and the Regional Church Committee for the Evangelical Church of the Old Prussian Union), 17 October 1935, in: Beckmann, *Kirchliches Jahrbuch*, p. 108. The Appeal was formulated by the committees in cooperation with Marahrens and handed over to Kerrl.
5 Kerrl's contacts with Bodelschwingh did not lead to Bodelschwingh's cooperation with the church committees, but he saw these as a chance of pacification; see Heike Kreutzer, *Das Reichskirchenministerium im Gefüge der nationalsozialistischen Herrschaft* (Düsseldorf: Droste, 2000), pp. 276-85.

Koechlin to Bell, 23 October 1935, Basel UB, NL 37, VI 101 (carbon).

My dear Lord Bishop,

I have been very glad to read you again and to hear from you what you very kindly tell me about your different important interviews in Berlin.

As to the advisability of an article to be written by you in the *Times*, I am a little hesitant and embarrassed to answer your question, as I have not been these last months in very close touch with the German Church developments and as I have in fact not been in Germany since the Dahlem Confessional Synod just a year ago. From what I know and feel I might be allowed to bring before you the following.

I am convinced that some day the State had to lay a new constitutional foundation for the official Church life in Germany. The old foundation of the constitution of Weimar and the new constitution of Wittenberg with the Reichsbishop were broken and the basis of the all too well-known Church elections of 1933, was on the one side impossible and on the other side hardly possible to be changed. The line of emergency Church law, taken in Dahlem, could not lead to a definite result without decisive cooperation of the State. I think also that Bishop Heckel was right in telling me that the new financial arrangement[s] taken by Minister Kerrl[1] were necessary, as the provisional arrangements inaugurated by Praeses Koch and others did not work sufficiently all over the place as to give to the State [a] real guarantee that the Church taxes were used in an irreproachable way.

The move of the State in creating the Church-Ministry headed by Reichsminister Kerrl was, as I feel, a real programme. The *ausschuss* chosen and put into office by Minister Kerrl cannot, as I feel, be opposed.[1] The effect of the Reichsbishop Müller being put aside was a happy one.[2] The men chosen offer[,] as a unit[,] strong guarantees. It seems to be certain that the election of this Reichs-Church-Executive took place not only in accord with Bishop Marahrens, but also with the two Bishops of Bavaria and Württemberg.[3]

As to the appeal it was new to me to hear that Bishop Marahrens was present when it was drafted. I do not think however that your information, according to which Pastor von Bodelschwingh approved it also, can be right. He seems to suffer from a complete nervous breakdown, complicated by a light pneumonia obliging him to leave every kind of work for weeks and possibly months. He cannot at any rate have been in the picture in an effective and really authoritative way. The wording of the appeal seems on the whole to be a not all too unhappy compromise. It gives me[,] however[,] some concern to see a sentence like the following:

We are staying to [or: standing at] the rebirth of the Nation on the foundation of race, blood and soil.

This concession to national-socialist ideology does not give any hope for the distress of non-Aryan Christians. It has to be noted that Reichsbishop [sic] Kerrl in two speeches soon after the issue of the appeal made very unclear and even dangerous statements. [On] the 17th of October he said in the German Academy for economic questions:[4]

> I do not [place] stress on the State Church because I wish an evangelical Church coming out of innermost conviction by its own free will to our State and *it has to come to it (!)* if it wishes to live, because it has to deal with the same members of the Nation with which we have to deal with the fellowship of the blood into which God has placed us . . . .. This Nation is marching with the Leader.[5]

In a second speech addressed to the press, Kerrl has emphasized also that the appeal has made the very happy and definite distinction between Christian doctrine and christian life, leaving the life to the State and the doctrine to the Church.[6] He has added words on the German Faith Movement being really astonishing [sic]. He said that this Movement could not be called to be godless, that, on the contrary, faith came in it to birth [sic] and showed how much national-socialism was a religious movement, standing everywhere for positive faith and life, also for positive Christendom.[7] [It] may be that he had to make concessions to the party ideology and party policy, going even a step further than the sentence of the Church appeal noted above. At any rate one has to remember that Kerrl is not party leader and that important party leaders like Rosenberg have a power he has not got in spite of his ministerial standing. Party interferences of [a] dangerous character are still very possible. For this reason I am glad to think that you intend to be as cautious as possible in any approval of the new Church appeal, because I wonder if you ought to back the new authority and not wait for some clear facts giving the true interpretation of the wording of the appeal. I know f[or]. i[instance]. that Bishop Dietrich of Hessen, in spite of orders given to him, did not allow last Sunday Confessional preachers to preach in their own parish and church and that he [was] said quite clearly to have a promise of Minister Kerrl that if he should go his own way, nothing would happen to him. Dietrich has a very strong position in the party.[8] In other counties [i.e. German states] the situation seems to be equally unclear.

Another important consideration to be borne in mind is that evidently Hitler needs peace in the Church and that his nearest friends like Hess and Ribbentrop see every interest in giving to the first steps of Kerrl and his Church-Executive as much weight as possible, even before the Church-Executive has come to act. They evidently have the greatest interest of [i.e.: in] having the authority of your approval on their side to be in a position to put in their papers words used by you in favour of the State efforts to bring about peace in the Church. Your name would become a weight on their side of the balance as it has been on the side of the Confessional Synod these last two years.

In view of all these facts I think the words 'wait and see' have their full right and importance. I quite understand and approve of your wish to acknowledge in a fair way good steps made by official Germany in the Church question, but after all one has seen and heard in the years behind us, one would like to wait for more guarantees that a really acceptable solution has been inaugurated by these very first steps, as important as they may be. At any rate you ought in writing [to] be very clear in your interpretation of what has been achieved in Germany, including even a strong advice as to the tendency which the next steps ought to have. In this respect I am very glad to think that you are in the possibility of writing at any time to the Ministers Kerrl and Hess.

If I should hear important facts arising out of the situation, I would be glad to let them be known to you.

With my very best regards,
cordially yours,

1 According to the Law on Asset Management in the Protestant Regional Churches of 11 March 1935 the finances of the Prussian churches, and later of most other churches, were controlled by Financial Departments. It is striking that Koechlin does not mention the Law on the Decision Procedure in Legal Matters of the Protestant Church of 26 June 1935, which deprived the Confessing Church of the possibility of appealing to the courts against measures taken by the state and the Gestapo.
2 The position of the Lutheran bishops against the Confessing Church following the decisions of the Dahlem Synod.
3 In fact, Müller was not deposed, and he retained his title. But he had to leave office and he no longer possessed authority.
4 It is unknown who suggested the persons of the *Reichskirchenausschuss* (Reichs Church Committee) to Kerrl. It is clear that in deciding who should chair it, Marahrens preferred the Westphalian *Generalsuperintendent* Wilhelm Zoellner to the Saxon *Generalsuperintendent* Johannes Eger.
5 Founded in 1925, the *Akademie zur Wissenschaftlichen Erforschung und Pflege des Deutschtums*, known as the *Deutsche Akademie*, was a private cultural-political association in Munich and the forerunner of the Goethe Institute, founded in 1951. To secure its funding, the Academy was given an Economic Council (*Wirtschaftsrat*) in 1935, to which it appointed patrons from industry and finance.

6   This speech is not published: see Bundesarchiv, R 5101/23753, fols. 51–62; summary, fols. 41–5; for an English version see fols. 61–77; summary fols. 63–5. Koechlin was probably quoting from a newspaper report. The underlining and the question mark here are both probably by Koechlin.
7   Kerrl's speech to the press was published in *Der Völkische Beobachter*, süddt. Ausgabe, 18 October 1935.
8   Against the anti-Christian tendencies in the party, this interpretation of the National Socialist movement disclosed Kerrl's basic assumption that Christianity and National Socialism were compatible, the basis of his policy of pacification.
9   The resistance against Regional Bishop Dietrich (Nassau-Hesse) was not limited to the Confessing Church. His arbitrary measures had provoked many critics. Because of this, Reich Governor Jakob Spenger took little part in the disputes and did nothing to maintain Dietrich in power.

Koechlin to Bell, 16 November 1935, Basel UB, NL 37, VI 102 (carbon).

Confidential
My dear Lord Bishop,

May I bring to your knowledge some particulars about the GESTAPO coming to the headquarters of German YWCA at Berlin-Dahlem. The secretary of the Burckhardt-House,[1] travelling in South Germany, came over the frontier yesterday evening to give me the information Pastor Riethmüller wished to be known by those backing outside Germany the evangelical youth work and the German Evangelical Church. It is of course not allowed to become known by any German personality that Riethmüller sent this lady over the frontier.

120 policemen of the GESTAPO came Tuesday, November 5th at 8 a.m. to the Burckhardt-House, jumped partly over the hedges, surrounded and entered the house. All the inhabitants and those doing their work there (girls attending a training course for youth work and girls attending the Bible lectures) were worshipping in a room of the first floor. A servant was down-stairs near the door. She was asked to give at once all the keys of the house and was threatened with imprisonment when she said that the keys were not in her hands. The police however allowed the devotional service to come to its end quietly before they entered the room and obliged all attendants of the service to stay there. In the meantime the search had begun in the offices down-stairs and went through the whole house from 8 a.m. to 5 p.m., every door and even the roof being occupied by policemen. They asked especially for confidential files, tried to find the foreign correspondence and seemed to be especially interested to discover [any] relationship with Roman-Catholic and Jewish movements. They also looked especially for suppressed books and other prohibited literature. They seized all the addresses of the girl groups in Germany and of their leaders and, which might become dangerous for some of these leaders, some questionnaires answered by them in writing on the action of the BDM (Hitler girls youth movement) and on the influence of some legislative acts of the Minister of Education. These papers written lately in connection

with the lectures given to girl leaders at Dahlem-House were in the desk of Pastor Riethmüller. The Police gave also close attention to the Publication Department. Very unkind words on Christian faith being a business article and so on were said. Many letters were copied by two secretaries coming with the police. The men were partly polite, partly very rough in their behaviour. They went along all day with their hats on and employed many tricks to catch some unfavourable utterance or by surprise some ungood attitude, but the whole behaviour of the Burckhardt-House seems to have been very correct and brave. The papers taken away were promised to be sent back, but it has not been the case yet.

The question if the Police hoped to find the theological faculty of the Confessional Synod is not clear. The whole action and attitude point to other directions. Of course the offices of Praeses Koch and the confessional brotherhood, being in the house, were searched very severely too, but one could not tell me with what result and possible consequences.

Pastor Riethmüller and Miss Zarnack seem to have the following judgement on the situations of the secret Police and on the actual situation of the work: As a D.C. man (*Deutscher Christ*) with his label was accompanying the secret Police, may be as one of its members, the D.C. are somewhat suspected to have by some calumny induced the secret Police to start this action. The Burckhardt-House, a beautiful building, with its very fine equipment and its splendidly organised Publication Department, had always been looked at as a very desirable object to get in [its] hands.[2] Its close connections with the Confessional Church and the fact that the leadership of the evangelical youth has passed from Stange [in]to Pastor Riethmüller's hands, have made Burckhardt-House one of the strongholds and main fortresses of the Confessional Church. The evangelical girl youth movement, headed by Fräulein von Zarnack and Pastor Riethmüller, is still unshattered thanks to a strong leadership and an excellent organisation. The young men youth movement is far less united. There could hardly be imagined a more dangerous stroke to the Evangelical Church than the suppression of Burckhardt-House and its work. The hope to find attitudes and papers proving so-called anti-state attitude and traitorship with foreign countries and the thought of using it against the German YWCA and the Confessional Church seems evident. The German YWCA as the German YMCA are still protected by law[s] regulating the life of all civil organisations, but a new law is said to come out, changing completely the legal situation of associations so that the present legal protection can at any moment come to its end, so that the State could act against YMCA and YWCA at its daily pleasure.

The Church Reichsminister Kerrl had evidently no power to prevent these happenings. It is quite possible that the party wing opposite to Kerrl initiated the action to show him the limits of his power. It is also possible that the more peaceful action of Kerrl and the war-like action against Burckhardt-House are again the two faces of the national-socialist sphynx. Nevertheless this action seems to be very symptomatic and dangerous. Pastor Riethmüller hopes that some clear-cut questions, brought before German representatives abroad, brought possibly also before German Church officials, might prove to be very helpful. Of course one would have to be very careful to compromise in no way Burckhardt-House.

I am simply sending to you this information, leaving it to your wisdom to act as you think best. For [the] purpose of very confidential information I am sending a copy of this letter to the headquarters of World's YWCA in Geneva and to Henriod.

With my very best regards,
cordially yours,

1 Hulda Zarnack (1883–1977): since 1924 director of the Burckhardthaus, the Berlin office of the YWCA, and between 1933 and 1953 its 'Superior'. An eminent figure, she had been vice-president of the YWCA in 1924. At the time of the Gestapo action Riethmüller and Zarnack were in London at a meeting of the YWCA; see Riethmüller's information in: Priepke, *Die evangelische Jugend*, p. 225.
2 See Hilda Rømer Christensen, 'When the YWCA entered the City: The Complexity of Space, Gender and Modernity', in *Pieties and Gender*, ed. L. E. Sjrup and Hilda Rømer Christensen (Leiden: E.J. Brill, 2009), pp. 196–9.

Koechlin to Bell, 28 November 1935, Basel UB, NL 37, VI 103 (carbon).

My dear Lord Bishop,

Since I wrote you about the German YWCA headquarters, Burckhardt-House in Berlin-Dahlem, I had two informations [*sic*] about it, which seem to prove that no imminent danger for the great evangelical youth work is to be expected. Pastor de Quervain of Elberfeld,[1] who is in the inner circle of the Confessional Church Pastors, told me that the leading men of the Confessional Church had taken this attack on their offices as they had taken other attacks, with calm spirit and without all too much anxiety.

The other information is stating that the secret police had heard of the questionnaire sent out by Pastor Riethmüller and Miss Zarnack concerning the religious and anti-religious influence of the Hitler-Youth and the effect of Minister Rust's legislation in the different parts of Germany. The police wished to get hold of the answers sent in to Burckhardt-House and of the names of those who answered the questionnaire. As you will remember the secret police succeeded in getting hold of these papers. This information too seems to point to the possibility that the state did not think of a dissolution of the German YWCA and its headquarters, at least not in a very near future.

Much more important are other informations [*sic*] I have got from a most trustworthy source in Berlin, being in closest contact with things going on in the *Reichsskirchenausschuss*. It is a fact that the statement published by the *Kirchenausschuss* was not allowed to be published before Minister Kerrl and Hitler had seen it.[2] It seems to be a fact also that when the members of the *Reichsministerausschuss* read their statement in the papers, they discovered that some sentences, important to them, were left out. You might have read, that Reichsbishop Müller, having lost his influence, was asked to leave his offices. In fact he was ready to do so in order 'to work undisturbed at home'. But as soon as he began to do so, he got a word - from whom?! - to go back to his office and to hold the place.

Reichschurchminister Kerrl failed until to-day in all his efforts to become the party leader for church questions. As he has not got yet the standing of a party leader[,] and as the party is the governing body in the State, he has to obey also in Church questions the party orders. According to Hitler's statement in Nürnberg the party is the State. For this reason the *Reichskirchenausschuss* was not allowed to elect in the sectional *Kirchenausschüsse* Praeses Koch and was obliged to elect [as] members of those *Ausschüsse* Minister Coch in Saxony[3] and Bishop Dietrich in Hessen. Bishop Dietrich has openly declared that being backed by the *Reichstatthalter*, the high official of the Nazi party in Hessen,[4] the *Kirchenausschuss* of Hessen would not be allowed to do anything in opposition with his views and would not be allowed to prevent anything he wished to see done [sic]. As you know, *Reichsminister* Kerrl had made the peaceful move to allow the confessional Pastors to preach again in their churches. It had been allowed in Hessen for a Sunday and the congregation was most grateful. The next Sunday these Pastors were not any more allowed to enter their churches. Bishop Dietrich, backed by party and State, said that the permission was only given for one Sunday. The little group of German-Christians of Baden has written to Berlin that its Bishop Kühlewein had not the confidence of the Church. Answering this denunciation, Kerrl and two of his men are coming these days to Baden to constitute a Badish *Kirchenausschuss*, much against the feelings of the great majority of the Church. A same denunciation has been sent by Württemberg German-Christians, where Bishop Wurm might also see his episcopal rights passing to a mixed *Kirchenausschuss*. It seems already certain that the Württemberg Church with few exceptions will strongly stand against such an *Auschuss* and that in Baden also, where the Church peace was assured, [a] new struggle will begin.

I read with great interest the other day in *The Times* your motion concerning the refugees.[5] I have to preside next week here [over] a great meeting, when Mr. McDonald, the high Commissioner of the League of Nations,[6] and Karl Barth will be the main speakers. Our people are awakening for the duty confronting them in consequence of the German racist and dictatorial policy. This whole realm of facts developing without mercy in the same direction, seems to prove that in the last analysis the anti-church policy of the Nazi State has not changed. The measures taken actually, giving the impression of moderation, are dictated by considerations of opportunity and tactics. The strategic aim is certainly still to destroy an independent evangelical Church, if possible even to destroy the Church as a whole. The pagan influence and infiltrations are going on with constantly renewed strength.

With kindest regards,
Yours very sincerely

1 Alfred de Quervain (1896–1968): Swiss Reformed theologian and pastor of Elberfeld since 1931; he was a friend of Karl Barth. He would move to Switzerland in 1938, later teaching at the University of Bern.

2 Here Koechlin errs. In his speech to the Gau chairmen of the *Deutsche Christen* on 15 October 1935 Kerrl even went so far as to declare that it was the happiest day of his life when he was given the Appeal of the Reich Church Committee and the Regional Church Committee for the Evangelical Church of the Old Prussian Union. See

Gertraut Grünzinger and Carsten Nicolaisen (eds), *Dokumente zur Kirchenpolitik des Dritten Reiches*, vol. III: 1935–37 (Munich: Christian Kaiser Verlag, 1943), p. 121. It is doubtful whether Hitler's approval of the appeal was necessary, since it was submitted by the members of the committees 'by state mandate as men of the church' for 'the leadership and representation of the German Protestant Church and the Protestant Church of the Prussian Union'. See Beckmann, *Kirchliches Jahrbuch*, p. 108.

3   Friedrich Coch (1887–1945): a member of the National Socialist Party since 1931, he became bishop of the Evangelical Church in Saxony in 1933 but was marginalized only two years later.

4   Jakob Sprenger (1884–1945): politician, Gauleiter of Hessen-Nassau. Since 1922 member of the NSDAP, he became Gauleiter of Hesse-Nassau-South in 1927 and after 1933 Gauleiter of Hesse-Nassau. According to the Reich Governors Law of 30 January 1935, he became Reich Governor of the *Volksstaat* Hesse, soon becoming President of the Government.

5   'Persecution of the Jews in Germany', Church Assembly, 20 November 1935; this motion, moved by Bell and supported by Archbishop Lang, provoked an important debate which became widely known for the dramatic intervention in support of the German Jews by Bishop Henson of Durham. See *Proceedings of the Church Assembly*, Vol. XVI, No. 3, pp. 466–78.

6   James Grover McDonald (1886–1964): an American scholar and diplomat, in October 1933 he was appointed high commissioner for refugees from Germany. The commission itself was an affiliate of the League of Nations. Unable to make headway, he resigned in December 1935. His future lay in Israel, and he became the first US ambassador there in 1949.

Koechlin to Bell, 3 December 1935, Basel UB, NL 37, VI 104 (carbon).

Dear Lord Bishop,

You will have read the new law of *Reichschurchminister* Kerrl issued yesterday in the *Reichsgesetztblatt*.[1] I am sending you under separate cover a copy of the *Basler Nachrichten* of to-day, December 3rd. You will find in it the speech Kerrl made to the members of the Prussian Brotherhood, also the 28th of November. The copies of that speech were seized in Burckhardt-House, Dahlem, but already one copy, may be the only one, had left Berlin for Basel. The text, even being in German, might prove to be useful for you.

I include a telegram Karl Barth sent this very morning to the *Svenska Morgenbladed*, which had asked him by cable to give his opinion, paying for a hundred words. I had with Barth this afternoon a long talk. He is of the decisive opinion that national-socialism means to give to the Confessional Church the decisive stroke and that the moment has come for the Churches outside Germany to issue without delay declarations expressing in the strongest and widest possible way their solidarity with the German Confessional Church.

Under the impression of these new events I have just telephoned to Henriod, who, as I hear, will be in London when this letter is reaching you. I hope it might prove possible to take decisive steps. Possibly we will vote a resolution to-morrow at the committee meeting of the Swiss Church Federation.

With kindest regards, yours very sincerely

Enclosure[2]

1. The fifth Decree for the Implementation of the Law for the Safeguarding of the German Evangelical Church, of 2 December 1935, pronounced the 'exercise of church regimental and church authority powers by church associations and groups inadmissible'. See Grünzinger and Nicolaisen, *Dokumente*, pp. 135–6. While Kerrl had previously tried to reach an understanding with the Confessing Church, this new decree turned against such efforts. He now found himself exposed to accusations that he favoured, and even supported, the Confessing Church.
2. This now appears to be missing.

Bell to Koechlin, 4 December 1935 (dictated 3/12/35), Basel UB, NL 37, VI 105 (typewritten).

My dear Koechlin,

Very many thanks for your most interesting letter of November 28th about the German Y.W.C.A. headquarters, and all that is going on in connection with the Kerrl Committee. The situation is an extraordinarily unsatisfactory one, and I suppose it is simply one rather outstanding illustration of the battle between the Radicals and the Moderates. Which will prevail in the end? I am very glad to hear that you are presiding this week over a great Meeting in Basel about the refugees. We are doing our best here to organise an appeal to the British public which will start, I hope, early in the New Year.

I wonder whether you are likely to be in England again in the next two or three months? Schönfeld and Henriod are in London on Thursday, and I shall no doubt hear something more from the former. Please let me have any news that is important. Privately I may tell you that on receiving yesterday's *Times* I telegraphed to Rudolf Hess preparing him for a strong letter which I sent by air mail yesterday, trying to call a halt, and showing how contrary the facts are to the assurances given and the hopes held out two months ago.[2]

Yours sincerely,

1. See Bell to Hess, 2 December 1935, Bell Papers, Vol. 7, fol. 482.

Koechlin to Bell, 23 December 1935, Basel UB, NL 37, VI 106 (carbon).

My dear Lord Bishop,

With very best thanks I received your letter of December 4th and have heard from Dr. Schönfeld, when he passed through Basel a week ago, something about the results of what you had tried to do through Reichsminister Hess.

In the Committee of the Swiss Church Federation we discussed the advisability of a special Swiss resolution, but because we heard through Professor Keller (I did not feel entitled to mention the confidential word you had written to me) of what you had done, we came to the decision not to do anything for the moment. It seemed that the situation had become less acute. If this impression is true, I do not know. The copy of a *post scriptum* addressed to-day to Miss Woodsmall, General-Secretary of the YWCA,[1] will give you some indications of the seriousness of the situation. I had written to Stange in a very cautious way, speaking of my desire to see Germany again after having stayed away since October 1934. Answering he is speaking of a quiet Xmas time and of some holiday weeks in the German hills up to the time when he will have to go to London for the administrative Committee of Life and Work.

This leads me to tell you that the meeting of the Officers Committee of YMCA, which I am bound to attend, will take place immediately following the administrative Committee, January 29th and 30th. My programme for the moment is to reach London in the afternoon of the 28th. As to my return, I cannot fix anything yet, but of course my London stay has to be short. I would be most grateful if I could have the possibility of seeing you at least for some moments of conversation as it was possible last year.

In the meantime I am sending you my very best wishes. Mrs. Koechlin and Elizabeth are joining me in asking you to remember us all to Mrs. Bell. With my very best regards,

cordially yours,

Enclosure[2]

1 Ruth Woodsmall (1883–1963): school-teacher and much-travelled leading figure in the American YWCA; she had that year become general secretary of the World YWCA. After the war she oversaw the work of the Women's Affairs Section of the U.S. High Commission for Occupied Germany.
2 This now appears to be missing.

Bell to Koechlin, 26 December 1935, Basel UB, NL 37, VI 107 (handwritten).

My dear Koechlin,

First a very warm message of goodwill and friendship this Christmas to you and your wife & daughter & family from us both!

Next most hearty thanks for your letter of 23rd received yesterday. I have heard nothing from Hess: but possibly there may have been some slight influences from my letter (with other co-sign[atories]) with the *apparent* improvement, or at least delay in deterioriation, of the Church situation. I had the opportunity a week ago of getting a further message which will, indirectly, reach him, as to the avoidance of coercion.

Bishop Ammundsen writes to me that the Confessional Church has split in two – (1) Prussia, and (2) the 'intact' churches led by Marahrens.[2] But is this really quite the case yet? Anything you can tell me about this – before I see the Archbp. of Canterbury on January 1 would be valued.

I shall look forward to seeing you in London Jan 28–30.

Yours ever

1 The definite split came after the Fourth (and last) National Confessing Synod at Bad Oeynhausen, 17–22 February 1936, provoked by the question of cooperation with the Church Committees.

Koechlin to Bell, 28 December 1935, Basel UB, NL 37, VI 108 (handwritten).

My dear Lord Bishop,

Your very kind lines came in this morning and after phoning with Karl Barth in order to get the latest and most accurate facts I hasten to answer your question concerning the split in the Confessional Church of Germany. Barth happened to receive a letter to-day, brought to him personally by a student coming from Munich. It is true that the Reichsbruderrat, that is the larger governing church council instituted at Dahlem Okt [i.e. October]. 1934 (20–30 men) could not any more agree on a common line of policy for the whole of Germany and dissolved.[1]

The Provisional Reichs-Church-Government headed by bishop Marahrens feeling that the very different situations in the so called 'intact' and 'destroyed' churches made for the time being a united action hardly – if at all – possible, resolved to withdraw from any active participation in the struggle, but resolved at the same time not to vote his own dissolution and not to go into any personal changes concerning its own membership. It did so in order to stay intact, if coming days rendered again necessary and possible united action. It did so secondly in order to give to the different provincial church governments [a] free hand to act according the needs of their particular churches and according [to] their own convictions.

In consequence the Provincial Bruderrat of Prussia, corresponding to the dissolved Reichsbruderrat for the whole north of Germany including Prussia, Mecklenburg, Schleswig, Hamburg and Oldenburg is again the only leading and responsible confessional church government for these areas. It means [a] free hand for Praeses Koch and his colleagues in Oeynhausen including Asmussen, Niemöller, Niesel.[2] The stronger line is again giving the head.

In Hannover being an intact church bishop Marahrens is still in possession of his rights and exercising his normal functions.

The same is true for the southern churches and their bishops. In Bavaria however the situation seems to become critical again. Minister Kerrl summoned bishop Meiser to allow the German Christian pastors he had dismissed to return to their former functions. It had to be done *sine conditione* and before Christmas, otherwise Kerrl would consider the church conditions in Bavaria as abnormal and would act accordingly concerning financial matters as well as administrative ones. Kerrl stated explicitly this quest [sic] to be a question of prestige for party and state. Bishop Meiser refused to submit but seems to have allowed two German Xian pastors, who without having left that group had acknowledged his church authority and had in consequence not been dismissed to preach tomorrow Dec. 29th the one in a church of Nuremberg the other in a church of Augsburg.

The views and policies seem to differ largely not only between North and South, but also between bishop Marahrens and bishop Meiser.

As to Dr. Zoellner it seems that the tension between him and Kerrl is still very unsettled. Dr. Zöllner's withdrawal is still considered to be very possible even probable.

In [sic] the whole the situation remains very uncertain and critical. The struggle is going on, the actions are not as united as it was the case for some time [sic], they are in consequence of the very different provincial situations separate, but nonetheless the confessional church stands true to its evangelical principles and is not losing ground.

May I in closing reiterate the very best wishes and grateful remembrances of all of us to yourself and Mrs Bell. May I also tell you that I am reading with the keenest interest and with growing sympathy your wonderful biography of the late Archbishop of Canterbury,[3] the most valued Xmas gift I received from Mrs. Koechlin.

Yours very cordially

1 See Koechlin's correction in his letter to Bell, 14 January 1936.
2 Wilhelm Niesel (1903–88): German reformed theologian and scholar of Calvin; since 1930 pastor of the Reformed congregation and inspector of studies at the seminary at Wuppertal-Elberfeld. Since 1934 he had been a member of the Council of Brethren of the regional Evangelical Church of the Old Prussian Union; in 1935 he became its effective chairman. From 1937 his position became increasingly precarious; briefly imprisoned several times, he was expelled from Berlin in 1940 and banned from speaking in the Reich. In 1946, he was elected moderator (chairman) of the Reformed Federation, a position that he held until 1973. From 1948 to 1963, he was a member of the Central Committee of the World Council of Churches (WCC). From 1964 to 1970 he was President of the World Alliance of Reformed Churches.
3 G. K. A. Bell, *Randall Davidson, Archbishop of Canterbury*, 2 vols. (London: Oxford University Press, 1935).This magnum opus would subsequently reappear in two single-volume editions, with revisions (1938 and 1952).

1936

12 January	Pulpit declaration of the Council of Brethren of the Old Prussion Union against the Church Committees.
19 January	Niemöller publishes the leaflet *Die Staatskirche is da*. Copies are confiscated.
21 January	Kerrl addresses a meeting in Hannover.
10 February	Gestapo actions are placed above the law.
14 February	A new appeal court for disciplinary cases is formed by the Reich's Church Committee.
18–22 February	The 4th Reich Confessing Synod at Bad Oeynhausen. The Provisional Church Administration splits over its response to the committees. The 'intact' churches will now co-operate with Kerrl; they now found the Council of the Evangelical-Lutheran Church of Germany (*Lutherrat*) while the 'destroyed' (or 'Dahlemite') churches reject Kerrl's committees as an intervention by the State.
7 March	The reoccupation of the Rhineland by German forces; the Treaty of Locarno is repudiated by the German government.
12 March	The Church executive is re-formed, but without representatives from Bavaria, Württemberg, Hannover, Saxony and Mecklenburg.
18 March	The creation of a new council and executive of a 'Lutheran Church of Germany' by the churches unrepresented in the new executive of the Confessing Church.
27 March	Reventlow leaves the German Faith Movement. Hauer also resigns.
10 April	Death of Leopold von Hoesch, German ambassador in London.
15 May	High state officials in Germany are prohibited from holding office in any church body.
28 May	The Second Provisional Government of the (Confessing) Church agrees to endorse an appeal to Hitler, complaining of the anti-Christian character of party leaders, the disruption of church order, the antisemitism of a government which presses the claims of blood, race and soil, the restrictions placed on church publications and the absolute claims of the state.
4 June	The memorandum of 28 May 1936 is submitted to the Reich chancellory.
17 June	Himmler is appointed head of the German police.

19 June	The administrative committee of Life and Work meets in Paris and discusses representation at the forthcoming Oxford Conference.
July	The memorandum of 28 May is published by the press abroad.
24 July	Ribbentrop is appointed ambassador to London.
August	The Confessing movement organizes a pulpit protest against paganism.
1 August	The Olympic Games open in Berlin.
6 October	Weissler and Tillich are arrested for leaking the 28 May memorandum to the press,
November–December	The abdication crisis in Britain
1 November	The announcement of the Rome-Berlin Axis.
13 November	A third man, Werner Koch, is arrested for leaking the 28 May memorandum to the press.
19 November	Hermann Muhs is appointed secretary of state and deputy of Kerrl in the Ministry for Church Affairs.
19–20 November	The Reich Church Committee meets in Berlin.
25 November	Germany and Japan sign the Ant-Comintern Pact.
13 December	Archbishop Lang broadcasts an address in the wake of the abdication of Edward VIII.
23 December	The Prussian Confessing synod demands the resignation of Kerrl and his administration.
29 December	*The Times* publishes a further letter by Bishop Bell reporting on developments in the German church struggle.

Bell to Koechlin, 9 January 1936, Basel UB, NL 37, VI 109 (typewritten).

My dear Koechlin,

I don't think I ever thanked you for your very kind letter just before my visit to the Archbishop of Canterbury. It gave me just the information I wanted, and was most interesting to the Archbishop.

I have received a letter from a Mr. Glanville, a fairly frequent correspondent, stimulated by a still more frequent correspondent – a friend of his – Dr. Kühn,[1] who, I gather, is a little bit of a nuisance from the amount of questions he asks and points he raises, even in Germany itself. Have you any advice to give me on the utility or otherwise of making such an enquiry as is mentioned on Page 4? I don't suppose really however that replies, whatever their nature may be, can be much more than paper assurances.

Yours sincerely,

1 No further information about Mr Glanville and Dr Kühn has been obtained.

Koechlin to Bell, 14 January 1936, Basel UB, NL 37, VI 110 (carbon).

My dear Lord Bishop,
Your letter of January 9th has reached me, but unfortunately I could not give you an answer at once. Dr. Kühn had already in April 1935 written to our Churches, asking for some intervention in favour of Pastor Lewek, who at that time was imprisoned for having read a prayer of intercession for the other imprisoned pastors. He was, as the letter of Mr. Granville is stating, [a] soldier during the war, was grievly [sic] wounded, is still partly lame, has seven children, the 7th of which was expected during those days. Three were ill. This letter in connection with other events led our Church authorities to ask our communities for prayers of intercession. Since then I had [sic] not heard of the case. May I say that in my view Dr. Kühn, in spite of the fact that he is certainly 'a little bit of a nuisance' in writing to all corners of the evangelical world, is a man of character and standing. The case of Pastor Lewek is certainly a serious one.

In spite of this fact I do not see the possibility for you to interfere in this personal matter. Many similar cases certainly could be mentioned. In asking in high quarters for a change of attitude, you would probably receive some kind of answer, which you hardly could oppose seriously. In dealing with many personal cases your influence in the main issues would in my view be weakened. To raise the principal questions mentioned by Mr. Granville would hardly lead to positive results. The whole situation in this aryan business is very unclear. The intermingling of the influences of Secret State Police, of political provincial leaders and church authorities is such, that one never can get hold of the really responsible authority.

The only thing possible would be, if someone, say Mr. Granville or another possibly more influential personality[,] could, based on really very clear facts, mention such a case in a paper and in such a way draw the official German attention to the very bad impression made by such dealings on foreign and especially English public opinion. It seems to be proved that personalities with some influential foreign relations are far less embarrassed and[,] say[,] persecuted than those standing only on themselves or on German relations. This is purely a suggestion as I do not like to be purely negative in answering your question and the suggestion of Mr. Granville.

May I add a word on the Reichsbrotherhood.[1] In my last letter I wrote to you that it had voted its own dissolution. This expression [which] I owed to a letter of Pastor Karl Immer to Karl Barth, was evidently too strong. It might only have been a resolution to meet not anymore again, as more or less unanimous decisions had proved to be impossible. As you know this Reichsbruderrat has been called together again for January 3rd and has with a majority of 17 to 11 voted [for] a resolution against the provisional Reichschurch-Government. The minority is relatively numerous. This might partly be explained by the fact that all five members of the Reichschurch-Government were voting members of the *Reichsbruderrat* and had voted with the minority. Compared with last year's result, when [in] late November 1934 only five members, Niemöller, Asmussen, Barth etc. had voted against the constitution of the provisional Reichschurch-Government, the change is notable, the majority of 17 being this time with Niemöller, Asmussen and the majority of November 1934 being this [?that] time (if you exclude the members of the provisional Reichschurch-Government) a minority of six. I mention this purely to indicate the change of general attitude. The Provisional Reichschurch-Government, stating that its power had only been partly given to it by the Reichsbruderrat, has resolved to stay in office as long as the independent Church Governments of the provinces and the Reichssynod, which at Augsburg had voted in favour of the Reichschurch-Government, would not take the actual attitude of the Reichsbruderrat. The situation, as I hear to-day from Miss van Asch van Wyck, the President of the World's Y.W.C.A., coming directly from Berlin, seems to be serious. They still hope to get a Reichssynod and there to find unity again. They have this hope the more as all parties of the Confessional Synod in the last analysis seem to be united in the view that the fighting against the Nazi State Philosophy will sooner or later come to the ultimately decisive state. The adherents of the Reichschurch-Government wish to give to the Reichschurch-Ausschüsse (Zöllner) and even to the State all chances possible to find an acceptable way towards peace before the definite break will have to come. The others seem to see no good in waiting and are inclined to force the issue for the present moment.

In sketching to you the situation as I see it after having heard this morning Miss van Asch van Wyck, who was sitting together with Pastor Riethmüller, Dr. Lilje, Kirchenrat Breit of Bavaria not later than yesterday night in the Burckhardt-House of Berlin-Dahlem, I do not pretend to have the real view of the situation. I am trying to investigate especially about the situation of the Southern Churches and am hoping to be able to write more to you before very long.

As to my present plans, I intend to arrive in London Tuesday, January 28th 3.21 p.m., staying at Kingsley Hotel, Hart Street, Bloomsbury. I will have to leave London on Friday of the same week at 4.30 p.m., at the latest at 11 p.m.

With kindest regards,
yours sincerely

Enclosure[2]

1 i.e. the Reich Council of Brethren.
2 Now apparently missing.

Koechlin to Bell, 6 February 1936 Basel UB, NL 37, VI 111 (carbon).

My dear Lord Bishop,

I have not written you anymore after the phone [conversation] we had together Wednesday evening of the last week, because I did not see any point rising which would have indicated towards another more active attitude. In fact the common feeling we seemed to have, seems to be confirmed *through more recent developments.* [underscored in pencil] Schönfeld, who, coming from Germany, has phoned to me yesterday morning, told of the greater possibility of seeing the Confessional Church including the Bishops of Hannover, Württemberg and Bavaria becoming united again. This is due partly to the attitude of Minister Kerrl, who, without letting know Dr. Zoellner and Bishop Wurm, asked Prälat Dr. Schoell from Württemberg[2] to come to Berlin and gave him instructions and power to constitute the *Kirchenausschuss* in Württemberg. Dr. Schoell, who seems to have wished in former years to become Bishop instead of Dr. Wurm, has accepted. The outcome of his effort is not clear yet. At any rate these proceedings have shattered even more the small confidence the Bishops and others had in the loyalty of Government Church policy.

Schönfeld told me another thing on which I wish to inform you as fully as possible. Dr. Lilje asked him to let me know that very probably Pastor Riethmüller would write to me these next days, asking me in very general terms to meet him somewhere in Germany. The point of Lilje was that such a call of Pastor Riethmüller would be sent to me in agreement with the provisional Church Government of Bishop Marahrens and, as I understood, other circles of the Confessional Church. They do not wish to send me an official invitation, but wish to have an opportunity of giving to me accurate all-round information on the situation to be passed to you. This call will be related somewhat to the *Reichssynod* of the Confessional Church to be held possibly about the 10th of February in some place of Western Germany.[3] It was not clear and probably cannot be clear that they will wish me to attend the session of the Confessional Synod. I am inclined to go to Germany if called by Riethmüller, but to go *in a purely personal capacity*, even if I am getting official information in Germany and even if I shall be invited to attend the meetings of the Confessional Synod. As far as I can see, the latter will hardly be the case and I certainly will in no way press our German friends in this direction.

You may feel certain that I shall do my utmost to underline the purely personal character of my coming due to a personal invitation and to keep your or the Oecumenical Council's responsibility completely out of my possible journey.

There is however a possibility that through the fact of my having been your official representative at the Dahlem Synod, it might be assumed by some people that my new coming might be due to a similar relationship. Doubtless the German friends would hardly have thought of sending me an invitation if you would not have asked me to go to Dahlem in 1934. If you should see a decisive difficulty in my going to Germany under those circumstances, please let me know by cable as soon as possible. I would fully understand a negative position of yours and would certainly in such a case follow your advice. I am not eager at all to assume a responsibility on [with] which I would not feel myself in agreement with you, remembering how great a responsibility and insight in the possibilities and dangers of the situation lies with you. As seen from my angle, I think if asked by the provisional Church Government to come to see them and to receive important information, it might be very important to go. Otherwise they would not think of calling me, which for them is always a somewhat risky thing. Second[:] I promised Riethmüller [at the] end of 1934, when he passed through Basel, to be at his disposal whenever he thought of needing my help either in Berlin or elsewhere. I took care to maintain intact the influence I might have, in avoiding any step giving the impression that I was mixing in an ungood way with German Church developments. In fact I have not been in Germany since the Dahlem Synod in 1934.

I will let you know if I am really called and will send you a report on my possible journey as soon as ever possible.

With kindest regards I am,
yours very sincerely

1   Jakob Schoell (1866–1950): prelate of Reutlingen and member of the church government since 1918, he retired to support a 'rejuvenation of the church Government' and to pacify the *Deutsche Christen* in 1933. Once a conspicuous figure, in 1924 and 1929 he had stood in the elections for the office of church president. In 1929 he was defeated by the later regional bishop Theophil Wurm. Schoell was widely known as a participant in world church conferences.
2   i.e. the fourth Reichs Confession Synod at Bad Oeynhausen.

Bell to Koechlin, 8 February 1936, Basel UB, NL 37, VI 112 (handwritten).

My dear Koechlin,

One line only in haste to thank you very much for your letter of 6th inst. I am deeply interested in what you tell me of a reunited Confessional Church. And I am particularly glad to know that there is a strong probability of your receiving a personal invitation to meet Pastor Riethmüller, in connexion with the Reichsynod [*sic*] of the Confessional Church this coming week. It would be a very good thing that you should go in this way to Germany; and I shall be most eager to hear any news.

With much goodwill and sympathy ἐν εὐχῇ [in prayer]

Yours ever

Bell to Koechlin, 5 March 1936, Basel UB, NL 37, VI 113 (typewritten).

My dear Koechlin,

I am looking forward much to hearing from you about the present position in the German Evangelical Church, and particularly as to what happened at the Meeting of the Reich Synod at Bad Oeynhausen. I got a summary of the proceedings most fully in *The Manchester Guardian* recording the resignation of the provisional government and the appointment of a temporary Commission. But now I see in to-day's *Times* that Bishop Marahrens has accepted appointment as Chairman of the State Committee for the Church of Hannover by Kerrl.[1] That, I confess, does rather surprise me.

I should be most grateful for any news.

Yours very sincerely,

---

1   In the event, the Synod of the Confessing Church could not agree on the question of cooperation with the church committees; nor could it decide on a binding directive for the churches. The looming split between the 'intact' Lutheran churches and the 'consistent' Confessing Church, especially in the Old Prussian Union, was not prevented. The two governing bodies broke apart. The Reich Council of Brethren, through a provisional committee, established a second Provisional Church Leadership as a purely confessional church body on 12 March 1936. As its counterpart, the Council of the Evangelical Lutheran Church of Germany was established by the Bishops Marahrens, Meiser, and Wurm as well as the regional brethren councils of Saxonia, Mecklenburg and Thuringia on 18 March. All of this was the result of developments since the 'Lutheran Pact' of 12 February 1935 and the 'Lutheran Day' of 5 July 1935.

Koechlin to Bell, 7 March 1936, Basel UB, NL 37, VI 115 (carbon).

My dear Lord Bishop,

I have to apologize for having not written to you sooner. The call which Dr. Schönfeld had phoned me [sic] to be possible even probable, has in fact not come to me. I had thought of writing to you after the Synod had taken place, but waited until I would have received news as accurate as possible.

Even to-day I cannot say that the whole situation is clear to me. The Synod has taken place, the Secret State Police being present all the time, even in the smaller committee meetings. The Synod has come to clear decisions and the break which could have been expected, has not taken place. This can be considered to be a very good result. Evidently the State is impressed by the attitude and the strength of the Confessional Church and does not dare to attack it openly. The decisions and messages draw the attention of all sections of the Church to the grave dangers inherent in the national-socialist aims. A clear voice has spoken and whatever might be the attitude of different Churches, they will have to take it into account.

The position of the so-called intact Lutheran Churches was not clear. Evidently Minister Kerrl had already begun consultations with the Church Authorities of Bavaria, Hannover and Württemberg before the Synod began. These consultations might have gone ahead during and after the Synod. It is a fact, which I did not know until to-day, that Bishop Marahrens has renounced to exercise his episcopal authority and has accepted to preside [over] a Church Committee, nominated by Minister Kerrl, a Committee exercising now the rights and authority of the former Bishop. In fact Bishop Marahrens is not any more Bishop in the former sense of the word, though he might maintain his title.[1] In the two Southern Churches this step has at any rate not been reached yet, but evidently Minister Kerrl has promised these Bishops not to interfere in their Churches if they accept the solution Bishop Marahrens has accepted. As soon as I know more of the definite attitude of the Southern Bishops, I will let you know. As far as I know, the Bishops Meiser and Wurm, possibly also Marahrens, have sent a man to Berlin, entrusted to maintain the contact with Kerrl and Dr. Zoellner on the one side and with the new provisional Government of the Confessional Church on the other side.[2]

On a long view all will depend on the attitude of national-socialism. If they maintain their anti-christian aims and if the State will try to enforce them on the Churches, the so-called intact Churches will have to join the Confessional Church. At present they might still have some confidence in a christian attitude of the State. In my impression they are mistaken and the concessions made now, might prove to be very dangerous.

With kindest regards,
yours very sincerley

1   This judgement of Koechlin is arguably too severe and is contradicted by Marahrens' reputation at this time.
2   The head of the Berlin office of the Council of the Evangelical Lutheran Church was Hanns Lilje.

Mason to Koechlin, 12 March 1936, Basel UB, NL 37, VI 114 (handwritten).

Dear Dr. Koechlin.

The Bishop thanks you for your letter of 7th March, and is much interested in what you tell him. He asks me to let you know that he has summoned an emergency meeting of the Administrative Committee of Life and Work to meet in London to-morrow afternoon, in view of the present international situation.

Yours sincerely

Bell to Koechlin, 29 April 1936, Basel UB, NL 37, VI 117 (typewritten).

I am sending you herewith a copy of a very important letter from Zoellner which was brought over specially from Germany to me by Dr. Wahl at the beginning of the month.[1] I had a message from the German Embassy asking whether I could see him. I was on the very point of leaving England for a cruise in the Mediterranean, the opportunity of which was a kind present to me.[2] Hence the delay in sending the copy to you, for I only returned yesterday. Wahl handed me the letter and expanded it *viva voce* to the general effect that there is now only one German Evangelical Church and Zoellner is its President. The split in the Confessional Church, and particularly the acceptance, as I understand, by the intact Churches of the Kerrl Committees, makes a considerable difference. I have told Wahl – and he fully agreed – that I could not answer such a letter on my own responsibility but that it must come before the Administrative Committee of Life and Work, which meets in the middle of June. I sent a kindly acknowledgement at once.

I shall be most grateful for any advice you can give me, for I am sure you have plenty of information with which to check what is there set out. I noticed in *The Times* of Monday the news of the cancellation of the suspensions of Dibelius[3] and others. I take it that there has been a very considerable mitigation of the attitude of the State so far as the use of coercion is concerned. How far freedom is real is another question, and how far the whole thing is a compromise of an unsatisfactory kind is also a question. I suppose still considerable reserve is necessary, though one does not like the idea of altogether failing to notice the new note of moderation.

Anything you can tell me with regard to the present position of the Confessional Church and generally would be most valuable.

Yours ever,

1 Bell returned to Chichester on 28 April 1936.
2 Otto Dibelius (1880–1967): since 1925 *Generalsuperintendent* of the Kurmark in the Evangelical Church of the Old Prussion Union; deposed by the State Commissioner August Jäger on 26 June 1933 (an act not rescinded until 1945); active in the Confessing Church since July 1934. In 1937 he was appointed member of the Old Prussian Council of Brethren instead of Martin Niemöller, who had by then been arrested. Dibelius had been an active participant in the international ecumenical movement, attending the 1925 Stockholm conference and the Lausanne conference of 1927. After the war in 1945 he became once more superintendent of the Kurmark and provisional head of Berlin and of Neumark/Oberlausitz. The Provisional Church Government of the Evangelical Church of the Old Prussion Union appointed him president of the High Church Council. When the Old Prussian Church was reorganized in 1947, the former church provinces became independent, and the church province of Mark Brandenburg became the Protestant Church of Berlin-Brandenburg under Dibelius, who now called himself bishop.

Enclosure:
Zoellner to Bell, 1 April 1936, Basel UB, NL 37, VI 116 (carbon).

Translation
My Lord Bishop!
You have had the kindness of repeatedly accepting informations on occurrences within our German Protestant Church. Allow me to outline in this letter the situation of the Church as it is to-day when in my opinion an important stage in the development within the German Protestant Church has been reached.

By a decree of the German Minister for Church Affairs on October 3, 1935, with the material provisions of which you are probably acquainted, the German Church Committee (*Reichskirchenausschuss* – *RKA.*) whose chairman I am was entrusted with the task of directing and representing the German Protestant Church.[1] The said decree created an absolutely new situation in our Church. For thereby the functions which according to the Constitution of the German Protestant Church were the Reich Bishop's and the Ecclesiastical Ministry's, viz. the direction and representation of the Church, were transferred to the RKA. Accordingly the latter assumes the full rights of the Church government of the German Protestant Church, although the decree of October 3, 1935 provides that this shall be subject to limits concerning both time and matter, in as much as the Church government shall only be in the hands of the RKA up to the time when a definitely organized Church may be given the possibility of solving her own religious problems in full liberty and peace.

Here I must briefly characterize the German Church Committee's position regarding the State. The statement that we are a Church government appointed by the State is not to the point. It is not correct too, as is sometimes alleged, that the German Ministry for Ecclesiastical Affairs had assumed *ex officio*, on behalf of the State, the control of the entire ecclesiastical life, thus constituting a sort of supreme authority of the German Protestant Church. It is just the reverse. In the first instance the German Ministry for Church Affairs, on behalf of the State, has only undertaken the tasks that formerly were those of the Kultusministerium and the German Ministry for the Interior respectively. By its institution no new law regarding the relations of Church and State (Staats-Kirchenrecht) has been created. With regard to the particular[ly] distressed condition of the Protestant Church, it is true, this German Ministry for Church Affairs has been set a *limited* special task, viz. the task of helpful legal redress for the restoration of order in the Church. The direction and representation of the German Protestant Church has been placed into the hands of the Church Committees. These Committees consist of irreproachable churchmen – as a rule they are duly appointed and ordained ministers of God's holy word. Thus the members look upon themselves as men of the Church in the State, not as men of the State in the Church. They perform their duties in accordance with ecclesiastical standards and constitute the Church government of the German Protestant Church.

As churchmen we have welcomed this form of legal redress offered by the State to the Church, as it alone could furnish the basis for preventing the impending schism which would divide the German Protestant Church into two Churches, an official Reichskirche and a Bekentniskirche (Confessional Church). To-day we can say that within the 4 ½ months of our activities we have succeeded in largely restoring order and authority within the German Protestant Church. The RKA and the Territorial and Provincial Church Committees appointed in connection with it are the lawful holders of authority in external and internal Church affairs, a condition precedent to the success of their work. In order to achieve the restoration of an orderly state of affairs in the various spheres within the shortest possible time and with complete success we have so far appointed Committees corresponding to the RKA for 6 Territorial Churches and within the old Prussian Territorial Church for 7 more Church provinces, which Committees have already succeeded, partly by way of decrees issued by them in settling the most urgent cases. For the Protestant Lutheran Territorial Churches of Hannover and Brunswick Church governments were instituted instead of Committees in order to create legitimate bodies for these territories.[2] All these Committees consist of trustworthy churchmen, among them many who come from the Confessional Movement. The Hannoverian Church government, for instance, is presided over by Landesbischof Marahrens.

This satisfactory progress of our work does not deceive us as regards the fact that to this day there exists a struggle of the various spiritual currents within our Church, although we think that we have definitely prevented a separation of the German Protestant Church into two Churches. It is not easy to outline these currents quite correctly. Besides a numerically insignificant group of determined 'German Christians' there is a group which must not be underrated of clergymen and congregations who have kept aloof from Church politics and have joined no group, without however having abandoned in any respect whatever the ground of the Church. The spiritual discussions within the Church are also quite materially influenced by the clergymen and congregations united in the 'Confessional Church', only the latter reflect spiritual and ecclesiastical movements greatly differing from each other.

From the outset the attitude of the 'Confessional Church' towards the work of the Church Committees has not been clear. Whereas at the beginning of our work individual members of the Confessional Church joyously agreed to become members of the Committees, and Landesbischof D. Marahrens declared on December 6, 1935, that he together with his Hannoverian Council of Brethren agreed to cooperate with and support the Church Committees, the attitude of the majority of the 'Confessional Synod' was reserved, temporizing and often negative. Even the 4th Synod of the Confessional Church which met at Oeynhausen from February 18 to February 22, 1936, has not really passed beyond this divided attitude of the 'Confessional Church'. For, whereas in the first theological statement made by the Synod, which contained a confessional statement in writing, an agreement was arrived at as to the organization and the duties of a genuine Church government, opinions differed widely when the practical problem had to be solved whether the work of the Church Committees should now be rejected unconditionally and from the outset or whether the individual measures taken by them should be tested on hand of Scripture and Creed, the attitude to be observed conforming to the result of such [a] test. The Synod's final resolution purporting that up to the definite reorganization of the Church the bodies of control appointed by the Confessional Church 'shall test on hand of the Creed the measures taken by the Church Committees and fraternally advise the congregations and clergymen on the attitude to be observed by them', has *not* been adopted unanimously by the entire Synod. For a third part of the members of the Synod (just the representatives of the moderate South-German opinion) had to depart before the conclusion of the Synod for reasons connected with their official duties. A further scanty third part had placed their personal diverging opinion on record in connection with the respective propositions in the theological statement. One of these members who made a separate statement is the Präses of the Confessional Synod, D. Koch, Oeynhausen. Some of these statements purported a radical No, others a readiness to cooperate with the Committees. Accordingly[,] two things are apparent:

1) The Synod has not been able to pass a resolution binding upon all, but is dissenting in itself.
2) The theological statement regarding the attitude of the Confessional Church towards the Committees is contradictory in itself, as it tries to couple the two views – the rejection and the recognition of the Committees. But even this statement, which at the conclusion demands a further testing of the Committees' acts by the controlling bodies of the Confessional Church, and accordingly not their rejection on principle, has been rejected by part of the members as being too strong. Therefore the report in the foreign Press that at Oeynhausen 90 to 95% of the Confessional Church had declared against the Committees is absolutely incorrect. If the attitude of the Synod towards the Committees shall be expressed in numbers it may be stated without exaggeration that most representatives of the Councils of Brethren of Old Prussia reject the Committees, it is true, whereas a large majority of the Councils of Brethren of South Germany and of the rest of Prussia are prepared to cooperate with them. This state of things was given expression in the fact that the *Vorläufige Kirchenleitung* ('Provisional Board of the Confessional Church'), of which Landesbischof D. Marahrens, Präses D. Koch, Oberkirchenrat Breit, etc. are members, resigned at the meeting of the Synod. The remaining radical group have appointed a new provisional board consisting of three members, all of them representatives of the radical opinion of the old-Prussian Councils of Brethren. This committee cannot be considered any longer a joint representation of the ecclesiastical circles hitherto united in the 'Confessional Church'. The attitude, by no means uniform, of these circles is illustrated *inter alia* by the fact that just a few days ago it has been possible, after some difficulties which existed at first, [and] had been overcome, to organize in the particularly difficult province of Westfalia a Church Committee consisting of four members presided over by a leading member of the 'Confessional Church'.

Recapitulating I may point out that for many years I myself in my ecclesiastical office, have defended a central prevalence of the Creed. Therefore I have always fully sympathized with the 'Confessional Movement', but I must disagree when from a *movement* within the Church, arising out of a momentary situation in a fight, and justified by it, the false thesis is deduced that the creation of a separate 'Confessional *Church*' was concerned. There are not – this is the clear result of the development in the Church during the last six months – *two* Protestant Churches in Germany but there is *one* Church, with a variety of ecclesiastical currents but with *one* legitimate Church government.

This Church government bears and exercises the responsibility and the representation of the entire Church. Of this responsibility I, as chairman of the RKA, am aware also as regards ecumenic relations [*sic*], and I am certain that the uniformly organized representation of the German Protestant Church has restored an essential clearness also for the ecumenic relations. I am happy that the German Protestant Church, as a member Church of Life and Work again can and will provide for its ecumenic representation in full ecclesiastical independence.

I am inclined to hope that also on the part of the Churches ecumenically connected with us this new situation will be fully appreciated, and the more so as there is now no longer any occasion for the doubts which temporarily were raised within the ecumenic community against a Church government of past days.

I have caused these statements to be translated into English for your convenience; a copy of the translation is enclosed herewith.

I remain, my Lord Bishop,
with sincerest regards,
Yours very truly,

1   The definition of the tasks is marked by two lines in the margin, probably by Bell.
2   The government of these churches was not instituted by the RKA, but by, or in agreement with, Kerrl.

Koechlin to Bell, 2 May 1936, Basel UB, NL 37, VI 118 (carbon).

My dear Lord Bishop,

Best thanks for your kind letter including a copy of Dr. Zoellner's letter addressed to you April 1st. Before I am writing more fully, I wish to get a still clearer insight in some aspects of the very complex question. In simply acknowledging to-day your letter, I might however express the view that the Oecumenical Council might be wise in dealing with Dr. Zoellner and his *Kirchenausschuss* as it has dealt these very last years with Bishop Heckel, Heckel having become the subordinate of Dr. Zoellner.

As to the Confessional Church my impression is that the resolution of Fanø still stands and that in consequence of Fanø Dr. Koch has been invited as a coopted member. I do not think that Dr. Zoellner could oppose such an invitation in asking you to go against a membership election due to a decision of the Council. And it would hardly be wise to mark at this moment a decisive change of attitude towards the Confessional Church.

I hope to send a fuller appreciation of the work and position of the Reichskirchenausschuss before long.

I am glad to think that you had the possibility of going southwards, possibly to Greece and I hope you came home with new strength for your great work.

As you take so kind an interest in me, I might be allowed to tell you that in addition to my church work I have been entrusted with the chairmanship of the Basel Mission. In realizing that the home base for 120 years is constituted by the Churches of Switzerland, South of Germany and Alsace, you will agree that we might be confronted from one day to the other with the greatest difficulties. The task is the more important from the oecumenical standpoint. I trust God might give us [strength] to stand together in his work in spite of the great tensions between Nations and possible different developments of Church life. Under these circumstances my nomination was to me a call of God to which I could not but obey.

With my very best regards,
yours sincerely

Koechlin to Bell, 28 May 1936, Basel UB, NL 37, VI 119 (carbon).

My dear Lord Bishop,

The letter you have written to me April 29th and the letter of Dr. Zoellner were constantly in my thought[s] during these last weeks. Without showing to him Dr. Zoellner's letter, I had yesterday an interchange of thought and views with Karl Barth, who, as you well [or: will] imagine, is still in close contact with the German Confessional Church and had only a few days ago here in Basel a short visit of Pastor Niemöller. I had also the opportunity of discussing the whole problem confidentially with another personality in closest contact with the Church life of Southern Germany and especially near to Bishop Wurm. As the result of these conversations I might state the following:

First I am not quite clear how far Dr. Zoellner is correct in stating that the 'right of directing and representing the Church' has passed into his own hands. The Kirchenausschüsse, as far as I know, are legally limited to regulating the organisational functions of the Church life without power of any spiritual direction of the Church. The Reichskirchenausschuss and the other Ausschüsse are institutions 'for time', limited to the date of autumn 1937 or, and even if they can guarantee earlier the normal functioning of organisational Church life before that date, bound to leave their place earlier. It is theoretically a fact that Reichsbishop Müller has not been legally destituted [sic], neither the Bishops created by him. There is of course some kind of understanding, probably approved and even desired 'for [a] time' by party and state according to which Bishop Müller and his men are living a private life, but ready at any time, without any legal change being necessary, to resume their former functions. The Reichsbishop still is signing his books and letters with 'Reichsbishop'. Bishop Coch and Dietrich are going about visiting parishes and allowed to do so by party-authorities in spite of all remonstrances of the Reichskirchenausschuss.

I do not wish to say that one might expect [to see] the Reichsbishop probably resuming one day again his functions, but the possibility still exists and evidently State and party at least do not wish to render such a possibility impossible.

It is certainly a fact that the Reichskirchenauschüsse have gone further than the limits legally traced to their activity and have very largely tried to direct and represent the German Evangelical Church. They certainly succeeded in many parts of Germany to bring about order and more peace, but it is equally a fact that very often when they tried to change impossible situations, agreeable to local State and party authorities, their power at once failed to get the desirable result. I know personally the President of the Hessen-Nassau Landeskirchenausschuss,[1] who, forced to allow the Bishop Dietrich to do what he, the President, desired to make impossible, and being obliged by the State to act against the Confessional Church, has become a broken man asking his friends to think of him in their prayers as of a man being a captive of the State, because in fact he is, as Zoellner is, a State employee.

The Oecumenical Movement would be mistaken in accepting definitely the Reichskirchenausschuss of Dr. Zoellner as being the definite legal authority directing and representing the German Evangelical Church. However it might in fact certainly be the case that this Reichskirchenausschuss has the largest power of all German Church authorities and that for the moment it has taken the place of the old Reichskirchenregierung of Reichsbishop Müller through which the Oecumenical Movement was until now connected with the German Evangelical Church as a whole. Heckel with his Aussenamt is certainly now dependent from [on] Zoellner.

For this reason I feel that the Oecumenical Council ought to accept the situation as such, deal with Zoellner instead of Heckel, but with all the reservations necessary to guarantee the possibility of another attitude if the situation should change again in Germany.

This possibility exists, seems even to be very probable. Hitler in one of his great addresses of March said, as different trusted men have heard through the radio, that the national-socialist Movement was bound to go his way over 'parties, states (Länder, i.e. Bavaria, Baden etc.) and *confessions*'. In the reprint of the address these words were left out. But the meaning of the Führer in this respect is very evidently clear. The school policy, the growing power of Rosenberg, the development of the Hitler Youth, the programme of the new national-socialist leader-training castles (Ordensburgen) are illustrating this fact. And there seems hardly to be anyone, even in the Reichskirchenausschüsse, who does not know that the decisive fight between Church and State, Gospel and National Socialism is still to come. It is nearly for all concerned only a question of *tactique*, if the Church might come into a better position for this fight in regularising with the help of the Reichskirchenausschüsse its situation, or if the way of Niemöller is the better one. In judging this situation, one has at least to bear in mind that the Reichskirchenausschüsse, in the last analysis and in spite of the personal integrity and view of the men leading them, are instruments of the State.

As long as the attitude of the State towards the Church is as unclear as at present, I think the Oecumenical Council has to be careful not to identify definitely the Reichskirchenausschüsse, being institutions of the State, with the Church itself.

As to the Confessional Church, we have to take into account the fact that the Churches of Bavaria, of Württemberg, of Baden, even of Hannover have not left the Confessional Church, even though Bishop Marahrens is working with Dr. Zoellner. The interpretation of the decisions of Oeynhausen may be different here and there and the practical[,] actual attitude towards the new Government of the Confessional Church might be different too. The fact is that Bishop Marahrens and his provisional Church Government ha[ve] passed over peacefully and completely the power and papers of the former provisional Church Government to the new Church Government instituted in Oeynhausen. It is equally a fact that the great Lutheran Churches, though they have come to a closer connection with each other ('der lutherische Pakt') have not instituted any sort and form of Church Government.

If f[or]. i[nstance]. Württemberg and Bavaria do not place themselves under the new Church Government of the Confessional Church, they do not either place themselves under the Reichskirchenausschuss, maintaining their [or: the] complete independence of an intact Church.

One might say that the different circles belonging to the Confessional Church are partly moving forward towards the Reichskirchenausschüsse giving to the so-called efforts of the State a fair chance and hoping in doing so to find their own chance. Others refuse to do it for reason of principle or reason of *tactique*. Those going forward, go forward partly one step, partly two and three steps, but all of them without an exception take care to leave the bridge behind them intact so that they might go back and lean upon the Confessional Church as soon as a new decisive fight has to be fought through. One might even say that for the sake of the whole Church it is urgently necessary that at least one wing (radical or extreme, as it may be called) is maintaining strictly the principle of the freedom of the revelation of God in the Gospel against the totalitarian claim of the State even over the Church.

Psychologically and politically it is natural that as long as the State is seeming to understand and to help the Church, the front of the Confessional Church is becoming less compact, but it is to be expected that with every new attack of the State[,] either on the Prussian side or in Munich or Stuttgart, the confessional front will become united again.

For this reason it would be a great mistake if the oecumenical Movement would not any more stand to [or: on] the decisions of Fanø. We might before long have in Germany again a situation very similar to that with which we were confronted in 1934 and it could be for the Confessional Church and for the German Evangelical Church as a whole of [the] greatest importance if the Oecumenical Council and yourself on its behalf could, based on official decisions taken and maintained, act as you have done these last two years.

May I add one further aspect illustrating the situation. The German foreign Missions are refusing absolutely to place themselves under the Reichskirchenauschuss, but are maintaining their very close contact with the Confessional Church without being organisationally and fully part of it. The Youth Movement is taking a similar attitude. Missions and the Youth Movement especially are under greatest pressure [*sic*] coming from the State.[2] The missionary societies with their literature and with other aspects of their work are in constant difficulties. The Reichskirchenausschüsse cannot help them. They are even a danger for them. Their hope is in the existence of the Confessional Church. I think they would not understand if the Oecumenical Council would give up its relationship with the Confessional Church of Germany.

Hoping to be able to give you more information after my interview with Pastor Riethmüller and my short visit in Stuttgart next week, I am yours very sincerely,

---

1 Rudolf Zentgraf (1884–1958): since 1925 member of High Custody and superintendent of the province of Rheinhessen; 1934–50 pastor at Bingenheim. On 5 November 1935 a Regional Church Council was formed in the Evangelical Church of Nassau-Hesse with three representatives each from the Confessing Church, the centre (from which Zentgraf himself was drawn) and the *Deutsche Christen*. Now in retirement, Zentgraf became its chairman. Meanwhile, the Regional Council of Brethren continued to regard itself as the spiritual authority of the church in the province while the ousted *Landesbischof* Dietrich, supported by his *Pfarrkameradschaft*, now virtually declared war on the *Landeskirchenrat*. Even an intervention by Zoellner could not bring success to Zentraf's attempts at mediation.
2 According to the Law on the Hitler Youth of 1 December 1936, all boys and girls now had to join the Hitler Youth. The youth work of the churches was ignored.

Bell to Koechlin, 5 June 1936, Basel UB, NL 37, VI 120 (typewritten).

My dear Koechlin,

I am most grateful for your extremely valuable letter of May 28th about Dr. Zoellner. What you say harmonises very much indeed with my own *primâ facie* view. I have had one or two opportunities of talk with Germans in this country, and I had an indirect idea of the views of Pfarrer Maas[1] from a Non-Aryan German teacher who has just come over. But your quotation from Hitler's speech in March is most significant, and what you say about the meaning of the Führer with regard to Confessions, as well as Parties and States, is very clear.

Somehow or other I think our Administrative Committee must make it clear to Zoellner that while for certain limited administrative purposes communications may be made with him, there must be no sort of final committal of the Universal Council, nor must there be any abandonment of the stand taken at Fanø. Nor must there be any discontinuance of the relations which we have had and enjoy with the Confessional Church.

The way of putting all this, with the necessary courtesy and the essential limitations, will require much thought. I should be most grateful for anything you can tell me after your interview with Pastor Riethmüller and your visit to Stuttgart. With all best wishes, and warmest thanks,

Yours ever,

1   Hermann Maas (1877–1970): courageous, left-leaning pastor, advocate of Jewish-Christian dialogue, member of the Confessing Church in Baden. Maas would later collaborate with the Grüber Büro in Berlin to save the lives of many German Christians of Jewish descent by arranging for official papers to facilitate their flight abroad. Later his contribution was acknowledged in Israel by the planting of a Hermann Maas Grove, and in 1966 Yad Vashem elected him Righteous Among the Nations. He was also honoured in his own city of Heidelberg and by the government of the Federal Republic.

Koechlin to Bell, 5 June 1936, Basel UB, NL 37, VI 121 (carbon).

My dear Lord Bishop,

I had [on] Monday night at Karslruhe two very good hours with Pastor Riethmüller of the Burckhardt-House, Berlin-Dahlem and [on] Tuesday[,] in his private house[,] a very good hour with Bishop Wurm in Stuttgart. Riethmüller, whom you know and to whom I put very clearly the question concerning the relationship of the Oecumenical Council to the Confessional Church, was very clear that the decisions of Fanø were at all costs to be maintained. The Reichskirchenausschuss, he said, had become for the State authority the power of directing and representing the German Church. The functions of the Reichsbishop had passed over to this *Ausschuss*, but the understanding had always been that this Reichskirchenausschuss could not interfere in purely Church matters of doctrinal and spiritual guidance. Zoellner himself had taken this view when accepting the call of Reichsminister Kerrl, but had been led to go much further than that. However, Riethmüller also is thinking that actually the oecumenical movement, desiring to maintain the contact with the official body, will have to deal with Dr. Zoellner instead of the Reichsbishop.

Without giving me fuller details, Riethmüller told me to be convinced that the Reichskirchenausschuss before very long will prove to be a great failure. He thinks that the start was wrong and that some successes Dr. Zoellner cannot advance any more. Dr. Zoellner seems to be very often at the end of his nerves, of his physical strength and of his capacity to dominate the situation. Riethmüller used the word that the Reichskirchenausschuss would personally end in a catastrophe of Dr. Zoellner. He asked me to be very cautious in all dealings from outside with Zoellner.

I asked Riethmüller for his opinion concerning the Confessional Church. He thought the view I had expressed to you in my last letter was right, though there are constantly changing situations allowing for relatively different judgements, but he underlines the fact that theoretically and partly practically the Confessional Church is still united. In the Youth Group connected with the Confessional Church and headed by him, all the evangelical Movements including the official Youth Movements of Bavaria and Wurttemberg, are still cooperating on the ground of the Confessional Church. The great group of missionary work and the Home Missions headed by Bodelschwingh take the same attitude, uniting all districts of Germany in one group. To see the Oecumenical Council still backing the Confessional Church means a great thing for Riethmüller and its Youth Movements and it would mean a very great loss if this backing would come to an end through a decision of any official character.

You might be interested in knowing that Burckhardt House got back from the Secret State Police all the papers taken away November 5th and that no step has been taken against it on the ground of the papers seized.[1] Riethmüller thinks that the sympathy expressed in England in those days was the real cause of the quiet months they had since.

I may say that I told Riethmüller that the Oecumenical Council would have to think over again the position it will have to take towards the different Church groups in view of the new situation and that you had asked me for information. I did so because I knew that he had seen you November last and that he could be trusted in any way.

As to Bishop Wurm I of course did not say a word of your letter. I did not wish either to press him with questions. I was in Stuttgart in my capacity of President of the Basel Mission and after one of the assemblies he kindly took me home and we discussed the relationship of our Mission to the Wurttemberg Church under the new situation. He told me that he of course did not allow the Reichskirchenausschuss to interfere in the Church life of Wurttemberg, this Church life being quite normal with one exception and this exception is that Bishop Wurm has still an Executive of the Synod with German Christians, able to stop financial measures. This is still a consequence of the elections of 1933. He needs a new Executive legally instituted and empowered to act and is hoping to get that in presenting a list to be approved by the Auschuss of Dr. Zoellner. So he is needing him for building up a new constitutional basis, but is not accepting his rule in any question of Church government. Bishop Wurm told me that Württemberg as well as Baden and Bavaria were paying their contributions to the new Reichs Church Government because they were all too glad to deal last of all with a man like Dr. Zoellner and not any more with men like Ludwig Müller, Oberheid,[2] Hossenfelder and Company.

Bishop Wurm spoke of Karl Barth with great gratitude and admiration, but regretted the all too radical attitude of him towards a tendency of arranging matters with the State. He however admitted that Karl Barth had seen clear[ly] concerning the substance of national-socialism in 1933 before the others had realized what was coming about.

Through another source I heard the following fact, which I can guarantee. In the Reichs Church Ministry of Kerrl they had prepared a new attack against Wurm and his Church Government, had a new Bishop and his new helpers ready. Oberkirchenrat Pressel,[3] Bishop Heckel's right hand, knew of it, went at once to Berlin, led [i.e. laid] the whole plan on the table of the Reichs Church Ministry and the men were perplexed, tried to say no, but were obliged to admit that this plan was existing. They were told that the whole Church of Wurttemberg would fight to the last if this plan was put into operation. Dr. Zoellner did not know anything of it. This happened not later than in the second half of May. That such a thing is possible is throwing a light on the real position of Dr. Zoellner. I found the Wurttemberg Church circles alarmed because the State is trying to take over all the children's schools until now in the hands of the Church.[4] They are fighting this measure because they are absolutely certain that the next step will go against the deaconesses.

I am going Saturday, June 13th to Kassel for the meeting of the Y.M.C.A.s,[5] where I am seeing Dr. Mott. As Henriod told me, he will go directly from there to Paris. Should I hear some facts of real importance, I would give to him a letter for Henriod or yourself.

Trusting that you will be guided by God in this important and in other great questions I am,

yours very sincerely

1 See Koechlin to Bell, 16 November 1935.
2 See Koechlin to Bell, 8 February 1934, fn 3.
3 Wilhelm Pressel (1895–1986): Lutheran pastor and leading member of the *Deutsche Christen* in 1933, he left the movement and became a close ally of Bishop Wurm, attending the Barmen Synod in May 1934. Expelled from the National Socialist Party a year later, he became a member of the Reich Brethren Council in 1936 and then Wurm's permanent representative on the Lutheran Council. After the war his relations with Wurm became strained and he became most active in church aid work and hospital chaplaincy work.
4 In Württemberg there were no church schools apart from the monastery schools at Maulbronn, Blaubeeren, Schöntal and Urach. Since 1933 Minister of Education Mergenthaler had been pushing for the conversion of the state denominational schools into community schools in order to establish 'only one German education'.

Since he officially promised to preserve denominational religious education, the churches did not oppose him. In 1936, change followed quietly, step by step, until the last confessional school class was abolished on 4 June 1937.

5 See Koechlin, 'Bericht über die Exekutivtagung des Weltbundes in Kassel-Wilhelmshöhe', Basel UB, NL 37, III 17a.

Bell to Koechlin, 12 June 1936, Basel UB, NL 37, VI 122 (typewritten).

My dear Koechlin,

I am very grateful indeed for your further full and most interesting and informing letter of June 5th, and thankful that you had such a very useful talk with Pastor Riethmüller and also with Bishop Wurm. It makes things much clearer to me than they had been. I am particularly interested in the prophecy which you report, that the Church Committee is likely before long to prove a great failure, and that it is not possible for Zoellner to make any advance; and I am very much interested in Riethmüller's opinion concerning the Confessional Church, and the conviction which you report that in the fundamental matters the Confessional Church is still united. I have had an interesting report from Henriod of his recent visit to Germany where he has had many talks with many people.

I am quite certain that there is no thought on the part of the Oecumenical Council of going back on the Fanø resolutions, or failing in any way to maintain its backing of the Confessional Church. I do not anticipate any possibility of an ending of that support through a decision of any official character. I am very sorry that I cannot myself be at the meeting of the Administrative Committee in Paris next week, but I shall be seeing Dr. Oldham beforehand, and also Schönfeld. The officers are to meet on Thursday, and will by themselves discuss the German Church situation. The Administrative Committee, including Krummacher,[1] will be meeting on the Friday and will discuss general questions, including the preparation for the World Conference. It is partly in connection with the preparation for the World Conference that the crux is coming. How is the German delegation to be chosen? Zoellner claims that he is the proper person to decide and to lead the delegation; nor is he at all likely to agree to two delegations, the other coming from the Confessional Church. Zoellner will himself very likely be at Chamby for the Meeting of the Council which will take the final decisions. I gather from Henriod that the Confessional Church leaders and the Church Committee leaders should hold an informal Meeting on neutral ground (though I do not quite know what neutral ground is) to decide on ways and means of a German Church delegation.

What you say about the possible new attack against Wurm and his Church Government, is very important and rather significant of possible new tendencies. Henriod tells me that Kerrl is a sick man and people talk of his being replaced even by such a personality as Hossenfelder. I am glad you are seeing Dr. Mott on Saturday.

With all best wishes,
Yours very sincerely

1   Friedrich-Wilhelm Krummmacher (1902–1974): theologian. In 1933 he became member of the National Socialist Party and in the same year he was appointed member of the foreign office of the Protestant church responsible for the German parishes abroad. 1939 he was conscripted as division pastor to the army. As prisoner of war he became member of the National Committee for a Free Germany and the Association of German Officers. In 1945 he returned to Germany as a member of the Ulbricht group.

Koechlin to Bell, 3 July 1936, Basel UB, NL 37, VI 124 (carbon).

My dear Lord Bishop,
   Bishop Wurm of Württemberg, who was in Basel these last two days in connection with our Mission Convention, had a long talk with me concerning the relation of the German Church towards the oecumenical movements, especially the Stockholm Movement. I think it important to let you know some main facts.
   Bishop Wurm underlined in a very decided way the fact that Dr. Zoellner had no legal authority whatever to deal on behalf of the German Evangelical Church with the oecumenical relations. When I mentioned the fact that he had written to you a long letter stating the contrary, he told me that he knew of it, but that all the Bishops had the very clear conviction that Dr. Zoellner had no right to write such a letter and that the content of it was very contrary to reality. He said that Bishop Meiser was especially opposed and angry about this letter and that he was in no way willing to accept Dr. Zoellner's leadership in oecumenical questions.
   I asked Bishop Wurm, with whom was the authority to deal with in oecumenical questions. He said it was very clearly with Heckel. That led us to speak of the extraordinary position Heckel is holding. He succeeded last autumn to get rid of [sic] the Reichsbishop *without coming under the rule of Dr. Zoellner*. He has a completely independent position, allowed to be independent by the State and financially provided for[,] partly by the State and partly by the Churches. Nothing has been changed concerning the competence of Heckel to deal with German Churches abroad as well as with the oecumenical relationship of the Evangelical Church. Bishop Wurm agreed however that Heckel has not [got] the Churches behind him. He saw a solution in bringing together the Lutheran Pact (the Bishops of the intact Churches) and the vorläufige Kirchenregierung of the Confessional Synod with Heckel and to come to an agreement as to the men able to represent the German Churches at Oxford. He thought that in fact the Lutheran Pact and the Confessional Church Government would have to provide the delegates including perhaps one or two men around Heckel.[1] He did not seem to be opposed to having one or two men of Zoellner included.
   When I asked Bishop Wurm once more what was his attitude towards the Confessional Church, he said very clearly that the Lutheran Pact was still part of the Confessional Synod and that it looked towards Praeses Koch as being the head of it. He said that in all principal issues the Confessional Synod was united but that the Lutheran Pact did not acknowledge the new vorläufige Kirchenregierung as being the Government of the German Church. He thought that a distinction had to be made

between the Confessional Synod itself and the group of men around Niemöller being the Executive of the Reichsbruderrat. The Bishops seem[,] however[,] to deal in many questions with this Executive of the Reichsbruderrat. In other questions they have to deal with Heckel and with Zoellner. Otherwise they would not be in a position to settle all their [or: the] questions involved in the task of their Churches.

I was astonished to see the very great reserve of Bishop Wurm towards Dr. Zoellner. He told me that Dr. Zoellner was going to make 'the greatest mistake of his life' in entering in close fellowship with Dr. Rehm,[2] a well-known German-Christian leader of very questionable methods.

Bishop Wurm will write to Bishop Marahrens and Bishop Meiser and possibly write to me afterwards. He saw that some agreement ought to be reached before the meeting of Chamby and he did not oppose the thought of the Oecumenical Council trying to help the different German circles to come to such an agreement.

The main result of this interchange of thought was the necessity for the Oecumenical Council to be even much more cautious in its attitude towards Dr. Zoellner, who at any rate in the oecumenical questions has not [got] behind him [n]either the intact Churches with the Bishops (Lutheran Pact) nor the Confessional Church, nor any legal authority.

As I have been now elected permanent representative of the Swiss Churches in the Oecumenical Council I think of coming to Chamby and am looking forward with greatest pleasure to seeing you there.

With kindest regards,
yours very sincerely

1   See Boyens, *Kirchenkampf und Ökumene*, vol. I, pp. 144–6; Gerhard Besier, *Die Kirchen und das Dritte Reich. Spaltungen und Abwehrkämpfe 1934–1937* (Berlin: Propyläen, 2001), pp. 551–3.
2   Wilhelm Rehm (1900–48): German pastor and high school teacher. Since 1922 he had been a member of the National Socialist Party and of the SA; from 1941 to 1945 he was a member of the Supreme SA Leadership in Munich, from 1943 as *Sturmbannführer*. In 1933 he became leader of the *Deutsche Christen* in Württemburg and from 1935 to 1938 Reichs-leader of the national *Deutsche Christen* movement.

Bell to Koechlin, 8 July 1936, Basel UB, NL 37, VI 125 (typewritten).

My dear Koechlin,

I am most grateful for your very interesting and important letter of July 3rd. What you say about Zoellner's position in the oecumenical relations is a real surprise. When Wahl came over on April 1st with the letter he certainly led me to think that Zoellner was now the authority for oecumenical relations, and that Heckel was under him. So it is most extraordinary to learn that Heckel has got rid of Müller without coming under Dr. Zoellner. This seems a quite unprecedented affair. Henriod thought that Heckel had in fact written Zoellner's letter to me. This I believe was not the case, for the letter was written by a much younger man who has been in touch with Confessional circles but is now with Zoellner.[1]

I am also very much interested in what you tell me about the Lutheran Pact being part of the Confessional Synod still, and looking towards Praeses Koch as its head. I wonder how he would justify however the distinction between the Confessional Synod itself and the Executive of the Reichsbruderrat? Your mention of Bishop Wurm's very great reserve, especially in connection with Zoellner's association with Dr. Rehm, is also very interesting. I am sending herewith a copy of my reply to Zoellner, so that you may see exactly what I said. Please keep the letter. I have heard from Krummacher since and enclose a copy of his reply.

I am delighted to hear that you are now the permanent representative of the Swiss Churches in the Oecumenical Council, and hope to come to Chamby. That will be a very great pleasure and help.

Yours ever,

1   Untraced.

Enclosure:
Bell to Zoellner, 23 June 1936, Basel UB, NL 37, VI 123 (carbon).

Copy
Dear Dr. Zoellner,

I am now in a position to write to you in reply to your very important and courteous letter of April 1st in which you were kind enough to give me an outline of the situation within the German Protestant Church in view of the fact that in your opinion an important stage had been reached in the development within that Church.

Once again I would thank you for that letter, and assure you of the deep interest with which I have read it.

The Administrative Committee of the Universal Christian Council for Life and Work met in Paris last week, and though most unhappily I was not myself able to be present at the Sessions, I have received a personal report from M. Henriod who has since stayed with me in Chichester. Moreover[,] as he had enjoyed the great advantage of personal conversations with yourself in Berlin, and had various opportunities of acquainting himself with the developments at first hand, I am in a much better position to reply than I was at Easter. I may say further that copies of your letter were in the hands of members of the Administrative Committee well before the Meeting. It is in the light of all these facts that I now send you an answer.

The Administrative Committee and the officers of the Universal Christian Council, in between the Meetings of the Council, are bound to be guided by any Resolution which may have been passed setting out matters of principle, should any situation arise to which such principle might be applied. On no occasion have principles been laid down with such clearness as on the occasion when the situation in the German Evangelical Church was considered at the last Meeting of the Council, held at Fanø in August, 1934. A Resolution of great importance was passed, and by this Resolution the Council and its various sub-Committees are bound, until any other decision is taken by the Council itself. This Resolution, amongst other things, expressed the Council's desire 'to remain in friendly contact with all groups in the German Evangelical Church'. It also instructed the Administrative Committee to follow up the principles which the Resolution set forth.

In the Resolution at Fanø the Council refrained from expressing a judgment with regard to the legitimacy of the different Church organisations then in existence. The Administrative Committee, in considering questions relating to the representation of the German Evangelical Church at oecumenical gatherings, and notably at the Oxford Conference on Church, Community and State, is not in a position to adopt any different procedure. The manner of representation must be decided within the German Evangelical Church itself, as these questions involve the constitution and authority of the Church. I entirely realise the extraordinary difficulties of the immediate situation, and of coming to a conclusion satisfactory all round with regard to the composition of a delegation representing the German Evangelical Church. I also realise that much has happened since 1934.

The members of the Administrative Committee are very much alive to the struggle of the various spiritual currents within the German Evangelical Church to which your letter alludes. I appreciate further the statement which your letter of April 1st makes, that the Church Committee over which you preside has been entrusted by the State with 'a *limited* special task', viz. the task of helpful legal redress for the restoration of order in the Church. Nor do I overlook all that you say with regard to the steps that have been taken and are being continued, and the hope that in due course a definite reorganisation may be achieved in the Church after a manner and following a method which will be welcome to all. But the very careful exposition in your letter to me of the various differences which are still unreconciled, makes it impossible to regard the present position as more than a provisional position, or as more than, to use your own words, 'an important stage in the development'.

Accordingly the Administrative Committee, in loyalty alike to the facts known to it and also to the Resolution adopted at Fanø, cannot cease to maintain the connection with the Confessional Synod of the German Evangelical Church which was there deliberately authorized and endorsed by the Council. In a very special section of the Fanø Resolution the Council assured its brethren in the Confessional Synod of the German Evangelical Church of its prayers and heart-felt sympathy in their witness to the principles of the Gospel, and of its resolve to maintain close fellowship with them. That Resolution must give us our direction to which we are obliged to adhere.

It seems to me however that this very fact lends great force to the suggestion which M. Henriod made personally when in Berlin, viz. that an agreement should be reached, in which the Confessional Synod would play its full share, for the adequate representation of the German Evangelical Church in oecumenical work. I would, with very great respect, and yet with very serious conviction, beg you to respond to this earnest suggestion.

With regard to the Meeting at Chamby itself, I am very greatly cheered to learn from M. Henriod that you have every intention of coming yourself. I hope very much that a full representation of the different currents in the Evangelical Church may be present at Chamby, in view of the grave importance of the matters to be discussed, and the laying down of the programme for the Oxford Conference. We rely much on your own help, and the help of your colleagues, in the whole task of preparation for the Oxford Conference. We also wish definitely that those who are identified most closely with the work of the Confessional Synod should come to Chamby, and we wish definitely that they may be represented under conditions and in a way in accordance with their own conscientious convictions. The members of the Universal Christian Council are usually chosen by the Sections, though the Council has power to co-opt a certain number of consultative members. In the judgment of the Administrative Committee it ought to be possible in these circumstances, by the exercise of goodwill on all sides and by an effort of mutual understanding, to bring it about, without implicating the Council in controversies internal to the German Church, that the Council at the next meeting, which will be concerned principally with the preparations for the Oxford Conference, should have the advice and help of persons representing different points of view, and enjoying the confidence of different parties, within the German Evangelical Church, who will be able to make the largest and richest contribution to the life and thought of the oecumenical movement.

I need hardly add that the work of Chamby will be constructive work, with the Oxford Conference almost entirely in view, and I should myself hope that matters of controversy may be avoided.

I remain, with sincerest regards,
Yours very truly,

Bell to Koechlin, 7 August 1936, Basel UB, NL 37, VI 127 (typewritten).

My dear Koechlin,

You may have seen my letter in *The Times* about the Confessional Church, on August 4th.[1] That very day I received a letter from Dr. Zoellner commenting very strongly on the statements made by the Berlin Correspondent on which I had based my letter. I enclose a translation of Zoellner's letter, together with the prints with which it was accompanied. I should be very grateful for any comments you could make on the denials of Dr. Zoellner.

I am sending a translation of Dr. Zoellner's letter to the Foreign Editor of *The Times* privately, in the hope of hearing something from him.

I am looking forward very much to seeing you at Chamby.

Yours ever,

1 The letter, written on 26 July and published in *The Times* on 4 August 1936, observed the new outbreak of intimidation in the churches: 'The Churches outside Germany . . . have no wish to intervene in domestic debates on secondary matters. But this issue is far graver. It is because they are convinced that fundamental Christian values are at stake that their interest is so keen, and their concern for the Confessional movement so deep. A blow struck at the Confessional Movement would be a blow struck at Christianity.' To Oldham Bell wrote on 31 July that the letter 'was intended as a question showing the German Government that we are watching.' Bell Papers, Vol. 8, fols. 204–5, 215.

Enclosure:
Zoellner to Bell, 29 July 1936, Basel UB, NL 37, VI 126 (carbon).

Copy
TRANSLATION[1]
Most honoured Lord Bishop,

The Berlin Correspondent of the *London Times*[2] in its issues of the July 18th and 21st (nos. 47430 and 47432) prints statements about the state of affairs in the German Evangelical Church which cannot remain unrefuted.

In the issue of the 18th, the *Times* Correspondent suggests *inter alia* that the Reich Church Minister has instructed the so-called Provisional Church Government (V.K.L.) to drop the title officially recognised last year by a German law Court. It is likewise suggested that the Reich Church Committee has ordered the Councils of Brethren of the Confessional Church to be closed.

So far as is known here, no instruction of the Reich Church Minister at all with regard to the *Firma* V.K.L. has been issued.[3] It is inaccurate to say that in the face of the so-called V.K.L. of the German Evangelical Church no justification of the leadership of this *Firma* has been given by a German verdict. The fact is simply that in answer to a complaint of the Reich Bishop against the V.K.L. for dropping this title, the ordinary law court declared that as this question was one of ordinary common pleas the courts were incompetent to decide and therefore the complaint was dismissed. The question whether the title could justifiably be held was never discussed at all. Moreover the *Gremium*, which now calls itself the Provincial Church Leadership, is not identical with the Provincial Church Leadership which stands under the Leadership of Landesbishop Marahrens at such times as he chooses. The latter in consequence of the split within the Confessional Church at Oeynhausen last February has retrograded. In consequence of the events at Oeynhausen so many circles have seceded that the claim of the present V.K.L. to be the continuation of the old simply cannot be upheld.

I have already had to tell you that we do not recognise the claim of the so-called V.K.L. to be sole lawful Leadership of the German Evangelical Church. Indeed no German Court would recognise it. A claim, now so utterly meaningless, makes [impossible?] our relations to the circles behind the V.K.L. and involves us all in guilt [*sic*]. Moreover it makes it more and more difficult for the State authorities to deal with remonstrances from these circles, however well justified.

Further details are contained in the Article on the present state of affairs in the Church, printed in No. 2 of the German Evangelical Church Paper, on July 16th, 1936. I add three specimens for your instruction and you will see that the *Times*' suggestion that the Councils of Brethren were forbidden by the Reich Church Committee is incorrect. Such a prohibition was never issued. The matter never arose at all.

I sincerely regret also the statement of the *Times*' Correspondent that the Memorandum of the so-called V.K.L.[4] was never laid before the Leader-Reich Chancellor.[5] The suggestion that for the publication of the Memorandum about which I too am still in the dark – it is very improbable that the Confessional Church possesses no means of its own.[6] Even in *Foreign News* e.g. Reuter's, for some time past such publication has frequently been granted to the Confessional Church: is it likely then that this news was spread by the police? Naturally the *Times* wants to prove the innocence of the V.K.L.

Especially[,] however[,] I regret that in this and other Foreign News' departments of the papers the 'Word of the Reich Church Committee to the Congregations' of July 10, 1936[7] – cf. my Appendix – is completely ignored. The Reich Church Committee claims that it clearly represents all justified demands and wishes, clerical or lay, in the ears of the State. This it does with all the means standing at its disposal which seem worthy. At the same time its use of publicity is limited because it knows that thereby it often does more harm than good.

Let me emphasize the fact that the *Times*, in the two last articles, in our view utterly fails to grasp their meaning. One-sided partisanship of a group does it the utmost harm.[8] All arguments that could be used in favour of the circles supported by the *Times* are rendered valueless by pointing to the inaccuracy of the Correspondent. Moreover great harm is done to the Reich Church Committee's efforts at reconciliation and above all to those of the Government authorities. Therefore I can from every point of view insist that its results are purely negative.

If you, most honoured Lord Bishop, have any chance in one way or another to lay before important authorities these representations and points of view, I should be extremely grateful to you.

1   This partly faulty translation was evidently made by Zöllner's staff.
2   Norman Ebbutt (1894–1968): since 1925 the *London Times* correspondent in Berlin; his reports emphasized the repressive policies of the National Socialist state and followed church affairs with close, and critical, attention. He soon found the force of his reports diluted by the newspaper's editor, Geoffrey Dawson, and in Germany itself he was accused of espionage by Goebbels and expelled from the country in August 1937.
3   This is incorrect: see 'Erlass des Reichskirchenministers an die obersten Reichsbehörden, Länderregierungen und die Reichsleitung der NSDAP, Berlin, 6 July 1935', in Grünzinger and Nicolaisen, *Dokumente*, p. 216.
4   That is, the 'Denkschrift der vorläufigen Leitung der Deutschen Evangelischen Kirche an den Führer und Reichskanzler' of 28 May 1936. This may be found printed together with further materials and information about the publication by the foreign press in Martin Greschat (ed.), *Zwischen Widerspruch und Widerstand* (Munich: C. H. Beck, 1987).
5   The question mark here added perhaps by Bell. Wilhelm Jannasch handed the memorandum to the head of the Presidential Chancellery in Berlin. But after some queries to secure an acknowledgement of receipt, the Secretary of State, Meissner, explained that it had merely been passed on to the Ministry of Ecclesiastical Affairs. No response followed. See Grünzinger and Nicolaisen, *Dokumente*, p. 200.
6   The meaning may be that the Confessing Church was itself responsible for the publication.
7   See Beckmann, *Kirchliches Jahrbuch*, pp. 141–2.
8   Exclamation mark here, added perhaps by Bell.

1937

1 January	Pastors of the Confessing Church protest against the exclusion of university students on its church training courses from the universities.
7 January	The Reich's Church Committee announces the arrest of nine pastors in Lübeck.
29 January	Bell meets Niemöller in Berlin for the first time.
30 January	The *Reichstag* extends the Enabling Act for four more years.
February	Zöllner tries to visit the nine Lübeck pastors but is prevented by the police.
12 February	The Reich's Church Committee resigns.
15 February	Hitler meets Kerrl at Berchtesgaden and orders free elections in the church.
17 February	The Provisional Church Government states its conditions for participation in the election.
19 February	Friedrich Weissler dies in Sachsenhausen concentration camp.
22 February	Hitler meets Kerrl again.
2 March	Hitler passes to Frick the regulation of the election.
11 March	*The Times* publishes a letter from a number of churchpeople protesting against the death of Weissler.
14 March	The papal encyclical, *Mit brennender sorge* is published.
20 March	Dr Werner, head of the church chancery, assumes the administration of the church until the election takes place.
24 March	*The Times* publishes a letter from Bell warning the German state not to interfere in the church elections and drawing attention to the papal encyclical.
April	The *Deutsche Christen* meet at Oberhausen.
6 April	A new interim Reich church administration is appointed jointly by the Lutheran and Confessing churches.
June	Frick criminalizes the contribution of money to the Confessing Church or to any other church organization not recognized by Kerrl.
22 June	The seventh *Report on the Affairs of Continental Churches* is submitted to the Church Assembly. Controversy follows.
25 June	Kerrl assumes responsibility over all church finances in Germany.
1 July	Arrest of Martin Niemöller.
5–6 July	Confessing and Lutheran leaders meet at Cassel and appeal to the state for a personal hearing.
11 July	A declaration prepared at Cassel is read out in the churches.
12–26 July	The International ecumenical conference on Church, Community and States takes place at Oxford.
17 July	Announcement of a new Anglo-German naval agreement.

3–18 August	The second world conference on Faith and Order takes place at Edinburgh.
29 August	A second declaration observing the state's refusal to respond to the Cassel declaration is read out in the churches.
17 October	The Prussian superior court declares that the Confessing Church is not a legal part of the German Evangelical Church.
7 November	A protest against the writings of Rosenberg and warning that confidence in Hitler is fragile, signed by ninety-six Lutheran and Confessing pastors, is held back from the public after Goebbels threatens charges of treason.
11 December	Kerrl confirms the appointment of Werner, made on 20 March.

Bell to Mrs. Koechlin, 6 January 1937, Basel UB, NL 37, VI 128 (typewritten).

My dear Mrs. Koechlin,

I have often thought of your husband at his great Meeting of the National Christian Council.[1] I know what a tremendous responsibility it is, and what tremendous opportunities there are. I read the other day of the opening reception by the Maharaja of Mysore;[2] and your husband's letter, written near Port Said, has been standing in front of me ever since I received it, in my basket; so that I have constantly had him in mind. I do hope you get good news of him, and that he is happy and well. I know he was going to undertake a fairly long tour in addition to the National Christian gathering itself. He told me that you and the family were very well when he left you, and he looks forward to seeing you in the same good health at the end of next month. I have not written to him direct, but if you are writing before he does start home, please give him my affectionate remembrance, and my very best wishes, and assure him of my prayers.

With all best wishes for the New Year from my Wife and myself & remembrance to your daughter!'

Yours very sincerely,

1. That winter Koechlin spent several months in India participating in the 21st World Alliance Conference of the YMCA in Mysore and the meeting of the National Christian Council. He also visited the work areas of the Basel Mission. See Koechlin's 'Bericht über die Indien-Reise, 24 April 1937', Basel UB, NL 37, II 31; his report to the National Committee of YMCA, 30 April 1937, Basel UB, NL 37, VI 4,6; id., Indienreise, Basel UB, NL 37, II 33; id., 'Die geistigen und geistlichen Grundlagen der Konferenz', *Der Ruf* (Zürich), no. 4, April 1937.
2. Nalwadi Krishnaraja Wadiyar (1884–1940): fourth Maharaja of Mysore, immensely wealthy he oversaw effective programmes of social and economic reform while becoming a patron of the arts and of education, in such a way that Mysore enjoyed a 'golden age', and one much admired by the British.

Koechlin to Bell, 3 April 1937, Basel UB, NL 37, VI 129 (carbon).

My dear Lord Bishop,

May I after my return from India write to you again, thanking you for the very kind words you have written to Mrs. Koechlin during my absence. It was a help to her as well as to me to know that your thoughts and prayers were with us. Once more I deeply appreciated your very great kindness to us.

I of course cannot write in full to you about the very great experience I had in India. Without trouble of health I could fulfil during the four months of my absence my whole programme. The World's Conference of Y.M.C.A. had especially in the questions concerning the relationship to the Churches very good results. The Y.M.C.A. brotherhood declared emphatically to be part of the Church and to be willing to work in the ranks of the Churches in view of the great tasks confronting christianity to-day.

The insight I got in the work of our Basel Mission, the close contact with the indigenous Church leaders were to me of the utmost value. I am also very grateful for all I was able to see of other Churches and their missionary work. The Bishop of Dornakal,[1] in whose house I stayed and with whom I had a room in common during the Mysore Conference, was very kind indeed and most interesting to meet. Bishop Moore of Travancore and Cochin,[2] Bishop Western in Tinevelly,[3] whose guest I had the privilege to be and the Bishop of Bombay,[4] whom I met occasionally, were also very kind. They helped me to see the developments of the Anglican communion in India as well as the possibilities and impossibilities of a Church-Union there. A man I was very glad to see was Rev. Stephen Neill[5] in Nazareth, certainly the most outstanding Christian personality in South India. You probably will have heard of him. At any rate remember his name, because he might be the personality to occupy some day any position in your Church.

Since I have come home end of February, I have had some days of rest with my wife in the Engadine and have come into close touch again with Church questions of Switzerland and the oecumenical problems. Adolf Keller told me of your common stay in Berlin.[6] Since then conditions have evidently changed again, as far as I can see not for the better.[7] The Church elections seem to be postponed indefinitely. Evidently the question to limit the right to take part in the elections to those who really care for the Church,[8] is hardly to be answered satisfactorily. The risk of party action in the elections can hardly be avoided. Maybe I am too pessimistic, but the thought of these elections is giving me greatest anxieties.

The other day I met the German Minister in Bern, von Weizsäcker,[9] a very fine man of the old type, personally connected with the Confessional Church of Württemberg and very anxious to help the German Church in its oecumenical contacts. Discussing a difficulty we have in the Basel Mission, he said very plainly that actually the German high officials did not care whatever for oecumenical relationship [sic], that every relation of the German Church with the Christianity outside Germany was making people nervous and that for the moment at least they were quite decided to follow their own way without taking into account the feelings of non-German Churches. This statement was indeed not hopeful, but it is worse to be taken into account [sic] in our efforts to help the German Churches. [It] may be that as in the past official Germany may sometimes listen for international political reasons to a word coming from England. But for the oecumenical movement as such and for individual Churches here and there, there does not seem to be left for the moment great opportunity of efficient help. [It] may be that Weiszäcker's judgment is rather personal, but as he has spent the whole winter in the Foreign Office in Berlin at a prominent place, his word has certainly some weight. I thought you might be interested to know of it.

In some days I am seeing Henriod and as the weeks will pass, I shall be looking forward more and more to the Oxford Conference and the important meeting of the Committee of 35.[10] I hope Mrs. Koechlin will be able to accompany me to England. Would you kindly remember me to Mrs. Bell and believe me

Yours very cordially,

1. Vedanayagam Samuel Azariah (1874–1945): since 1912 the influential, evangelizing bishop of Dornakal; his international relationships grew from his early association with the YMCA; for many years he steered the work of the Joint Committee on Church Union in South India, work which would create the new Church of South India two years after his death.
2. Edward Moore (1870–1944): bishop of Travancore and Cochin, 1925–38; he first worked in southern India as a missionary for the C.M.S. and committed much of his ministry to promoting education and healthcare and supporting those from the Scheduled Castes (Dalits).
3. Frederick Western (1880–1951): Bishop of Tinnevelly, 1929–38; he had come to India as a part of the Cambridge Mission to Delhi in 1904.
4. Richard Acland (1881–1954): bishop of Bombay, 1929–47; once a soldier he had joined the USPG and travelled to India in 1912, thereafter become Secretary to the Society there, 1925–9.
5. Stephen Neill (1900–84): a gifted scholar, he succeeded Frank Weston as bishop of Tinnevelly in 1939; active for uniting the churches in South India, he resigned in 1944; deputy secretary general of the WCC 1948–51. In 1954 Bell would be instrumental in dispatching him, abruptly, to Geneva where he worked for the WCC until 1962. See Dyron B. Daughrity, *A Worldly Christian: The Life and Times of Stephen Neill* (Cambridge: Lutterworth Press, 2022).
6. See for Bell's discussions from 28 January to 1 February Jasper, *Bell*, pp. 215–17.
7. On 12 February 1937 the Reich Church Committee resigned after conflict broke out openly between Zoellner and Kerrl. On 15 February Hitler announced new church elections.
8. Koechlin refers to the request of the Provisional Church Government's circular letter of 17 February 1937: the Confessing Church would refuse to take part in church elections 'that give the masses dominion over the church and take away the believing community's right in the church'; quoted by Meier, *Kirchenkampf*, vol. 2, p. 149.
9. Ernst von Weizsäcker had become ambassador there in 1936.
10. In October 1936, a working team of thirty-five members from Life and Work, Faith and Order, the International Missionary Council, the World Alliance for Friendship among Churches and the YMCA was set up to prepare a binding connection between the different branches of the ecumenical movement. This committee, which included Koechlin, met in London, on 8–10 July.

Bell to Koechlin, 28 April 1937, Basel UB, NL 37, VI 130 (typewritten).

My dear Koechlin,

It was a great delight to get your letter of April 3rd. I was away in the Lakes[1] having a holiday when it came. Hence the delay in replying. I rejoice in what you say about your experiences in India. It must have been a wonderful time, and I am very thankful that your health was maintained and that all the material side went well. Still more thankful am I to learn of the fine relationship developed as between the Y.M.C.A. brotherhood and the Church.

It must have been very stimulating to see the work of not only the Basel Mission but of the other Churches too. I am hoping to see the Bishop of Dornakal who is over in England at this time, and I am very glad to read what you say about Stephen Neill.

I know about him, but I have never actually met him. When he was in Cambridge he was considered one of the most brilliant men of his time. I am very glad of the great impression that he made upon you.

I was very much interested in what you tell me about the German Minister in Berne, and the present position. What he says about the German high officials, and their indifference to oecumenical relationships, is important. I confess that when I have been talking with German officials I have been struck with their wish to keep in touch with England, and I suppose the Church of England, and that they look at things no doubt politically, and for this reason a word coming from England may be of service.

I am looking forward to seeing you in July, and it will be a great pleasure to Mrs. Bell and myself to see you and Madame Koechlin again.

With all warmest remembrance from us both to both of you.

Yours very sincerely,

1   i.e. The Lake District in Northwest England.

Koechlin to Bell, 26 May 1937, Basel UB, NL 37, VI 131 (carbon); LPL, Bell Papers, Vol. 2, fols. 241 (r and v).

My dear Lord Bishop,

Saturday last Dr. Reinhold von Thadden, one of the leading laymen of the Prussian Confessional Church and of the German Confessional Church as a whole, has been here in Basel for some hours and came to see me in connection with the attendance of the Oxford Conference. As you certainly know, the Secret State Police has seized the passports of different appointed delegates to the Oxford Conference (Dibelius, Niemöller and others), to prevent them from going to England this summer. Other delegates, also belonging to the Dahlem group of the Confessional Church have still their passport[s]. But they decided not to attend Oxford unless all appointed delegates were able to attend. This decision seems to be a definite one.

Dr. von Thadden has spoken Thursday last in Berlin with Dr. Lilje and Dr. Lilje told him that the Lutheran Council was considering the possibility and advisability of taking the same attitude. That would mean that the Bishops Wurm, Meiser, Marahrens would not attend Oxford unless all representatives of the Dahlem wing were allowed to attend also. This in order to manifest very clearly at this important occasion the oneness of the Confessional Church in Germany.

The hope evidently is also, to oblige by such a position the State to give permission to Niemöller, Dibelius and others to exercise their oecumenical mandate at Oxford. Dr. von Thaddden suggested himself that I might write to you unofficially about the communication he made to me after consultation with Dr. Lilje. He was very cautious in wording what he said about the Lutheran Council. Evidently no decision has been taken there yet.

You will probably receive official communication from both bodies concerned before long, but I think it is important that you know already now what might take place. It would indeed be most awkward and disagreeable to have the German Church in such a case only represented by Bishop Heckel and his men.

Dr. von Thadden spoke also of the Committee of Thirty-Five, whose members he and Dr. Lilje have been appointed to be. His question was if they ought to go to that meeting even if they did not attend Oxford. I advised him that they ought to do so. No other member of the Confessional Church is concerned there. The question of solidarity with those being prevented from leaving Germany, is not arising and the possibility of having at least at that occasion the cooperation of the Confessional Church in Germany and the direct contact with prominent members of it, would be, I said, of the utmost importance for all concerned with the Conferences to be held. He seemed to agree with this point of view.

If I am hearing more about this important matter, I will let you know at once.

With kindest regards,
yours very sincerely,

Bell to Koechlin, 28 May 1937, Basel UB, NL 37, VI 132 (typewritten).

'Private'

My dear Koechlin,

Very many thanks for your letter of May 26th. I know Dr. von Thadden and am very glad to know first-hand from you what he has said. I am afraid the situation is very serious. As a matter of fact I had a letter a fortnight or so ago from Karl Barth, telling me that Niemöller was in grave danger, and urging me to take action. I asked Karl Barth for details of the danger, but he has not yet replied. Only I at once got into touch with Ribbentrop and von Blomberg, and have heard from Graf von Durckheim,[1] Ribbentrop's right-hand man. The last named tells me that Niemöller has not been arrested, nor has Dibelius, but suggests that they are trying to be martyrs. He writes also (though he marks the letter confidential) that the prospects of a German delegation coming are exceedingly remote. I am following it up with him, for he has promised to send me more details when he has found out more.

But in the meantime Henriod, who was in Berlin in the earlier part of the month, is coming to England next Tuesday or Wednesday, and I am hoping to arrange a meeting between him and Oldham and Sir Walter Moberly[2] and myself, and any other person who is knowledgeable and available. The Germans whom Henriod saw are very anxious to keep in continuous touch with England by a succession of short visits. They also want us to say something, but not at once. I think they want us to say something when it is finally settled that a German delegation is prohibited. It is possible that it may be well for one or two individuals to say something, but I think the most authoritative statement must be made at Oxford.

I am inclined to suggest on Friday night – and on this I should very much like your reaction – that the Oxford Conference should send a special delegation immediately after Oxford to Berlin, to see the Church leaders and to speak to them, not only in a private way but in a public way, though not necessarily asking for any public answer from them. My thought was possibly that if this seemed a reasonable line of policy, a few people should, well before the Oxford Conference, think out the character of such a statement, and then that a Committee should be appointed at Oxford with regard to the absence of the German delegation, this Committee being able, if so disposed, to make a recommodation for such a delegation to the Oxford Conference. Whether we could have a session of a Section of the Conference in Berlin rather than the delegation, I do not know. But there is something to be said for an adjournment to Berlin to deal with this special point. I wonder what you would think of any statement indicating a recognition on the part of the members of the Conference of a sense of the real reasonableness of some of the political desires of the German people, quite apart from the Nazi régime.

I entirely agree with what you say about Bishop Heckel who must certainly not be allowed to come if others do not come; and what you say about the Committee of Thirty-five. I wonder what will be the position of Martin Dibelius[3] and others who are officers or Chairmen of Commissions. Will *they* be allowed to come to the Conference?

Yours ever,

1 Karlfried Graf Dürckheim (1896–1988): after a vivid early career as a soldier, then a member of the *Freikorps* and then an academic drawn to mysticism and psychology, he settled for a diplomatic career and came under the wing of Ribbentrop. With the passing of the Nuremberg Laws in September 1935 Durckheim became, awkwardly, a 'Non-Aryan'. Ribbentrop arranged for him to work in Japan, where he found much to fascinate him, and he lived there between 1938 and 1947.
2 Sir Walter Hamilton Moberly (1881–1974): British academic philosopher and vice-chancellor of the University of Manchester, 1926–34; first full-time chairman of the University Grants Committee, 1934–48; Principal of St Catherine's Foundation, 1949–55; between 1949 and 1952 chairman of Church of England Committee on the Relations between Church and State. An active ecumenist, Moberley was a member of Life and Work and also J.H. Oldham's Council on Christian Faith and the Common Life.
3 Martin Dibelius (1883–1947): professor of New Testament studies at Heidelberg, 1915–47, an internationally recognized liberal theologian and a leading light in the new school of Form Criticism, a development much disliked by Bishop Headlam and, probably, many other Anglican bishops. Even so, his work was profoundly influential in the universities, and it did not leave the intellectual ground unaltered in the English theological colleges. From the conference in Lausanne in 1927 he was also engaged in the ecumenical movement for Faith and Order. During the Third Reich Dibelius had sympathies with the Confessing Church but he did not become a member of it, remaining a figure of the centre ground. See Hans Bringeland, *Religion und Welt: Martin Dibelius (1883–1947)*, Vol. 2: *Dibelius in seiner Heidelberger Zeit (bis 1933)* (Münster: Lit Verlag, 2013), 246–8, and Vol. 3: *Dibelius im Dritten Reich und in der Nachkriegszeit* (Münster: Lit Verlag, 2013), pp. 51–3.

Koechlin to Bell, 1 June 1937, Basel UB, NL 37, NL 37, VI 2 (unpaginated) (typewritten); VI 133 (carbon).

My dear Lord Bishop,

I have spent three days in Southern Germany and saw Bishop Wurm yesterday morning in Stuttgart. When I came home yesterday evening, your very kind letter of May 28th was awaiting me. May I thank you very heartily for sharing with me your thoughts about the German situation.

My visit to Bishop Wurm was due to a suggestion of Henriod, who phoned to me Thursday last, asking if I could not get some particulars about the developments of the German situation.

Bishop Wurm seemed to be very depressed by the actual situation. He was quite explicit in stating that there was no hope and no question of a German delegation going to Oxford. He had seen Mr. von Neurath lately, who could not promise any help in the matter. The Lutheran Council had stated to Neurath as well as to other high officials how deplorable it would be for Germany if no delegation could be present in Oxford. They had at the same time stated that they would only be in a possibility of going, if the Government would give them an assurance of a fair policy in Church matters and if the delegates of Oxford would be assured to be protected afterwards against unfair attacks. They have not been able to get such an assurance and such a promise. Bishop Meiser and Bishop Marahrens seem to have had the most difficult stand after their journey to America in connection with the World Council of Lutheran churches. Bishop Wurm said that in his view Bishop Marahrens would in no case get his passport for England and that the same had to be expected for the others.

We spoke of the great address of Mr. Goebbels and Bishop Wurm told me that in his utterances Goebbels had also been very vehement against the Evangelical Church, stating f[or] .i[instance]. that it was a well-known fact that those attending church services were only reactionaries and Bolshevists. If one knows what these words mean for national-socialism, such a statement means nothing less than that the Church is the enemy of the State. Not a word of this 'evangelical' part of Goebbels' speech has however been reprinted in any German paper, a fact which is not yet explained. Bishop Wurm however was inclined to see in the utterances of Goebbels the true attitude of highest party and Government circles.

The third and as he underlined the greatest concern was the impossibility of coming to an agreement with the Dahlem wing of the Confessional Church.[1] He assured me that the Lutheran Council had done everything possible to understand and to take into account the position of the Dahlem people, but that always again new suspicions were arising, rendering in the very last minute an agreement, which had seemed to be settled, impossible. He was very outspoken in his judgement about Niemöller and Karl Barth. I do not think we can help from outside at the present moment, but my hope is that men like Otto Dibelius and Lilje might be able to prevent an irreparable break in the midst of a front which more than ever has to stay united. Bishop Wurm gave me the copy of a letter of Kerrl stating that he alone was allowed to speak for the German Evangelical Church as a whole. I am including a copy of it in German and English.

I asked Bishop Wurm, what attitude the Oecumenical Council ought to take before and during the Oxford Conference. He thought that we could hardly do anything to bring a German delegation to Oxford and that even if you in England could lead the Government to allow some people to go out, the situation of such representatives would most easily be an impossible one. But according to his feelings the Conference ought to feel very free to make on the German Church situation and on the attitude of the Government a very explicit statement.

Thinking now of your suggestion in the light of what I heard from Bishop Wurm, I think the administrative Committee of the Oecumenical Council ought to follow most closely the situation between now and the beginning of July. I think also that it will be quite natural and necessary to have a group of people appointed officially at Oxford to deal with the reasons of the absence of the German delegation and to present possibly a report and a resolution. As far as ever possible such a resolution ought to grow out of the general work of the Conference and to be so to speak the application on the special German case of the great principles agreed upon.

As to a delegation to be sent to Germany soon after Oxford, I think it might be a most valuable and necessary step. But as the situation is changing so constantly and rapidly, it will hardly be possible to take the final decision before the end of the Oxford Conference.

Your thought of an official meeting to be held in Berlin, is so new to me that I do not dare to give a definite judgment to-day. To be quite frank, I do not think that in view of the attitude of the Government it would practically be possible to realize it. To suggest to the Conference to deal with some political desires of the German people – I think of the colonies – seems to me rather dangerous and could lead to other suggestions concerning other desires of other Nations. But this being my very first reaction to your thought, please do not take it as my definite attitude.

As to the presence of Bishop Heckel, Bishop Wurm told me that Heckel himself would not be willing to go without the other Bishops. Though I do not know, I think that men like Professor Martin Dibelius, Stange and others would not and should not come if the official delegation was prevented from coming.

Very cordially,
Yours

P.S. As to the captivity of the members of the provisional Church Government (Dahlem wing), Bishop Wurm confirmed what our newspaper said, that a reason of [or: for] it is a document delivered to the foreign press and containing a speech of Dr. Gross in Munich. The Secret State Police wishes to know who has delivered this document, the Confessional Church and its leaders being suspected.[2]

1 i.e. the part of the Confessing Church mostly in Prussia which insisted on the resolutions of the second Reich Synod of the Confessing Church at Dahlem (19–20 October 1934) and in consequence formed the Second Provisional Church Government after the Confessing Church split at the Reich synod at Oeynhausen (17–22 February 1936). This so-called 'consequent Confessing Church' stood against the Lutheran Council or the Lutheran wing of the Confessing Church.

2 On 14 May 1937 pastor Wilhelm Jannasch, a staff member of the Provisional Church Government, was arrested for disclosing a report on the speech of Dr Groß, head of the office for racial politics of the National Socialist Party. In Munich he had spoken to Bavarian health officers about the future methods of propaganda by which the church might be undermined. Other arrests of leading members of the Confessing Church followed, culminating in the arrest of nine members of the Reich Brethren Council on 23 June. On 1 July Niemöller was arrested by the police.

Enclosure:
Kerrl to the leading officials of the German Evangelical Provincial Churches, 19 May 1937, Basel UB, NL 37, VI 2 (unpaginated) (carbon).

Copy[1]
The Minister for Church Affairs of the Reich and for Prussia

In a letter dated April 8th 1937–1531 – you have communicated to me the decision taken April 3rd 1937 by a conference of church-leaders,[2] according to which some of 'the actual leaders of the Provincial Churches (Landeskirchen) have asked you to unite in cooperation with Bishop D. Wurm – Stuttgart, Präses Zimmermann – Berlin[3] and Landessuperintendent D. Dr. Hollweg – Aurich[4] the whole of the Provincial Churches having as a common base Art. 1 of the Constitution of the German Evangelical Church in their common task and to act as official representatives of the German Church'.

I have to let you know that in consequence of the law concerning the position and protection to be given to the German Evangelical Church of September 24th 1935, I have under October 3rd 1935 empowered the Reichskirchen-Ausschuss to represent the German Evangelical Church. After the resignation of the Reichskirchenausschuss the Führer, by a decree of February 15th 1937, has entrusted the German evangelical church people themselves with the election of a General Synod in view of the elaboration of a constitution. This new constitution will decide upon the government and the representation of the German Evangelical Church.

It is not possible and I am not willing to allow the decisions of the General Synod to be prejudged. For this reason I have in the 13th decree of March 20th 1937 renounced [or: resolved] to appoint a new representation, but I have recognized the existing provincial Church-Governments in their legal position and in such a way given them the possibility to go on with the legal business of their respective Churches, restricting however their powers to their respective Churches. This regulation is guaranteeing the normal functioning of the current business. This settlement has to be considered as a final one.

To make everything quite clear, I wish to state that a restricted circle of church-leaders has neither legally nor ecclesiastically the legitimation to constitute a representation of the German Evangelical Church. For this reason decisions like that of April 3rd cannot be recognized by me.

To Landesbishop Marahrens, Hannover.[5]

I am sending to you this copy for your information.
By order: Ch. Muss (?)

1 Translated by Koechlin; German version: Basel UB, NL 37, VI 2 (unpaginated) (carbon).
2 On 3 April the Church Leaders' Conference protested against Kerrl's 13th decree on the implementation of the Law on the Safeguarding of the German Evangelical Church (20 April 1937). This transferred the state-church administration to the juridical president of the Old Prussian Superior Church Council, Dr. Friedrich Werner, while dictating that the administration of the church regime should remain vacant until church elections announced by Hitler. The regional churches were now allowed only to act as an administration of the church regime as far as current affairs were concerned.
3 Richard Zimmermann (1877–1945): superintendent of Berlin City I 1927 to 1943 and 1935–37, chairman of the Provincial Church Committee of the Mark Brandenburg and member of the Regional Church Committee of the Evangelical Church of the Old Prussian Union. He was an unacceptable figure to the Confessing Church.
4 Walter Hollweg (1883–1974): from 1927 regional superintendent of the Reformed Church of Hannover; after 1939 president of the regional Church Council of the Evangelical Reformed Church of the Province of Hannover at Aurich.
5 The letter was sent to Marahrens because he, as the longest-serving regional bishop, had informed Kerrl of the decisions of the conference.

Bell to Koechlin, 30 July 1937, Basel UB, NL 37, VI 2 (unpaginated) (carbon).

My dear Koechlin,

A line to say that I should be grateful if you would ask Bishop Marahrens if he has any objection to the Archbishop of Canterbury publishing the letter of thanks for the Message to the German Evangelical Church[1] signed by himself, Dr. Fleisch[2] and Pastor Müller.[3] I think it would be of very real value if this letter could be published, and of course the sooner the better.

When I saw Archbishop Eidem at the Garden Party at Lambeth, I showed him this reply from the German Evangelical Church and he was very pleased, as was also the Bishop of Copenhagen[4] and others to whom I showed it. Archbishop Eidem spoke of the possibility of his going to see Bishop Marahrens later on, though he could not do it this or next month. I asked him whether it would be possible at the end of October when Archbishop Germanos[5] would be in Germany and I could join him. He said it is not impossible, and was interested in the idea, though he carefully refrained from committing himself. It would not do of course to load Bishop Marahrens to expect Archbishop Eidem with the deputation, but the bare possibility that he might conceivably come is something.

I do hope your visit to Germany will prove fruitful and informing, as I feel certain it will.

With all the best wishes and ever so many thanks for your constant friendship and good counsel and co-operation,

                                                            Yours very sincerely

1   The letter of 23 July 1937, sent to the Archbishop of Canterbury, may be found in Boyens, *Kirchenkampf und Ökumene*, pp. 358-9. It was written on behalf of the committee which was founded at Kassel on 6 July 1937 as a new attempt at church unification. Its members comprised Bishop Marahrens, as representative of the Church Leaders' Conference, *Oberkirchenrat* Breit of the Lutheran Concil and Pastor Friedrich Müller as member of the Provisional Church Government. See the pulpit declaration of the committee for Sunday 11 July 1937, in Beckmann, *Kirchliches Jahrbuch*, p. 194.
2   Paul Fleisch (1878-1962): since 1932 spiritual vice-president of the Evangelical-Lutheran Church of Hannover; in 1933 he was compulsorily retired but in 1937 he was rehabilitated. He had remained a member of the Lutheran Council since 1934, in 1936 becoming its vice-chairman.
3   Friedrich Müller (named Fritz Müller-Dahlem) (1889-1942): co-founder of the Pastors' Emergency League in 1933; in 1934 member of the Council of Brethren of the Confessing Church of the Old Prussian Union and in 1935 of the Reich Council of Brethren. In 1936 he became chairman of the Provisional Church Government and chairman of the conference of the Regional Councils of Brethren. Between 1937 and 1940 he was often disciplined by the church institutions and repeatedly imprisoned.
4   That is, Hans Fuglsang-Damgaard (1890-1979), bishop of the diocese of Copenhagen and *primus inter pares* of the Danish bishops, 1934-60.
5   Lukas Pantaleon Germanos (Strenopoulos) (1872-1951): Greek-Orthodox metropolitan of Thyateira, since 1922 Exarch of the Ecumenical Patriarchate of Constantinople for Western Europe, based in London. Since 1920 he had been a leading representative of Orthodoxy at international ecumenical conferences.

Koechlin to Bell, 3/4 August 1937, Basel UB, NL 37, VI 2 (unpaginated) (handwritten), LPL, Bell Papers, Vol. 2, fol. 490-3 (r and v).

My dear Lord Bishop,

I have to report to you on my mission to Hannover and Oeynhausen. Yesterday, Thursday morning I had at least two hours of quiet interchange of thoughts with bishop Marahrens, and in the afternoon I was from 2.15-4.30 with Praeses Koch in Oeynhausen. Both received me as cordially as possible and seemed most grateful for my visit. I had arrived at Hannover very early in the morning and left with the night train, to arrive here in Basel this morning 11 o'clock. I met no difficulties whatever neither at the frontiers nor in Hannover, at no moment had I the impression of being watched. My conversation with bishop Marahrens dealt point after point with the different aspects of the conference action. He took careful notes, so that he might report to a group of church leaders including the Dahlem wing, with whom he said he would meet these very next days. He evidently avoided to take definite positions before having consulted with them. On my side I did not insist for it and avoided also to ask for detailed information, bishop Marahrens did not give me on his own initiative. I promised that everything, he would tell me, would be dealt with confidentially.

1. As to the *message* sent to the brethren in the German Church[1] I explained very fully, what had led to it, what was its meaning and purpose and how we had

worked for it. I pointed to the unanimity of the Conference in this respect, which had been evident from the opening speech of the Archbishop of Canterbury up to the end. I told him of the attitude of Dr. Aubrey[2] and of the isolated position of the German Free Churchmen.[3] – The bishop was very grateful for the message and approved warmly of it. He only would have preferred, if the Roman Church would not have been mentioned, its position and attitude being in fundamental points very different from the evangelical ones. He however didn't lay great stress on this matter. And though he understood quite well, what you had meant[,] and approved of it, he said the mentioning of the Russian sufferings in your introductory speech had given the opportunity for regrettable press attacks.

As to the *publication of the message* in Germany the situation proves to be very difficult. Orders have been given by the state that the message is not allowed to be published in any paper, including church papers, without adding the protest of the Free Churches and the official comment given by the State to the Oxford decisions. To publish it in the official Church papers (*Amtsblatt*) would very probably lead to the repression of these papers at least for some months, and that would mean to deprive the church government of the only possibility of making known their decisions and their legislation to the pastors and to the laymen in official positions. It is thought of reading the message from the pulpits. It would have to be everywhere on the same Sunday, without enabling the Secret Police of knowing and preventing it beforehand [*sic*]. In any decision to be reached in this respect, the very serious actual situation will have to be taken into account very fully. I underlined the fact that we wished to help and strengthen the Church in Germany and not to add to their difficulties and sufferings, so the responsible Church leaders should feel free to take the line, which would best serve the church. The desire to make known the message throughout the churches was evident as well with bishop Marahrens as with Praeses Koch. They certainly will do what they can.

2. As to *the Delegation* I pointed to the fact that the time and the procedure of it was not decided yet, not even its composition, that we had thought of the second part of October as of a possible term and that as to the procedure to be followed your mind was quite open to any suggestion or wish from the German side. I mentioned, that without binding ourselves, we had thought to meet at any place to be proposed by them with the delegation which ought to have come to Oxford as with any group of men called together by the German Church leaders for that purpose. I said however that it would be most difficult to give up the delegation and that the latest possible term for it seemed to be November or early December 1937, with which bishop Marahrens completely agreed. He sincerely approved of the delegation and also seemed to agree with the possible procedure as mentioned by me. On his very explicit question I told him that you would lead the delegation, that Archbishop Germanos would probably join it, that a Scandinavian representative was to be asked and if possible a representative personality of the American churches and that I myself was to be a member, but that five were thought of as a maximum. I of course did not mention the name of the Archbishop of Uppsala. I did not either speak of the possibility of his individual visit to Hannover. After consultation

Bishop Marahrens will let you know[,] directly or indirectly, what the German Church leaders have to propose. I might add that the bishop as well as the Praeses was decidedly of the opinion, that the postponement of the delegation was for the moment the best course to take.

3. As to the *letter sent to the Archbishop of Canterbury* as an answer to the message and signed by the three leaders of the three groups of the Confessional Church, bishop Marahrens was inclined to think that its publication in the *Times* would create new difficulties. Personally he didn't feel free to approve of the publication, but on this point too he will consult with his colleagues. The question is the more delicate as pastor Müller is in prison.

4. That leads me to say a word on *the general situation*. It is most serious at the present moment. Monday of this week Generalsuperintendent Dibelius has been imprisoned also.[4] The trial of pastor Niemöller has to take place at the days of August 10th, 12th and 16th. Praeses Koch felt sure that the sentence wouldn't be less than six months. Asmussen is free again. Beginning of July – this is to be very confidential – a new evidently very strong and decisive letter has been addressed by the whole Confessional Church to the State.[5] Its text and content is kept strictly secret. An answer hasn't come yet. A reminder will be sent these days. The second part of August might be most decisive and difficult.

   Actually the press utterances against Oxford, its message and its proposed declaration are part of the struggle. The protests are welcome if not asked for and are officially published in all the papers in spite of the fact that the message and even your speech is not allowed to be known.

5. The attitudes of *the Free Church representatives* have created a very great harm to the Church of Germany. Though they are not surprised and though they realize that the words of bishop Melle[6] were misused in a way he didn't foresee – for lack of knowledge, insight and vision – the Church leaders profoundly deplore that the Free Churches have so utterly failed at this maybe decisive juncture of German Church history. Bishop Melle will be asked questions not easy to answer. I gave as full and – I hope – as fair an account on what had happened as I could.

6. As to the *Committee of 7* to deal together with the Edinburgh-Committee of 7 with the realisation of the Central Committee I urged very strongly, that in view of the German cooperation bishop Marahrens should if ever possible attend the meeting of August 19th in London. It is however doubtful if he will be able to do so. The very days after the proceedings against Pastor Niemöller might necessitate his presence in Germany. Furthermore he has to preside August 26th [over] the Executive of the Lutheran World Confederation in Amsterdam where Archbishop Eidem will be present. Two absences would in any case be difficult. Furthermore the bishop can't risk his passport being taken away from him *before* Amsterdam, which could be quite possible if he went to London contrary to the wish of [the] Government. I told him that Archbishop Eidem was ready to take his place. But as he himself emphasised the importance of German participation, I told him that in the case of his inability of going, there was most certainly the possibility of Dr. Lilje attending the meeting either in his place or in another capacity. In saying that, I realised, that it was not quite in accord with the Oxford

decision, but I felt that some flexibility was possible and *that it was of the utmost importance to have if ever possible a Germen present at the meeting of August 19th.* For this reason I venture to ask you[,] very emphatically, to use your influence in favour of such a solution.
7. I said a word explaining, why I hadn't gone to *Berlin*. The bishop agreed that it was better I hadn't gone just now. He had seen pastor Böhm[7] the day before and promised to give him an account of my visit. He felt sure the Dahlem brethren would understand and approve.
8. I said also a word that, in a letter addressed to Henriod, bishop Heckel had protested that the message had been sent to him only 'for information' and not officially. Bishop Marahrens wondered at it, because not long ago he had very distinctly said to Heckel, that the foreign department of the Church couldn't be more than a department and that it was not entitled to expect to be regarded as representing fully the German Church. Bishop Marahrens said to me that after Dr. Zoellner's resignation he regarded himself in his capacity of Senior-Bishop of Germany as being the first representative of the German Church and that Heckel had no authority except through him. Without arguing the legal foundation of such an assumption, I think it is corresponding with the actual reality and I think we have to conform to it, as in fact we have done in recent days.

My *conversation with Praeses Koch* did not add much to what I had learned from bishop Marahrens. It was more general, less ordered and less official, more of a frank, confidential and friendly talk on main issues. As ever the Praeses made the impression of a brave, fearless, fighting man with a profoundly sound judgement. Nevertheless he is greatly burdened, his health evidently not all too good. He is very pessimistic as to the tendency and final goal of the Party and State in Church matters. Two of his words will interest you. He said the Church situation in Germany was always the best barometer for the good or bad condition of German-English relationship. In connection with the visit of the Dean of Chichester,[8] one of the pastors present at the famous evening conversation, cross-questioned in prison had been laughed at by a member of the secret police in the following words 'Haven't we been very clever to hear everything that was said. Only a pity that we didn't take hold of a real conspiracy!' How the police took hold of the conversation can't yet be explained. You might tell the Dean, that bishop Marahrens was really in an impossibility of receiving him at the day proposed and that Praeses Koch had waited for him at the station of Oeynhausen.

I hope my report might be of some use to you. At any rate I think my visit[,] apart from it being a sign of friendship and sympathy, will have enabled the German Church leaders to see clearer and to make in the light of what I could tell them proposals for future actions. How these proposals might come to you, I can't say. As far as possible directly. Bishop Marahrens knows, that if my going once more to Germany could be of service, I would be ready to come.

In the meantime I am leaving Basel tomorrow morning for Hotel Margna, Sils in the Engardin, where I hope to stay until August 26th.

Dr. Mott has asked me to write to him after my German visit, so that he might be able to give information to the Archbishops of York and Uppsala. I will give him some impressions of general interest, but I prefer to leave it entirely to you, to forward the more detailed and confidential information of my report to whom you think good. Please excuse my handwriting and don't forward faults in grammar and orthography I might have made. I am sitting in an empty and closed house without the help of my trusted secretary.

And finally let me thank you most heartily for all your kindness and confidence and also for your very friendly letter received just before I left London Monday morning. In thinking of all the privileges I enjoyed in connection with the Oxford Conference I remember with a very special gratitude what it meant and always will mean to me to have been close to you in very important questions and to have learned and received so much from you during these days.

With my best regards
Yours very sincerely

1. The text of the official message may be found in J. H. Oldham and W. A. Visser 't Hooft, *The Churches Survey Their Task* (London: SCM Press, 1937), pp. 275–6.
2. M. E. Aubrey, a leading figure in the British Baptist churches; he had attended the Fifth Baptist World Congress in Berlin in August 1934 and returned deeply sceptical of the situation in Germany.
3. While representatives of the Evangelical Church were not prohibited from attending the conference only two Germans were present: Bishop F. H. Otto Melle (1875–1947) of the Methodist Church, as official delegate of the Union of the Evangelical Free Churches, and the director of the Baptist Federation, Paul Schmidt (1888–1970).
4. Dibelius had sharply criticized Kerrl in an open letter at the end of February; 10,000 copies of this were printed and circulated. See Beckmann, *Kirchlichhes Jahrbuch*, pp. 158–61. The criminal proceedings consequently brought against Dibelius by Kerrl ended in an acquittal on 6 April 1937 after a trial at the Moabit criminal court in which Kerrl himself appeared as a witness.
5. In this Koechlin is incorrect.
6. At first the delegates of the Free Churches agreed to take the letter to the German Church, but then they decided that they could not. Melle caused a stir by praising National Socialist politics and speaking of the appearance of Hitler as a sign of divine providence. He insisted that there was religious freedom in Germany.
7. Hans Böhm (1899–1962): Lutheran pastor in Berlin, member of the Pastor's Emergency League and speaker of the Confessing Church in 1934; since 1936 he worked for the Provisional Church Government with Niemöller and Albertz. He had been known to Bell since attending a preparatory meeting for the 1937 Oxford conference in London in February 1937.
8. Duncan-Jones had, at short notice, flown to Germany to ask leading figures in the German church whether they would welcome an envoy who might deliver a message from the Oxford conference. He returned with qualified support for this step.

Bell to Koechlin, 23 August 1937, Basel UB, NL 37, VI 2 (unpaginated) (typewritten);
LPL, Bell Papers, Vol. 2, fol. 572-5.

Private

My dear Koechlin,

You will like to know how matters have advanced with regard to the World Council, and whether I have heard anything about the delegation. I hope you have had, and are still having, a really refreshing holiday.

(1) *World Council.* The Committee of the 14 met last Thursday. Unfortunately Faith and Order had put in several rather heavy brakes. I enclose a print of the Edinburgh comments.[1] You will see that the main brake is that which involves a submission of the completed plan to the Continuation Committee of Faith and Order. The Committee of 14, after a good deal of discussion, in which Dr. Oldham pointed out the difficulties in which Life and Work was placed, agreed that a provisional Conference should be held in Holland, May 9-13, for the purpose of drawing up a Constitution for the proposed World Council, and to make provision for the maintenance of the work of the two movements during the period until the proposed General Assembly has been convened. The Provisional Conference is to be formed by means of an invitation being sent to the Churches asking them to send representatives, on the lines laid down in the Report of the Committee of 35. The scheme for the World Council circulated to the Churches will embody the conditions laid down by Edinburgh.

It was pointed out that the Faith and Order movement could not participate unless the final scheme had been approved by the Faith and Order Continuation Committee. It was also pointed out on behalf of Life and Work that the Oxford representatives would have power to go ahead in the event of failure or serious delay in the meeting of the Conference. Dr Adams Brown, on behalf of Life and Work, and the Archbishop of York, on behalf of Faith and Order, have signed the letter of invitation.

(2) *Delegation to German Church.* During the week preceding the Meeting of the Committee of 14 (August 19th) Schönfeld had been in Berlin and had been on the telephone with Oldham. He had seen Bishop Heckel a good deal, and was most anxious that Heckel should come to the Committee of 14. I said, when Oldham asked me, that it was impossible unless Heckel were to be nominated by Bishop Marahrens who had been chosen by Oxford and had the right to nominate anyone to take his place. To cut a long story short, after various comings and goings Heckel arrived on Wednesday with Schönfeld. He came down to Chichester to see me. Schönfeld had fifteen minutes alone with me at first, and said that Marahrens wanted Heckel to attend the Committee, that Heckel was the only person who could come without question from the German Church to England at this juncture so far as State departments were concerned, that it was important that the German Church should be involved in this transitional stage, for if a new organisation were created in which they had not been co-operating in forming, it might be very difficult to get permission for the Church to join. It would be very different if the German Church had somehow been co-operating throughout and if the new were a clear development of the old. Schönfeld also said that Marahrens was particularly anxious that Heckel should come, and had said that Heckel was a man in whom we could all have confidence now, though he had made mistakes in the

past. Schönfeld gave two illustrations of ways in which Heckel had recently battled on behalf of Marahrens and the Church, though I have no means of checking this – (1) Rosenberg had sent two of his men to Oxford to report on the Conference with a view to giving a very unfair account of the Oxford Conference in the German press. Heckel had gone to the Foreign Office, and on their instructions Ribbentrop had ordered these two men of Rosenberg's to leave England. (2) Muhs,[2] being very angry at the letter signed by Marahrens and Müller and Fleisch in response to the Message of the Oxford Conference, had written Heckel a very brutal letter demanding a copy, which Heckel was to take to Marahrens. Heckel went at once to Muhs, insisted on the withdrawal of this brutal letter and said that if he did not withdraw it he would take the matter up with various State departments. As a result Muhs capitulated and tore up the letter in Heckel's presence.

I said that as long as Heckel came at Marahrens['] request the Committee of 14 could not possibly take exception to it. I suggested that as Heckel had not brought a letter from Marahrens, Heckel himself might write to the Secretary of the Committee of 14, or the President, stating that as Marahrens had not been able to come he, Heckel, had come at Marahrens' request and with his approval. This he agreed to do. So Heckel attended the Committee of 14 though he did not take any very active part.

It is however with regard to the delegation that I wanted to inform you particularly. You will remember Heckel's objection to the delegation on various grounds. Now however he is in favour, only he wishes it to be not a 'delegation' but 'a visit of friendship'. Apparently, perhaps partly as a result of Oxford, the moderate members of the Nazi party are getting much disturbed about the anti-Christian attitude of the radicals. They see that they cannot break with the Christian Church and the Christian religion, and so are rallying together in opposition to Rosenberg and Co. This, Heckel says, would make a visit of friendship particularly opportune. Only it could require very careful preparation. The implication was of course that Heckel should do the preparation. Heckel also was rather anxious that the visit should include a reception at which State Ministers should be present, and that a good deal should be made of the whole visit. I rather think he did not want me to go – indeed he suggested the Archbishop of York, the Bishop of Novi Sad[3] and the bishop of Copenhagen, and intimated that friends in a State department whom he had consulted said that they would most readily co-operate in making the best possible arrangements for a visit of such visitors. I said that we were anxious to arrange the visit in such a way as to be most useful to the German Evangelical Church, and that we should be perfectly satisfied with an entirely quiet meeting, say at one centre only, e.g. Hannover, in which the Message could be delivered and in which we could confer perfectly quietly with those who Bishop Marahrens and Dr. Müller wanted us to confer with; and I said that I was a little shy of anything to do with Statesmen. It was not our business. And I made other remarks which are summarised in a letter which I enclose.[4] Heckel and Schönfeld had a talk with Oldham on Wednesday night, and I think Oldham was more persuaded than I was about the term given to the visit of Oxford representatives. On Thursday I said to Heckel – as we had been hoping to follow up the conversation but there was no time – that as there was no time I hoped to write him a note giving the principal points, so that it might be a help to him in discussing the matter with Marahrens. I said the same to Schönfeld. Each said separately 'It is not [in] the least necessary'. In other words it seemed to me that Heckel did not want anything in writing. It made me all the clearer that something should be put down in writing. My main point is that whatever is done must be done with the entire approval of Marahrens and Müller. I should be a little surprised, I own, if the Dahlem people were ready to give Heckel *carte blanche* and while I should not want to go to Germany if it were better that I should not go at this stage, I am rather anxious that the people who do go should not be exploited for political ends.

I accordingly wrote a letter to Heckel. I enclose a copy[5] I had told Heckel about your visit to Marahrens. Heckel was to see Marahrens in the next few days, so I felt it could do no harm for me to write to Marahrens a very short letter saying that we were sorry he could not come to the Committee of 14 but thoroughly understood that his engagements prevented it, and that I had given a note of certain points to Bishop Heckel which Bishop Heckel would no doubt communicate to him. I cannot help feeling that it is really necessary to safeguard oneself and the Oxford position. Though Schönfeld meant me to be impressed I am afraid I was impressed in a rather different direction from what he hoped when he reported Gerstenmaier[6] as saying to him, about the reception, 'Perhaps Hitler would come'!

Yours ever,

1 Hermann Muhs (1894–1962): a German lawyer, since 1929 a member of the National Socialist Party; in 1933–5 president of the district government of Hildesheim and subsequently Secretary of State of the Reichministry for Ecclesiastical Affairs. After Kerrl's death in 1941 Muhs would become effectively responsible for church politics.
2 Bishop Irinej Ciric of Novi Sad (1884–1955), in the Serbian Orthodox Church; by this time a regular participant in ecumenical gatherings and a good friend of Bishop Headlam, whom he invited to Serbia and who had stayed there for a month the year before.
3 This enclosure is evidently missing.
4 Also missing.
5 Also missing.
6 Eugen Gerstenmaier (1906–86) worked between 1936 and 1944 in the office of foreign affairs of the German Evangelical Church under Bishop Heckel. In this capacity he was involved in preparations for the conference in Oxford in 1937. As member of Heckel's staff he was suspected of being a supporter of the *Deutsche Christen*, not least by Dietrich Bonhoeffer. Yet Gerstenmaier was also connected with Bishop Wurm. After 1939 he worked part-time in the cultural policy department of the Foreign Office where he met Hans Bernd von Haeften and Adam von Trott zu Solz. These relationships opened a door to the Kreisau Circle around Helmuth James von Moltke and Peter Count Yorck of Wartenburg. On 20 July 1944 Gerstenmaier was in the centre of the plot against Hitler. He escaped death at the People's Court, was imprisoned and subsequently freed by the US Army. In 1945 he founded the main relief organization of the Protestant Church, which he directed until 1951. Between 1949 and 1969 he was a member of the *Bundestag*, becoming president of the German Parliament in 1954–69.

Koechlin to Bell, 30 August 1937, Basel UB, NL 37, VI 2 (unpaginated) (typewritten); LPL, Bell Papers, Vol. 2, fols. 585–7.

My dear Lord Bishop,

I have to thank you most heartily for your two letters, the one dated August 8th [1] and the second August 23rd. I was very grateful to know that you agreed with what I had said and done August 2nd in Hannover and Oeynhausen and was wondering how the things had developed afterwards, when your second letter came to give me a very full and most interesting information. I received it just before leaving my holiday-place after a good rest of 21 days.

May I give you my reaction on what you are telling me. To be quite frank, I think it is most unfortunate that Bishop Heckel, clever as he is, succeeded in taking into his hand the question and maybe the preparation of the Oxford delegation and I really cannot understand Dr. Schönfeld that he entered so fully in such a line. The two points mentioned in favour of Heckel might be true. It was always evident that he tried to prevent extreme measures of Government personalities and that he was anxious to protect himself against being called a German Christian. But it is certainly equally true and will remain equally true, that he was leaning on two sides and that in many cases he did purposely a great harm to the Confessional Church. In fact he was much more anxious not to be called in official Germany a confessional churchman. I cannot help being convinced that to a large extent the Confessional Church would not trust Bishop Heckel to handle in a good way the very delicate question of the Oxford delegation, though very certainly in some quarters he is judged less severely than in others.

I wrote to you that Bishop Marahrens put Heckel into his place when the latter tried to pretend to be the real official representative of the German Church dealing with other Churches. On the one hand he certainly considers him as the secretary for foreign relations and would not like to eliminate him completely in dealing with the oecumenical movements. So Bishop Marahrens might have thought Heckel to be the only personality to be allowed by the State to leave Germany in order to represent him in London August 19th and he might have instructed him to talk over with you the matter of a delegation.

Nevertheless we on our side have to take the utmost care to protect ourselves. Personally I am very grateful for everything you said and did. I think we ought in no case to depart from our fundamental position which was to speak and to act exclusively from Church to Church without any desire to go into politics and to speak to the State. The Oxford Delegation ought to state very clearly that its only desire and its only mandate is to see the German churchmen who were prevented from coming to Oxford and to report to them and to those they might wish to include on the Conference. It is in my view out of any question that we could at the present moment meet with State officials, except to be received by them officially, as long as 50 to 100 Churchmen are suffering in prison due to the action of these same State representatives. Meeting State officials could only mean to bring to them the protest of the Conference in view of these sufferings. After earnest thinking we did not wish the Oxford Message to be such a protest. To protest personally would of course be more courageous and for this reason a more proper thing to do, but the protest would have to be announced at the start, before meeting the State representative, even before entering Germany. Would we then be in a good position for protesting? Would we not be obliged to listen to all State grievances, to all official explanation and justification, to very long speeches? What would and what could then our answer be, uninformed as we are officially and unable to use private information we have got?

And then the composition of the delegation. It is to me as clear as sunshine that you yourself are the only personality for leading the delegation. That was the thought of Oxford. That is in the line of the whole action of the Oecumenical Council these last years and is an impossibility to admit that a German[,] even tacit[,] desire could be allowed to eliminate you. We cannot submit to such a change, because it could and would be interpreted as if we were changing policy and not any more standing behind the official action of the Chairman of the Administrative Committee, mainly responsible for what has been done and said during these last years and weeks. It is not in the main analysis a question of personality. It is a most important question of principle and I am most anxious that you should not yield in this matter to any suggestion trying to entrust the leadership of the delegation to another personality. Furthermore it seems to me impossible to think of the Archbishop of York for leading the delegation, because he is representing Edinburgh and not Oxford,[2] in Heckel's eyes very officially the Anglican Church.

As to my own participation, I am still willing to be at your disposal if the main lines laid down at Oxford are maintained. I think I could be willing to consider the delegation as a 'friendly visit to the Church', which it was always meant to be, but certainly not as a 'friendly visit of Churchmen to German State officials' under the present circumstances and I do not think I would feel free to go to Germany under another leadership than yours. On the other hand I am anxious to ask you to feel completely free as to my personality. I am quite in another position than yourself and the Delegation can very well do without me. It might even be better to choose a representative of another Church. My visit to Germany August 2nd is in no way binding you to stick to my participation. I am ready to serve the cause if I am asked to do so in participating and am of the same willingness to serve it in abstaining from participation if that seems to be the better course to take. If I am not bound by duty to do it, I am not in the least anxious to accept a responsibility which is not an easy one and which most certainly is a delicate one.

I hope Bishop Marahrens will have taken benefit of his stay in Amsterdam to write to you personally about this whole question. I confess to be somewhat astonished that he had not sent to you a word before. The notes he took during my visit were very full and he promised to bring the matter before his colleagues, to discuss it with Böhm and to let us know what was the German Church view on the question. I underlined our desire that the proceedings should go on in full agreement with the Dahlem brethren and he agreed expressively with it. What Heckel has brought forward, is most certainly going in another line.

As far as I can see the situation has not changed very much since beginning of August. It is becoming more and more serious as well generally as in personal questions. The end of August might have passed relatively quietly because the Party Days September 7th to 14th might bring the watchword for the future policy in church matters. That is at least expected to take place. It might at any rate be wise to postpone any final decisions on our side until middle of September. If I am getting important news, I will let you know at once. According to my present plans I am here in Basel during these next weeks. Except special necessity, which I do not foresee for the moment, I do not intend to go to Germany before middle of October, when I have promised to give a missionary lecture at Herrnhut near Dresden.

Hoping that you might have before long a good holiday, I am with my kindest regards

yours very sincerely

August 31st 1937

P.S. I have just seen a German personality coming from Berlin and having seen some people near to official State attitude. He told me that the present great tension was between the Reichs-Church-Minister on the one side, desiring to maintain the official public status of the Church in the meaning that the Church ought to be completely a State department and the 'Braunes Haus', i.e. the Party, represented by Rosenberg, Goebbels, Himmler, Ley[3] *and Hess*, desiring to separate completely Church and State and to give to the Church only the character of a private association. He did not thinkt that the Party Day would already bring about the solution of this tension. Evidently he had not seen Church people to tell him about reactions of the Oxford Conference and I did not feel free to press upon him this question.

1   This now appears to be missing.
2   i.e. the Faith and Order movement as assembled at the Edinburgh Conference, which Temple chaired, and not the Life and Work movement at its Oxford conference.
3   Robert Ley (1890–1945): virulently antisemitic member of the National Socialist Party, which he joined in 1923; *Gauleiter* of Southern Rhineland since 1925; Leader of the Reich Organisation of the Party since 1932 and head of the German Work Front (*Deutsche Arbeitsfront*) since 1933. By the beginning of the Second World War he had lost much of his influence.

Koechlin to Bell, 25 September 1937, Basel UB, NL 37, VI 2 (unpaginated) (typewritten); LPL, Bell Papers, Vol. 2, fols. 644–6.

My dear Lord Bishop,

I have to thank you for your letters of September 7th and 22nd.[1] I did not answer earlier because I was not certain enough about your address and because I wished to wait until my friend Thurneysen, who had gone to Germany for lectures to the students of the Confessional Church, had returned home and had been able to give me newest information.

Let me begin in saying a word on the attitude of Bishop Marahrens. I confess to have been most disappointed when Dr. Hartenstein, Director of our Basel Mission, told me that Dr. Knak of the Berlin Mission had seen Bishop Marahrens on his way to London about July 28th and that Bishop Marahrens had told him quite explicitly that a delegation of the Oxford Conference could not possibly be received by the German Church under the present circumstances. Hartenstein, who knew of my visit, told Dr. Knak that Bishop Marahrens had not told me a word pointing to such an attitude and asked him if Marahrens had really been so very explicit. Knak answered that Marahrens' words had been unmistakable. This negative position of Marahrens is confirmed by what you have written to me in your letter of September 7th. Why did he speak to me as if he would take with his colleagues our proposal in quite favourable consideration? It was at least my impression that he would do so. Why didn't he give his full thought so that we might have been clear about his judgement and helped by it?

Thurneysen, who has seen [in] these last days Praeses Koch, Bodelschwingh and many other personalities, told me that, though respecting Marahrens as a spiritual personality, everyone he saw regretted that he was lacking in power and courage of decision. He was in everything most anxious not to bind himself in any direction, so that no one knew exactly what was his thought and line of policy. That seems to be the reason why he is not a leader trusted by those who in fact would like to follow him.

As you also say, it seems to me to be most important now to get at Bishop Marahrens. But the man to do that seems to be the Archbishop of Uppsala, who through the Swedish Embassy and the very clever Pastor Forell of the Swedish Embassy would be in a position to bring before the senior Lutheran Bishop of Germany the question of the delegation in a way Bishop Marahrens would have to answer by yes or no. I think that even for Archbishop Eiden it is very important to know as directly as possible how the German Lutheran Bishops would receive a delegation headed by him, the Lutheran Primas of Scandinavia. Would Archbishop Eidem be willing to go to Germany knowing that the official Lutheran Churches did not wish to meet him? Certainly Bishop [sic] Eidem as no one else would have the authority of pressing the question on Bishop Marahrens and the other Lutheran Bishops. At any rate I feel that after the experience of August 4th my authority with Bishop Marahrens would not be sufficient. If f[or]. i[nstance]. Forell could go to Bishop Marahrens with a mandate of Archbishop Eidem and of yourself, it would probably be the easiest way if he, staying and living in Berlin, could also deal with the confessional leaders of whom, as far as I know, only Böhm is out of prison now.

As to Heckel, Thurneysen brought to me from different sides, even from those having been closest friends of Heckel, very unfavourable judgements. His ambitious character has led him to even brutal actions if someone was standing against his plans.

According to my programme I have to be in Herrnhut Monday evening or Tuesday October 10th/11th. It would be possible to go there via Berlin about the 10th or return via Berlin about October 16th. I could of course also manage to stop at Hannover if really necessary. To go to Germany before that date, would be very difficult and in fact only possible in case of serious emergency. Sunday 17th I have to be in Stuttgart and can very easily manage to see Bishop Wurm then. Let me know if around these dates I can be of service to you and if using f[or]. i[nstance]. the services of the Anglican chaplain in Berlin I can send you news at once, without being obliged to wait until I have left Germany about October 20th.

As to the task of the delegation, my reaction is, that to go there with the wish to be reconcilers between the Reichschurch-Minister Kerrl and the Church, is a hopeless undertaking. It seems to me even to be dangerous to acknowledge officially these State Church authorities. I am afraid they will be in a position to dictate the situation and to prevent us from doing what we have to be most anxious to do and to say. Not to speak of the press propaganda, which will be entirely in their hands, and might bring us in a most awkward position.

How, evidently with Kerrl's knowledge, the pastors are treated, may be illustrated by one striking fact brought to my attention by Thurneysen. I think I told you that Pastor Immer had a stroke in prison. It happened after having been most painfully questioned through hours without having been allowed to sit or to lean on anything; after having been together with common criminals; after having been photographed like a criminal *not* in his clothes, after his fingerprints having been taken. Returned to his little prisoner's room, his excitement was such that the stroke happened. He was then brought to a hospital to avoid his dying in prison. The doctor noticed then that his blood pressure evidently had been too high before and that Immer had not known of it. He is recovering now.

Another fact concerning the lectures to the students. You know that the confessional theological school of Asmussen in Berlin has been prohibited and cannot be reopened.[2] In Elberfeld they succeed in continuing somewhat the lectures. Holiday lectures ought to have taken place in Berlin. They were prohibited. It was tried to start them in Bethel-Bielefeld, Bodelschwingh's place. It was not possible to do that either. Then the about 80 students were scattered in villages near Oeynhausen. They were lectured here and there, always 20 together, changing places again and again, so that the State Police could not get at them. Professors of Marburg, who had been asked to lecture, were asked by the students not to do so, because they would have lost their places at once, if their participation would have come to the knowledge of the State Police. Thurneysen went to the rescue on his own risk and I as his Church President did not prevent him from going. He was glad to have been able to render this service, but his impression is, that the training of theological students has become a desperate thing. He thinks that State violence will more and more prevent the Confessional Church to do its work. This is also the impression of other people I have heard of. You will understand that under those circumstances I doubt very much the advisability of trying any reconciliation in Germany.

Evidently the visit of Wahl and Krummacher will throw a new light on the situation. I hope my letter will help you a little bit to face their questions and proposals. It is indeed very difficult to find our way in this delicate matter of delegation. I pray that God may give us his guidance.

As to the possible dates mentioned by you, I think I could be in Berlin November 8th. But please do understand it if I am leaving the question of my participation open until I know if with my convictions I can really fit into the definite task and programme of the delegation. You may be certain that I wish to go with you as far as I ever can.

With kindest regards, yours very sincerely

1   These two letters now appear to be missing.
2   After the banning of the church colleges at Berlin and Wuppertal in November 1935, and Kerrl's prohibition of examinations by organs of the Confessing Church in his fifth Ordinance to the Law for the Safeguarding of the German Protestant Church of 2 December 1935, the Reich Ministry of Education sought to prevent the participation of lecturers from the theological faculties in any substitutions and examinations put on by the Confessing Church. With a further circular of 17 November 1936, he forbade theology students from attending any such courses altogether.

Bell to Koechlin, 4 October 1937, Basel UB, NL 37, VI 2 (unpaginated) (carbon); LPL, Bell Papers, Vol. 2, fols. 672–3.

My dear Koechlin,

This is just a provisional reply to your very kind and informing letter of September 25th. I have written, as you suggest, to Archbishop Eidem, to see whether he can get Pastor Forell to tackle Bishop Marahrens and Böhm and others as soon as possible. It looks to me as though the situation is worse rather than better now. Krummacher and Wahl threw no fresh light on the situation. They had nothing particular to say about anything. They did not know much about the delegation. They only felt pretty clear that Bishop Marahrens was against it, and they also felt that any move by the foreign Churches just now, or by the Oecumenical Movement, was likely to lead to a cutting off of the German Evangelical Church by order from all Churches abroad, snapping the somewhat precarious links which still join us.

The situation seems to be worse in Germany with the closing of the Confessional schools etc. I understand from my sister-in-law, Miss Livingstone, who is in Berlin on non-Aryan Christian relief matters, that I am *persona ingratissima* to the Nazis.[1] I will let you know what Archbishop Eiden says. He has not yet replied on the question of date – the date suggested by me being, in view of his own engagements, somewhere about November 8th.

There is one point on which I should be rather glad of your special advice. You may have opportunities, in the same way as you had after the most useful consultation with Thurneysen, for knowing how welcome this proposal would be. We have to hold a Meeting of the Administrative Committee of Life and Work before the end of the year. It is at present arranged for December 11th, I think, in London, but it has occurred to me (and I know Otto Dibelius said that a Meeting of one of our Oecumenical Committees in Germany would be a real help), that the Administrative Committee might meet and do its ordinary work in some German town – not necessarily Berlin.

There is one point which I ought to mention as a point that I gathered from Krummacher and Wahl, namely that if a visit were made to Germany and its object was the future – the World Council and the co-operation in the Oecumentical Movement of the German Evangelical Church – that would make all the difference; and I think that we might see a way through thus: If our delegation, or representatives of the Administrative Committee meeting in Germany, could lay most of its emphasis on that part of the proceedings of the Oxford Conference which looked to the future. It is an extremely difficult and delicate situation. One does not want to make a false step; nor does one want by inaction to give the appearance of weakness or betrayal.

My sister-in-law's address in Berlin is:-
>Miss L. M. Livingstone,
>>Pension,
>>>Kantstrasse 149
>>>>Berlin-Charlottenburg.

This letter is being signed on my behalf so as to get to you as soon as possible. I entirely understand about the impossibility of reconciliation with Kerrl. I do not think that was in Archbishop Eidem's mind. It was only that he wished to preserve his independence. It would be madness to go to Kerrl in ordinary or present circumstances.

Yours very sincerely

1   For Laura Livingstone (1889–1970) see James Radcliffe, 'Bishop Bell of Chichester and Non-Aryan Christians: The Role of the Berlin Quakers, the Paulusbund, the Grüberbüro and the German-Jewish Emigration Office', *Kirchliche Zeitgeschichte/Contemporary Church History* 21, no. 2 (2008): pp. 277–86.

Koechlin to Bell, 5 October 1937, Basel UB, NL 37, VI 2 (unpaginated) (typewritten); LPL, Bell Papers, Vol. 2, fols. 690 (r and v).

My dear Lord Bishop,

I am just receiving from Pastor Forell in Berlin a letter dated October 2nd and asking me if I could receive a friend of his Saturday next, October 9th, 11 a.m. He would like to speak to me about 'urgent personal matters'. I have just answered that I would gladly be at his friend's disposal.

I suppose that it is a man of the Confessional Church who wishes to come here to give me important news. In view of this possibility, of which I am of course not absolutely certain, I would be grateful to hear from you so that I might be in a position to talk to him in a way which would be in agreement with your plans and to take, if advisable, the opportunity of his going back to Berlin to let our friends there know what our plans are.

May I furthermore remind you that according to my plans I am leaving Basel Sunday evening for Herrnhut, where I am due Monday evening for the *Missionswoche*. I have to be there until Friday midday. Sunday afternoon I have to speak in the Stiftskirche of Stuttgart. It would be possible for me to go to Berlin for a very short visit Monday next, October 11th, or Friday/Saturday, October 15th/16th. In Stuttgart I will most probably see Bishop Wurm.

Sunday last Hartenstein brought some news from Stuttgart, where he had seen Bishop Wurm. The situation in the villages, where the pastors have not any more been allowed to give the Bible teaching in the school and where German believing teachers (Rosenberg paganism) have been authorized to give the religious teaching, the teaching which the children have all to attend, seems to be most excited.[1] The parents assembled in large crowds for manifestations. The police intervened and arrested larger numbers of people. Bishop Wurm seemed to think it not impossible that some day in the great excitement someone would shoot and that then things of greatest gravity would happen. In the office of the Ministry of Cult and Education in Stuttgart the feelings against the Church are becoming more and more full of hatred, because they feel that they cannot overcome the resistance of the people in the villages and because they of course are making the Church responsible for that.

You will have read in the papers that Himmler as great chief of the GESTAPO has prohibited every lecturing of the Confessional Church to the students, even simple holiday lectures.[2] It might be the answer to the lecturing in villages attended by Thurneysen, which had been prohibited for Berlin and for Bethel-Bielefeld.

I am glad to have the opportunity of going out to Germany, to have personal contacts again and to feel out myself what the atmosphere is. You will of course have news very soon after my return, October 20th.

Hoping you have received alright my letter of September 25th, addressed to Hotel Royal, Paris, I am,

yours very sincerely

1   The prime minister of Württemberg and Minister of Culture, Christian Mergenthaler (1884–1980) was an antisemite and an opponent of Christianity. His first attack on Christian influences came in 1936 with the transformation of the confessional schools into community schools (*Deutsche Volkschule*). See Koechlin to Bell, 5 June 1936, note 4. One year later, the campaign against religious education began in earnest, in contradiction to requirements of the constitution. On 28 April 1937 Mergenthaler issued a further decree setting out how education must express the spirit of National Socialism itself. The next step followed an order of the Reich Minister of Education of 18 March 1937 that all clergy who gave religious education in public schools without being appointed as civil servants must take an oath of allegiance to the Führer. To this Mergenthaler allowed no reservations. Mergenthaler's goal was the introduction of a National Socialist *Weltanschauungsunterricht* as a compulsory subject for all. It was generally introduced by a decree of 5 April 1939.
2   Heinrich Himmler's decree of 29 August 1937 had banned theological education by the Confessing Church altogether: to be found in Beckmann, *Kirchliches Jahrbuch*, pp. 205–6.

Koechlin to Bell, 9 October 1937, Basel UB, NL 37, VI 2 (unpaginated) (carbon); LPL, Bell Papers, Vol. 2, fols. 713–4 (r and v).

My dear Lord Bishop,

Best thanks for your important letter of October 4th, answering in advance my letter to you dated October 5th.

As I thought, the interview announced to me by Pastor Forell was very important. It was Dr. Hanns Lilje, who came in the name of Bishop Marahrens himself to let us know how things stand and to make clear proposals. I am trying to give you as exact an account as possible. I will excuse [sic] if I am relatively brief. It is Saturday afternoon. I have to preach to-morrow morning and to leave in the late afternoon.

1. *The booklet written by Rosenberg against the Protestant Church*[1] is laying a very dangerous emphasis on the oecumenical movements, attacking Oxford, the Lutheran World Council and different not German oecumenical leaders in the strongest terms. The theme 'international Christendom' will be dealt with very thoroughly this winter in the schooling of all the national-socialist organisations (army, youth movement, working people). A small group, composed by von Soden,[2] Asmussen and Lilje, has written an answer to this whole book, dealing of course also with other matters, which will be circulated as a manuscript and if possible printed before long.[3] But the danger of cutting down all relationships between the German Church and the other Churches, to which Wahl and Krummacher seem to have pointed, is very imminent. Dr. Lilje suggested that possibly one could give expression to a protest to the different embassies of Germany in England, Sweden, America and so on.
2. *In the Church Ministry* the tension between the Minister Kerrl and Dr. Muhs, a new man, seems to be very strong. Kerrl wishes to make of the Church as a whole strictly a State Department. Muhs is inclined to give the leadership to the German Christians. Wherever he has power to do so, he is giving places of influence to members of this group. He is for the moment the stronger man and it seems possible that Kerrl will be transferred with the 1st January to another place. The former tendency to have Bishops, is not anymore welcome. The State does not wish to have Church leaders, only simple pastors, the whole leadership remaining in the hands of State and Party.
3. *The theological training* is in greatest danger. The free faculties and free training cannot be maintained. The tendency of the Churches, even of the Dahlem wing, seems to be to send the students to the more or less intact faculties (Tübingen, Erlangen, Marburg) and to give to the students of Prussia the possibility of passing their church examinations, which they cannot pass f[or] .i[nstance]. in Prussia, in the intact Churches like Hannover, Württemberg, Bavaria. The difficulty still remains to make it possible for these men to come to parishes, all pastoral elections being more and more either in the hands of the German-Christians or in the hands of State officials.
4. The so-called *'Kassel-Convention'* of early July 1937, uniting the three groups of the Confessional Church, seems to work well. In matters of principles the whole thinking is made together. Decisions are not taken without agreement or at least mutual consultation.
5. *Bishop Marahrens* wishes you especially to know that his silence is not due to lack of consideration or to negative attitude to Oxford and the plan of a delegation. He did not wish to speak or to write before things were clear and had of course to be most cautious in all his dealings. He is not 'very much against' the delegation. He is in favour of it, provided some conditions are fulfilled.

a) It is of course impossible for the German Church to invite the delegation to come. The delegation has to announce officially to the German Church its intention to come in fulfilment of the mandate received by the Oxford Conference. I said that this was the natural way to take.
b) The date of November 8th seems too early. The Rosenberg attack against oecumenical work is going just now at its fullest. The *Reichstagung* of the German-Christians is taking place to-day and to-morrow at Eisenach. Backed by Party and State, the German Christians have got full possibility of public expression in the newspapers! It seems wise to wait until the atmosphere has become a little more quiet and until the effect of the Church reaction to these attacks is felt somewhat. The time around the first advent, that is November 28th, seems more appropriate. In fact they propose such a date, provided the development is not going in an unexpected way. The practical difficulty to overcome will be to announce the arrival of the delegation at a date on which a previous agreement with the German Church has been reached, so that we may avoid to place [*sic*] the German Church in the disagreeable situation to tell us that we cannot be received just now. But I think this difficulty can be managed.
c) As to the character of the delegation, Lilje could only give me his personal impression. He is however feeling that others and specially Bishop Marahrens will agree. He is seeing some danger in giving to the delegation too demonstrative a character. These last weeks even Church services of special character have been prohibited. It could possibly be the case even for a Church service at which the Archbishop of Uppsala would intend to preach. As no publication can be made before or after the service, the effect of such a demonstration would not be far-reaching. The official propaganda on the other hand would have every possibility of making a most disagreeable use of such a demonstration.

The real thing to do, according to Dr. Lilje, is to have a closed meeting with the German delegation appointed to Oxford, some other Church people and with representatives of some State Department being invited as guests. That was the way used when a visit of the Lutheran World Conference took place in the offices of the Lutheran Council in Berlin. Very good things were said at that occasion and listened to by the State representatives. Nothing had to be kept secret and no bad effect whatever was felt afterwards, on the contrary. I could only tell Dr. Lilje that we had always thought of such a line and that I had suggested it in your name to Bishop Marahrens.
d) As to the composition of the delegation, the first thing Dr. Lilje wished me to tell you, was, that in no way Bishop Marahrens or any one in any group of the Confessional Church had ever thought that you ought to stay away. On the contrary, they wish you most strongly to come. The proposal made by Heckel, to appoint the Archbishop of York, was entirely due to his own initiative and Bishop Marahrens had not known anything of it until a few days ago, when he got the news indirectly from me through Dr. Thadden. They are quite in agreement with Archbishop Eidem leading the delegation,

the names of Archbishop Germanos or the Bishop of Novi-Sad. They favour also my joining the delegation and would like to have the Bishop of Copenhagen included. Not only for his personal and spiritual value and his being Bishop of Copenhagen, but also because born and brought up in the German part of Denmark, he was *Reserveoffizier* of the German army and had earned in the great war the 1st class iron cross!

6. *Heckel, Wahl and Co.* After the 4th of August Bishop Marahrens had appointed Dr. Lilje to be his representative at the meeting of August 19th, but Heckel protested in such an angry and dangerous way and would have been able to make so great difficulties in the future, that finally Bishop Marahrens and Lilje agreed that it would be better to let him go. But he has not got any instruction to negotiate with you about the delegation and no instruction whatever to negotiate about it with some State officials, as he seems to have done before coming to you.

   As to the English visit of Wahl and Krummacher, Bishop Marahrens heard of it purely by chance, going to Heckel's office some days ago. He was told that the two had received by cable an invitation to come and had accepted this invitation. I could only quote to Dr. Lilje, who asked me if I knew anything about it, what you had said in your letter written in Paris and according to which you seemed to have been surprised yourself by the announcement of their coming to Chichester. It did not seem impossible to Dr. Lilje that an invitation had come to Wahl and Krummacher through Dr. Oldham or Schönfeld. Very personally and confidentially he showed a certain anxiety that Schönfeld was going his own ways and making accordingly his personal suggestions to Dr. Oldham, who in this case owing to your absence on holiday might have acted without consulting you. These independent dealings of the office of Heckel and his people are disagreeable to all parts of the Confessional Church in Germany and they wish us to know that we ought in no way to encourage them.

7. Dr. Lilje asked me why the answer of the Confessional Church to the Oxford Message, signed by Bishop Marahrens, Müller and Fleisch, had not been read publicly at the Oxford Conference. He wished to know if a special reason had led us to such a silent attitude. He seemed to regret our not reading it publicly. I could only tell him that we had been very glad to receive this letter and that no intention unfavourable for the Confessional Church had led us not to read it.

Dr. Lilje has gone to Zürich this evening. He will be back in Berlin Tuesday. Friday next the Cassel Committee (including all groups of the Confessional Church) is holding a meeting in Halle. They will give further thought to all the matters discussed to-day in my house and we agreed that I would meet Lilje and if possible Böhm Friday evening, October 15th, at the *Mission House of the Leipzig Mission, Karolinenstrasse 19 in Leipzig*, so that I might hear what they have agreed upon in Halle. It is possible that our meeting may also last [until] Saturday morning. Definite news will reach me at the address of Bishop Baudert at Herrnhut.[4]

I nearly forgot to answer your question concerning the *Administrative Committee* to be held in Germany. Lilje thought it would be far better to stick to the delegation. A

Committee would in no way be free to do its real business and would be suspected to be the official body of the Oxford Movement investigating the German Church situation.

As to the emphasis to be laid on the future work, he thought it would of course be one of the points to be spoken about, when the delegation would meet with the German Church leaders, but in his view not the main point. The best thing to do, according to his insight, is to come in the name of the Church universal to greet the German Church, which had not been in Oxford and to state that the unity of the Church of Christ was such an unquestionable reality that it had to be manifested at that occasion in view of the present as well as in view of the future. Within other words, we ought to remain in our lines and to avoid all problematic and opportunistic thinking.

I promised to write to you at once so that you might be able to give me your reaction until Friday. You could possibly do it in a way allowing the Halle meeting to know of your reaction. Lilje will send a trusted person about Thursday evening to your sister-in-law, Miss Livingstone, to ask her if a letter had arrived for me or for Dr. Lilje. In the latter case he would use your letter at the Halle meeting and bring it to me in the evening. In the first case I would receive your reaction in time to discuss it with Dr. Lilje and those he wishes to include in our meeting. You can of course send two letters. We thought that you would be in the position to use the channel of the diplomatic service going to the English Embassy in Berlin. To reach me through Basel would not be possible. A direct word would, if you should chose that way, best go to *Bishop Baudert, Herrnhut*. It will hardly be time for you to communicate with Archbishop Eidem, but if you see some way to do it, he might send his reaction directly to Pastor Forell in Berlin. Dr. Lilje will be in touch with him also before Thursday evening.

As soon as I am back in Basel, you will receive further news. In the meantime I am as always

yours very sincerely

1. Alfred Rosenberg, *Protestantische Rompilger. Der Verrat an Luther und der Mythus des 20. Jahrhunderts* (Munich: Hoheneichen-Verlag, 1937).
2. Hans Freiherr von Soden (1881–1951): since 1924 professor of New Testament studies and church history at Marburg University. From the beginning he was an opponent of the National Socialist Party and, together with Rudolf Bultmann, he played a leading role in criticising the Aryan Paragraph of the Theological Faculty of Marburg University in 1933. Chairman of the Regional Council of Brethren of Kurhessen-Waldeck and member of the Reich Brethren Council from October 1934, he was a leading light in the Confessing Church.
3. See also the instruction of the parishes by the Confessing Synod of the Rhineland in Beckmann, *Kirchliches Jahrbuch*, pp. 214–19.
4. Samuel Baudert (1879–1956): bishop of the Moravian Congregation of Herrnhut 1929–45; organizer of the Mission Weeks at Herrnhut.

Bell to Eidem, 11 October 1937, Basel UB, NL 37, VI 2 (unpaginated) (carbon): LPL, Bell Papers, Vol. 2, fols. 718–19.

My dear Archbishop and Brother,

I am very grateful for your letter this morning and for your telegram in answer to mine. By the same post I had a very long letter from Dr. Koechlin. In it he described a visit just received from Dr. Hanns Lilje, sent by Bishop Marahrens himself. From this letter it is quite clear that Bishop Marahrens is after all definitely in favour for [sic] a delegation coming to the German Evangelical Church under certain conditions. There should not be a Church Service, nor should the delegation have too demonstrative a character in view of the unscrupulous methods of official Nazi propaganda. The visit should take the form of a closed meeting with the German delegation appointed to Oxford, and including some other Church people, and with representatives of some State department being invited as guests. This was the way used when the visit of the Lutheran World Convention took place in the offices of the Lutheran Council in Berlin. Very good things were said then, and listened to by the State representatives. Nothing had to be kept secret, and no bad effect whatever was felt afterwards – rather the contrary. Dr. Koechlin explained to Lilje that this was really the conception we had always formed, and which he had actually suggested on August 4th in my name in his conversation with Bishop Marahrens.

The question of the date has a certain difficulty. At the present moment there is a very hot propaganda going on, and a Rosenberg attack against oecumenical work, and the German Christians have a great demonstration this week at Eisenach, backed by the Party and the State. Lilje thought it might be wiser to wait until the atmosphere had become a little more quiet, with a view to seeing the effect of the Church reaction to these attacks. So they propose somewhere about November 28. As the two or three days round about November 28 were impossible for me I put the date forward a little and telegraphed to you about the first week in December. I am very glad indeed that you could come from December 8 onwards. That period would also if necessary suit me. I have told Koechlin these two dates. I cannot help thinking that in a way the sooner we go the better, and that the first of the two periods is the best. But you shall hear as soon as ever I hear. Koechlin is in Germany this week and is to meet representatives of the various groups on Friday.

I ought to add that there is a good deal of indignation about Bishop Heckel's activities. He seems to have been acting entirely on his own, and to have forced himself on to the Committee of Fourteen, though Bishop Marahrens was himself most anxious that Lilje should go and not Heckel – he only agreed to Heckel because of the angry way in which Heckel spoke of what might happen if he (Heckel) did not go. They would very much like the Bishop of Copenhagen to come, and they attach great importance to the Lutheran representatives. I am also writing to the Bishop of Novi Sad and Archbishop Germanos.

Yours affectionately,

Bell to Koechlin, 11 October 1937, Basel UB, NL 37, VI 2 (unpaginated) (carbon); LPL, Bell Papers, Vl. 2, fol. 721.

My dear Koechlin,

I am extremely grateful for your very important and illuminating letter of October 9th. I write direct to Herrnhut as that seems the best way.

I am very glad indeed of the plan which you have sketched, and the willingness of the principal personalities whom you have mentioned to see us. The plan which you sketch is excellent, and you may tell anyone that I whole-heartedly agree. I have heard from Eidem to-day. He was most anxious to be reassured about our friend's attitude after the information which I gave him, based on your former letter. In view of what you say he would be most definitely willing and anxious to come. As to dates, I have telegraphed to him to-day about dates and other matters, and have received his reply before writing this letter to you. The days Nov. 2–11 suit him. He could not manage the latter date mentioned, but the period commencing December 8 would be possible. So far as I am concerned, my possible days are November 8–11 inclusive, and the period following December 8. I am communicating at once with the other persons named. It may be the case that the earlier date would be the better if we can obtain the persons specially important.

If I have any further news, by telegram or otherwise, you shall hear. I may add that there is an Anniversary Celebration of Gustavus Adolphus at Leipzig on November 6 which Eidem would like to combine if possible with a visit. By the way, please tell Lilje that their reply to the Message did not arrive in London till after the Conference was over. If it had arrived in time it would undoubtedly have been read. My first sight of it was at the Lambeth Garden Party. It was dated from Berlin and Hannover, July 23, so you will see it was too late.

I look forward to hearing from you. Please remember me most warmly to our friends, and my cordial greetings to Bishop Baudert.

Yours very sincerely,

Koechlin to Bell, 20 October 1937, Basel UB, NL 37, VI 2 (unpaginated) (carbon); LPL, Bell Vol. 2, fols. 745–9.

My dear Lord Bishop,

I came home yesterday night after a nine days stay in Germany. Saturday morning October 16th from 10 to 12 I met Dr. Hanns Lilje and Dr. Böhm in Leipzig. Your letter dated October 11th had reached me in the afternoon of October 14th at Herrnhut, so that I could base our discussion on the opinion expressed by you. Thanks also for the kind lines of October 16th awaiting me yesterday here.

The result of my conversation was not as I hoped it would be, because the committee of the Kassel Convention had to be postponed from Friday last to Friday of this week. It was nevertheless an advance to be able to see Lilje and Böhm together and to know that on the side of our German friends they were really making their plans for our visit together. We came to a full agreement on the following points:

1. The visit of the Oxford Delegation has to avoid any ungood demonstrative character, hurting unnecessarily the feelings of State and Party. It ought however to be a demonstration of oecumenical unity in which the German Evangelical Church is most anxious to remain included. It is also anxious to let the Party and State know that in no case the German Church will accept to be cut off from the body of Christ. A meeting, possibly two meetings, will be held with those who had been delegated to Oxford as well as those who will be mainly responsible for the work following up Oxford and Edinburgh.
2. Our German brethren wish also to have at least one more official meeting to which they think [it] wise and good to invite some representative and carefully chosen people of the Foreign Office, possibly also of the Party and even of the Gestapo, so that these people, who as a rule are very little and wrongly informed, might be present, see the representatives of the oecumenical movement and hear them speaking of their main concern. This meeting would only be accessible for especially invited people. On their question if we would accept to speak at such a meeting, I answered in the positive, provided that the Church would have the whole thing in [its] hands and that it was understood that the whole proceedings would go on on church lines. I indeed think we have every interest to avoid any secrecy and to have the possibility, in speaking mainly to church people, to let the others know what is our great concern. The German brethren insisted on the fact that our accepting such an opportunity of speaking also to representatives of the secular world, would be a great help to them. In taking such a position, I said however that I would submit to you this plan.
3. There was not yet complete agreement about the desirability and possibility of the Oxford delegates speaking or preaching at a church service. Dr. Böhm very strongly emphasized that to bear witness in a church service of the unity of the body of Christ would be very important and very useful. He does not think that the Police or the State would try to intervene. It would, as he said, be the very first time that in church service matters a State or Police intervention would take place. Böhm was underlining his point of view in saying that strong forces desire to embody the Christian community in Germany entirely and exclusively into the German *Volk* and that it was highly necessary to bear public witness just now in Germany of the universal Church of Christ. Lilje, though agreeing in principle, saw possible difficulties and asked me if we on our side would be prepared to take the risk of the Police not allowing us to speak in a church service. In reserving entirely Archbishop Eidem's and your opinion, I said that in my personal view we should be prepared to preach the gospel in a German Church if asked to do so and to bear the witness of Christ and his Church universal if the situation in Germany according to the opinion of all concerned was calling for such a service. And we should not be afraid of the possibility that even in the last minute we should not be allowed to speak. The condition would however be that the

situation would be entirely legal and that the whole service, for which all parts of the German Church included in the Kassel Convention would have the common responsibility, would in no way be aggressive or polemic, but in the contrary [sic] entirely a positive preaching of the Gospel. Lilje asked me if possibly the English or other Government would use its influence in asking some delegates not to speak publicly. I said that provided the conditions laid down were fully taken care of, that would not be the case.

Finally we agreed that the Kassel gremium being the responsible gremium for arranging such a service, our German brethren ought to deliberate more fully about it and to bring before us definite proposals. There was however already [on] Saturday unanimity between our German brethren that the Oxford Message ought not to be read. Such a reading would have too provocative an effect.

4. As to the date, I underlined your reasons and the desire of Archbishop Eidem to come if possible [on] November 8th. But again Lilje and Böhm thought this early date to be impossible. Time was lacking to arrange properly the things and the press situation was at this moment not in favour of the undertaking. They said in fact that they could not receive us [in] early November and sticked [sic] to the proposal of early December. The date mentioned by you, beginning with December 8th would suit them. I think we have just to submit to their reasons and necessities.

5. As to the general programme of the visit, we spoke of our arriving in Berlin f[or]. i[nstance]. [on] December 8th in the evening, leaving the evening free for consultations amongst ourselves and possibly with very few leaders of the German Church. The morning of the 9th: meeting with the German Church representatives concerning future and effective cooperation, may be [or: involve] other important questions. In the afternoon: a larger gathering with State representatives and speeches of more official character. In the evening: eventually [a] church service. December 10th: at least the morning free for further consultation with church leaders and possibly other emergencies. In the evening: departure from Germany. Of course Berlin would under those circumstances be the meeting place. I insisted that we ought not to stay longer than necessary for the fulfilment of our task. To stay longer would at once give the impression of a commission of inquiry.

Böhm had the thought of sending the delegates individually to different parts of Germany for services f[or]. i[nstance]. December 12th, but he gave up this plan and saw that it would give a wrong impression of what we wish to do.

6. As to the composition of the delegation, they once more agreed with the names already discussed with Lilje here in Basel [on] October 9th.

As already mentioned, the Committee of the Kassel Convention will discuss these proposals and fix the plans Friday next. Lilje has to be in Southern Germany in the first days of November and I arranged to meet him again [on] November 4th, possibly November 2nd in Karlsruhe, a city of two hours railway distance from Basel. Would you kindly give me until that date your and possibly Archbishop Eidem's reaction on this plan, so that I might as far as ever possible come to an agreement about all questions involved. I regret that when we arranged this new meeting, I did not think of Archbishop Eidem going possibly to Leipzig [on] November 6th. I of course leave it very gladly to him, if he wishes to take into his own hands the further negotiations. A word giving up the Karlsruhe meeting will very easily reach Lilje. On the other hand to see Lilje again would possibly clear the questions so that the definite agreement could more easily be reached at Leipzig by Archbishop Eidem himself a few days afterwards.

There is one other question we have to bear in mind in connection with this whole delegation and its purpose. I spoke in my last letter of the tendency of Heckel's office to go independently its own way. I asked Lilje and Böhm to do whatever they could to avoid such a possibility in having constant contact in this whole matter with Heckel and his office. We have however to be aware that the same tendency – may I say quite naturally – is existing in our own Geneva office. Schönfeld being responsible for the going on of the whole research work, has to stay in contact, at least partly on his own initiative, with the office and with the personalities responsible in Germany for the oecumenical work. He stayed these last days in Germany, saw Böhm and Lilje the day before I saw them, spoke with them also about the delegation, was even questioned by them about it. On his way home to Geneva he called on me unexpectedly this very morning when I had already begun to dictate this letter. I told him how matters stood viewed from my experience, because I thought that everything had to be done to avoid new misunderstandings coming up. I did not go into all details and not into aspects of the question which I thought to be confidential. In listening to Schönfeld and speaking to him, a question arose in my mind, which I of course did not bring before him. Wouldn't it be wise to have Schönfeld with us in Berlin? He will have to deal with all the people we meet. He ought to deal with them according to the decisions and the policy laid down by our delegation in Berlin. We are going to discuss there questions for which he has been in the past and will be in the future our responsible man, at least as long as the new organisation will not have come into being. His advice will be of importance to us, especially as at least some numbers of the delegation do not know very much of the oecumenical research work, of the special difficulties it has to face in Germany and of the imponderabilia of the situation there. And very certainly the temptation to follow too personal and too independent a policy, would be considerably lessened. As far as I see, he could not be a full member of the delegation, but attached to it in his official capacity as research officer.

I am not quite aware that in asking Schönfeld to join us, the question of Henriod has to be taken in account, but as much as I wish to help Henriod, I cannot see that under the present circumstances his presence would be a strengthening of our group and in fact it would not either strengthen his own position.

I am going for a lecture on India and for Y.M.C.A. business to Geneva [on] Thursday, October 28th. I hope to see Henriod if he is back from his Balkan trip and to discuss with Schönfeld some questions of the work in Switzerland, which we had no time to discuss this morning. If you wish me to give to Henriod a full account of what I have seen and done, please let me know. I shall be grateful for every advice you will kindly give me in this connection.

The day before yesterday I saw Bishop Wurm in Stuttgart. We had no long interview. He wished especially to see clear about Bishop Melle, with whom they have many difficulties just now. We very briefly spoke of the delegation. He seemed to agree with what has already [been] said about the Lutheran Convention.

The situation in Germany is very difficult to analyse. Evidently Rosenberg and his people have a very great influence just now, but other forces are at work also. A great uncertainty is still existing about the elections taking place or not taking place. A sudden decision of the State concerning church matters is still possible. In the meantime the fight about religious teaching in the schools and Rosenberg's influence in every quarter is going on and everywhere the power of State machinery is felt.

In Herrnhut we had however a very good missionary week with about 250 people. In spite of increasing difficulties the German missionary people are unitedly [sic] convinced that they have to hold firm to the task entrusted to them. They manifested a wonderful confidence that ways and means may be found to continue, though on a smaller scale, at home and on the mission field[,] their work. The whole meeting was looking to Hangchow[1] and on the willingness to go forward with the *Una Sancta*. I had to give one of the main lectures on 'The way leading to Hangchow' and was, as I hope, able to help all those listening to me to come to a clearer insight into the substance of oecumenical work.

I felt how important it is to be based on the biblical and truly church foundation and to avoid the secular international speaking [sic]. It will certainly be of the greatest importance for our visit to Germany to come amongst ourselves to a full agreement and to a clear vision on what we have to say and how we have to say it.

With kindest regards,
Yours very sincerely,

1 The meeting of the International Missionary Council, planned to take place at Hangchow, had to be relocated to Tambaram in India after the Japanese invasion that July. It eventually took place on 12–29 December 1938.

Bell to Koechlin, 25 October 1937, Basel UB, NL 37, VI 2 (unpaginated) (carbon); LPL, Bell Papers, Vol. 2, fol. 764.

My dear Koechlin,

Very many thanks for your letter of October 20th with its extremely interesting Report. I will not give you my reaction upon all the contents of it at this moment, but content myself with acknowledging and saying how very grateful I am. Immediately I received it I wrote to Archbishop Eidem to tell him what you had said, and asking him for his reactions. On hearing them I will write to you at once. This means writing again in a day or two I expect. Praeses Koch was due to arrive in London yesterday for a local German Church Jubilee, and I am expecting him to stay Wednesday night here. He may have news of the Conference of Church leaders on Friday.

I do not quite know about Schönfeld and Berlin, but I will think this over. The trouble is that Schönfeld is, I am finding, so very much under Heckel's influence. It was through him that Heckel came to the Committee of Fourteen, and I am afraid he is somewhat suspect to our Confessional friends. Schönfeld also wanted the official Report actually to omit the Message to the German Evangelical Church, and here again he was speaking for Heckel. Of course if Böhm and Lilje would like Schönfeld, that alters the matter very much. But still, very likely it may be wise to have him on the ground that he will in the future be our responsible man. I will think about it and let you know. I do not think that it would be at all wise to have Henriod with us in all the circumstances. I have no objection to your seeing Henriod and telling him what you have done when you are in Geneva on Thursday. I ought to warn you that he is in a very sensitive condition at the moment. He is feeling very much that he is being overlooked, and especially he feels that he is being subordinated to Schönfeld. There is great tension, I gather from correspondence with him, between Schönfeld and Henriod.

I am very glad to hear that there are other forces in Germany at work in addition to the forces of Rosenberg.

I have a letter from the Bishop of Novi Sad to-day saying he would like to come with the delegation, but he cannot say definitely until we know the date.

Once more with ever so many thanks,

Yours ever,

Koechlin to Bell, 4 November 1937, Basel UB, NL 37, VI 2 (unpaginated) (carbon); LPL, Bell Papers, Vol. 3, fols. 14–17 (r and v).

My dear Lord Bishop,

I have to thank you for both your letters of October 25th and 30th, the letter accompanied by Dr. Schoenfeld's letter, which I am enclosing again.[1]

Saturday night I received a message from Dr. Lilje to meet him in Karlsruhe Tuesday instead of to-day. It was too late to let you know in good time, so your letter arrived here in Basel just when I was sitting with him for [a] good two hours in a hotel hall at Karlsruhe.

Our discussion was quite worthwhile, but we did not fix anything in view of Archbishop Eidem's visit to Germany which is taking place during the week-end and will give him fullest opportunity to discuss and maybe to decide finally the matter with Bishop Marahrens.

The German situation in view of the delegation seems still to be uncleared [sic]. In connection with the *Reichstagung* of the German Christian group in Eisenach, October 10th, quite a vehement attack has appeared in the press against Bishop Marahrens and these very last days Bishop Wurm has been attacked by Church-Minister Kerrl in an open letter published in the press and given through by [sic] the radio.

During the furlough of Bishop Wurm, the Wurttemberg *Oberkirchenrat* had written to the pastors to avoid common manifestations with the Methodists as long as the attitude of Bishop Melle in Oxford had not been cleared between him and the Church

Government.² In answer Kerrl is issuing the statement which I am enclosing. You will note the very strong words used against us oecumenical people.

It has not become clear yet if the statement viewed primarily the oecumenical question or tried to weaken the position of Bishop Wurm. Dr. Lilje – and I am inclined to think he is right – is of the latter opinion in view of the fact that Bishop Marahrens also has been recently attacked, in view also of the other fact that deliberations between different ministries have taken place recently aiming at a solution of the Church question. The outcome of these deliberations is not known. The Church circles are inclined to think that a very dangerous solution was viewed and decided in principle, but that the formal and legal way of getting it through, had proved to be all too dangerous and impossible as soon as the legal advisers had gone through the matter. To get rid of the provincial Church Governments, seems certainly one of the great aims of the central Reichschurch-Ministry and one might say of State and Party. The attacks against the Bishops are a symptom of a step forward in the developments.

For this reason Dr. Lilje felt that the German Evangelical Church ought not to be afraid of receiving the friendly visit of the Oxford delegation. Bishop Marahrens however seems to be more hesitant – as is his nature – and wishes if possible to wait until the development of the action of Kerrl is clearly seen.

2. Another aspect has to be taken into account. The Foreign Office evidently knew of the delegation. When Bishop Marahrens announced there personally Archbishop Eidem's visit for the 6th of November, hesitation was shown to accept it and they said to Bishop Marahrens that they had heard Archbishop Eidem would lead the Oxford delegation which was expected to come to Germany November 8th. Bishop Marahrens answered that this supposition was certainly wrong, as he did not know of an Oxford delegation visiting Germany at that date. He did not – I am following Lilje – say another word of the delegation. Lilje did not exactly know how the Foreign Office knew of the matter. We have to count with the possibility that it was through Heckel and we have certainly to count with the fact that if our visit remains fixed for December 8th, the Foreign Office will know it very soon, other Government circles very soon afterwards and that the propaganda will be in a possibility of fighting in the press against the delegation well in advance of our visit. The possibility of keeping the thing secret[,] until our friends in Germany will have announced it themselves in inviting to a meeting State and Party officials, proves to be impossible.

Under those circumstances it is also very regrettable that our Dahlem friends are very careless in their utterances. Schönfeld asked me by phone these days if really the delegation was to go to Germany December 8th. Ehrenström,³ passing through Berlin, had heard of it. I simply answered that [,] as far as I knew, nothing was fixed yet.

Dr. Lilje felt, and I was agreeing with him, that the uncertainty of possible imponderabilia and many always possible risks could again and again postpone the delegation until our visit would become impossible, that evidently always the presence of the delegation in Berlin would be a risky thing, but that on the other hand it would be if not fatal though quite grave to allow the other side to render our visit impossible. It would be a good thing neither for the German Church nor for the oecumenical movement and the future relationship between the two. We felt that to stick to decisions taken, was according to the experiences on the long run always the best course to take.

For this reason Dr. Lilje is in favour of our coming. But of course it will be for Bishop Marahrens and Archbishop Eidem to decide.

The question of the programme of our visit has under those circumstances not been advanced.

3. And now a word to Schönfeld's attitude. Finally I have not seen him in Geneva last week. My time was taken up very much by other engagements. Henriod had not come back to Geneva from the Balkans. An interview with Guillon had shown me that the personal relationship in the Life and Work office was, as you mentioned in your letter, not at all what it ought to be. Guillon who quite sees some weaknesses in Henriod, is regretting very much Schönfeld's attitude to him. I was struck how far he is distrusting Schönfeld and how he feels that Schönfeld, going constantly to Germany and having the full confidence of Dr. Oldham, is trying to get through all his thoughts also concerning the delegation, in bringing Heckel into the picture in Germany and in throwing Dr. Oldham's influence in the balance in England. That his attitude is causing difficulties to our German friends, was confirmed to me by Dr. Lilje, who was most anxious that you might convince Dr. Schönfeld not to go against your plans and to ask him to induce Heckel that the latter might not stand against the intentions of the Kassel Convention, but in the contrary to accept the leadership of it.

To enable you to have if possible a thorough discussion about this matter together with Dr. Oldham and Dr. Schönfeld, we agreed that Dr. Lilje should ask Archbishop Eidem to write to you as quickly as possible after his return, so that you might have in your hands the result of the coming German visit of the Archbishop at the date of Schönfeld's stay in London.

The main point for Schönfeld seems to be that he is with nearly complete exclusiveness looking at the possibility of his German study circles dealing with the results of Oxford. He is laying greatest emphasis on every single possibility of such a research action and intellectual educational process. The thought of losing only one of these possibilities, is leading him rather to give up the whole delegation. In Dr. Lilje's view, Schönfeld is exaggerating greatly the effectiveness of many of these possibilities. On the other hand Dr. Lilje confirmed to me that certainly Heckel had, at least for the moment, financial and other possibilities of publishing papers, which the Kassel ring had already lost. He frankly admitted that the publication of Dr. Gerstenmaier's book[4] had been a notable personal success of Heckel, for which they were grateful.

But Lilje was certainly right in pointing to the fact that Schönfeld and Heckel could not do their work without the effective help and the moral backing of the men and the leadership of the German Church as represented by the Kassel Convention and that the whole research work – the exclusive concern of Schönfeld – was on the long run impossible if the official and generally accepted relationship of the German Evangelical Church in the oecumenical movement was not manifest. It is a wrong policy to give up the Oxford Conference, its message and delegation[,] and to think that the research work can go on effectively on a basis of oecumenical reality.

I think we have certainly to take into consideration Dr. Schönfeld's concern, but to give him his real place in the whole picture and to act accordingly.

As to Schönfeld's participation in the delegation, I was thinking aloud when I wrote to you about it. I had not come myself to a conclusion and was anxious to clear my thought in getting your reaction. I still feel hesitant and would hardly be prepared to answer the question in the affirmative just now. The developments of the very next weeks might best show us how to act.

4. May I say a word on the letter I have written September 14th to Dr. von Thadden in Italy, a letter I had already mentioned when writing to you October 9th. I had written very frankly to Dr. von Thadden, knowing that he was anxious to hear what had been done and decided. As he was [a] member of the provisional Church Government of Dahlem, appointed member to the Oxford Conference and appointed member of the Committee of Thirty-Five, I thought I was entitled to give him pretty full evidence. I spoke on my visit to Hannover and Oeynhausen August 4th. I said that we had no direct news of Bishop Marahrens, but that we had heard he was against the delegation, though he had not expressed any such view in my presence. I spoke of Heckel's coming to London August 19th and our surprise of it [sic]. I have also said that Schönfeld and Heckel had spoken of State officials receiving the delegation and that Heckel had proposed that the Archbishop of York should lead the delegation, without mentioning your name anymore.

Thadden, returned to Germany, has sent this letter direct to Bishop Marahrens, who in consequence had sent Dr. Lilje the first days of October to see me in Basel. Unfortunately Dr. von Thadden, as it seems to be the custom with our Dahlem friends, had spoken of my letter to Böhm and others without having anymore the text of it in his hands. Böhm had spoken of it to Schönfeld, blaming the latter's attitude. Böhm also, without having seen my letter, has, as Dr. Lilje told me Tuesday, attacked Bishop Marahrens in a Committee meeting of the Kassel Convention, basing his attacks on the content of my letter. This seems to be unfortunate and I might not have been cautious enough in writing to Dr. von Thadden whom I considered to be one of the leading responsible people, able to use confidentially a personal letter so that the common cause might be served and not hindered. I feel sorry that Bishop Marahrens might have felt hurt by the form in which I had written and by the use made of my letter. I told it [to] Lilje and asked him to tell it to Bishop Marahrens. I evidently will take the first opportunity possible to tell him a word myself. I should also be very sorry if you too should feel annoyed by the way I proceeded. At any rate I have learnt a lesson.

On the other hand it seems to be certain that my letter gave a move to the whole development, which was highly necessary[,] and that it stopped some ungood developments connected with the delegation business. It opened the eyes of Bishop Marahrens for some dangers he did not see clearly enough and overcame some of his hesitations. So it might in reality not have been a hindrance, but possibly a good thing. Lilje told me also that other letters quite independent of mine, coming from Germany and dealing with Heckel's visit in London, had come to Bishop Marahrens, f[or]. i[nstance]. from Sasse in Erlangen,[5] and had strongly underlined the view expressed by me in my letter to Dr. von Thadden and had led the Bishop to trust definitely my general judgement in this whole question.

5. Guillon told me that you had thought of holding the Administrative Committee in Berlin. Though I am not concerned in it, I have put the question to Lilje, if he thought the holding of such an official meeting in Germany advisable. He was very clearly of the opinion that you would in no way be free in your moves and even in your

deliberations and that furthermore the holding of such an official Committee meeting in Berlin, following the visit of the delegation, would give the wrong impression of an inquiry committee. I feel that it would be much more cautious to fix this meeting outside Germany.

6. About the trial of Niemöller nothing is known, but some ten days ago he seems to have had a collapse and to have fainted, certainly a very grave symptom.[6]

With kindest regards,
Yours very sincerely

Enclosures.[7]

1. The letter of 30 October and the enclosure are now missing.
2. Methodist Bishop Melle's statement emphasized the freedom of religion in the Third Reich against the Confessing Church. Consequently the Upper Church Council of the regional Church of Württemberg instructed the congregations to refrain from joint events. This decision was sharply criticized by Church Minister Kerrl, who wrote to protest to Bishop Wurm.
3. See Eugen Gerstenmaier (ed.), *Kirche, Volk und Staat. Stimmen aus der Deutschen Evangelischen Kirche zur Oxford Weltkirchenkonferenz* (Berlin: Furche Verlag, 1937).
4. Nils Ehrenström (1903-84): Swedish pastor who joined the ecumenical movement in 1930 working for the Universal Christian Council for Life and Work as Henriod's assistant; 1934 deputy director of the Study Department; 1940 co-director, from 1946 director, of the Nordic Ecumenical Institute at Sigtuna. He would later play an important part in Bell's momentous meeting with Bonhoeffer and Schönfeld in Sweden in May 1942.
5. Hermann Sasse (1895-1976): Lutheran theologian, participant in the World Conference on Faith and Order in Lausanne in 1927. From 1933 he was associate professor of church history at Erlangen University, becoming a full professor in 1946. Protesting against the membership of the Lutheran Church of Bavaria in the new Evangelical Church of Germany and against the Barmen Theological Declaration, Sasse converted to the Old-Lutheran Church and immigrated to Australia, where he became a professor at Immanuel Theological Seminary in Prospect, North Adelaide, 1949-65.
6. For Niemöller's experience of imprisonment, see Wilhelm Niemöller (ed.), *Martin Niemöller, Briefe aus der Gefangenschaft Moabit* (Frankfurt/M: Lembeck, 1975).
7. These now appear to be missing.

Bell to Koechlin, 9 November 1937, Basel UB, NL 37, VI 2 (unpaginated) (carbon); LPL. Bell Papers, Vol. 3, fol. 24.

My dear Koechlin,

Very many thanks for your extremely interesting and important letter about your talk with Lilje. I look forward eagerly to hearing from Bishop Marahrens on his return to Sweden.

I think probably what seemed the unlucky passing by Dr. von Thadden to Bishop Marahrens of your letter to Dr. von Thadden, has turned out for the best. It is a very great pity, I think, that Bishop Marahrens is so extremely circumspect. I daresay the

Dahlem people are too rapid in their movements, but I am sure it would be a real disaster from the point of view of the German Evangelical Church and the oecumenical movement, if the delegation were to be postponed into another year. I think we ought to go in December, and I hope that Archbishop Eidem will have been able to persuade Bishop Marahrens that it really is a vital matter that we should adhere to somewhere about December 8th.

I will write to you as soon as I hear from Archbishop Eidem. In the meantime ever so many thanks. I am deeply interested by all you tell me, including what you say about Bishop Wurm.

Yours ever,

Bell to Koechlin, 11 November 1937, Basel UB, NL 37, VI 2 (unpaginated) (carbon); LPL, Bell Papers, Vol. 3, fol. 44.

My dear Koechlin,

Just a line in haste. I have heard this morning from Archbishop Eidem. The Swedish Minister at Berlin told him that the Foreign Office had sent for the Minister and had told him that if Archbishop Eidem did come as the head of a delegation to the German Evangelical Church, it would be regarded as a very unfriendly act. He also said that it would hurt the Confessional front. The Archbishop saw Bishop Marahrens and talked the whole situation over with him. Marahrens was hesitating, but at the same time said that the position of the German Church was so grave that he did not think anything could hurt it. It was arranged between them that the Archbishop should write a letter direct to Marahrens from Sweden, not referring to previous conversations in any way, and should ask him whether he (Marahrens) could arrange for the reception of some foreign Churchmen by the German Church leaders. The Archbishop, in his letter, would be quite general, but would refer to the anxiety of foreign Churchmen, and the great danger of losing connection between the German Church and other Christian Churches. Opportunity would also be taken, it would be pointed out in the letter, to talk over some of the issues arising out of the Oxford Conference.

I have written back to-day urgently, very much on the lines that you wrote to me in your letter, saying that I felt it would be very bad from the point of view both of the German Church and of the oecumenical movement if the delegation were to be still further postponed, or not to go at all. I really feel that we ought to take our courage in our hands and go. Of course Bishop Marahrens and his colleagues must decide, but I think it really would be bad if no delegation was to go to Germany.

I ought to have said that Marahrens was going to confer with Wurm and Meiser and others as soon as he receives Archbishop Eidem's letter. You shall hear as soon as possible.

Yours ever,

Koechlin to Bell, 15 November 1937, Basel UB, NL 37, VI 2 (unpaginated) (typewritten); LPL, Bell Papers, Vol. 3, fol. 57 (r and v).

My dear Lord Bishop,

Very best thanks for both your letters of November 9th and 11th. I was very glad to hear of the agreement reached between the Archbishop of Uppsala and Bishop Marahrens and I hope that it will prove to be possible for the delegation to go to Berlin in December, though I realize how very difficult it is for the German Church to accept the risks involved in it.

Saturday last, November 13th[,] Henriod came to see me and we had a very good talk of two hours. I gave him pretty full information of the steps taken in view of the delegation. He on his side spoke to me very frankly and in an excellent spirit of the decisions of the Westfield College,[1] of his actual position and his personal relationship to Dr. Schönfeld. Everything he said proved that he has not lost the high standard of attitude he had when answering the Archbishop of York's speech the last day at Westfield College. Evidently the difficulty for him is lying in the fact that Life and Work has more or less passed over the leadership of the movement to the Committee of Fourteen, that the latter had not been able to make real steps forward in August and had entrusted Dr. Oldham with the responsibility of taking the necessary decisions and that Dr. Oldham is working with his research-secretary Schönfeld, who is not the administrative executive officer of Life and Work. And Henriod, who still is formally the general-secretary of Life and Work, is in fact put aside.

Henriod was very grateful for letters he had lately received from yourself and Dr. Oldham and he is hoping that the meeting of the Administrative Committee will clear his situation for the remaining months of his Life and Work activity.

Henriod is going next week to Czechoslovakia in his capacity of secretary of the World's Alliance. He intended to return by the way of Berlin and had already written to Rev. Diestel[2] in order to meet him there. I asked him very instantly to give up this plan and to meet if necessary Dr. Diestel elsewhere. Realizing the very complicated and delicate situation, created in Berlin in view of the possible coming of the Oxford delegation, he agreed that his presence in Berlin these very next weeks could call for all kind[s] of unfavourable and possibly dangerous interpretation. When leaving, he was clear to ask Dr. Diestel to meet him at Nuernberg. I think he will stick to this decision. At any rate I insisted on my part that he might in no case go to Berlin without your knowledge and approval.

I am looking forward eagerly to hearing from you about the definite decision of our German friends and am in the meantime,

yours very sincerely

1 On 8–10 July 1937 a preparatory conference took place at Westfield College in Hampstead, London, to work on the forthcoming world conference of Faith and Order.
2 Max Diestel (1872–1949): superintendent of the church district of Kölln-Land I in Berlin from 1925 to 1948; in 1931 he had been appointed deputy and in 1935 executive chairman of the German association of the World Alliance for International Friendship through the Churches. He was member of the Brethren Council of Berlin from 1935.

Bell to Koechlin, 4 December 1937, Basel UB, NL 37, VI 2 (unpaginated) (carbon); LPL, Bell Papers, Vol. 3, fol. 82.

My dear Koechlin,

I have not yet heard from Archbishop Eidem as to what Bishop Marahrens' letter contained. So I do not know the grounds on which he has asked for a postponement of the visit. In the meantime I have a very pathetic letter from Pastor Hildebrandt, who is a young German Pastor in London, saying that he has heard a rumour of postponement and feeling that this means that the Oecumenical Movement is *stumm*, and feeling rather desperate about the future.

I hope that postponement is not simply due to extreme caution on Bishop Marahrens' part. It seemed to me possible that the new tone taken in Kerrl's recent speeches may be due to some change of front on the part of the State towards the whole Church problem. But how far these changes, though they hold out hope for a moment, are really changes in the permanent outlook, one does not know. We have been so often deceived and disappointed that we must not be too hopeful. On the other hand I quite understand Bishop Marahrens, with his temperament, desiring to make the fullest use of any grain of comfort, and being unwilling therefore to embarrass a possible reconciliation or amelioration by the arrival of visitors from foreign Churches.

It seems to me quite probable that the letter from Archbishop Eidem, which was carefully worded and spoke about the anxiety of foreign Churches, and the desire of a certain number of Church leaders to have fellowship with German Church leaders, may have been useful. It would presumably have been shown to people in the Foreign Office, for it was an open letter, and it made a definite proposal with regard to a delegation, and gave the names of the delegates.

I was able to see Lord Halifax[1] privately for a good talk about the German Church situation before he saw Hitler, and I think that was useful.

I wonder if you have any news? I should be most thankful for your own opinion about the present prospect.

Yours very sincerely,

1 Edward Wood, since 1934 Viscount Halifax, after 1944 1st Earl of Halifax (1881–1959): British Conservative politician, Foreign Secretary between 1938 and 1940. In 1936–8 he was one of the architects of the policy of appeasement of Hitler, working closely with Prime Minister Neville Chanberlain. After *Reichskristallnacht* in 1938 he became more deeply convinced of the need to deter further German aggression. Between 1940 and 1946 he was British ambassador to the USA.

Koechlin to Bell, 10 December 1937, Basel UB, NL 37, VI 2 (unpaginated) (typewritten); LPL, Bell Papers, Vol. 3, fol. 105–6 (r and v).

My dear Lord Bishop,

We ought to be in Berlin to-day and I do not realize without regret that once more our visit has been postponed. Your two very kind messages, for which I have to thank you very heartily, do not speak of the reasons of the postponement and I have not heard through any channel anything explaining to me the attitude taken by our German brethren. All I hear is that the party policy, aiming at destruction of the Church, is going ahead and that the tendency to prevent and to destroy the oecumenical relationship of the German Church is still very strong. It is of course not difficult to imagine that under those circumstances the postponement of the visit of the Oxford delegation seemed to be more cautious.

May I however express my opinion that we ought as strongly as ever possible [to] declare our desire to come without further delay and to urge upon our German brethren to receive us in any way which may seem to be possible. The situation is becoming very important and even dangerous.

We on our side have a mandate of all the Churches of the world to establish a direct contact with the German Evangelical Church and to make it evident in Berlin itself through our visit that nothing can prevent our unity in Christ with the Church of Germany. If we give up this mandate, the trust in the decisions of Oxford and in the divine guidance we believe to have had there and in the obedience to a mandate which might not only be human, is questioned and shaken. In principle we ought to go to Germany in spite of the fact that the Germans are unwilling to receive us. We ought to bring them courage and strength in their hesitation to make on their side manifest their unity with us.

On the other hand it seems to me most important for the German Church itself to receive our visit and to give witness of the reality of their oecumenical unity in spite of all hindrances and attacks coming from State and party. Is it the State and party or is it the Church to decide in such a matter? Is the Church giving up the freedom to have unity with other Churches?

I of course realize that our visit might be disagreeable for every one of us – in this respect I am not unhappy to be in Basel instead of Berlin – and call for new attacks in Germany against the Church, but the more I think of it, the more I am convinced that to be cautious has never been a strength for the German Church; on the contrary. To act even boldly, obeying God's orders, has proved to be the only salvation for the Church. I think that the Oxford delegation would be well inspired in following these lines and in giving to our hesitant German brethren a lead in this direction.

In expressing my thought, I realize that I do not know all the facts. I do not wish to judge, but simply to give you in my capacity of one of the delegates my own impression. Would it be possible to have confidentially a copy of the correspondence between the Archbishop of Uppsala and Bishop Marahrens? To read these important documents, would help me to see how things stand.

I can still dispose of my time in February and am ready in principle to join the delegation then, provided that I can be of use and that the character of the delegation will not be changed.

It may be my last letter before Xmas. May I send you my heartiest wishes and give once more expression to my gratitude for all your kindness this ending year. Mrs. Koechlin is joining me in sending the best greetings to Mrs. Bell.

Very cordially yours,

Bell to Koechlin, 13 December 1937, Basel UB, NL 37, VI 2 (unpaginated) (carbon); LPL, Bell Papers, Vol. 3, fol. 111.

My dear Koechlin,

I am very grateful for your letter of the 10th inst. received to-day. Like you, I am dreadfully disappointed. I have only just received from Archbishop Eidem a copy of Marahrens' reply and I send copies of Eidem's letter and Marahrens' reply for you to read and return, together with Eidem's letter to me and my reply to him. You can keep the copy of my reply to Eidem if you wish,[1] but please return the other three letters. You will see from my letter to Eidem that I am entirely with you with regard to the situation. It is extremely disappointing. As you say, it is most important that we should bring the German Church courage and strength in their hesitation, and that the German Church itself, for its own sake, should receive our visit.

Could you please tell me what would be possible in the way of dates for a visit to Berlin in February? In a way no doubt one must be prepared to give up any appointment if the situation demanded it, but what would be most convenient, and what would be possible, for you?

With all warmest remembrance, and very best wishes for Christmas to you and Mrs. Koechlin and your family, in which my wife joins me,

Yours most sincerely,

1 The copy now appears to be missing.

Koechlin to Bell, 16 December 1937, Basel UB, NL 37, VI 2 (unpaginated) (typewritten); LPL, Bell Papers, Vol. 3, fol. 116 (r and v).

My dear Lord Bishop,

Very best thanks for your letter of December 13th and the correspondence between Archbishop Eidem, Bishop Marahrens and yourself. I am glad to retain the copy of your letter of December 13th to the Archbishop and am returning the other letters.

It is indeed very disappointing that Bishop Marahrens did not see his way to welcome our delegation in December. He was evidently consulting or negotiating with Kerrl, whose newest strong ordinances against the Confessional Church are expressively maintaining the actual relative independence of the intact Churches.[1] What on one side is interpreted as an improvement of the situation, is interpreted by others as a means to divide the confessional front in two parts and to weaken the Churches' strength of resistance. I am decidedly of the opinion that the latter interpretation is the right one. At any rate Bishop Marahrens' negotiation with Kerrl and the relative success he has had will weaken if possible even more the rest of [the] confidence he possessed. It will not make [it] easier for us to deal with the whole Confessional Church of Germany through him.

I agree however that we ought to try once more to fulfil our mandate, but showing to Bishop Marahrens very clearly that a new postponement would mean a definite *refusal to receive the delegation of the foreign Churches*.[2]

Best thanks for your very kind wishes. We both reiterate them very heartily.

Yours very sincerely,

Enclosures.[3]

P.S. As to the date in February, I can arrange at [sic] any time convenient to you, provided that it can be fixed before all too long. The 2nd and 3rd of February I might come to London for an Officers' Committee of the World Y.M.C.A. As soon as I know definitely if I am attending this meeting, I will write to you in order that I might if possible have the opportunity of seeing you.

1   By the 17th ordinance on the implementation of the law to safeguard the German Evangelical Church, Kerrl expanded the church's administration by transferring leadership in the German Evangelical Church, and in the churches where the leadership was not clearly clarified, to state administrative bodies. The 'intact' regional churches of Bavaria, Württemberg and Hannover were not affected by this measure, but from this point they no longer had direct contact with the Brethren councils of the 'destroyed' churches. See Grünzinger and Nicolaisen, *Dokumente*, pp. 149–50.
2   From 'refusal' to the end of the sentence is underlined, apparently by Bell.
3   These now appear to be missing.

Bell to Koechlin, 31 December 1937, Basel UB, NL 37, VI 2 (unpaginated) (carbon); LPL, Bell Papers, Vol. 3, fol. 138.

My dear Koechlin,

I have heard from the Bishop of Copenhagen as well as Archbishop Eidem and yourself, that we four at any rate can go to Germany in February. But I am still waiting to hear from the Bishop of Novi Sad and Archbishop Germanos. I will let you know as soon as anything definite comes.

I should be grateful for any further news you can tell me since the latest attack on the Confessional Church. I do not know what the release of the Pastors at Christmas implies, but I expect nothing very important. I have rather refrained myself from writing to *The Times* about the German Church, mainly because I should be with the delegation to Germany, and it probably would be unwise to write in too critical a tone before going to Germany. I do not know what you feel about this. On the other hand I am not at all sure that in the special circumstances it might not be well for me to try and get the English bishops, who meet in Convocation in the middle of January, to express themselves in a sympathetic Resolution with regard to our earnest sympathy with, and care for, the fellowship of the Germen Evangelical Church. Anything you would like to say to me, and could write to me straight away, would be most valuable.

With the best wishes for the New Year,

Yours sincerely,

P.S. This letter had already been typed when a letter arrived from the Bishop of Novi Sad. He is very anxious to go to Germany with the delegation, and he thinks it probable that he would be free in the second half of February. He has promised to give me full information as soon as possible. The reason for his uncertainty about [the] date has been that the Bishops have been convoked for January 23rd in connection with the election of a new Patriarch, and the Convocation has to deal with the Church situation generally. It may last three weeks, he says, but it might well last a shorter time.[1]

1 On 21 February 1938 Gavrilo Dožić (1881–1950), Metropolitan of Montenegro and the Littoral, became Patriarch Gavrilo V.

1938

19 January	At convocation Archbishop Lang observes the continuing oppression of Christians in Germany.
February	A. S. Duncan-Jones, dean of Chichester, and W. G. Moore, a British Congregationalist, fly to Berlin in an attempt to see the trial of Martin Niemöller.
4 February	Joachim von Ribbentrop is appointed foreign minister.
2 March	Niemöller is acquitted of all but three minor charges and is released. He is promptly taken back into custody and imprisoned in a concentration camp.
5 March	Kerrl orders that all ordinances in the church, excepting those concerned with ritual or doctrine, must now be submitted to the Ministry of Church Affairs for approval.
11 March	*Anschluss* between Germany and Austria. It is confirmed by a plebiscite on 10 April.
20 April	Werner orders that all pastors in the churches of the Old Prussian Union should now swear an oath to Hitler.
9–13 May	Life and Work conference at Utrecht.
July	Angry letters between Bishop Headlam and Bishop Headlam about Martin Niemöller are published in *The Times*, culminating on 26 July in the publication of letters between Bell and Archbishop Lang stating that Headlam's views are not those of the Church of England itself.
17 July	Joint Christian and Jewish intercessions take place across England for the persecuted Jews of Germany.
27 July	Bell makes his maiden speech in the House of Lords, speaking about the refugee crisis.
31 July	The Confessing synod of the Old Prussian Union recommends pastors to take the new oath of loyalty to Hitler.
15 September	The British prime minister, Neville Chamberlain, flies to Germany to see Hitler and prevent war over the Sudeten crisis.
18 September	Nationwide intercessions in Britain for peace.
22 September	Chamberlain and Hitler meet a second time.
27 September	The second Provisional Government of the Confessing Church issues a special order of worship and prayer for peace.
28 September	Archbishop Lang broadcasts a call to prayer.
29 September	International conference at Munich.
30 September	Agreement is announced at Munich.
2 October	A day of national thanksgiving in Britain.
5 October	The German government announces that the passports of Jews will now be stamped with a 'J'.
29 October	The Lutheran bishops, Wurm, Marahrens and Meiser, are summoned by Kerrl. The prayer of September is now criticized

	as treasonable. The bishops consent to sign a new statement of repudiation.
7 November	A German diplomat, Ernst von Rath, is murdered in Paris.
9–10 November	*Reichskristallnacht*, a pogrom against Jews across Germany and Austria, follows.
12 November	Archbishop Lang immediately publishes a letter of protest in the *Times*.

Koechlin to Bell, 7 January 1938, Basel UB, NL 37, VI 2 (unpaginated) (typewritten).

My dear Lord Bishop,

Very best thanks for your letter of December 31st. I am glad the Bishop of Novi Sad seems to be able to join the delegation about middle of February. I am keeping my time free as far as ever possible to be at your disposal at any time which will prove to be possible for our going to Germany.

As to the actual situation in the Confessional Church, I had news this morning through the son of Pastor Hesse in Elberfeld,[1] who is studying here and spent his Xmas holidays at home. The news he brought to me are not good [sic]. It is true that all pastors who had been imprisoned for business of church collections and such kind of things, were released. Fifteen others who are imprisoned for their preaching are not free and have to be judged by a special Court. As to Nicmöller, no one knows what might happen. The Reichsminister for Justice seems to have read the main papers and does not seem to take the risk of calling the Court to judge the case. He is even said to have brought the matter before Hitler without getting from him any decision either to ask for judgement or to release. It is more or less expected that before long, maybe even in January, the Confessional Church might be prohibited.

The financial situation of the Confessional Church seems to become most difficult. In fact Hesse asked me probably on his own initiative if financial help could be got from foreign Churches. Until now the Church refused always to take into consideration such a possibility, because no graver accusation can be thought of in Germany than to be dependent from [sic] foreign money. It would, as far as I can see, also be most difficult for us to help in an efficient way on the long run the German brethren. Evidently this problem has to be thought of and possibility discussed with the German Church leaders.

In view of the Oxford delegation I am rather concerned by other facts,[2] Hesse mentioned to me. The Dahlem people seem to have decided to call a new confessional Synod of the Reich. The main lines of action and policy have already been drafted. Those who wish to attend the Synod, will have to declare their agreement with these principles beforehand. Invitations to attend will go to the intact Churches, but at the same time to oppositional groups inside the intact Churches, f[or] i[nstance] in Württemberg to the so-called *Pfarrersozietät*,[3] attacking Wurm constantly for not going fully with the Dahlem provisional Church Government. New very considerable tension might arise between the Bishops and the Dahlem people. These tensions had already grown in December and if this Confessional Synod will take place, as it is proposed, either in January or beginning of February, possibly before or soon after the Confessional Church will have been prohibited by the State, we might find, to use a very mild expression, a most complicated and embarrassing situation. Pastor Hesse, according to what his son told me, thought that this Confessional Synod might say a word to the foreign Churches and even suggested the possibility that we on our side might try to get into contact with this Synod. The Synod seems to think of pronouncing against Reichschurch-Minister Kerrl a similar judgment the Dahlem Synod has pronounced against Reichsbishop Müller and Dr. Jäger. In December the Confessional Synod of the Rhineland has taken place and seems already to have voted resolutions in the same direction.[4] But until now it has not proved possible to print anywhere these resolutions. They are kept secret until an appropriate publication is assured. I might hear more about it to-morrow, going to see at his request one of my friends somewhere in the Black Forest, who is a member of this Synod.

Under those circumstances I think you are wise not to publish anything in *The Times*. But of course changes in the situation might make a public word from you advisable from one day to the other, in spite of your being a member of the proposed Oxford delegation.

As to a resolution to be voted by the Convocation of the Anglican Bishops, I do not see a decisive reason why such a resolution should not be voted. I wonder however if it would not be more appropriate to ask in some way or another your Pastors and congregations for prayers of intercession. This might of course be implied and even the purpose of your resolution.

Included I am sending you a copy of a pamphlet sent out before Xmas to all Swiss pastors and written by Karl Barth.[5] It has been backed by those whose names are printed on the last page. It is calling the Swiss pastors to make intercession in their Sunday services for the German Church in this most critical situation. I hear that since then about 500 pastors have declared to be in full agreement with the paper. The Council of the Swiss Churches has decided the day before yesterday to write a letter to the different Swiss Churches, to express their agreement with the main purpose of this pamphlet. I am sorry that I cannot translate it for you. I think the Dean of Chichester or someone else will be glad to give you the content of it in some detail.

As mentioned above, I am going to see to-morrow at Königsfeld a friend of mine who is pastor in Düsseldorf. Sunday I have to preach and to give an evening address in Karlsruhe for the Basel Mission. I will see Bishop Kühlewein of Baden and meet also privately some leaders of the confessional group. I hope to get some deeper insight in the situation and will write to you Thursday next after my return. But I felt I ought not to wait in giving you the informations already in my hands.

With kind regards,

yours very sincerely

Enclosure.[6]

1 Helmut Hesse (1916–43): the son of Hermann Albert Hesse (1877–1957), he was a student of Theology between 1935 and 1940. As a member of the Confessing Church he refused to be examined and ordained by commissions of the official Church, instead asking that he be ordained by the consistory of the presbytery of the Confessing parish at Elberfeld. During the war, in consequence of a sermon against the persecution of the Jews, he was detained together with his father and imprisoned at the concentration camp at Dachau. He died in the hospital there, without medical care, on 24 November 1943.

2 The following 'facts' seem to owe more to hopes for what should be now done than anything actual and sound.

3 The *Kirchlich-Theologische Sozietät* in Württemberg was a theological working group that emerged in 1930 from the circle of friends around the pastors Hermann Diem, Heinrich Fausel, Paul Schempp and Richard Widmann. In the Third Reich the group represented the position of the Confessing Church on the basis of the declarations of the Confessing Synods of Barmen and Berlin-Dahlem. With its theological statements,

it repeatedly came into conflict with the Württemberg church leadership under Bishop Wurm, for example in 1938 when the church refused to take the oath of allegiance to Adolf Hitler.
4   The sixth Confessional Synod of the Rhineland took place from 9 to 11 November 1937 at Barmen, but did not pass such resolutions. It protested only against Himmler's degree of 29 August, which had banned theological education by the Confessing Church altogether. It also commented on expulsions and interdictions of preaching by pastors.
5   This memorandum on the German church struggle was a declaration of solidarity for the Confessing Church. Karl Barth had edited, but not written, the text. By the end of March, 532 German Swiss and 173 French Swiss pastors had signed it. At the beginning of Niemöller's trial it was circulated to all cantonal church councils and church officials.
6   Now apparently missing.

Bell to Koechlin, 11 January 1938, Basel UB, NL 37, VI 2 (unpaginated) (carbon).

My dear Koechlin,

Very many thanks for your letter of January 7th. I am most grateful for it. It so happened that yesterday I saw Dr. Rieger, one of the German Pastors in London, a great friend of Böhm. He was off to Germany for two or three weeks and was due to spend a few days with Praeses Koch to-day; and he was going to see Böhm in a few days' time. I took the opportunity of saying that what you had told me made me rather anxious, for it would be very embarrassing for some of the foreign Church friends of the German Evangelical Church – the Confessional Church in its larger meaning – if there were to be a split. Dr. Rieger said that Böhm and Müller of Dahlem were both taking a much more prominent position in the Kassel-Gremium – as he put it, 'playing the first violin'. It was that which gave me the cue to say that there was a danger of there being no second violin, and then I went on to emphasise the good advice which your letter contained.

Dr. Rieger said that there was every hope that the Oxford delegation would be received in February, and Böhm was very anxious it should come. I gave Dr. Rieger a letter for Böhm in which I said, in a way that it might be convenient for him to have unofficially from myself, that the oecumenical Church representatives would have reluctantly to conclude that further postponement would mean an inability to receive. I said that it was now six months since the Oxford Conference had passed the Resolution, and while the delays were, up to a point, understandable, we should have to conclude from a further delay, inability to achieve the Resolution – and that would be very unfortunate from the point of view of the fellowship of the oecumenical Church with the German Church.

I was grateful for your words about a letter to *The Times*, and also about a possible Resolution in Convocation. I had to send in a notice of motion some few days ago, in order to get it on the printed paper. I enclose a copy. I think you will find that it is in the kind of spirit which you would approve, as it is especially a request for intercession.

Dr. Rieger said that the Minister of Justice had received a very large number of letters from all over Germany asking what is the date of Niemöller's trial. He suggested that it would be very useful if letters from foreigners also were addressed the Minister of Justice. His address is: –

Dr. Gürtner
Berlin-Dahlem
Cecilienallee 26.

He also suggested that it would be very useful if a good number of friends from abroad sent congratulations to Martin Niemöller for his birthday, which is on Friday, January 14th. I am going to send him a message. Perhaps you could send him one too. I believe he is 45.[1]

I am compelled to leave this letter for my secretary to sign, as I am away all day after dictating it. If you have further information after your return from Germany I should be most grateful. Rieger told me that at the present moment there are only fifteen pastors now in prison. Of course any hints you could give me with regard to material for my speech would be most acceptable.

Yours ever

1 Niemöller, born in 1892, became forty-six years old on 14 January 1938.

Koechlin to Bell, 12 January 1938, Basel UB, NL 37, VI 2 (unpaginated) (typewritten).

My dear Lord Bishop,
My visit in the Black Forest and in Karlsruhe did not give me the deeper insight in the German situation I had expected. My friend, Pastor Lahusen of Düsseldorf, had for reasons of health not been in a position to attend the Confessional Synod of the Rhineland and had no knowledge of the proceedings, which the young Hesse had given to me. He however told me that Dr. Werner,[1] using to the fullest the administrative and financial powers given to him by the Reichschurchminister, had put in the church office of Düsseldorf a new man coming from outside and having left the Church three years ago.[2] The consistorium had been rebuilt by him, so that the gulf between the local and provincial church government on the one side and on the other side the congregations and pastors standing to by the confessional Church, is wider than ever.

In Karlsruhe I noticed that the situation is relatively quiet and easy, one reason being that the Church is paying all its expenses by church taxes without financial contributions of the State. Most of the pastors are following under the leadership of Bishop Kühlewein more or less a middle line, which however by many is judged to be dangerous, because in school and elsewhere the national-socialist ideology is pushed forward with power and skill. One little incident: Bishop Kühlewein was announced in the papers to have a Xmas sermon December 24th in the evening. He had given in his text and had delivered beforehand his address into a phonograph, the speeches being often delivered by gramophone. Without having received any notice either beforehand or afterwards, without any change having been announced in the papers or in the radio, this speech was replaced by a speech of the well known German-Christian pastor Schneider in Stuttgart.[3] Bishop Kühlewein ought to have protested much more vigorously than he evidently has done. He seems only to have asked the pastors to say [on] December 31st that the speech had not been delivered by him.

I had asked through the representative of the Basel Mission in Karlsruhe to see Bishop Kühlewein and he received me very kindly Sunday morning in his house. But very characteristically he received me together with his daughter, to avoid any officiallity [sic] of my visit and any conversation dealing with any delicate problem. I think all that is very characteristic for him.

His predecessor, Dr. Wurth,[4] who had withdrawn [in] 1933 being then already 72, came to my church service and asked me to see him if possible. I know him for many years and called on him in the afternoon. He is much more the type of a man like Praeses Koch and expressed very frankly his fears as to the future and his anxiety that the attitude of the actual church Government was not strong enough. Being still very vigorous in body and mind, he evidently regrets being not anymore in the front-line and may not be fully objective in his judgement. I have nevertheless the impression that he has a very clear vision of the dangers. He was by the way the man having settled the whole financial business for the Church of Baden in good time on a basis independent from State finances. His Church has now all the profit of this far-sighted policy and has not to fight the very difficult situation the Württemberg Church is financially going through now.

Much more important in view of the Oxford delegation are the news I received yesterday from Dr. Freudenberg,[5] coming from Berlin and asked by Albertz,[6] Asmussen and Böhm to see me. Dr. Freudenberg was until 1933 in the diplomatic service and hold posts in Italy and in the Foreign Office in Berlin. The German Minister in Bern[7] was his colleague and spoke to me the other day in high terms of him. His wife being not fully Aryan, he preferred to leave the service in time and to study theology here with Karl Barth. He told me that the Dahlem people in Berlin are firmly counting with the coming of our delegation in February. As to the postponement of the delegation in December, the Dahlem people do not seem to see quite clear. At any rate they have not given formally their agreement to the postponement and are inclined to think that Bishop Marahrens interpreted the powers given to him all too elastically. They do not see however a reason to fight him on this ground, but they are not willing to allow another postponement in February.

The Kasseler gremium seems to be stronger that I was inclined to think after having seen Hesse. The provisional Church Government does not wish to lose again the contacts created last summer and the possibility of influencing as well the intact Churches as also other church groups going their more or less independent way like the Church of Baden and smaller Churches of Lippe-Detmold etc. As a whole they think the experience made with the Kassel Convention was a good one. The aim of Dahlem is to strengthen its position and influence in the Kasseler gremium and to get at the same time a stronger position also in its fight with the State.

The plan of a Reichschurch Synod has to be judged in the light of this policy. In preparing the Synod, consultations are going on with all those in the Kasseler Convention, the theological and other leadership being with the Dahlem people. A thorough preparation with clearly faced issues seems to be indispensable and some measure of agreement, reached in advance, seems at least highly desirable. Dr. Freudenberg, who has a very balanced and sound judgement, has not heard anything leading him to think that the Dahlem people wish to be unfair to the intact Churches and their Government. The young Hesse had also spoken to him, but Dr. Freudenberg was inclined to think that the father Hesse had always, even in the Dahlem circle, taken an extremely critical attitude. On the other side he was inclined to distrust any move towards united action with the intact Churches and on the other side his aim was to force the intact Churches to go all the way along with the Dahlem people. The young Hesse, as it is the right of youth, might even be more extreme than the father. As the result of my thinking I am inclined to have to-day a more optimistic judgement than when I wrote to you my last letter.

Dr. Freudenberg did not hear anything about financial help. It will at any rate be better not to do anything in this respect before having been in Berlin. He spoke much more of the great anxiety they have in Berlin concerning the training of their students, the situation in the universities becoming worse every month and the secret training of the Confessional Church having become nearly impossible. Even the possibility of studies outside Germany, is in danger to be eliminated by State measures.

Dr. Freudenberg, in speaking of our delegation, insisted that we ought, if ever possible, [to] try to speak to some State Ministers and mainly to approach the Minister of Justice in view of the imprisoned pastors. He hopes we will do the utmost in trying to see personally Niemöller, who by the way will have his birthday Friday next, and a Superintendent Bleeke[8] being imprisoned since June without getting his judgement. Niemöller seems to be in good conditions again. He had asked for permission to spend Xmas with his family at home. But no 'leave' was given to him. He seems to have received in prison about 500 cards and letters for Xmas and 800 for New Year. Being in Berlin, we certainly will not be allowed to ignore his situation.

I of course did not ask Dr. Freudenberg about the advisability of your writing in *The Times* and of a resolution to be taken by the Convocation of Canterbury. My impression is still that you ought to restrain from writing publicly just now, but that a sign of remembrance and especially a call to prayer issued by your Convocation would be a good thing.

Pastor Forell is in Switzerland just now. I am seeing him beginning of next week on his return to Berlin and could give him – using of course much caution – some informations for the Dahlem people, if you wish me to do so. As I wrote to you December 16th, I plan to be in London during the first week of February, arriving in London at the earliest Tuesday afternoon, February 1st. The meetings of the Officers Committee of Y.M.C.A. are fixed for the 2nd and 3rd. I am anxious to be at home for the week-end, but would be glad to arrange my plans so that I might see you, if you on your side see any possibility for it.

With kindest regards,
yours sincerely,

P.S. Your letter of yesterday morning⁹ is just coming in after I had already signed my letter. I think the informations I can give you to-day, are not only more or less confirming Dr. Rieger's impressions, but answering your questions.

As to your resolution, may I simply tell you that whatever I was asked in Germany about the Oxford Message, people wondered at the mention of the Roman-Catholic Church. At present those who suffer most, are certainly the Protestants, the situation of the Catholics having been very much improved since Mussolini's visit. But I can easily understand that a resolution[,] voted at the Convocation of the Anglican Church, can hardly avoid mentioning the German Roman-Catholic Church. I always expressed to our German brethren that the Oxford Conference could not close its eyes in view of what our brethren in the Catholic Church had also to suffer. My only impression is that our evangelical brethren ought to feel that your thoughts are going to them in the first line.

A second question arising in my mind is, if the sentence 'in the persecutions which they are now suffering in the hands of the German State' is quite necessary to be said in such a strong form, if you speak afterwards of imprisonment. The main danger you do not mention, is the skilful propagation of the anti-christian national-socialist beliefs. Compared with that the 'persecutions' are of a relatively small importance. It may be that you cannot and do not wish to change in any way the wording of the resolution. Possibly you could stress these points in your speech.

Excuse me for writing so straight away and without having had time for quiet thought. I wish the letter to leave this evening.

1   Friedrich Werner (1897–1955): lawyer, in 1933 acting president of the Evangelical *Oberkirchenrat* (Church government) of the Church Senate of the Old-Prussian Union, and also member of the Church Office of the German Evangelical Church; between 1937 and 1945 he was the leader of the Evangelical Church of the Old-Prussian Union and of the German Evangelical Church. These positions made him a figure of impressive, but highly problematic authority in the church.
2   i.e. Hans Friedrich (Hansfritz) Sohns (1907–90): Nazi functionary. A participant in the march to the Feldherrenhalle in Munich in 1923, he had worked for the National Socialist party on a full-time basis since 1932, barred from completing his legal studies because of a crime. In 1935 he entered the SS (later rising to the rank of *Sturmbannführer* in 1943). Since 12 November 1937 he had been the head of the finance department in Düsseldorf.
3   Georg Schneider (1902–86): town pastor at Stuttgart, from 1934 a public advocate of radical *Deutsche Christen* views. See Rainer Lächele, *Ein Volk, ein Reich, ein Glaube. Die 'Deutschen Christen' in Württemberg 1925–1960* (Stuttgart: Calwer Verlag, 1994), pp. 91–116, 172–80.
4   Klaus Wurth (1861–1948): president of the Evangelical *Oberkirchenrat* of the regional Church of Baden 1924–33.
5   Adolf Freudenberg (1894–1977): lawyer who worked in the Foreign Office until 1934, but then had to retire from the civil service in view of the Jewish descent of his wife.

He now turned to study theology. Ordained by the Dahlem Brethren Council, he immigrated to London. In January 1939 the Provisional Committee of the WCC (in Process of Formation) entrusted to him the care of the German non-Aryan Christians, work which brought him to Geneva in the summer of 1939 to set up the Council's refugee relief organisation. In 1947 he returned to Germany. See Martin Stöhr and Klaus Würmell (eds), *Juden, Christen und die Ökumene. Adolf Freudenberg 1894–1994. Ein bemerkenswertes Leben* (Frankfurt/M.: Spener, 1994).

6   Martin Albertz (1883–1956): leading member of the Confessing Church and opponent of the Third Reich. From 1931 to 1953 he was superintendent of the church district of Berlin-Spandau, being dismissed by the *Deutsche Christen* Church Government between 1934 and 1945. In 1935 he became a lecturer of New Testament studies at the ecclesiastical High School in Berlin; until 1941 he was head of the examination office of the Confessing Church Berlin-Brandenburg. Between 1936 and 1945 Albertz was a member of the second Provisional Church Government. After 1945 he was professor of Reformed theology at the ecclesiastical High School in Berlin.

7   Otto Carl Köcher (1884–1945): as successor of Ernst Freiherr von Weizsäcker German minister in Bern between 1936 and 1945.

8   Philipp Bleek (1878–1948): since 1935 head of the church district of Saarbrücken. As a nationally minded pastor he sought common ground between National Socialists and Christians, in 1935 signing an agreement with Reich Commissioner Josef Bürckel on the cooperation of state and church. He was, even so, a member of the Confessing Church and an opponent of the *Deutsche Christen*. In accordance with the Reich Council of Brethren's call for a boycott of the church elections and in view of the statement of the Saarbrücken Confessional Synod, Bleek joined other members of the Confessing Church in calling for a boycott of the new elections in a leaflet on 24 June 1937. On 27 June, the day of the elections, he was imprisoned and charged with violations of the *Heimtückegesetz*, but on 28 February he was released and was subsequently expelled from the Saarland – even though proceedings against him continued. After suffering a heart attack in Dortmund, he and his wife secured papers to emigrate to Argentina in 1939. See Klaus Michael Mallmann and Gerhard Paul, *Das zersplitterte Nein. Saarländer gegen Hitler* (Bonn: Dietz, 1989), pp. 25–31; also Joachim Conrad, 'Philipp Bleek (1878–1948)', *Biographisch-Bibliographisches Kirchenlexikon* 23 (2004): cols. 92–102.

9   The letter now appears to be missing.

Koechlin to Bell, 28 January 1938, Basel UB, NL 37, VI 2 (unpaginated) (typewritten).

My dear Lord Bishop,

Best thanks for your letter received this morning.[1] I intended to write to you anyhow to-day, as I have met yesterday afternoon in Freiburg Dr. Reinhold von Thadden, who had asked me to meet him there.

The news he gave me without having a mandate to discuss with me the matter of the delegation, did not give me good prospects for our going to Berlin. He told me, what has been confirmed to me from another source to-day, that the trial of Pastor Niemöller, which is to begin February 7th, will last at least four weeks, possibly longer and that the court will be in session four days of each week. Forty cards have been given out to representatives of the foreign press and rumours seem to go around Berlin 'that the Bishop of Chichester has asked permission to be present and watch the proceedings all along'! Dr. von Thadden expressed the personal opinion that it would not be advisable for a foreign Church delegation to come to Berlin as long as this trial will last, that it would even be very difficult to make during that time the necessary preparation for a reception of the delegation coming soon afterwards. That would mean the earliest date to be end of March, beginning of April.

Furthermore von Thadden said quite explicitly that evidently Bishop Marahrens and even some of his colleagues are against the coming of the delegation. As to the Dahlem people, the situation seems to be very difficult. They have not any more their office [sic]. The sessions of the Provisional Church Government are rendered nearly impossible, because the members residing in Berlin like Böhm, Müller, Albertz have received strict police orders not to leave anymore the city of Berlin and the members of the Provisional Church Government, residing outside Berlin, are not anymore allowed to come to Berlin. Both parts seem to be decided to go against this order, to meet in spite of it and to take the risk of imprisonment. But to receive under those circumstances a foreign Church delegation, is, to say the least, most difficult for the Dahlem people.

I had the clear impression that the whole plan is becoming more and more a cause of great embarrassment for our German brethren. In thinking of the continual postponement, they have the feeling that justice has not been done to our friendly willingness of coming to see them. In thinking of the future, they have the feeling that they ought to do the utmost to make our coming possible, to avoid an unpoliteness, but they do not see the way of acting according to their desires.

Realizing this situation, I underlined the fact that I had no mandate whatever to speak either in your name or in the name of the Archbishop of Uppsala, but that I felt personally that a definite decision had to be reached before long. The delegation had either to be received before Easter or the whole plan had to be liquidated in a way if possible honourable to both parts. With 'honourable' I mean a solution reached in agreement with both parties, leaving no bitterness on either side and allowing to take up the plan of a visit on a new ground without being bound to the Oxford mandate. Accordingly I said to Dr. von Thadden that if the Kassel gremium came to the unanimous opinion that the delegation could not be received very soon, we certainly did not wish to embarrass them and to come contrary to their willingness to receive us. We were anxious to help them and not to make things more difficult for them than they already were. I added that if they would express to us their regret of not being in a possibility of receiving us before Easter, as they should have liked to, and if they would give us some reasons for it, we would certainly be willing to withdraw our proposal of coming to see them, so that the definite position would be taken by us and would not be imposed on them. It ought however to be understood on both sides, that the plan to meet under new circumstances, in a way dictated by the occasion, would still stand. We thought of a Reichs-Church Synod or of some other occasion not to be foreseen now.

In suggesting such a line of action, my point of view was, that before the representatives of the Churches will meet in May in Holland, the plan of the Oxford delegation will have either to have been realized or to have been killed. Better kill it in time and to have the way free for the future, than to stick to it until time and circumstances will have deprived it of reality, meaning and life. Such unrealized and probably unrealisable plans, laying in the way of the future, can be a great hindrance. In the special case such a situation would certainly not be in the interest of the oecumenical movement.

To give up the plan, would certainly mean a lost battle, but could not be decisive from the strategical point of view, if lost under honourable circumstances.

Von Thadden will take up the matter with Dr. Lilje and others on his own personal responsibility. Confronted by the letter of Archbishop Eidem and with this possible solution, our German brethren will have to decide without losing time and we will know where we are.

As to the Reich-Church Synod, it seems to be postponed. The willingness of the Lutheran Council to have it called before long, does not seem to be very great.

I hope that saying to Dr. von Thadden what I said, I did not act against your plan. Before coming to my suggestion, which of course I had not prepared in advance, I very strongly emphasized the desirability of realizing the delegation if ever possible and I pointed up to the end of our conversation to the gravity of the decision to be reached. But: *ultra posse nemo obligatur*.[2]

May I in closing tell you that I am due in London Tuesday next, February 1st, in the afternoon, staying at the Kingsley Hotel, Hart Street, Bloomsbury Square, W.C. 1. The meetings of the Officers Committee of Y.M.C.A. will last until Thursday afternoon about 4 p.m. I intend to leave London Friday evening. May I ask you to send me a word to my hotel, telling me if there is any possibility of meeting you without unduly taking your time?

With kindest regards,
yours very sincerely,

1 The letter now appears to be missing.
2 i.e. nobody is obliged to do more than they can.

Koechlin to Bell, 29 January 1938, Basel UB, NL 37, VI 2 (unpaginated) (handwritten).

My dear Lord Bishop,

Confirming the letter I wrote to you yesterday, I have to forward a message received this morning through a Swiss pastor, who had been in Berlin this week. It is coming from Böhm and his colleagues, who in spite of the police orders had met for a session of the Provisional Church Government in Berlin Tuesday last.

1. The Kasseler Gremium seems to have answered the question of the visit of the Oxford delegation negatively.
2. Nevertheless the Provisional Church Government calls us urgently and heartily to come as soon as possible and to be its guests. The church situation seems to be alarming and a friendly visit of foreign church leaders would mean a great help – especially in view of the Niemöller trial!
3. If the Oxford delegation should not be willing to come of [or: over], finally, the individual visit of church leaders should seriously be considered. One of them at least ought to follow the Niemöller trial, either having received due permission to do so – or getting a card through a Journalist! The presence of a representative of foreign churches would be of great help and value.
4. The confessional church can't any more give work to theologians and pastors being only half-Aryan or having half-Aryan brides or wives. The foreign churches ought to study, if and how those men could get work in churches or missionary work outside Germany.

I am asked to forward to you and through you to the archbishop of Uppsala and the bishop of Copenhagen this message. Personally I don't think it possible for the Oxford delegation to go to Germany under these circumstances. The combination of Oxford delegation and Niemöller trial seems extremely dangerous. My impression that we ought to finish as quickly as possible with the Oxford mandate is strengthened by the fresh news. The question [of] how to act on a new ground is the more urgent.

I have arranged to be absent from Basel if necessary until Sunday or even Monday morning, hoping that such arrangements would make it more easily possible to see you.

With kindest regards
Cordially yours

Koechlin to Bell, 5 February 1938, Basel UB, NL 37, VI 2 (unpaginated) (handwritten).

My dear Lord Bishop,

We just had lunch together: Henriod, Sparring-Petersen[1] and I. Petersen is taking your letter and going today to Berlin in order to give the necessary advice to Blauenfeld (?)[2] and to see Dr. Lilje and possibly Böhm about the question of the delegation. He will report to you direct as soon as he will be in Denmark again. So that you might hear the latest news. I phoned with Pastor Rieger. He told me our brethren in Berlin to be very confident [sic] in view of the Niemöller-trial. As to the Oxford delegation he said that the Provisional Church Government had been anxious to have the visit of the 'delegation', bishop Marahrens and his followers didn't wish to have it, but were anxious to have 'the men'. Both finally agreed to receive us and to see how best to deal with us, once we would be in Berlin. I understand now the contradictory impressions I had in hearing from both sides and I am inclined to let things go as they are, hoping they will develop all right. On this question too Petersen will report to you.

May I, before leaving the English shores[,] thank you once more for receiving me so kindly in Chichester. The evening of yesterday and the sunny morning of today around the walls of your palace and the towers of your beautiful cathedral will long and gratefully be remembered.

Yours cordially

1   Gunnar Sparring-Petersen (1900-94): Danish theologian and ecumenist; since 1923 secretary of the Danish department of the World Alliance for promoting Friendship through the Churches and since 1937 member of its Executive Committee. From 1940 he was a member of the Board of the Nordic Ecumenical Institute at Sigtuna.
2   J.V. Blauenfeld: Danish pastor at Berlin, whom Bell had asked to attend the Niemöller trial as a representative of the ecumenical movement.

Koechlin to Bell, 11 February 1938, Basel UB, NL 37, VI 2 (unpaginated) (carbon).

My dear Lord Bishop,

I received yesterday quite unexpectedly the visit of Dr. Lilje, who came in the name of the Kasseler gremium with the decisions taken by it concerning the Berlin visit of representatives of foreign Churches. He also gave me the latest news about the Niemöller trial.

As to the *visit in Germany*, he told me that the reason for the putting off in December had been that Dr. von Bodelschwingh and Dr. Breit looked forward to have most important deliberations with Reichschurchminister Kerrl at exactly that date.[1] Though the majority of the gremium had been of the opinion that our visit ought not to be put off, Dr. Breit asked so strongly to think of his and Dr. von Bodelschwingh's responsibility, that they gave way. In the meantime the situation has become more difficult. The Government has issued an ordinance stating that the Führer (Hitler) did not wish the Germans to speak outside Germany about the German Church question. This ordinance was issued to stop all lectures of German theological professors and Church leaders in foreign countries. The Niemöller trial is aggravating the situation even more.

Under those circumstances the Kasseler gremium *unanimously* decided a fortnight ago, about the time I saw Dr. von Thadden, to propose a change in the character of the visit. It should not anymore be a visit of the delegation of the Oxford Conference, but a meeting arranged to study how the cooperation of Germany with the oecumenical Movement could be arranged. They have especially at heart to study with us the question of the German attendance at the Utrecht Conference to be held May 9th to 13th. In order to make it evident that the character of the visit has been changed, they think that the personalities coming to Germany ought to be chosen accordingly. They are anxious to have Dr. Oldham as a member of the delegation and are very anxious too to have Archbishop Eidem. They also thought of the Bishop of Copenhagen and of yourself, though they realize that it might not be quite agreeable for you to come to Germany in an official capacity after all the attacks you had to undergo in the German press and after the recent visit of the Dean of Chichester in Berlin, which has not rendered your personal situation in Germany easier.

I do not know if Dr. Oldham will be in a possibility of coming. I hope very much indeed he will. But if so, he must of course have the liberty of choosing those to work with him in Germany on a question particularly entrusted to him by all the Churches. I do not need to say, that I am very willing to withdraw myself in order to give him the possibility of another and better choice.

A last remark was that in any case the visit should include the name of a representative English Church leader, the more as our German brethren still think of a meeting, to which they hope to invite some representatives of the Ministry for foreign affairs and possibly other people.

As to the date, Dr. Lilje proposed March 15th. That would suit our German friends best. It would, that is his hope, also facilitate Archbishop Eidem's coming. It would also give time to settle the relationship between the Kasseler gremium and Bishop Heckel. Bishop Marahrens has pressed on him last week a solution quite honourable to him, but making it perfectly clear that the responsibilities and decisions were laying with the Kasseler gremium and not with him and his office. A second meeting with him ought to have taken place this week, Bishop Wurm and Bishop Meiser being present, but Heckel very characteristically has written that the political situation had in the meantime changed so much, that this meeting had become useless!

For Bishop Marahrens and the Kasseler gremium there is still a difficulty in the fact that Heckel has through Schönfeld and Dr. Oldham a direct channel for dealing with the oecumenical Movement, without taking any notice of the German Church itself and its leaders. A word of warning to Schönfeld, coming from your side, would be felt to be a real help. If the German Church can settle directly without foreign interference its relationship with Heckel, then and then only a normal functioning of oecumenical relationship, even in research work, can take place.

May I add that the Kasseler gremium will certainly have Heckel and his office present at the deliberations with representatives of the foreign Churches.

If the date of March 15th should not be acceptable, it could be, but only as a second possibility, March 8th.

Lilje, who came to Basel yesterday morning at 11 o'clock, proceeded at 4 o'clock to Wengen, where he is the guest of a Swiss pastor. He will stay there about 10–12 days and then come to Basel again. He should like to get through me the reaction to his proposal and if possible the definite answer about our coming visit, to take it with him to Germany. During his stay in Switzerland, he is in easy reach of Basel. I can consult him by phone or otherwise. Would you kindly in consultation with Dr. Oldham take the necessary decisions and let me know if possible before the end of next week.

As to the *Niemöller trial*, the Dean of Chichester will probably have given you important details. Lilje was very pessimistic. He said that the second day, when he was still, together with Diestel, Böhm and Breit, allowed to attend the proceedings, the attitude of the three judges had been very unkind to Niemöller. The first day the attitude had been much kinder. Evidently the judges had received instructions to be stricter. And then the fact that they yielded to the proposal of the attorney to exclude the members of the Confessional Church, is very grave. The attorney based his proposal on an article of *Le Temps* and stated, that only people sitting in the room could have given to *Le Temps* the facts published. In consequence the representatives of the Confessional Church had to be excluded. The lawyers of Niemöller pointed to the fact that the article in question was dated January 24th (!) and containing only facts known by everyone. The article had nothing to do with the fact of having attended the deliberations of February 7th. In spite of that the Court decided as it was asked to do by the official attorney. Also on a proposal of the attorney, all those present got a command of absolute silence, an imprisonment of 6 months being fixed in case this command being not obeyed to. Niemöller's lawyers, having no possibility of any other protest, decided to protest in laying down their mandates in order to make it absolutely clear that the proceedings were so unfair as to make it impossible for a lawyer to carry on his grave responsibility. Niemöller and his wife expressively [or: expressly?] agreed with it in spite of the fact that the situation is becoming for Niemöller much more difficult. Now Niemöller is alone in the court, all the galleries being full of Party and government officials and mainly of all those having in many ways been the men representing the attacks against the leaders of the Confessional Church. All the Government and Party pressure is in such a way necessarily exercised in a terrible way on the poor three judges.

Lilje agreed that I should rectify the wrong news published evidently under the influence of the Propaganda Ministry in our papers, but after having thought of it, I do not dare to expose him to the dangers involved, as the Secret Police certainly will know sooner or later that he has passed through Basel for his stay in Switzerland. But if the real facts could be brought to an influential paper before long, I think that it would be a good thing. I would be very grateful to have your reaction on that point.

1 See report of the conversation of Kerrl, Muhs and Stans with Bodelschwingh and Breit in the Reichschurch Ministry, 2 December 1937, in Gertraut Grünzinger and Carsten Nicolaisen (eds), *Dokumente zur Kirchenpolitik des Dritten Reiches*, vol. IV, 1937–39 (Gütersloh: Christian Kaiser Verlag, 2000), pp. 132–41.

Bell to Koechlin, 14 February 1938, Basel UB, NL 37, VI 2 (unpaginated) (carbon).

My dear Koechlin,

I am most grateful for your letter of February 11th received to-day. I heard from Sparring-Petersen, but he did not put anything very definite in his letter, except that he had seen the Dean of Chichester and that means would be taken to keep one informed from time to time. He did not mention the delegation. The Dean of Chichester had seen Otto Dibelius and reported to me what you have said, viz. that the delegation was very definitely wanted, that it should be private, that its object should be how the German Church can be related to the Oecumenical Movement in the future, that it should take place in March, and could all be done in a couple of days.

I am most grateful for your very much fuller account, after your talk with Lilje. I am writing at once to Oldham asking him to take the matter up this end and to make sure of being able to go himself. I am afraid that March 8th and March 15th are both impossible dates for me, owing to other engagements which I cannot escape. But in any case I think that probably it is wiser that in all the circumstances I should postpone coming to Germany till a little later, making a more personal visit, so to speak. I am telling Oldham exactly what you say about an English Church leader, and everything else. I am also writing at once to Archbishop Eidem and to the Bishop of Copenhagen. Anything that Oldham says in reply I will let you know at once.

Yours ever,

Koechlin to Bell, 21 February 1938, Basel UB, NL 37, VI 2 (unpaginated) (typewritten).

My dear Lord Bishop,

I have still to thank you for your kind letter of February 14th. Soon afterwards I got two letters from Dr. Oldham dated February 15th and 16th. You are finding the reaction of Dr. Lilje to all these three letters in my letter to Dr. Oldham, whose copy I enclose for your information.

May I give you the wording of Dr. Lilje concerning your visit in Germany:

> I think the proposal of the Lord Bishop to come later in a more private capacity instead of joining the delegation is excellent. Possible misinterpretations of his coming at the present moment are avoided. It is becoming very clear that nothing is changed in our close relationship to him and we will not seem to have yielded to stronger influences from outside. We would dislike very much indeed to see the name of a Church leader, who has done so much for us, simply disappear from the list of those visiting us. The first visit (the delegation) will certainly leave many questions unanswered, which will have to be cleared at a later moment. I feel certain that this will be the case for some questions concerning our own Church situation (Heckel etc.).

May I add to this a personal word? You know how strong my feeling always has been against your not being yourself one of the leaders of the delegation. Even now I do not like thinking of your postponing your going to Berlin. On the other side the impression is getting stronger on me that owing to all you have done to help our German brethren, any pressure to bring you in a most delicate and difficult situation, would be ungrateful and unfair. For this main reason I can agree to the new proposal. To know that you will before long also go to Germany with the possibility of approaching some people you hardly would have been able to approach just now, is of real comfort, because I feel certain of a special efficiency of such a personal private visit of yours.

As Dr. Oldham has asked me to join him when he will go to Germany, I accepted and hope to be of some help to him and to those joining the delegation.

With my very best regards, I am,
cordially yours

Enclosure:
Koechlin to Oldham, 21 February 1938, Basel UB, NL 37, VI 2 (unpaginated).

Copy

My dear Dr. Oldham,
In the light of a letter received this morning from Dr. Lilje, I cabled to you:

Visit Berlin end March even early April possible. Lilje leaving Switzerland Thursday.

In his letter he is emphasizing the following points:

1. There seem to be no difficulties whatever for our German brethren to receive our visit in the second half of March. It might even be easier for them at that date. Even the first week of April would be possible, though the nearness of Easter week would render it to many of the pastors more difficult to be at our disposal.
2. The thought of the Bishop of Chichester, to come possibly later in a more private capacity, is heartily welcomed, because there will still exist many questions to be settled after the first more official meeting, and the Bishop of Chichester, if such a later visit would be announced, would still appear to be the trusted leader to deal with the German Church in the name of the other Churches. The German brethren are most anxious to avoid every impression as if, to please party circles, it would have been suggested to the Bishop of Chichester to stay away.
3. Your own presence at this first meeting is under those circumstances most needed. Lilje is of the opinion that the importance of our visit for the continuance of the work of the World Council is such, that even a high demand on you would be justified by it.
4. If the Archbishop of York could make it possible to come to Germany, it would be most important. In this connection Lilje is thinking of the possibility of approaching Ribbentrop in London when he is taking his leave,[1] not only to speak to him of the proposed visit, but also to get some clear understanding about the possibility of oecumenical relationship of the German Evangelical Church. Possibly Lilje thinks such a question or remark could also be brought forward by personalities like Lord Halifax or Lord Lothian.[2]
5. Lilje still agrees that my joining the delegation could help your task.

As to the exact date, may I tell you that the two weekends Saturday/Sunday March 19/20 and April 2/3 would be most difficult for me, but in both cases I could manage, if necessary, to be in Berlin early Monday morning.

Lilje is coming here on his way home Thursday early afternoon. The more the questions involved in the delegation can be cleared before that time, the better.

You won't mind my sending a copy of this letter to the Bishop of Chichester for his information.

With my best regards,
yours very sincerely,
sig. A. Koechlin.

1   On 4 February 1938 Ribbentrop succeeded Neurath as Reich Foreign Minister.
2   Philip Henry Kerr, 11th Marquess of Lothian (1882–1940), known as Philip Kerr until 1930: British politician, newspaper editor and diplomat who showed favour to the Hitler regime until 1938. A leading supporter of Appeasement, his outlook altered in 1939, the year in which he became ambassador to the United States. He died only a year later. See J. R. M Butler, *Lord Lothian, Philip Kerr (1882-1940)* (London: Macmillan, 1960).

Koechlin to Bell, 25 February 1938, Basel UB, NL 37, VI 2 (unpaginated) (typewritten).

My dear Lord Bishop,

Dr. Oldham, to whom you had passed my letter of February 11th, was kind enough to correspond with me on the possibilities for a visit to Germany, in order to discuss there with the Church leaders the future oecumenical relationship of the German Evangelical Church. Unfortunately considerable difficulties seem to stand in the way of realizing the plan in a way which could really meet as well the difficulties as the desires of our German brethren.

Discussing yesterday with Dr. Lilje, who has left again for Germany, the whole situation and all the implications involved, we came to the conclusion that the best, possibly the only way to come in good time to a clear understanding of the situation, would be that I, if possible together with Lilje, should discuss with yourself and Dr. Oldham the whole problem. There are very delicate and confidential aspects of it, which cannot without risks of different kind be dealt with by writing.

For this reason I am asking Dr. Oldham in a letter leaving Basel by the same mail, to grant to me the possibility of meeting with him and yourself at a date convenient to both of you. In writing to you these few lines, I simply wish to give you this direct information and to urge upon you personally to be kind enough to give favourable consideration to our proposal and to make your presence at such a meeting possible.

With kindest regards
yours very sincerely

Koechlin to Bell, 5 March 1938, Basel UB, NL 37, VI 2 (unpaginated) (typewritten).

My dear Lord Bishop,

Best thanks for your lines of February 28th.[1] In the meantime I announced to Dr. Oldham by cable my coming to London Thursday afternoon, hoping to meet him and yourself any time in the evening after 5 o'clock. I am staying at the Rubens Hotel, Buckingham Palace Road. For different reasons I ought to leave again either during the night or Friday morning by air.[2]

In Swiss Church circles the new turn of Niemöller's trial is causing much anxiety.[3] Special services of intercession are prepared and everyone expects that the oecumenical

Movement might not lose its opportunity of acting in every way possible. It is especially expected that a visit of foreign Church leaders, asking for information in Berlin and trying to see Niemöller, might take place without delay. Under these circumstances this visit is getting a new aspect, which we will have to discuss very thoroughly Thursday next.

A leading pastor of the Dahlem wing in Württemberg has just come to see me in order to tell me that at this juncture the Confessional Church is looking for our help and is expecting the visit of churchmen whose name and position is carrying weight in Government circles of Germany.

May I confidentially in this connection share with you the main anxiety Lilje and myself had when discussing a week ago the last letter of Dr. Oldham? Though he was willing and even desirous to go himself to Berlin in order to discuss the question of the World Council with the German Church leaders, he let us feel that the state of his health did not allow him in good conscience to make the journey and that he was needed at any moment in London in view of possible difficulties concerning the establishment of cooperation of the English Churches being the essential condition of any larger scheme. He pointed to Dr. Mott's visit in April and did not seem to take into account sufficiently the real dangers existing in Germany and consequently on the Continent, even for the proposed World Council.

His final proposal was that William Paton[4] and Eric Fenn[5] would be in Berlin end of April anyhow and that under those circumstances his own presence would not be necessary. He did not say a word about the Archbishop of Uppsala or the Bishop of Copenhagen, in spite of the fact that even looking over the scheme of the World Council it would be essential to have these outstanding Lutheran leaders present in Berlin, in order to come to a satisfactory solution. It seems to me very evident that, looked at from every angle, it might be absolutely necessary to try our best to have these men present in Berlin. A delegation consisting of Paton, Fenn and myself is simply inacceptable [sic] for Berlin and I have to say myself that under these circumstances I would not be willing to go.

Under those circumstances there was no hope to come to a clear understanding and to a sound solution by correspondence. Hence the proposal to come to London for personal consultation. Hence my desire to have you present at such a meeting. I wish of course to be very fair to Dr. Oldham, the more as I have for him the highest and affectionate regards, but I know that, having taken at heart a responsibility of central importance, he is inclined to follow all too exclusively this one line without taking sufficiently into account other questions and aspects, as important and decisive as they might be.

Pardon, if I am sharing with you confidentially this my anxiety. As it will hardly be possible to see you before we meet together with Dr. Oldham, I was however anxious, especially under the new circumstances, to let you know what I have at heart and to allow you to give to it some thought.

With my best regards. yours very sincerely,

1. This letter now appears to be missing.
2. Bell, Koechlin, Lilje and Oldham had planned the delegation that Thursday night. See Bell to Henriod, 14 March 1938, in Besier, *Intimately Associated*, p. 61.
3. The Niemöller trial ended on 2 March. He was sentenced to a detention of seven months, and as he had already been held in custody for that long the sentence was practically equivalent to an acquittal. But Niemöller was immediately sent to Sachsenhausen concentration camp as the 'personal prisoner of the Führer'. Bell now worked to organize world-wide protests across the Churches. See Andrew Chandler, *British Christians and the Third Reich: Church, State and the Judgement of Nations* (Cambridge: Cambridge University Press, 2022), pp. 209–12, 222–3.
4. William 'Bill' Paton (1886–1943): missionary and ecumenist; first secretary of the National Christian Council of India, 1922–6. He then succeeded J. H. Oldham as Secretary of the International Missionary Council (1927–43), as Oldham became more involved with the Life and Work movement. Paton would play a vital role in the creation of the World Council of Churches, in 1939 becoming secretary alongside W. A. Visser 't Hooft. His premature death in 1943, at the height of his career, came as he was participating in discussions about the reconstruction of Europe.
5. Eric Fenn (1899–1995): English Presbyterian minister; in 1937–9 assistant to J. H. Oldham in organizing 1937 Oxford Conference; 1939–45 assistant director in the Department of Religion at the BBC.

Bell to Koechlin, 25 March 1938, Basel UB, NL 37, VI 2 (unpaginated) (carbon).

My dear Koechlin,

This just to say you that the delegation is on a fair way to completion. The following are ready to go:

Dr. Koechlin
The Bishop of Copenhagen
The Bishop of Visby[1]
Dr. J. H. Oldham
The Bishop of Chichester.

Unfortunately Archbishop Germanos cannot come as our Easter Week is the Orthodox Passion Week involving many services. I expect that I shall hear that the same reason will prevent the Bishop of Novi Sad. The Bishop of Visby has been deputed by the Archbishop of Uppsala. He says that he could not come if the delegation were postponed, but he could come in those days after Easter.

So would you, of your kindness, arrange with Lilje in such a way that the delegation should arrive in Berlin on the afternoon of Wednesday, April 20th, with a view to a private meeting together and consultation with one or two of the Germans. I take it that Thursday, April 21st, is the day of the formal conference, and that Friday, April 22nd, will be given up to informal talks, and that we leave that evening or next morning. Would Lilje be able to arrange for our hotel accommodation, or whatever other accommodation he thinks right?

Yours ever,

1   Torsten Ysander (1893–1960): bishop of the Diocese of Visby, 1936–47, and bishop of the Diocese of Linköping, 1947–59.

Koechlin to Bell, 29 March 1938, Basel UB, NL 37, VI 2 (unpaginated) (typewritten).

My dear Lord Bishop,
   Best thanks for your letter of March 25th received Saturday morning. I have written at once to Berlin to let Lilje know its content. In order to be as cautious as possible, my secretary has written by hand and signed the letter, has addressed it to the private address of Dr. Lilje's secretary, given to me expressively for such a purpose, and has posted it in German territory in Freiburg, so that it might not be regarded as a foreign letter to be suspected by the police.
   I offered to meet Lilje or someone personally in Germany, so that we might fix every detail in advance and that the members of the delegation might reach Berlin as prepared as possible for their task, I will of course write again as soon as news from Berlin will have reached me.

With best regards I am,
very sincerely yours,

Koechlin to Bell, 8 April 1938, Basel UB, NL 37, VI 2 (unpaginated) (typewritten).[1]

My dear Lord Bishop,
   Henriod came back from Berlin to Switzerland Wednesday noon.[2] I could not see him, as I was not in Basel, but had a conversation with him by phone. His news after having seen Lilje are as following.
   The delegation consisting of yourself, the Bishop of Copenhagen, the Bishop of Visby, Dr. Oldham and myself is expected in Berlin in the afternoon of Wednesday, April 20th.[3] The meetings to be arranged with German Church leaders will all have a private character, as it does not seem possible to arrange something on an official and larger scale. Our German friends however look forward to arrange on a small scale for Thursday, April 21st, a meeting to which a representative of the Foreign Office will be invited. Heckel will probably not be present at the meetings, as he is refusing to see us together with representatives of the Dahlem wing. We will have to see him separately.
   Bishop Marahrens is trying to clear the situation with Bishop Heckel and to convince him to be present at a common meeting, but it is doubtful if he will be successful.[4] After having settled with Heckel this delicate question, Bishop Marahrens will call on the Foreign Office, speak to it of our coming and invite it to meet us. As soon as that will be done, I shall receive further news.
   Lilje did not say anything of the hotel where we could stay together. I am writing to him again at once, to remind him of this particular question.
   As to Pastor Niemöller, Henriod told me that he is under [a] very severe regime, alone in a prisoner's room, allowed only to receive one letter every fortnight. A letter

of Mrs. Niemöller had been sent back, because Niemöller had already received a letter some days before. Dr. Schacht[5] and some generals have asked Hitler to change this state of things – but in vain. Again and again pressure is exercised on Niemöller to sign a promise not to speak anymore publicly, but he is refusing. The whole treatment evidently is trying to bring him to a state of health and mind, in which he might at last sign such a paper. Otto Dibelius and many churchmen not belonging to the Dahlem people, are asking the foreign Churches to continue to manifest their sympathy and to call for prayers for Niemöller, so that his name might constantly be mentioned in the Churches abroad. The hope of German national-socialist circles evidently is that he might be forgotten and that the Austrian, the plebiscite-questions[6] etc. might help to fulfil this end.

I am sending a copy of this letter to Henriod, so that he might correct possible misinterpretations of his phone and complement what might seem necessary to him.

With kindest regards,
yours very sincerely,

1   Also in Besier, *Intimately Associated*, pp. 64–5.
2   See Henriod's report on his journey through Austria, Germany and the Scandinavian countries in his letter to Bell, 8 April 1938; ibid., pp. 66–70.
3   See Bell's Memorandum on his visit to Berlin and Hannover in Chandler, *Brethren in Adversity*, pp. 144–9.
4   See Marahrens' letter to Heckel, 4 April 1938 in Boyens, *Kirchenkampf und Ökumene*, Vol. I, pp. 375–6.
5   Hjalmar Schacht (1877–1979): banker, politician and co-founder of the German Democratic Party in 1918; president of the Reich bank, 1924–9 and 1933–9, and Reich Minister of Economics, 1934–37. See John Weitz, *Hitler's Banker. Hjalmar Horace Greeley Schacht* (Boston: Little, Brown, 1997).
6   On 13 March 1938 German troops invaded Austria in an act of forcible annexation. On 10 April a plebiscite confirmed Hitler's triumph by allegedly securing 99 percent of the votes cast.

Bell to Koechlin, 9 April 1938, Basel UB, NL 37, VI 2 (unpaginated) (carbon).

My dear Koechlin,
I am very grateful for your letter about the visit to Berlin.
This is to say that I am most anxious to know what hotel you are going to stay in. I have already had one letter asking me if I know[,] and I must let the Bishop of Visby and the Bishop of Copenhagen know during the next few days, for they have to make their plans. Would it be too much trouble for you to telegraph name and address of hotel and possibly also the nearest station. I am leaving Chichester on Saturday to spend Easter and the two following days in Bruges with my wife. I am proposing to catch the Tuesday night train from Bruges to Berlin, but I could catch the Tuesday morning train if that were more useful from the point of view of talks before our Conference.

I am dreadfully disturbed about what you say about Niemöller. I am asking the Archbishop of Canterbury to write to Ribbentrop direct, as Ribbentrop called on him when he was saying good-bye in London a month ago. I cannot very well write to *The Times* myself before I go to Berlin, but I am trying to get other people to make a stir.

Yours ever,

Koechlin to Bell, 11 April 1938, Basel UB, NL 37, VI 2 (unpaginated) (carbon).

My dear Lord Bishop,

Best thanks for your letter of April 9th received this morning. It came in together with a letter of Lilje's secretary with the following content.

Our German friends are wanting a real communication that they may count on our coming. 'We should like to know it officially (Augustus)'. As Augustus is the nick-name of Bishop August Marahrens of Hannover, it means that the time has come to announce [to] him officially, directly and by post our coming to Berlin. As Bishop Marahrens wishes to invite for one of the meetings representatives of the Foreign Office, he wishes evidently to show a letter written officially to him, certainly in careful terms, allowing him to underline the fact that all initiative and responsibility is lying with the foreign Church leaders and not with him. I am of course leaving it to you to write to him.

As to the hotel, the letter says: 'I am advising you to go to the Christliches Hospiz, Mittelstrasse 5. I have inquired there and made sure that for all of you there will be rooms on Wednesday afternoon (definite)'. This word 'definite' evidently means that our rooms are definitely booked. I know the Hospice at the Mittelstrasse, a very good and quiet place in the centre of the city, close to the University, in a street running parallel and nearest to the *Linden*. The situation is such that it does not matter at which station you arrive. The only difficulty might be that Wednesday is the birthday of Hitler and that due to some military or other demonstration the circulation might be interrupted. But it is also possible that Hitler might spend his birthday in Vienna and call there for that date the new Reichstag of the whole of Germany 'elected' yesterday.

As to the programme the letter says: 'The plans for our visit are very simple. Wednesday evening we should like to spend the time personally with you. Thursday morning free for work. In the afternoon we are having tea and are hoping that we might succeed to invite for it some prominent visitors.' That means that reaching Berlin Wednesday in the afternoon is time enough. And the tea party with prominent visitors means certainly the meeting with some official representatives of the Foreign Office, maybe of the Party. I tried to cover the main points in cabling you this morning as follows: 'Christian Hospice Mittelstrasse 5 booked Wednesday afternoon, centre city, station irrelevant. Official announcement to Marahrens of our coming expected.'

As to Niemöller, I have heard that for some reason he had to be brought to the Gestapo prison at Alexanderplatz and that there Mrs. Niemöller was allowed to see her husband. I do not know anything of a leave he had to go home and I do not believe that that happened. As to the rumor of his being transferred to a fortress, it was mentioned in our papers, but in no ways confirmed. I hope we might see a possibility of doing something for him in Berlin, at least to call on Mrs. Niemöller.

Another concern in connection with our Berlin visit is the attitude of Heckel. As I wrote to you in my last letter, Henriod pointed to the fact that we would have to see him separately. My feeling is that we ought at all costs to avoid calling on him. If we ought to see him, he ought to call on us. This as well as other delicate questions might arise in Berlin, but cannot be settled before we meet there.

May I add that I am leaving Basel Tuesday night, reaching Berlin Wednesday 3.19 p.m. I am writing to Lilje to-day the time of my own arrival and that you are probably arriving already with the night train from Aachen and am asking that he might arrange to come in touch as soon as possible with those coming in.

I am glad to know that you are looking forward to some days of rest in the wonderful old Bruges. In view of Lilje's programme it is certainly not necessary that you are travelling before Tuesday night.

With kindest regards,
yours very sincerely,

Bell to Koechlin, 13 April 1938, Basel UB, NL 37, VI 2 (unpaginated) (carbon).

My dear Koechlin,

Many thanks for your letter of April 11th. It crossed one from me. I hope that the letter which I have written to Marahrens[1] was of the right kind.

I am very glad that all is in order about the Hospice at the Mittelstrasse. I shall arrive on Wednesday morning about 8 o'clock and will go straight to the Hospice. If Lilje or any other friends would like to call there after breakfast, it would be very nice. My wife and I are going to Bruges early on Saturday. We shall be there for two or three days. I hope very much that the Hitler Birthday Celebrations will take place in Vienna, rather than in Berlin.

As to Heckel, I think he certainly ought to come and see us and, of course, he ought to be associated with other Church Leaders. I suggest that our proper line is to expect Heckel to be present at the ordinary Conference or one of them, and if he is not there to let it be known that if he cares to come and see us, that will be alright. But that we should not go to see him, unless the other Church Leaders definitely desire to do so. That is my first reaction, so to speak. I hope there will be no difficulty now.

I am looking forward very much to seeing you on Wednesday.[2]

Yours very sincerely

1   See Bell to Marahrens, 12 April 1938 in Besier, *Intimately Associated*, p. 74.
2   The long-planned meeting with representatives of the German Church took place on 20–22 April 1938, but the delegation consisted only of Bell and Koechlin, who had long discussions with representatives of the Confessing Church, especially Otto Dibelius and Hans Böhm, and also met Heckel. They also visited Else Niemöller and emphasized that Christians all over the world were united in intercession and solidarity with her husband. On the return journey they met Marahrens in Hannover. See Chandler, *Brethren in Adversity*, pp. 144–9.

Koechlin to Bell, 28 April 1938, Basel UB, NL 37, VI 2 (unpaginated) (typewritten).

My dear Lord Bishop,

I hope you reached Friday night allright Bruges again and will have enjoyed further good holidays together with Mrs. Bell. I had to change trains at Fulda and enjoyed there very much a stay of nearly two hours, giving me the opportunity of seeing this great centre of German catholic life, the place of St. Bonifazius, the great missionary of Germany. I had special pleasure in seeing the delightful old little chapel built in the 9th century.[1] Just before midnight I was at home again, grateful in more than one respects for the three days spent in Germany. It was a great privilege for me to share with you in the oecumenical task we had to fulfil and I wish to thank you for all your kindness and confidence. Though some impressions were rather depressing, I think we could render to our German brethren and to the oecumenical movement a valuable service in going to Berlin and Hannover. To have this new insight in the situation, will be of great value for me and, as I hope, for the decisions to be taken in Utrecht.

May I mention to you that Hartenstein has received from Dr. Knak in Berlin a letter concerning the Gossner Mission question.[2] The German Evangelical Missionary Council is alarmed by the attitude of the Gossner Mission. The council was already to discuss with Gossner ways and means to help them and expected that two representatives of the Council would be invited to meet with the Committee of the Gossner Mission. Instead of receiving such an invitation, Lokies[3] is writing that they do not need any more such a common sharing of the difficulties as the oecumenical Movement, especially as yourself and Professor Keller have proved to be willing to help the Gossner Mission. Under those circumstances they could do without the help of the German Evangelical Missionary Council.

The difficulties of all German Missions are growing. These difficulties can only be overcome if the solidarity between them is maintained. Special arrangements of one of the Missions with either foreign countries or an oecumenical Movement can create the gravest difficulties for all German Missions. Some aspects of the missionary problem are even more delicate than the Church problem. I therefore venture to suggest to you to be in this matter as cautious as ever possible. Knak and Professor Schlunk are complaining that the Gossner Mission entered in negotiations through Schönfeld with Keller and yourself without saying one word of such a possibility to the colleagues of other Missions and to the Council to which they belong. Though it would have been an unaccustomed proceeding, it would have been more natural to use the channel of the I.M.C. to solve this missionary problem. Probably the Gossner Mission purposely has avoided to do so. I am writing to you after having discussed the matter with Hartenstein, who is agreeing with this letter.

Looking forward with great pleasure to seeing you again in Utrecht, I am

yours very sincerely,

---

1   i.e. St Michael (Michaelskirche), one of the oldest churches in Germany, built in 818–22.

2   The Gossner Mission had been founded in 1836. Dedicated to the training of missionaries, and based in Berlin, it was – unlike the other missionary societies – non-denominational. Mutual collaboration never proved easy.

3   Hans Lokies (1895–1982): German theologian, co-founder of the Pastors Emergency League and leading member of the Confessing Church. Lokies had been inspector of the Gossner Mission in 1927 and he became its director in 1938, remaining in that position until 1961. He was head of the school board of the Confessing Church and after 1942 he served as head of the German Federation for Christian-evangelical Education.

Bell to Koechlin, 30 April 1938, Basel UB, NL 37, VI 2 (unpaginated) (carbon).

My dear Koechlin,

I am most grateful for your letter of the 28th April. I did so very much enjoy our visit together to Berlin and Hannover. Far more thanks are due to you from me, than the other way. I am seeing Oldham on Wednesday, and will give him an account of our visit. But you will be able to supplement it in various ways at Utrecht, where, I am afraid, it is almost certain I cannot be, owing to the very heavy programme to which I am absolutely committed here.

I am very much worried about the Gossner Mission and Schönfeld. I think that he and Lokies are trying to use us most unfairly. I enclose a letter which I have just received from him. Please show it to Hartenstein, or anybody else you think relevant. I also enclose a copy of my letter to Schönfeld.

Yours most sincerely,

[Two Enclosures]

Bell to Schönfeld, 30 April 1938, Basel UB, NL 37, VI 2 (unpaginated) (carbon).

My dear Schönfeld,

Many thanks for your letter of April 28th. I note what you say about the Gossner Mission. I do not know anything about any proposals which may have come from the S.P.G.[1] But I do not think the situation as between the S.P.G., and the Gossner Mission in terms of future collaboration, can be quite so simple as you suggest.

In any case, however, I do feel rather strongly, that the Universal Christian Council must not attempt to intervene in Missionary questions of this kind. Dr. Koechlin and I had a great deal of talk together in Berlin on this very subject. And as you know I have been in communication with Paton. I am rather startled to hear, that Mr. Lokies has actually refused to receive two representatives of the German Evangelical Missionary Council to discuss ways and means, on the ground that the Oecumenical Movement, especially the Bishop of Chichester and Professor Keller, have proved to be willing to help the Gossner Mission. I hope that you will tell Mr. Lokies, that he is under a grave misapprehension. The Missionary question must really be considered by the proper authority, that is the International Missionary Council. That body knows the whole field in a way that the Universal Christian Council cannot possible know it. And I am afraid that I must say, so far as I personally am concerned, I could not approve of the Universal Christian Council dealing with the matter at all.

I am sorry to have to write in this way, but misunderstandings grow unfortunately, unless one is clear. And I am quite certain that the line stated in this letter, is the right line.

Yours very sincerely,

1 Society for the Propagation of the Gospel in Foreign Parts: the S.P.G. The Society was founded in 1701 with the aim of financing and coordinating the Church of England's missionary work abroad.

Schönfeld to Bell, 28 April 1938, Basel UB, NL 37, VI 2 (unpaginated) (typewritten).

My Lord,

Thank you very much for your letter of April 13 and for all you have done in this matter. I do not want to take too much of your time, nor do I know whether you had an opportunity to discuss these questions in Germany. I would therefore like only to state some facts, the knowledge of which may help to clear the situation.

1. Paton has had no representation from the German Missionary Council (!) in which the Gossner Mission had no (!) personal representative. There is behind the scenes very deep and far-reaching disagreement between Dr. Knak, the Chairman of this Council, and Mr. Lokies, the really responsible leader of the Gossner Mission. Dr. Knak is also the Director of the *Berliner Mission*, into which they have long since wanted to incorporate the Gossner Mission, the Berlin Mission having no missionary field in India. But the parishes supporting the Gossner Mission had strong objections to this procedure, and under the devoted and very successful leadership of Mr. Lokies the work of the Gossner Mission has been flourishing again since 1928, after having nearly died in the years before. I wanted only to call your attention to this situation, which should be taken into account.
2. When the Society for the Propagation of the Gospel helped the Gossner Mission with its gift, negotiations were initiated by the representatives of the Gossner Mission and carried through in order to secure very close cooperation or even federation between the Kols-Church and the Anglican Missionary Church in the same field. From the Anglican representatives the following conditions for any close administrative and organisational cooperation or federation were laid down: re-confirmation of the members of the Kols-Church and re-consecration of the pastors of the Kols-Church. The native members and representatives of the Kols-Church did not want to accept these conditions. What then could the

representatives of the Gossner Mission do? They also negotiated with the Swedish Lutheran Mission Church (Bishop Sandegren[1]), but the Swedish Missionary Societies were already supporting the work of the Leipzig Mission in India.

What were the responsible representatives of the Gossner Mission to do in this situation: on the one side the impossibility of coming to a closer cooperation and reorganisation in the mission field, and on the other, the severe restrictions on the part of the State as regards the sending of foreign exchange to the mission field, with more and more, behind these restrictions, at first secretly and then more or less openly, the intention finally to hinder German missionary work in India.

Mr. Lokies has done all he could to secure, in spite of all these difficulties, the necessary funds for the foreign exchange, and he succeeded for some years. Besides this, it was he again who mobilised all the available forces in order to get the help of the Lutheran Churches in North America. Here again he was successful, but first of all the grant secured was only to support the Kols-Church itself, and not the missionaries.

I have just received a letter from Dr. Long,[2] telling me that, according to a request from Mr. Lokies, in the face of the intolerable situation of the missionaries, they have agreed that a good deal of their contribution sent in March to India may be used also for the missionaries.

I wanted to bring these facts before you, for they seem to me to help to make it possible to understand the whole situation.

3. Finally, may I simply say that I did not conceive this whole question which I submitted to you as a possibility to help the Gossner Mission, but as a possibility of helping one of the younger churches against the totalitarian claims of the State, and at the same time of supporting one of the most urgent tasks within the German Evangelical Church. During these days I have been reading the first chapters of Dr. Kraemer's new book *The Christian Message in a Non-Christian world*,[3] and I was deeply impressed by the vision given by him of how the organic relationship between the living Christian community and the missionary work has to be reconsidered in a new way and, I may add, in the Gossner Mission the ideas developed here are already being carried into reality, in building up a remarkable Christian lay work, through which the Christian lay forces in the parishes have been educated, strengthened, mobilised in a very quiet, deeply religious and very effective way. Perhaps you have also heard about the lay groups (miners, peasants and other groups), coming to the *Staatsministerium* in Berlin in order to say what they feel about Niemöller. This is only one striking instance of the effects of such a work among lay people.

Just *now* the pressure put upon Mr. Lokies to resign, and so to open the way for the disintegration of this whole work, is becoming stronger and stronger. And therefore it is a question whether just at this very time, as a kind of symbolical action, a small gift of ten to fifteen pounds from churches of Christians in different countries, could not be sent to India, in order to show that a real oecumenical cooperation is beginning against the totalitarian claims which endanger the life of the Kols-Church. These gifts could be sent directly to Lloyds Bank Ltd., Calcutta, Gossner Mission Ranchi, c/o Herrn Missionar Kerschis, Ranchi India. If such gifts could be sent during the immediate future, it would encourage the missionaries in the Kols-Church to stay on and not to leave this Church (which is what the radical representatives of the national socialist cell in Calcutta and their helpers in Berlin hope will happen). And it would show them that the churches and Christians are here helping each other against such totalitarian claims. It is to be hoped that the Executive Committee of the Lutheran World Convention[4] will deal again with this situation at the end of May in Sweden, but in the meantime such gifts would be a very special help.

I am sending a copy of this letter to Dr. Keller, whom I hope to see at the beginning of next week.

Yours very sincerely,

1. Johannes Sandegren (1916–1966): Swedish pastor and Bishop of Tranquebar in the Tamil Evangelical Lutheran Church (TELC) in Tamil Nadu, South India, 1934–56.
2. Untraced.
3. Hendrik Kraemer (1888–1965): Dutch Reformed mission theologian and historian of religions. From 1921 to 1935 he was a research assistant for the Dutch Bible Society in the colony of the Dutch Indies. After his return from colonial service, he entered the service of the Dutch Missionary Council in 1936. From 1937 to 1947 he worked as a professor of religions at Leiden University. From 1948 to 1955 he was head of the new Ecumenical Institute of the World Council of Churches in Bossey. *The Christian Message in a non-Christian world* (London, 1938), written at the request of John Mott, became his most influential book.
4. The Lutheran World Convention was founded in 1923 by members of the National Lutheran Council in the United States and members of the Allgemeine Evangelische-Lutheran Konferenz in Germany. It served to foster and oversee their collaboration in areas of relief work in the wake of the First World War. The Convention was succeeded in 1947 by the Lutheran World Federation.

Koechlin to Bell, 5 May 1938, Basel UB, NL 37, VI 2 (unpaginated) (typewritten).

My dear Lord Bishop,

Best thanks for your lines of April 30th. Included I am returning your correspondence with Dr. Schönfeld. I have shown it to Hartenstein, who is very grateful that you have written as you did. These last days Dr. Knak has had a conversation with Lokies in which Lokies seems to have seen the dangers involved for the whole German missionary work in his attitude. Dr. Mott, who is meeting to-day with the missionary leaders of Germany, will certainly have the opportunity of looking into the matter and give as far as that is possible effective counsel and help for the solution of the problem.

I still hope it might be possible for you to be at Utrecht.

With kind regards,
yours very sincerely,

Enclosures.[1]

1 See Bell to Koechlin, 30 April 1938.

Koechlin to Bell, Utrecht, 13 May 1938, Basel UB, NL 37, VI 2 (unpaginated) (handwritten).

My dear Lord Bishop,
  Before leaving Utrecht[2] I should like to return the letter of Schönfeld, you have sent me through your chaplain. I need not go into details, but simply state, that before writing to you, I had read the letters exchanged in this business between the leaders of the German Missionary movement. I hear through Dr. Warnshuis,[3] who came here direct from Germany and who has talked over matters here with Dr. Knubel, the chairman of the American Lutheran Convention,[4] that the latter has voted to send direct to the Mission Field of Gomera in India the 9,000, Dollars, necessary for the maintenance of the work in 1938. They are inclined to continue later on.
  I have been asked this afternoon to present to the Administrative Committee of Life and Work a short report on our visit to Berlin and was glad to state, that the mandate entrusted to you had been fulfilled as far as the conditions permitted.
  I can't go into the proceedings of the Conference. May I only say, that we made an important step forward and that many problems, for which we had seen no solution have been cleaned in a wonderfully harmonious and satisfactory way. We most certainly were under the lead of the Spirit of God. – All regretted very much your absence.

With kindest regards,
Yours very cordially

1 Koechlin had attended the Utrecht Conference from 19–12 May, which took the crucial decisions for the planned constitution of the WCC and elected Visser 't Hooft as General Secretary. See Koechlin, 'Oekumenische Konferenz in Utrecht 1938', *Basler Nachrichten*, 17 May 1938; some further notes in Basel UB, NL 37, I 5.
2 A.L. Warnshuis (1877–1958): American church leader, formerly Secretary of the International Missionary Council, from which he retired in 1942. Warnshuis would visit Europe in 1944 to fortify preparations for what became the Department of Reconstruction and Inter-Church Aid.
3 Frederick Hermann Knubel (1870–1945): Lutheran Clergyman and the first president of the United Lutheran Church in America, 1918–44.

Koechlin to Bell, 8 July 1938, Basel UB, NL 37, VI 134 (carbon).

My dear Lord Bishop,
  Before leaving my work for my holiday time, I am anxious to send you a few lines, first to thank you for your word of July 5th concerning Miss Livingstone's work in Germany. I knew of it, trusted it fully and have already acted in consequence. Would

you kindly give Miss Livingstone the letter I enclose,[1] as she told me in her last letter that she would spend her holidays with you, beginning July 12th.

Second I wish to mention to you some facts concerning the *German Church Situation*. As I have heard, the state of health of Pastor Niemöller is not good and is causing real anxiety. Mrs. Niemöller seems to have had a complete breakdown not long ago, after she had been allowed to see him. But all petitions are in vain, because Niemöller is a personal prisoner of Hitler. We can but pray for him – and Hitler!

For the intact Churches[2] the great danger consists in the fact that Dr. Werner in Berlin is taking into his hands the complete financial control over the Church. Four weeks ago five men from Berlin came to Karlsruhe, took over the whole organisational and financial control over [or: of] the Church, wrote to all the pastors that they had to obey strictly all regulations coming from them and that to speak of this matter in the pulpit or elsewhere, would be considered to be misuse of the pulpit and punished as such. The whole correspondence between the pastors and parishes on the one side and the Church Council and the Bishop of Baden[3] on the other side has to go through this financial control, so that these gentlemen might examine if any question of finance or organisation is involved. They have power to stop everything they think to be contrary to their intentions and powers. The Bishop and the Church Council cannot dispose of even one Mark without [the] consent of these gentlemen who are in closest possible connection with Party and State. The members of the congregations are led to believe that this control is only dealing with finance and organisational structure. It is very difficult to show them that the Church has no liberty anymore. Bishop Marahrens seems to have accepted for Hannover this change even without consulting with the other Bishops. He had been promised that his own old Hannoverian men could manage the whole thing, but very soon after his return from Uppsala new men from Berlin were sent and the main old men were dismissed by order of Dr. Werner.

In Württemberg and Bavaria Bishop Wurm and Bishop Meiser are up to now resisting successfully this attempt of financial control, but it is very evident that Dr. Werner is only waiting for the best moment to jump in there also and that the hope is relatively small to make it impossible.

Under these circumstances the tensions inside the intact Churches are even more serious. They became again very grave in connection with the question of the oath.[4] Bishop Wurm and as I know also Bishop Meiser have come to an arrangement with the State, according to which the oath of consecration is not touched by the new oath. Nevertheless an oppositional group does not accept this compromise and seems decided not to take the oath. It is in fact the tension between the intact Churches and Lutheran Council on one side and the provisional Church Government of Dahlem having its group of intact Churches on the other side. In Württemberg four weeks ago the minority group of 80 pastors read a paper in the pulpit against Bishop Wurm and his Church Government. The official Church Government the next Sunday prevented these pastors from preaching and sent in these parishes representatives of their own to read another paper.

I confess that even having many [items of] news, it is most difficult to come in these questions to a clear judgment.

Last week we had our Basel Mission Convention. As usual about 800 people from Germany came over the borders in spite of the fact that they knew that the secret

State Police had aimed at preventing this Convention to take place. Passports were not renewed. Other passports were taken away from some people. Journeys in common by cars and special trains as usual were not allowed to take place. It is remarkable that under these circumstances people had the courage of coming[,] nevertheless. Until now the missionary work can go on in Germany in spite of many existing difficulties. But how difficult the situation is, has been shown by the fact that the Jewish Mission, whose annual meeting is taking place the same week, had thought of asking Karl Barth to preach a sermon. Karl Barth being prohibited in Germany, the Jewish Mission being prohibited in Germany and the programme of the Jewish Mission being on our programme, the majority of our Committee has thought that this would be too great a danger for the work of the Basel Mission and for coming annual Conventions and has asked the Jewish Mission and Karl Barth to renounce [sic] on this sermon. The thought was that under no circumstances we would separate and distanciate [sic] from the Jewish Mission, but that the name of a man was not in the same way a fundamental question. The Jewish Mission accepted, Karl Barth made no difficulties. But all over Switzerland a great storm arose that to please the Third Reich we had thrown out Karl Barth. I am quite clear for myself that we ought to have taken another way, though I have to admit that such a programme could possibly have been misused in Germany against the Basel Mission in a most dangerous way.

This also might show you how terribly difficult the situation is. Most of those coming from Germany were grateful that we had acted as we have done. They were convinced that[,] otherwise[,] difficulties might have arisen, which to overcome would not have been possible.

Hoping that you might also have a good holiday, I am

with kindest regards,
yours very sincerely,

P.S. I will be back about August 14th. All letters will be forwarded.

1 Now apparently missing.
2 i.e. those four churches (of Bavaria, Hannover, Württemberg and Westphalia) which had not fallen into the hands of the *Deutsche Christen* in the elections of 1933.
3 i.e. Julius Kühlewein.
4 See Angelika Gerlach-Praetorius, *Die Kirche vor der Eidesfrage. Die Diskussion um den Pfarrereid im 'Dritten Reich'* (Göttingen: Vandenhoeck & Ruprecht, 1964).

Bell to Koechlin, 11 July 1938, Basel UB, NL 37, VI 135 (typewritten).

My dear Koechlin,

Very many thanks for your letter of July 8th. I am grateful for what you say about Miss Livingstone. I am also disturbed to hear about Pastor Niemöller's health and the anxiety which it is causing. I had news on Friday in the *News Chronicle*,[1] coupled with a note from Sir Walter Moberly which he had received in German from a friend in Germany, that Niemöller was in a very sad way, and that the one hope was his immediate removal to a Sanatorium. I do not know whether this is really the case. I rang up Pastor Rieger, whom I had seen only the day before in London. I had asked him particularly whether the rumour passed on to me by Sir Walter Moberly was justified and he said he had heard nothing at all of an anxious character about Niemöller's health, and he would have been sure to have heard had there been cause for anxiety. On Friday I rang him up about the report in the *News Chronicle*. He said he was going to Holland last night and would find out more news there. Any news you have will be most welcome. We had a Service of intercession in St. Martin's-in-the-Fields, London (Dick Sheppard's[2] Church) on July 1st. I enclose a print of what I said.[3] There was a very good congregation.

Thank you very much too for what you say about the general situation and Dr. Werner's activities and financial control. I am very glad that Bishop Wurm and Bishop Meiser are resisting. I saw Bishop Meiser in Uppsala. He was present at the Consecration of the three Swedish Bishops, though he was not actually taking part. We had a word together and I liked him very much. Bishop Marahrens and I walked in the procession in Uppsala Cathedral side by side.

I am very much interested to hear of the wonderful pilgrimage from Germany to the Basel Mission Convention. That is most gratifying. The situation with regard to Karl Barth and the Sermon is very significant. Please give him my warmest regards when you see him. I am wondering what you think of the Conference at Evian.[4] Keller is there, and we have two English representatives taking care of the Non-Aryan Christians and acting on behalf of the International Christian Committee – Mrs. Ormerod and Walter Adams.[5] We are also planning to make a much stronger organization in this country for Non-Aryan Christians, and have got a splendid Chairman.[6]

Yours ever,

1. *News Chronicle*, a popular liberal daily newspaper created in 1930 and owned by the Cadbury family. It would cease publication in 1960 and so offer further proof of the decline of British liberalism as a cultural force.
2. H. R. L. ('Dick') Sheppard (1880–1937): prominent and popular Anglican priest, most famously as a BBC broadcaster, vicar of St Martin-in-the-Fields in central London (1914–26) and leading light in the pacifist Peace Pledge Union, which he created in 1936.
3. The print is now apparently missing.
4. i.e. the Évian international conference, 6–15 July 1938, promoted by the Roosevelt administration in the United States to devise a concerted response to the growing numbers of refugees from Germany and Austria. It ended without success.
5. Mary Ormerod (1894–1975): British Labour politician in London, civil servant and a leading figure in the International Christian Committee for German Refugees; Walter Adams (1906–75), historian and Secretary to the Academic Assistance Council, 1933–8; afterwards he worked for the London School of Economics (1938–46) while holding other political and advisory positions.
6. i.e. the new Christian Council for Refugees from Germany and Austria, established on 6 October 1938. This united four committees under the joint presidency of the Archbishop of Canterbury, the Moderators of the Free Church Federal Council and the Church of Scotland and (later) Cardinal Hinsley. The chairman was Sir John Hope Simpson (1868–1961), once a Liberal politician but now a formidable figure in the administration of international bodies.

1939

January	Ecumenical conference in Paris.
9 February	The Church Assembly of the Church of England debates religious persecution abroad.
15 March	German forces occupy Prague.
18–21 March	Werner publishes four decrees. The consistories are empowered to transfer pastors against their wishes; parishes lose the right to choose their pastors; minorities in each parish are granted the right to demand the use of the church's premises; dictatorial powers are assumed by the president of the consistory.
20 March	Archbishop Lang speaks on the international situation in the House of Lords, controversially referring to the Soviet Union.
23 March	German forces occupy the county of Memel.
25 March	All Germans between the ages of 10 and 18 are conscripted into the *Hitler Jugend*.
22 May	Hitler and Mussolini sign the 'Pact of Steel'.
28 May	The Confessing Church issues a public protest against Werner's four decrees.
5 June	Archbishop Lang and Bell speak in a debate on the refugee crisis in the House of Lords.
11 June	Confessing leaders appeal to all pastors to declare themselves either for the Confessing Church or the *Deutsche Christen* movement.
July	Rust tries to close the Divinity Faculties at the universities of Heidelberg, Leipzig and Rostock.
23 August	Molotov-Ribbentrop Pact.
29 August	The Spiritual Consultative Council (*Geistlicher Vertrauensrat*) is constituted, comprising Bishop Marahrens, Bishop Walther Schultz (*Deutsche Christen*), Senior Consistory Councilor Johannes Hymmen (neutral), and later Otto Weber (reformed confession).
1 September	German forces invade Poland.
1 September	Archbishop Lang speaks on the invasion of Poland in the House of Lords.
3 September	The British government declares war on Germany.
8 November	Assassination attempt by Georg Elser on Hitler in the Munich Bürgerbräukeller.

Koechlin to Bell, 11 January 1939, Basel UB, NL 37, VI 136 (carbon).

My dear Lord Bishop,

For many months I had no real opportunity of writing to you and more than once missed the close contact which I had the privilege of having with you until summer 1938. But my thoughts went to you very often, following your work especially amongst the non-aryan Christians with greatest gratitude. May I assure you that I will feel near you also in future in the great work you are doing in so many respects for the Church Universal of Christ. I am praying that God's blessing may rest upon your work and your home abundantly.

If I am writing to-day, I am asked to do so by Professor Martin Dibelius, whom I saw the day before yesterday in Heidelberg. I had not been in Germany for some months, otherwise I would probably have given you my impressions. Missionary calls led me to go to Stuttgart and Heidelberg the first days of this year. I had in church services great congregations, evidently most grateful to partake in the vision of world-wide missionary work and promise and to listen to someone coming from outside preaching the good news of Christ's victory. I felt the privilege of rendering such a service, though the feeling of the extraordinary general situation was constantly present. The developments seem to be driving towards some great catastrophe and the imminent dangers surrounding the Church and its Ministers are very evident. The 10th of November has proved it in a terrible way.[1] Everyone I saw was deeply concerned and really ashamed, but powerless to react otherwise than in private, except the pastors daring to say even in pulpit courageously and cautiously at the same time the truth of the Gospel. I ought to have seen in Stuttgart Bishop Wurm, who had asked me to call on him, but who unfortunately had just to go to Berlin for the most important deliberations with Kerrl you might have heard of and the results of which are not known yet.[2]

In Heidelberg I stayed in the house of Pastor Maas, certainly the most exposed man in the city and one of the very very few dealing constantly with non-Aryan Christians coming to him from Frankfurt, Karlsruhe, Stuttgart and all parts of Southern Germany. It seems nearly miraculous that he is still in liberty.

As to Professor Martin Dibelius, of course in a quite different position, he was mainly concerned about the oecumenical theological work. He had at heart to let you know a concern of his which he did not dare to put in a letter posted in Germany. He had received your last letter with the post-scriptum dealing with the *societas studorium Novi Testamenti*,[3] presided [over] in England, if I am right, by Dr. Dodd[4] and in Germany by Professor Kittel.[5] His great hope is that this *societas* might succeed in establishing again the effective theological cooperation between Great Britain and Germany and that especially the German Government would agree to it. Professor Kittel, as Dr. Dibelius said, is definitely decided to condition his cooperation by the Government approving the cooperation of Professor Bultmann in Marburg[6] and of himself (Dibelius). If Kittel is succeeding, Dr. Dibelius might get his passport again or at any rate the permission to go to England for a meeting of this *societas*.

This would in his view prepare the way to [or: for] the general theological Conference to be held according to your plans as soon as possible in Chichester under the direct or indirect auspices of the Oecumenical Movement. But he feels very clearly that this cause could best be served if no official relationship between the *societas studiorum Novi Testamenti* and this other Conference would become evident. He has the strong impression that if the German Government circles would read in the invitation of the *societas studorium Novi Testamenti* your name and read between the lines that a theological Conference of the official oecumenical movements were propagated under a new name, the permission for the new creation would never be got.

Dr. Dibelius was also somewhat concerned that your plan might be to give up your study conference in favour of the *societas studiorum Novi Testamenti* in uniting the two. This would in his view be a great loss. For this reason he is hoping that you might, though favouring personally but not officially and not in giving your name to the *societas studiorum Novi Testamenti*, let this experience as well as the time work towards the realization of the other project.

I hope to be clear in my statement and to give accurately the thought of Dr. Dibelius. It might hardly be necessary to say that in asking me to write to you, Dr. Dibelius was especially anxious to let you know how grateful he is for everything you are doing and to assure you that his proposal in no ways should be interpreted in another way. I told him that having dealt with you in the matter of the Oxford delegation, I knew that you were quite aware of the fact that in German Government circles your name actually was not helping a most desirable favourable decision of the German Government and that certainly you would understand his suggestion.

I hope that when meeting you at the end of the month, I might[,] better than it is possible in this letter, let you know the feelings of deep gratitude and friendship Dr. Dibelius and all others I met in Germany have for you and the invaluable services you rendered and still are rendering to the German Church. But I did not like to wait, because you might have to take your decisions possibly in the next days.

With kindest regards,
yours very sincerely,

1   i.e. *Reichskristallnacht*, 9–10 November 1938.
2   On behalf of the Conference of Church Leaders, the regional bishops Wurm and Marahrens and the regional superintendent Hollweg presented Kerrl with a memorandum on 11 January 1939 as a last, unsuccessful attempt to bring about a common order of the German Protestant Church; Beckmann, *Kirchliches Jahrbuch*, pp. 276–82; see too Meier, *Kirchenkampf*, vol. III, pp. 71–3.
3   The *societas studorium Novi Testamenti* was an international scholarly society which was just coming to life at this time: it would be formally founded in 1939. The Society published the journal *New Testament Studies*.
4   Charles Harold Dodd (1884–1973): eminent New Testament scholar and professor of divinity at Cambridge, 1935–49; he was a Welsh Congregationalist minister who was much influenced by German thought and who had studied with Harnack in Berlin; he would go on to play a fundamental role in the production of the New English Bible.
5   Gerhard Kittel (1888–1948): eminent and controversial Tübingen New Testament scholar who had openly embraced the National Socialist movement and, in particular, its antisemitism: his 1933 lecture *Die Judenfrage* became notorious. Although Kittel's academic work was widely known and admired in Germany and abroad his political

enthusiasms and affinities discredited him as a public figure and after 1945 he was firmly marginalized. See Robert P. Ericksen, *Theologians under Hitler: Gerhard Kittel, Paul Althaus and Emanuel Hirsch* (New Haven: Yale University Press, 1985); Manfred Gailus and Clemens Vollnhals (eds), *Christlicher Antisemitismus im 20. Jahrhundert. Der Tübinger Theologe und 'Judenforscher' Gerhard Kittel* (Göttingen: Vandenhoeck & Ruprecht, 2020).

6   Rudolf Bultmann (1884–1976): professor at Marburg, 1921–51, and an active supporter of the Confessing Church; he was widely recognized for his central place in the new movement of Form Criticism; his work became influential in the English-speaking world after 1945. See Christof Landmesser (ed.), *Bultmann Handbuch* (Tübingen: Mohr Siebeck, 2017).

Bell to Koechlin, 14 January 1939, Basel UB, NL 37, VI 137 (typewritten).

My dear Koechlin,

I am very grateful for your letter of 11th instant. I have often thought of you during these last months and of our time together, especially in Berlin at Easter. How much has happened since then. I am looking forward very much to seeing you in Paris at the end of the month.

I am very grateful for the message from Dibelius. Professor Dodd was here last Sunday, and the full explanation of what was in Dibelius' mind is a real help, for it was not absolutely clear from the correspondence, though Dodd and I both thought that what comes out clearly in your letter, was the wise and the desired course. All shall be done, I feel certain[,] as Dibelius desires in the terms of your letter.

With all warmest remembrance from us both to you and your wife,

Yours very sincerely,

Bell to Koechlin, 11 September 1939, Basel UB, NL 37, VI 138 (typewritten).

My dear Koechlin,

You and I have not exchanged letters for some time but I have constantly thought about you, and when Markus Barth[1] was here for a weekend your name naturally came up. This is just intended to say that I do very much want to keep in touch with you during this time of war. I also should heartily welcome any means of friendship and fellowship with our brothers in the Confessional Church. I do not know whether this will be possible through, for example, your mediation, but anything that you think I can do on my side I shall be only too happy to do. And I do want you to know this. My affection and fellowship for them is, as indeed goes without saying, unchanged and unbroken.

The new Bishop of Tinnevally, Stephen Neill, was here yesterday. I think you met him at the Madras Conference. He is a quite first-rate man. I had heard much about him but had never met him before. We had a long talk and he was most anxious to do anything he could on the spot, for the German missions in India. He is hoping to see the Secretary of State for India, Lord Zetland,[2] before he returns to India, which is quite soon on account of the war, and I have told him that he ought to see Paton. He thinks, and of course I agree, that everything possible should be done to enable their work to continue.

Yours ever,

1. Markus Barth (1915–94): first son of Karl Barth and at this time a student; he would become a Reformed pastor and a distinguished theologian in his own right, after 1953 in the USA and between 1973 and 1985 at the University of Basel.
2. At this time Lawrence Dundas, Second Marquess of Zetland (1876–1961): conservative politician and member of the Anglo-German Fellowship; he was Secretary of State for India, 1935–1940.

Bell to Koechlin, 9 November 1939, Basel UB, NL 37, VI 139 (typewritten).

My dear Koechlin,

Very many thanks for your most welcome letter of 17th October.[1] It took ten or fourteen days to arrive. It is a real pleasure to maintain personal contact with you. I do hope we shall keep the correspondence continuing during the war. I am very glad you were able to tell a trusted friend about my feelings towards the Confessional Church and am much cheered by his own emotion and feelings as a result. I am also very much interested to know of the possibility of greater freedom where the army has taken control.

We had a most moving service for refugees in St. John's Church, Westminster on October 28th.[2] It was very largely attended. Two German Pastors, one aryan and the other non-Aryan took part, and a Methodist and myself. There was one sermon in English by me and another in German. The strong desire was expressed that such services should be continued and this will be done. A prayer fellowship was started, bearing refugees especially in mind, and I hope it will have a wider ambit as well.[33]

You will be glad to know that the Home Office has released five of the six German Pastors who were interned.[4] They heard their appeals before those of any other Germans and indeed gave them priority over a number of others. They could not have been more considerate. These, of course, are the official German Pastors, I have seen them all since their release and they are most grateful. The non-Aryan German Pastors who have come over to England have all, I think, been freed from all restrictions, with one or two cases pending, and are regarded as 'friendly aliens'.[5]

With all warmest regards from my wife and myself to Mrs. Koechlin and you,

Yours most sincerely,

1. Now apparently missing.
2. i.e. St John's Church in Smith Square, Westminster.

3   A tantalizing glimpse but no very certain information has emerged. Among German pastors the two obvious candidates are Franz Hildebrandt and Julius Rieger while the Methodist minister might well have been Henry Carter, who was by now overseeing the work of Bloomsbury House, or William Simpson.
4   The exception was Fritz Wehrhan.
5   Internees were categorized in terms of risk. 'Friendly aliens' were usually refugees and were considered to be of only the slightest danger to national security. The policy of internment was a cause of embarrassment to the government; Bell became one of its most effective critics in the House of Lords.

Koechlin to Bell, 20 November 1939, Basel UB, NL 37, VI 140 (carbon).

My dear Lord Bishop,

It gives me very great pleasure indeed to congratulate you for the academic honour which our Basel theological faculty had the most happy thought to confer upon you.[1]

We are indeed not a very great city of outstanding importance, but in the Europe and the church situation of today our faculty has nevertheless a standing not unworthy to ask you to accept a close connection with it. And it might be symbolic to think that you belong to us at the end of the terrible battle-lines, ready for spiritual help to both sides and the same time deeply concerned in view of the sufferings here and there.

Best thanks also for your very kind letter of November 9th which reached me November 15th. I had the visit of a student close to Pastor Albertz, who brought messages from there, telling that after some weeks of some kind of relief the Confessional Church again was under greater hardship. A pastor whom even the Gestapo had given free [sic], was conferred [sic] to court by the Consistorium and is now in [a] Concentration Camp. The authorities nominated by Werner are rendering most difficult any independent action of Confessional pastors. And amongst the younger generation the tendency towards total unity of State, Nation and Church is growing in connection with the war.

In our country the Church tries to be awake to the duty to which God has called it at the present time, in rooting its life more and more in Christ and his holy word. The question discussed just now of entering into the Oecumenical Council with the basis 'Christ our God and Saviour', though creating some difficulties, is helping to clear the situation. We too have to be aware of possible dangers of a somewhat national religion based on our independent history, our whole tradition in the foundation of our commonwealth. It was indeed remarkable how these two last years and especially this summer a deep consciousness of the sources of our own life and a strong attitude against foreign influence have built up a new strength, but the danger to make of it a religious belief has already become evident.

The world-wide missionary responsibility is also becoming more and more living. I am especially concerned about it and in every respect heavily burdened with the responsibility for the Basel Mission, which now entirely rests upon the Swiss Churches and is under exclusively Swiss leadership.[2] After a common past of more than [a] hundred years with the South-German and Alsacian Churches you will realize how many problems are arising. But it is becoming more and more clear that the deepest unity in Christ can only be maintained in facing realistically and with a spirit of consequence the present situation and standing with heart, both feet and head loyally and without weakness [,] on the new foundation. But we cannot hope to get through unless God is present amongst us with his mighty help.

My wife and Elisabeth are joining me in sending to Mrs. Bell and to yourself our best greetings.

Very sincerely yours,

1 For the reflections of the Basel Faculty see Visser 't Hooft to Bell, 24 November 1939, in Besier, *Intimately Associated*, Part One: 1938-1949, p. 171: 'it was generally considered an extremely bold action on the part of the Faculty, because the official Swiss attitude is rather not to show any particular sympathy for citizens of belligerent nations ... you had proved by your action of these last years what it really means to be the Church on an ecumenical scale.'

2 With the outbreak of war in September 1939, most of the German staff of the mission were interned, while the Swiss missionaries were left to fend for themselves.

Bell to Koechlin, 8 December 1939, Basel UB, NL 37, VI 141 (typewritten).

My dear Koechlin,

Your letter of November 20th gave me the greatest pleasure, and I do most heartily appreciate the very generous words which you use. I was surprised and delighted by the honour which Basel University has conferred upon me.[1] The Theological Faculty of Basel has an eminence in the whole world altogether of its own; to be associated with Basel in this most honourable way is to have a relationship of which any man might be proud. I am exceedingly proud that it should have been paid to me at this very time, and in the very midst of war. I value what you say regarding me as belonging to you at the end of the terrible battle-lines, deeply concerned and ready for spiritual help wherever it can be given.

I am very much interested to hear what you tell me about the Confessional Church, and your recent contact with a student close to Pastor Albertz. The Archbishop of Canterbury always asks me whenever I see him what news I have, and I was glad to be able, the other day, to give him this last news, though it is sad news.

What a heavy task falls upon your shoulders now with regard to the Basel Mission and the whole world-wide missionary responsibility in which you take so energetic and devoted a share. These days are tragic days and testing in every sort of way.

I am very glad the Archbishop of York[2] has decided to summon the Provisional Committee to meet in a neutral country on February 1st and 2nd.[3] I hope most earnestly that nothing will turn up to prevent such a meeting. Bishop Berggrav[4] has cabled to say that he is coming to London today. I had a long letter from him on Wednesday suggesting Anglo-Scandinavian and German-Scandinavian conferences in different places at an early date. He will, no doubt, have something to say about these when he comes. But those conferences were proposed at a meeting in Oslo on November 22nd and 23rd when Professor Gulin of Finland[5] was present, with the three Primates. But Finland has become a victim since then. I expect that Berggrav's visit is more immediately concerned with Finland and Norway than with the general oecumenical task.

My wife joins in warmest greetings to you and your wife and Elisabeth,

Yours most sincerely,

P.S. I expect to see Berggrav tomorrow. Paton tells me the *Administrative* Committee meets in Holand Jan. 6-7.

1   Only on 25 February 1946 could Bell present his University of Basel lecture, 'Germany and Christendom', at a formal ceremony there. See here Koechlin to Bell, 16 March 1946, with enclosure, and Appendix 2.
2   William Temple (1881-1944): Archbishop of York, 1928-42; he became Archbishop of Canterbury in 1942 but died in office two years later; a popular bishop and archbishop who published widely, he was perhaps best known by his book *Christianity and Social Order* (1942), which set out an Anglican social theology and a vision of what would constitute a just post-war society. He was a principal figure in the Faith and Order movement, where his role matched that of Bell in Life and Work. The two were close friends.
3   This meeting of the Provisional Committee of the WCC (in the Process of Formation) took place in Zilven, in the Community of Appeldoorn, on the German border, in January 1940. Bell flew there in the company of Temple, the Presbyterian William Paton and the Methodist Henry Carter.
4   Eivind Berggrav (1884-1959): primate of the Church of Norway and bishop of Heligoland since 1928. He would play a courageous part in the church's resistance to the German occupation after the invasion of April 1940. See Gunnar Heiene, *Eivind Berggrav. Eine Biographie* (Göttingen: Vandenhoeck & Ruprecht, 1997); Edwin Hanton Robertson, *Bishop of the Resistance. The life of Eivind Berggrav, Bishop of Oslo, Norway* (Saint Louis: Concordia, 2000).
5   Eelis Gulin (1893-1975): professor of New Testament studies at Helsinki University, 1933-45 and subsequently bishop of Tampere; he was deeply involved in ecumenical work and, in particular, Finnish-Anglican negotiations.

1940

6 January	Bell and Koechlin attend a meeting of ecumenists at Apeldoorn, in the Netherlands, looking to agree a statement on Peace Aims.
13 March	Moscow Treaty concludes the Finnish-Soviet War.
April–June	Norwegian campaign.
30 April	First Polish ghetto established in Lodz.
15 May	The Dutch government surrenders.
10 May	German forces invade France and the Low Countries; the Dutch government surrenders on 15 May; France surrenders on 25 June.
July–October	Battle of Britain and the beginning of the 'Blitz'.

Koechlin to Bell, 26 March 1940, Basel UB, NL 37, VI 143 (carbon).

My dear Lord Bishop,

I need not tell you that since we met last in January I very often have thought of you, of your work and also of our discussions in Zilven. The development of events with which we were deeply concerned at that moment, have again and again called back to my mind the possibilities and impossibilities we had to consider there. Though I felt deeply that we could not come to a common mind concerning our duty as representatives of the Churches of Christ, I remain grateful for those memorable days of nevertheless deepest unity in our faith in Christ in the midst of a most tragic world situation.

Those days in Holland have given me the possibility of thinking of Finland and of the Scandinavian countries as it would not have been possible for me otherwise. I realized their truly tragic situation and our possibly not less tragic situation to have no possibility whatever to help them effectively. I have often asked myself if the position I had to take in Zilven was the right one, but even to-day I do not think that it would have been right and wise to follow the Scandinavian lead.[1] The Church Universal might now be called away from great words and acts to much smaller and humbler services; it might be called to wait and to pray so that it might be better prepared to render later on the services God at his time will permit her to render to a poor broken world.

I very seldom am hearing something of the German Confessional Church. I had these days however the visit of Pastor Peters,[2] Secretary of the German Church Committee for Prisoners of War and Internees, still a young man, having been for six years pastor in Nizza, where he evidently had real christian fellowship with French pastors. His judgement is deeply influenced by this fact and I was very glad to hear through him that German officials having to deal with questions of German prisoners in England had confidence that they might be well treated because they had confidence in the truly christian character of English men they knew. You might be glad to hear that amongst others your name had been mentioned in this connection.

As Peters is part of Heckel's Foreign Office, I did not wish to go into questions of German Church politics with him, the more as our whole time was taken up with the question of prisoners of war. He is willing to help as much as he can in the Chaplaincy work amongst the English and French prisoners of war in Germany. I trust his sincerity and hope that his influence will be effective.

Here in Switzerland week after week is passing, our country more and more a fortress, the men under Arms, the economic life deeply affected, a time of great uncertainty not easy to bear, but we have reason to be most grateful in spite of the dangers surrounding us. My family is well. After a pretty hard winter I intend to go now for a week to the Lake of Geneva, the country of Chamby and Clarens. Hoping that Mrs. Bell and yourself are well also, I am always yours most sincerely,

1   i.e. the lead given by Bishop Berggrav in favour of peace negotiations.
2   Hans-Helmut Peters (1908–87): travelling preacher based in Nice in southern France, 1933–9. On 1 November 1939 he moved to the Church Foreign Office of the German Protestant Church as an auxiliary worker and became secretary of the Protestant Aid Organisation for internees and prisoners of war. From July 1940 to 1944 he was pastor of the German Lutheran Christuskirche in Paris and Special Representative of the German Church Foreign Office in France.

Bell to Koechlin, 19 April 1940, Basel UB, NL 37, VI 144 (typewritten).

My dear Koechlin,

I was very glad to receive your letter of the 26th March and to read your news and your judgments. Even since you wrote the situation in Scandinavia has got so much worse and such terrible things have happened.[1]

I, too, have often thought of our time together in Holland. I learnt much then, and such opportunities give one a wonderful chance of sharing feelings and judgments. I certainly came away a wiser and a spiritually richer man. I have often thought of your words with regard to the remarks I myself made on the responsibilities of churchmen when governments have taken such deep and costly decisions. You are a very wise and far-seeing man.

Most unfortunately I was hundreds of miles away from home when Berggrav came back from his visit to Berlin.[2] I had a letter from him but he did not seem to have got much in Berlin or been allowed to have much free conversation with church leaders; though I think he had a very full talk with Weizsäcker.[3] I am told, however, since then by Canon Thompson Elliott of the World Alliance[4] that he was much more sanguine about what Germany said as to peace possibilities and that he was disappointed by the British attitude. I do not know myself anything about this at first-hand. I wonder whether you have heard anything, especially since Norway was invaded? The *Daily Telegraph* of April 17 said that he had joined the 'Puppet Government' at Oslo and had broadcast urging Norwegians to make peace. I cannot believe that this represents his attitude. I think that the *Telegraph* (so far as I can judge from the *Times*) has misrepresented the administration at Oslo as a Puppet Government. It seems to be a care-taking administration under Governor Christensen and not under any Germany control.[5] If Bishop Berggrav made a broadcast, I should imagine it was to encourage and comfort the people and urge them to have patience. If you have news, do please tell me.

I was glad to have your news of the Confessional Church and also of the attitude taken in Berlin with regard to the friendly character of church leaders and reliance on our doing our best to help German prisoners. What you reported about Peters was therefore encouraging on that score.

I have enquiries from time to time from Archbishop Eidem as a result of enquiries to him from Heckel, and I replied to the best of my ability. I think the arrangements for spiritual ministrations to the prisoners in various camps are pretty regular and sound. One of the German pastors has been for some time ministering to the women prisoners and has now been authorised to minister to certain camps for men prisoners.

Pastor Wehrhan[6] has had to be re-interned. He was one of the Pastors who were released on representations made to the Home Office, but he behaved so indiscreetly that they had to re-intern him. I think that he will probably be re-partriated.

In the meantime, you will be interested to know that the German Church Committee has offered the post of German Priest in his Church in London to Pastor Büsing.[7] He is a refugee married to a non-Aryan wife, a quite admirable man, and he has made it understood to the Committee that he will welcome refugees at the Church and he will indeed be a most useful centre of spiritual help to Germans of all kinds.

I can imagine how difficult the position in Switzerland must be. I do trust that you and Mrs. Koechlin and the family keep well and are standing the strain. May all good be with you. Please let me hear again.

Yours ever,

1   German forces had occupied Norway and Denmark on 9 April 1940.
2   For an account of Berggrav's activities see Heiene, *Eivind Berggrav*, pp. 89–113; also Peter W. Ludlow, 'Scandinavia Between the Great Powers: Attempts at Mediation in the First Year of the Second World War', *Särtryck ur Historisk Tidskrift*, 1974.
3   Berggrav met Weizsäcker in Berlin at last on 18 March 1940, but the Secretary of State declared that not much could be done to prevent war; see Gunnar Heiene, 'Bishop Berggrav's Peace Initiatives at the Beginning of the Second World War', *Current Research on Peace and Violence* 13 (1990): pp. 210–19; see too Arne Hassing, *Church Resistance to Nazism in Norway, 1940–1945* (Seattle: University of Washington Press, 2014), p. 38.
4   William Thompson Elliott (1880–1940): Anglican priest and active international ecumenist who became a canon of Westminster, 1938–40.
5   Ingolf Elster Christensen (1872–1943): Norwegian lawyer and conservative politician and governor of Oslo and Akershus, 1929–40. After the German invasion he was appointed chairman of the Executive Council, acting on behalf of the Norwegian Supreme Court in negotiations with the German state. He withdrew from public life after these failed.
6   Fritz Wehrhan (1872–1951): pastor to the German Protestant Christ Church and to the Lutheran St Mary's Church in London, 1911–44; he was the senior figure of the German pastorate in Britain. He retired in January 1945. Briefly influenced by Bonhoeffer to favour the Confessing Church, from 1936 Wehrhan supported the vision of a German Reichchurch.
7   Wolfgang Büsing (1910–94): after his first examinations in the Confessing Church, in 1935, he served his curacy in a Berlin parish while studying at the Finkenwalde seminary under Dietrich Bonhoeffer. In 1936, with the support of Franz Hildebrandt, he became curate at the German-Lutheran St Georg Church in London; in 1938 he married Erika Danckwarth, who was now, according to National Socialist law, to be categorized as 'Half-Jewish'. After further examinations in Berlin, Büsing returned to London and in 1938 the Committee for Non-Aryan Christians of the Church of England appointed him pastoral counsellor of Non-Aryan Christian refugees in London. Between 1940 and 1949 he was vicar of Christ Church in Whitechapel, in East London. In 1949 he and his family migrated to Canada. See Hartmut Ludwig and Eberhard Röhm (eds), *Evangelisch getauft – als 'Juden' verfolgt. Theologen jüdischer Herkunft in der Zeit des Nationalsozialismus. Ein Gedenkbuch* (Stuttgart: Calwer Verlag, 2014), pp. 68–9.

Koechlin to Bell, 27 April 1940, Basel UB, NL 37, VI 145 (carbon).

My dear Lord Bishop,

I have to thank you very heartily for your most kind letter of Apr[il]. 19th. I am grateful indeed to share with you the questions both of us have so deeply at heart.

As to Bishop Berggrav I have not heard anything definite except the telegrams you have also mentioned, indicating that he is at least working and speaking under German control, and that he evidently is used by the German invaders in their interest, without probably having the possibility of maintaining fully enough his independent judgment and speaking. But I confess that thinking of his whole attitude I am not as certain as I should like to be concerning his conviction of strong resistance against the spirit prevailing in Germany. There was in his all too great comprehensiveness of the actual German attitude something very strange which made me feel uncomfortable, and in addition to that an aiming at the peace *à tout prix* which was more in the line of [the] Oxford Group mentality than of a clear theological and biblical position.[1] I might think that this great uncertainty of attitude, this evident leaning on the German side must have been characteristic for the whole northern atmosphere, until this month. Otherwise the motionless collapse of Denmark and the evident cases of treachery in Norway would not have been possible to such an extent and with such a disaster as this.[2] A strong injection of Karl Barthian conviction in this question would have been of decisive importance for the northern churches as well as for the nations.

What happened to Bishop Berggrav is a question that makes me think a great deal. As bishop of Oslo he certainly had to remain there. But at once he had lost his freedom and was bound to come into a dependant position, asked to do and say things which to refuse would not only to himself be of utmost danger, but also be dangerous for the immediate welfare of the flock entrusted to his pastoral care. At once a conflict between the duties of the bishop of Oslo and those of the Primate of Norway must have arisen for him, and if in addition some pacific conviction led him to believe that the Church could not back the nation's war, the danger of being used by the German invaders must have become tragic.

Until now I was convinced that at all costs I had to stay here in Basel at my post. But I confess that what [has] happened now in the north is making me hesitating somewhat [*sic*], though neither a bishop nor a primate, my position could of course in a much similar way become similarly dangerous and impossible. The choice in reality might be to save outside the occupied city the freedom of action and speech, or to fail in the clear witnessing at the very day of our militation [struggle], or to go the way leading behind the locked door.

Maybe we have no choice at all. May God give [us strength] to be led by Him and to get by His Grace the strength to stay upright whatever might happen. When we are thinking of such possibilities which might one day become one's own, one is led to become humble and to refuse any judgment on others.

Please do not think that in consequences of the recent developments we are getting nervous in Switzerland. Life is going on day by day steadily, though of course one is acting and thinking in order to be ready for any possibility. I am glad to hear what you say about Pastor Büsing whom I do not know.

As hard as it might be to stay interned possibly through years I think those who have not a very clear position are better there, than exposed to many temptations and difficulties. I feel that way also for missionaries, and we have in the Basel Mission the following line: Exercise no pression [pressure] on our men of German nationality to give parole. It means more: Those who nevertheless accepted parole have done it for their own responsibility and conviction. In such cases our leading Swiss men can with good conscience guarantee for the liberated missionaries. I am glad to say that these were in the great majority.

I saw Dr. Visser 't Hooft last week. We felt – and this is confirming what you say – that the work for the prisoners of war is in good shape, especially because the churches feel their ecumenical responsibility in this connection. Fortunately, we have some money in cash, but are waiting to spend it until we see more clearly how things develop in the north. As for general Y.M.C.A work for prisoners, the Danish pastor Christensen, who fortunately had begun in German camps, amongst Poles and others already [at the] end of February, can at least for the moment continue without difficulties.

Mrs. Koechlin and Elisabeth are joining me in sending to yourself and Mrs. Bell our kindest regards.

Ever Yours very sincerely

1. i.e. Protestant conservative evangelical in the mould of Frank Buchman, who had been criticized for being too accommodating to National Socialism.
2. On 9 April 1940 Germany gave both Denmark and Norway an ultimatum with the assurance that their territorial integrity and political independence would not be touched if they capitulated immediately. Norway refused; the Danes accepted, after some hours of fighting, and were thus able to ensure that the government remained in office. In Denmark King Christian X remained in the country, while in Norway King Haakon VII and his family, as well as the government and its gold reserves, escaped to London. It was not until 10 June 1940 that the military engagement was finished. Josef Terboven was appointed as the Reich Commissioner for occupied Norway, while Vidkun Quisling, the leader of the *Nasjonal Samling* party, served as prime minister of Norway from 1942 to 1945.

Koechlin to Bell, 19 August 1940, Basel UB, NL 37, VI 146 (carbon).

My dear Lord Bishop,

As it seems possible to send a word to England I am most anxious to let you know that I am constantly thinking of your work, of your great responsibilities, of Mrs. Bell and yourself. How terribly events have developed since January! Nations and churches under the judgement of the hand of God, as – so it seems – never before. I am trembling in thinking of what has happened and still might happen but trusting however that God even in these times of judgement is with His Church every day and that He will strengthen those who in all this are trusting Him.

Let me say that it is a great comfort to me to think of you and to know that you also are remembering us here in Switzerland. May God keep and preserve you in His Strength and Peace.

Yours very sincerely

Bell to Koechlin, 1 October 1940, Basel UB, NL 37, VI 147 (typewritten)

My Dear Koechlin,

It was a great pleasure to get your letter of August 19th. The Fellowship of fellow Churchmen of other countries means a very great deal at this time. I shall never forget you and your friendship. Events have indeed moved apace since we last met, all of us under God's judgement. We hope and pray may God unite us all and bring us together again before too long.

My wife's greetings also to your wife and daughter

Yours affectionately,

1941–7

22 June 1941	German forces invade the Soviet Union.
7 December 1941	The United States enters the war.
October 1941	Ecumenical offices in Geneva receive reports of the mass deportations of Jews in the occupied countries.
13 May 1942	Bell flies to neutral Sweden, there meeting Dietrich Bonhoeffer and Hans Schönfeld; he returns 1 June.
17 December 1942	The Allied governments publish a joint statement on the mass murder of the Jews of Europe.
14 January 1943	Casablanca Conference: Roosevelt and Churchill meet and agree that Allied policy should demand the unconditional surrender of Germany; the conference ends on 24 January.
28 November 1943	The three Allied governments meet at Teheran until 1 December.
6 June 1944	The Normandy landings bring the long-awaited Second Front and, in time, the liberation of France.
9 February 1944	Bell speaks against 'obliteration bombing' in the House of Lords.
20 July 1944	German resistance circles attempt to overthrow the Hitler regime.
9 April 1945	The death of Dietrich Bonhoeffer.
8 May 1945	War in Europe ends.
17 July 1945	The Potsdam Conference of the Allied governments begins; it concludes on 2 August.
27–31 August 1945	Conference of Protestant church leaders at Treysa. Foundation of the Protestant Church in Germany
18–30 October 1945	Bell and Koechlin visit Germany and with other ecumenical representatives attend the meeting at Stuttgart.
February 1946	The first post-war conference of the Provisional Committee of the World Council of Churches takes place in Geneva and a new age is inaugurated by a great service at St Peter's Cathedral. Bell receives his honorary degree from the University of Basel. The World Council of Churches creates the Commission on International Affairs and the new international conference and study centre at Bossey.
10–14 June 1946	Bell returns to Germany and meets with Bishop Marahrens.
1 October 1946	The first International Military Tribunal at Nuremberg concludes. Between 1946 and 1949 further tribunals follow.
16–30 October 1946	Bell visits the British Zone in Berlin.
1 January 1947	The British and American Zones in occupied Germany amalgamate.
5 June 1947	The Marshall Plan is announced in Washington.

Koechlin to Bell, 16 March 1946, Basel UB, NL 37, VI 148 (carbon).

My dear Lord Bishop,
    It is very kind of you to write to me as you have done February 28th.[1] I appreciate very highly the feelings you express and count it as a great privilege to have shared after all we had in common during the last 13 years the memorable days of Geneva so intimately with you. Your visit in Basel[2] also will not be forgotten. It was a great service you rendered to the Faculty and Church of our city and it was a great pleasure to have you personally amongst us as a most honoured and beloved guest.
    With kindest regards,

yours very sincerely,

P.S. Would you kindly express to Mrs. Bell the gratitude of Mrs. Koechlin for the kind lines she has written to her.

1 This letter now appears to be missing.
2 It was on 25 February 1946 that Bell presented his University of Basel lecture.

Bell to Koechlin, 18 March 1946, Basel UB, NL 37, VI 149 (typewritten).

My dear Koechlin,
    I am sending you herewith a copy of the text of my lecture at Basel, as you kindly asked.[1]
    I wonder if you have been able to get the photographs from the Basel newspaper of the procession into the Cathedral in Geneva?
    With all warmest remembrances,

Yours very sincerely,

1 The text is reproduced here as Appendix 2.

Koechlin to Bell, 27 March 1946, Basel UB, NL 37, VI 150 (carbon).

My dear Lord Bishop,
    Best thanks for your kind words and the text of the address you delivered in Basel on Germany. I hope to reprint at least parts of it in some of our Swiss Church papers.
    Excuse me please for not having sent earlier the *Basler Nachrichten* with the pictures. You [will] receive it under separate cover. As you will see the names of the second picture are hopelessly mixed up. It is nevertheless a good souvenir for those who put right everything.
    With kindest regards also to Mrs. Bell, I am,

always yours very sincerely,

Koechlin to Bell, 6 June 1947, Basel UB, NL 37, VI 151 (carbon).

My dear Lord Bishop,

I received these days the book you so kindly promised to send me and which I indeed am very glad to read and to include in my library.[1] I have given a great part of my last quiet Sunday afternoon to read your speeches in the House of Lords, some at least of your other addresses and of your sermons. I was most grateful to hear your voice and to realize that it had a hearing not only in the church field, but also in the political world and could possibly, maybe not immediately, influence directly those who were and are responsible for the grave decisions to be taken. I was deeply moved in thinking how difficult and delicate it must have been on many occasions to say what you had to say and to say it in the right way as a disciple of Christ and representative of his Church.

To follow the development of your thought, from 1939 to 1946 which remains substantially the same thought, but applied to the evolution of circumstances, is very illuminating, showing not only what God has laid in the depth of your heart and on your conscience, but also the great vision of God's coming and at the same time eternal plans with mankind.

I felt afresh the great privilege to be allowed to be connected to you through all these years. You may be certain that I am most grateful in thinking that you will grant me the same privilege in the years to come.

Very sincerely yours,

1 This was *The Church and Humanity, 1939-1946* (London: Longmans, 1946).

Bell to Koechlin, 12 December 1947, Basel UB, NL 37, VI 152 (typewritten).

My dear Koechlin,

I am much touched by your letter, and by that from your niece.[1] Please thank her warmly for her letter, and tell her how glad I am to know that she has arrived safely. I can imagine something of the immense relief it must be to her after all these tribulations.

Thank you also very much for your most kind Christmas message. My wife and [I] warmly reciprocate this greeting to yourself and Mrs. Koechlin and the family. I cannot tell you how deeply I value your friendship. I look forward eagerly to seeing you again at the Provisional Committee in Geneva next month.

I have an extra cause for writing at the present moment, having heard from Pastor Menn[2] about Schönfeld.[3] He has sent me a copy of his letter to Pastor Boegner as President of the Administrative Committee, which certainly tells a very sad story of Schönfeld's health. Things seem to be going very ill with him: for the fourth time, I gather, he has broken down seriously after a brief attempt to do his oecumenical job in Germany. I cannot help feeling rather troubled about Schönfeld and our responsibilities to him. I think that Visser 't Hooft will have received a copy of Menn's letter to Boegner; but anyhow I think it can do no harm to send you a copy. I would ask you to let me have it back when you have considered it, with any comments.

With all warmest greetings,
Yours very sincerely,

1 It is not clear who this might be. The Koechlins were a large family.
2 Wilhelm Menn (1888–1956): active member of Life and Work. He was pastor and superintendent in Andernach, 1934–50, from 1946 and from 1947–56 the head of the Ecumenical Central Office of the Evangelical Church in Germany in Frankfurt/Main.
3 In 1948 Schönfeld became senior consistory councillor and ecumenical officer in the Church Foreign Office at Frankfurt, where he built up the Ecumenical Central Office. By now an ill man, he retired in 1951.

Koechlin to Bell, 20 December 1947, Basel UB, NL 37, VI 154 (carbon)

My dear Lord Bishop,
Very many thanks for your letter of December 12th which arrived beginning of this week just before I had to go to Geneva for a two days meeting of the Reconstruction Committee.[1] There I had the possibility of discussing the question [of] Schönfeld with Visser 't Hooft as well as with Dr. Gerstenmaier. The two had already spoken about it before I arrived and had reached an important conclusion. 't Hooft had not seen Pastor Menn's letter and Dr. Boegner had not written to him about it.

But now the decision we reached:
Gerstenmaier, who by the way said that he had to hold himself completely to the opinion expressed by Pastor Menn, declared that the family of Dr. Schönfeld would have to come at the latest May 1st 1948 to Germany and that the German *Hilfswerk* would take care of them.[2] As to Dr. Schönfeld himself, his health needs special care. He will possibly have to go to some kind of *clinique*, first in Switzerland and, if it should prove to be necessary, later on even in Germany. For him also *Hilfswerk* would take the material responsibility from May 1st on. That means of course that the responsibility for the family until May 1st remains if not legally so in fact and morally with the Ecumenical Council.

If Gerstenmaier offers this solution and in his very energetic way is willing to realize it, the main reason for it is that according to his conviction neither Schönfeld himself nor his family will be able to find their equilibrium in Geneva. He sees the further work of Schönfeld in the ecumenical headquarters apart from considerations of health as impossible. He knows him enough to see that as long as a clear-out decision is not taken once for all, Schönfeld will always come back to old ideas, hopes and more or less unclear considerations. It was of interest to me to hear that Dr. Schönfeld's mother had periods of psychic lability and that her ways of thinking had always been most complicated and even contradictory. Dr. Schönfeld's health is evidently not good. He must have had rather serious heart troubles after the first world war. The strain of the years 1933–1946 and then his personal difficulties arising out of the decisions of the Provisional Committee in Geneva[3] were evidently too much for him.[4]

Now as to the actual situation until May 1st. 't Hooft as well as myself, we are still convinced and the development of work seems to prove it, that the decision of February 1946 had to be taken in the interest of the work to be done for Amsterdam.[5] But we agree with you that we have a serious responsibility towards Dr. Schönfeld and his family. It is regrettable that Dr. Michelfelder[6] from one day to another declared with great strictness, that from January 1st he was not willing to give a cent for Schönfeld. As he has left Geneva already[,] December 14th[,] for the States, I could not see him. It is possible that his real intention was to put an end to the endless postponements and enforce on all concerned a definite solution. If this was his real intention, he has succeeded but 't Hooft hoped that he would be willing to help a little more in order to overbridge the gulf. 't Hooft will also speak to Dr. Bush,[7] hoping that some American Presbyterian money might be made available. From my side I hope to help also though it will not be possible to offer a great amount. 't Hooft does not see the possibility to charge the accounts of the World Council. At any rate you might be assured that the situation is met until the Provisional Committee is meeting January 20th. We might see then together with others what ought to be done.

Best thanks for your message to Rosemarie John.[8] She is coming for lunch Tuesday next and will certainly appreciate it very much.

And now last but certainly not least I wish to express to yourself and Mrs. Bell our heartiest wishes for Xmas and the New Year. Christ, the light of the world, is certainly shining in the darkness of our days, hidden to many and not manifest in the larger national and international developments, but very real for those believing in him. It is our great comfort and strength in the days to come.

With best regards,
yours very sincerely,

***Enclosure.*[9]**
Letter Menn concerning Dr. Schönfeld

1. Koechlin had been a fundamental figure in the establishment of the Department for Reconstruction and Inter-Church Aid in Geneva in 1942. See W. A. Visser 't Hooft, *Memoirs*, pp. 173–81; Antii Lane, Juha Meriläinen and Matti Peiponen, 'Ecumenical Reconstruction, Advocacy and Action: The World Council of Churches in Times of Change, from the 1940s to the early 1970s', *Kirchliche Zeitgeschichte/Contemporary Church History* 30 (2017), pp. 327–41.
2. This arrangement was probably a consequence of Gerstenmaier's friendship, and intensive contacts, with Schönfeld since their common time in Heckel's Foreign Office of the German Protestant Church and then in the resistance movement during the war.
3. No further information.
4. See also Bell to Visser 't Hooft, 26 January 1948, in Besier, *Intimately Associated*, p. 397.
5. i.e. the first General Assembly of the W.C.C. at Amsterdam, 22 August–4 September 1948.
6. Sylvester C. Michelfelder (1889–1951): American minister and general secretary of the Lutheran World Federation, 1947–51; he had been invited to represent the American section of the Lutheran World Convention in Geneva in 1945.

7   Dr Bush represented the Presbyterian Church of the USA at the meeting in Geneva.
8   Untraced.
9   The enclosure is now apparently missing.

Bell to Koechlin, 30 December 1947, Basel UB, NL 37, VI 155 (typewritten).

My dear Koechlin,

I am most grateful for your letter about Schönfeld, and for all the trouble you have taken. I am very glad I wrote just when I did. What you say seems very hopeful of a solution. I am very glad that you have had the opportunity of discussing the whole question with Visser 't Hooft, as well as with Gerstenmaier.

I am looking forward very much to seeing you at Geneva in the third week of January.

With all warmest good wishes for the New Year,

Yours ever,

1948–58

1–6 April 1948	Bell visits Germany.
23 June 1948	Bell speaks in the House of Lords on the continuing war crimes trials.
24 June 1948	The Berlin blockade begins, ending 12 May 1949.
22 August 1948	The first General Assembly of the World Council of Churches begins in Amsterdam.
May 1949	The Federal Republic of Germany is created; the Democratic Republic is set up in October.
15–19 July 1949	The Central Committee of the World Council of Churches meets in Chichester.
25 June 1950	War breaks out between North and South Korea.
9 July 1950	The Central Committee of the World Council of Churches meets in Toronto.
1–8 January 1953	The Central Committee of the World Council of Churches meets in Lucknow.
August 1954	The second General Assembly of the World Council of Churches takes place at Evanston; Bell meets Koechlin for the last time and subsequently attends the Anglican Congress in Minneapolis, 4–13 August.
3 October 1958	Bell's death.

Koechlin to Bell, 15 December 1950, Basel UB, NL 37, VI 153 (carbon).

My dear Lord Bishop,

I received these days your very important printed letter of December 9th addressed to the members of the Central Committee.[1] I am deeply grateful to you for addressing yourself to us in such a way. The call to stand together, to pray together and to give to each other signs of living fellowship, is a real help. I will try my best to be true to it. At any rate you may be assured that I am thinking of yourself and the great responsibilities you are carrying for the World Council as well as for your own diocese, Church and Nation in these indeed very anxious times.[2] May the Xmas days and the great Gospel it brings to us from heaven prove to be for you too, as for all of us, the strength, the help and the lead on which we solely and wholly rely.

The text of the prayer you have proposed to the member Churches of the World Council has come to us these days and has already passed to our cantonal Churches. I trust it will be widely used in all our communities.

I also received just this morning through Visser 't Hooft your proposal to hold, previous to our Executives session, an unofficial meeting of 2 to 3 days in order to discuss in a more informal way the great issues evolving from the dangerous international tension. For this very timely initiative we have reason to be grateful to you. I am glad it seems to be possible for me to be present. I am at any rate arranging my plans in accordance.

Finally, I have still to thank you for having sent me very kindly the book containing your Olaus Petri lectures of Uppsala.[3] I have not quite finished to read them because other things constantly came between and so I missed the right moment to tell you how much I appreciated your gift and how grateful I was for this new kindness of yours. In what I have read I learnt a great deal about Anglican history and its present attitude linked to the past and nevertheless looking to the future. We cannot have enough insight in one another's Church. Every new glimpse is helping us to better understanding. This understanding again is placing us in the reality. Without it we cannot effectively work together for the future of the Church of Christ.

As this will be the last letter I am writing to you in this closing year, I cannot but give expression to my gratitude for all the inspiration and confidence and friendship I received from you during the past months and especially in the days I was privileged to be with you together in Bossey and Toronto.[4]

With my heartiest wishes for Mrs. Bell and for yourself, in which Mrs. Koechlin is joining,

I am,
Yours very sincerely,

1 Printed in Besier, *Intimately Associated*, pp. 692–4.
2 Koechlin refers to Bell's letter emphasizing the 'moment when "contending world powers" are in such tragic conflict, and the reconciliation of East and West has become even more important since Toronto'.
3 G. K. A. Bell, *Christian Unity: The Anglican Position* (London: Hodder & Stoughton, 1948). The text of Bell's Olaus Petri lectures at Uppsala University, October 1946.

4   The Executive Committee of the WCC met in the Ecumenical Institute in Bossey, 21–23 February 1950 and the Central Committee in Toronto, Canada, 9–15 July 1950. Bell and Koechlin were members of both committees.

Bell to Koechlin, 19 February 1953, Basel UB, NL 37, VI 156 (typewritten).

My dear Koechlin,

I was much touched by your letter[1] arriving on my 70th birthday, February 4th – and not least by the fact that one of your laymen regularly remembers me in his prayers because you have been so kind as to include my name in the prayer booklet.

But I value your good wishes and your prayers in a very special way. We have been close to one another ever since the days of the Stockholm Conference in 1925. I vividly remember your visit to Chicester, and the stimulus it gave in my own thoughts and actions about the Nazi regime. But you are really too good in what you say about my influence in your personal life and in your work. Believe me that the feeling and the debt are mutual.

You may like to see a copy of my Pastoral Letter read in all churches of the diocese last Sunday.[2] Please don't bother to reply – but it will show you what we are trying to do in the diocese of Chichester this year.

My wife joins me in warmest remembrances to you and your wife and the family.

Yours very sincerely,

1   Evidently now missing.
2   This was *The Word and the Sacraments* (1952), Bell's last episcopal charge written for clergy of the Diocese of Chichester.

Bell to Koechlin, 25 September 1954, Basel UB, NL 37, VI 157 (typewritten).

My dear Koechlin,

I was greatly touched by your letter, which I found on my return to Chichester last week-end.[1] I too was very sorry at not being able to say a personal goodbye. I had to leave the Steering Committee rather quickly for an appointment, and somehow I did not realise (though it was foolish of me) that I should not see you later that day. It must have seemed rather abrupt and odd that I left without saying farewell. But I was very glad that Cooke[2] made an opportunity of saying something about you at the luncheon meeting, and gave me also the opportunity of saying something, very inadequately, by way of supplement. I thought your impromptu response was admirable, and the warmth of feeling amongst the members present must have been felt by you.

Our relationship ever since 1925, and our growing friendship, which has become such a very strong bond, particularly since our co-operation in helping the Confessional Church in Germany, has been one of the happiest and most treasured possessions in my life in the ecumenical movement. I do very much hope that the coming years will give other opportunities for meeting from time to time. I should value this very greatly. If you are in England, do let me know – and I will certainly let you know if there is any chance of my coming to Basel.

You will have had plenty of work in helping D'Espine[3] and your other colleagues to interpret the Message of Evanston to the Swiss Churches. I was very glad to meet D'Espine, and was much struck by his personality and ability. I do greatly hope that he may play a vigorous part on the Central Committee and in the ecumenical councils generally.

Mrs. Bell joins in sending warmest regards and remembrances to you and Mrs. Koechlin.

Yours ever sincerely,

1. Evidently now missing.
2. Leslie E. Cooke (1908–67): British Congregationalist lay preacher, social worker and leading light in the early reconstruction programmes of the World Council of Churches.
3. Henri D'Espine (1895–1982): professor of practical theology at Geneva University, 1937–64; one of the leading figures in Swiss Protestantism during and after the Second World War, he succeeded Koechlin as president of the Federation of Swiss Protestant Churches from 1954 to 1962 while also serving as a member of the Central Committee of the World Council of Churches.

Appendices

Appendix 1

In the House of Lords on 13 December 1939 Bell promoted the case for a negotiated peace in a debate following by a motion by the Earl of Darnley. This responded to the offer of mediation made by the King of Belgium and the Queen of Holland. (See *Hansard, House of Lords Debates*, Fifth Series, Vol. 115, cols. 252–6 (13 December 1939).) In Switzerland, Karl Barth was not impressed. On 16 December 1939 he wrote to Bell, 'In our Basel papers we [are] reading a most astonishing and incredible report of the events . . . in the House of Lords last Wednesday . . . *Your* name was mixed up in a deeply unpleasant manner with a crowd of "Nazi-Freunde und Pazifisten". I do not believe a word of it.' Barth thought this must be the Bishop of Gloucester, or that the reports must be completely misleading. Bell replied on 23 December 1939, writing that he had sought 'to plead simply for a way of negotiation "as soon as negotiation can be made" instead of "a war to the bitter end". I said very decidedly that I was not a pacifist, nor was I in favour of Peace at any price. I also condemned the "brutality" with which the Nazis began and continued the War.' (See Bell Papers, Vol. 74, fols. 6–8.) Barth, still mystified, turned to Koechlin for a further explanation.

Koechlin to Karl Barth, 19 January 1940, Basel UB, NL 37, VI 142 (carbon).

Lieber Karl,

Beiliegend den Brief Chichesters und die Parliamentary Debates des House of Lords zurück. Bei der Rede Chichesters wundert mich, dass er von neutralen Freunden so manches über deutsche Friedenswilligkeit gehört haben will. Ich vermute das sind die skandinavischen Quellen, von denen wir Dienstagabend zu reden Anlass hatten. Abgesehen davon, dass diese Quellen nicht uninteressiert sind an einer sofortigen Mediation, dürfte doch auch ziemlich klar sein, dass die Friedenswilligkeit, von der sie reden, kaum etwas Anderes meinen kann als den Frieden der Deutschland seine Eroberungen sichert und Hitler gestattet, im Sattel zu bleiben, seine Position zu stärken und seine gesicherten Erfolge weiter auszubauen. Mir scheint, Chichester übersieht die Grundhaltung, die Methode und Dynamik des Nationalsozialismus, sonst müsste ihm vor den Folgen eines solchen Friedens mehr bangen als es der Fall zu sein scheint.

Zum anderen scheint es mir so zu stehen, dass er die äusseren und unmessbaren geistigen und religiösen Folgen des totalen Krieges als ein unübersehbares, nicht einzudämmendes, nicht wieder gut zu machendes Uebel ansieht, das grösser und in seinen Folgen schwerwiegender ist als irgendein Friede, der jetzt geschlossen werden mag. Das ist jedenfalls die Haltung, die ich bei ihm herausgespürt habe, als ich mit ihm zusammen war.

Während Chamberlain Anfang September am Ende des für ihn tragbaren Entgegenkommens und Wartens stand, ist offenbar Chichester nach seiner Sicht an diesem Enden noch nicht angekommen. Er sieht oder hofft wenigstens noch auf eine Möglichkeit des Zuwartens und Einrenkens der gegenwärtigen furchtbaren Situation. Dabei stellt er aber auf Eindrücke und Erwägungen ab, die meiner Ansicht nach nicht richtig sind. Er rechnet damit, dass, je länger der Krieg dauert, desto mehr Hitler das deutsche Volk zur unlösbaren Einheit zusammenwachsen[,] und hofft, dass man[,] wenn der Friede geschlossen werde, die Ablösung des Volkes von Hitler, die vor dem Krieg eingesetzt habe, weiter und zum guten Ende gehen werde. Das scheint mir aber ein verhängnisvoller Irrtum in der Beurteilung der Lage zu sein. Recht mag Chichester menschlich gesehen höchsten darin haben, dass das Ende des Krieges im Westen Deutschland frei machen könnte von seiner Verbundenheit und Abhängigkeit mit Russland. Ob aber damit die braune Bolschewisierung Deutschlands ihr Ende hätte, ist eine andere Fragen. Chichester scheint das anzunehmen, während er in der Fortsetzung des Krieges die unaufhaltsame Gefahr der direkten völligen Bolschwisierung Deutschlands sieht.

Natürlich wird Chichester zu seiner Haltung auch dadurch bestimmt, dass er sieht, welch immer weitere und fruchtbare Kreise die Dämonie und das Chaos des Krieges zieht[,] und es wird ja wohl so sein, dass wir alle einstweilen noch diese Folgen in ihrer Grauenhaftigkeit nicht erkennen. Ob er aber dem gegenüber nicht zu wenig rechnet mit dem Hereinbrechen anderer Kräfte, an das wir glauben dürfen, wenn wir ganz einfach im Gehorsam des Glaubens stehen und handeln und zum Weitergehen des Krieges im jetzigen Augenblick noch ja sagen? Finnland wäre ein Zeichen dafür, dass das auch zu Wendungen der Kriegslage führen kann, die wir in unserem Kleinglauben viel weniger vorauszusehen vermögen als die schweren Folgen des Krieges.

Ich weiss nicht, ob Dir diese Ueberlegungen etwas zu sagen vermögen. Wenn ich Chichester zu antworten hätte, so würde wohl meine Antwort sich ungefähr in der Linie dieser Gedanken bewegen.

Mit herzlichem Gruss,
Dein getreuer

Dear Karl,

Please find enclosed the letter from Chichester and the Parliamentary debates of the House of Lords. During the speech I wondered that he claimed to have heard so many things from neutral friends over a German willingness for peace. I suspect that these are the Scandinavian sources, of whom we had reason to talk on Tuesday night. Besides the fact that these sources are not interested in immediate mediation, it should also be quite clear that the willingness for peace of which they talk can only mean a peace in which Germany secures its conquests, allowing Hitler to remain in the saddle in order to strengthen its position and continue to build on its successes. It appears to me that Chichester overlooks the basic approach, methods and dynamics of National Socialism, otherwise the consequences of such a peace would be of more concern to him than they appear to be.

On the other hand, it seems to me that he regards the external and immeasurable spiritual and religious consequences of a total war as an incalculable, irreparable evil, and one that is greater and more serious in its consequences than any peace that may now be made. In any case, that is the attitude that I sensed when I was with him.

While the limits of Chamberlain's patience came at the beginning of September, Chichester's mind has not yet arrived at that point. He sees, or at least hopes, that there is still a chance of waiting, and sorting out, the present, terrible situation. Yet in that, he relies on impressions and considerations which, in my opinion, are not right. He expects that the longer the war goes on the more Hitler will and the German people will grow together into an indissoluble unity, and hopes that if peace is made Hitler and the people will be divided, as was the case before the war, and that there will be a good outcome. That seems to me to make a fatal error in judging the situation. In human terms, Chichester may well be right that the end of the war in the west could free Germany of its association with, and dependence on, Soviet Russia. But whether that would end the bolshevization of Germany is another question. Chichester appears to accept this, seeing in the continuation of the war the inexorable danger of the direct, entire, bolshevization of Germany.

Of course, Chichester's view is determined by seeing that in the ever-growing and spreading demony and chaos of such a terrible war, there will be consequences the horror of which we have yet to recognize. But does he not reckon too little with the intervention of other forces, in which we may believe, if we now say that we will simply stand and act in good faith and go on with the war? What happens in Finland might lead to changes in the war situation, and such things we, with our little faith, are much less able to predict than the serious consequences of the war.

I do not know if these reflections can tell you anything of value. If I had to reply to Chichester, my answer would be broadly along these lines.

With kind regards,
Yours truly,

Appendix 2

GERMANY AND CHRISTENDOM, Bell's address to the University of Basel on receiving his honorary doctorate, 25 February 1946.

Basel UB, NL 37, VI 149 (typewritten).

It is a great privilege to speak in Basel tonight. I owe much to Basel, and especially to the Chairman, and to my friends in the theological faculty for the honour they paid me at the commencement of the war:[1] so when I was invited to come here from Geneva, I accepted with delight.

I have come from a meeting of the Provisional Committee of the World Council of Churches.[2] It was a peculiarly enriching experience to re-knit the links with old friends, from whom I had been separated for six long years. But the occasion was most welcome because here was gathered an Assembly of Christendom, apart from the Church of Rome. Here there met not a World Church, but a sort of microcosm of the Orthodox and Protestant Churches, cutting across the boundaries of nations. Men and woman, therefore, from America, Russia, Great Britain, China, France – from Germany, Greece, Norway, Romania, Denmark, Holland, India, Switzerland and Sweden – who, in spite of national divisions, found a centre of unity in Christ. And there are few things more important to bring out to-day than the community of Christians.

I have taken as my theme for to-night's meeting 'Germany and Christendom'. Many have written and spoken about the place of Germany in Europe. It is a subject full of difficulty: and with France on one side, and Germany on the other, you in Basel must necessarily be the receptacle of many rumours, and of many views. Yet the proper treatment of Germany is vital to the future peace of Europe and therefore of the world.

Christendom in former times was almost a synonym for Europe: and though now, with the great experience of the Christian religion on the one hand, and with the great secularization of Europe on the other hand, it has a wider application, I shall address myself to my theme first as a European, and next, in the broadest sense of the word, as a Christian.

Here in Basel you received many refugees before the war broke out, who were victims of Nazi oppression in Germany. I have no doubt also that you knew very well the horrors of the concentration camps. Nor can there be any illusion about the magnitude

---

[1] i.e. the honorary doctorate awarded to Bell by the university on 17 November 1939; see Bell to Koechlin, 20 November 1939.
[2] See *Minutes and Reports of the meeting of the Provisional Committee of the World Council of Churches held from February 21st to 23rd 1946*; the constitutional documents of the WCC with an introduction by W.P. Visser 't Hooft (Geneva, 1947).

of the Nazi cruelties. I know too how sharp was the suffering, and how prolonged the strain which the Nazi war-mongers inflicted on the United Nations. England has suffered much. I read with pride of the enthusiastic reception which Switzerland has just given to Field Marshal Montgomery. But other nations have suffered on a far more terrible scale. Russia's sufferings are colossal. Poland, Norway, Yugoslavia, Greece, and all Central Europe have gone through fearful agony through the oppression, and violence, and slavery of their occupation. I mention these facts in order that you may realise that I know something of Germany's vileness – I have seen some of those who have been tortured – I have had victims of the concentration camps staying with me in my house, bent low with misery. I do not underestimate the gravity of the problem of the right treatment of Germany.

I said that I address myself to my theme first as a European. It is impossible to hope for a lasting solution of the German problem unless you tackle it as the crux of the problem of Europe.[3] A nation is composed of its men. Is there any evidence of European-minded men in Germany? We have had only too much evidence of the Nazi-minded man. But there has been a tradition of European-ness in Germany for centuries. And by European men, I mean sons of the great poets, writers, musicians, philosophers and scholars. There was that older and better Germany in former days: many of its leading representatives were killed by Hitler during the years from 1933 onwards, including the thousands of victims of the July 20 Plot.[4] But it is true enough that the younger generation is infected with the poison of Hitlerism. The boys and girls of the Hitler Youth, the young men and women up to 25 and 30, were all exposed to the ghastly offensive of the Nazi *Weltanschauung,* and – though there were some remarkable exceptions, notably in the South of Germany,[5] the great majority, knowing no other way, followed the Führer, and became fanatics for race and blood and war. I was in Germany before Christmas, as a delegate of the World Council of Churches.[6] The military governor of one of the largest towns in the British zone said to me in the course of conversation: 'There are two factors to be remembered as you look at Germany today. The first is that the whole population is stunned by the terrible devastation which the bombing has caused. The second is the problem of leadership.' For 13 years the Germans of energy and initiative, speaking generally, became

---

[3] See Bell's discussions with Gerhard Leibholz in Gerhard Ringshausen and Andrew Chandler (eds), *The George Bell–Gerhard Leibholz Correspondence. In the Long Shadow of the Third Reich, 1938–1958* (London: Bloomsbury, 2019).

[4] For a comprehensive study see Peter Hoffmann, *The History of German Resistance 1933–1945*, 3rd ed. (London: Macdonald and Jane's, 1977). After the war the numbers of those killed in consequence were placed high including the victims of the 'Gewitter action' by which many members of the former parties were talken prisoner, but historians have since concurred at an estimate of around 200 killed while around 700 were arrested in connection with the conspiracy.

[5] Bell probably had the White Rose Group in mind here, reports of whose story had been published in Britain, not least in William Bayles, *Seven were Hanged: An Authentic Account of the Student Revolt in Munich University* (London: Victor Gollancz, 1945).

[6] Bell visited Germany on 18–30 October 1945; the main purpose was the meeting with the German Church leaders at Stuttgart on 18–19 October; see Koechlin's and Bell's reports in: Clemens Vollnhals (ed.), *Die evangelische Kirche nach dem Zusammenbruch. Berichte ausländischer Beobachter aus dem Jahr 1945* (Göttingen: Vandenhoeck & Ruprecht, 1988), pp. 204–33; also see E. Gordon Rupp, *I seek my Brethren. Bishop George Bell and the German Churches* (London: Epworth Press, 1975), pp. 24–8; see too R.C.D. Jasper, *George Bell*, pp. 293–5.

members of the Party. With those men now disqualified from leadership, the reserves from which to draw men to the responsible posts in the restoration and education of Germany are pitifully small.

Well, no one who has visited German towns as I have done can be under any illusion as to the volume of destruction which the bombing has brought. Very nearly all towns of any substantial size have been anything from 50 to 90 per cent gutted. And the systematic destruction of railway bridges and lines of communication by the retreating German army has added to the disorganization. The population goes on living in cellars and shelters, with whole families crowded into single rooms. It is no wonder, apart from the shortage of food and fuel, that with this great mass of ruins always before their eyes, the Germans should be stunned. Other countries, I know, have suffered terribly at the Germans' hands. There is nothing here like the incinerator chambers: nothing here like the perpetual walking death in the person of the Gestapo: no sadistic cruelty or torture: no slave labour, or mercy killing. But simply destruction – simply a feeling of impotence – simply misery and despair.

And the question which I ask myself and ask you is, from the European point of view, how is such a problem to be tackled?

The perpetuation of such a desperate situation in the centre of Europe is an invitation to war. It is a task in the end, of course, for the Germans themselves. But at present the responsibility rests with the occupying Powers. They, in their four zones, are the Government of Germany. I can only speak of the British Military Government with any real knowledge. But I would express my great admiration of the public-spirited and conscientious way in which the leaders of the Military Government in the British zone approach and discharge their task. The task is partly educational, partly moral, partly political. On the educational side, from the European point of view, I hope that everything possible will be done to supply the schools and universities, as well as readers of every age, with the classics of German literature: and not only with German classics, but with other European classics as well. Also I hope that what has been written outside Germany in various branches of literature and scholarship since 1933 will be supplied as well. In both these ways a beginning can be made in breaking down the isolation of Germany from the rest of the world. And I would also like to see a re-entry, on a modest scale, of foreign newspapers to German libraries – especially from Switzerland. If only 500 daily newspapers – or even less than that – were permitted to be sent to selected recipients, it would be a valuable contribution to the education of the German mind. This is only, of course, a very small part of the educational task. It depends above all on securing the right German teachers. It involves the giving of generous democratic ideas, training in freedom and practice in social and political responsibility, an entire re-writing of many textbooks, and a radical transformation of the curriculum.

But of course beneath everything else lies the moral task. There is a conflict in the German soul, as in every soul, between the Devil and God. But an extra tragedy appears in the German soul: for while the good elements abound in many Germans, there has been a tendency at certain times in certain persons to the diabolical, and the evil, of which National Socialism has been the most terrible expression. And the question is, how can you discourage or extinguish the diabolical, and encourage the healthy and good? It cannot be by leaving the Germans alone in their present catastrophe. That will only deepen the despair. It cannot be by simply condemning the past, and philosophy of the past. It must be by giving them an active example of a better philosophy and showing in actual personal dealings evidence of the true way of life. I shall speak of the religious situation later, when I turn to the handling of the whole problem of recovery essentially as a Christian. But speaking as a European, I would say it is a task in which all men of good will, and all believers in spiritual values, must co-operate. I would say that while warning against militarism and National Socialism, and gangsterism, we must give grounds for hope, we must avoid incurring resentment and hatred, and give an incentive to work, holding up our policy as an illustration of a Western democratic outlook.

I believe that the main task is a cultural task, with the moral and spiritual as the essential factors. But these factors are profoundly affected by, as they also of course affect, the political and social structure of the nation. So, I have to look at the theme of Germany and Christendom, as a European, from that angle also.

Germany is the very heart of Europe. Amputate Germany, and you amputate Europe. Make the economic and social existence of Germany intolerable, and there will be the gravest repercussions, in the long run, on the economic and social fabric of Europe. It is the unity of Europe which is the real issue. We must regard Europe as *one*, and not either as a collection of fragments to be fitted together in a jigsaw puzzle, or as an assortment of entirely independent sovereign states, walled up and fortified against all the other states, similarly sovereign, self-centered and exclusive. And we must look at Europe's unity not primarily from a political, but from a cultural, and next, from an economic, point of view. Therefore when we are considering the treatment of Germany by the Allies, whether in Peace Treaties, or in any other post-war plans, we ought not, I suggest, to consider it from the point of view of whether treatment or the peace is hard or soft, but whether, in the long run, it is going to lead to the ultimate welfare of Europe, and therefore of the world.

1. It is fundamental that it is made as near impossible as men can devise for Germany to become a military power in any foreseeable future. Since the discovery of the secret of releasing atomic energy, the whole meaning of military power has been transformed. And, in theory, a small nation could, once in possession of the secret, destroy the greatest of the Big Three before there was any chance of counteraction. So it will be necessary to take special precautions so that any attempt at securing the secret of atomic energy on Germany's part be forestalled.

2. As Mr. Attlee[7] has said, no system of safeguards can itself provide any protection against would-be aggressors. The real security against a revival of militarism in Germany is an industrious and contented German people: as certainly a resentful and aggrieved Germany would take every step to stir up trouble between the Great Powers, and would be only too ready to suggest that it would be to one of the Great Powers' interest to have an armed Germany on her side.

---

[7] Clement Attlee (1883–1967): Labour politician, Deputy Prime Minister, 1940–1945, and Prime Minister, 1945–1951.

What are the conditions of a contented Germany now? I would say, generally speaking, these: -

(1) That Germany, from the purely economic point of view, should be united.
(2) That it should have enough industrial goods to export to enable it to pay its way.
(3) That it should not be overcrowded with surplus populations from other states.
(4) That there should be enough work for all able-bodied men to find something to do.

We should all like that, you may say. And there are many other countries belonging to the United Nations which would give a great deal for such an end. There is no reason why all countries should not have that modest requirement if the states of Europe were working together in a whole-hearted economic way, and if the American continent took its share. In Germany's case, there is also all the rebuilding of houses to be done, which will take many years: and all the education on liberal principles to be achieved. But there is this further difficulty affecting the boundaries and the population.

By the Potsdam decisions[8] – which the Peace Conference is expected to confirm – the total area of Germany is reduced by one quarter – that is from a pre-war 181,465 square miles to 135,500 square miles; but with the population of the whole of the quarter, plus another 3,000,000 from Czechoslovakia and Hungary to be accommodated in the Rump which is left, and to find work and houses, when in the great towns half the houses are destroyed and the work does not go round. And – this again from the European point of view – for that 42,000 square miles annexed by Poland from Germany the population of Poles available is at least 30 per cent less than the former German population, and far behind the Germans in ability to work the soil. In addition, the manner in which the mass expulsions of the 11,000,000 to 14,000,000 men, women and children liable to expulsion, are being carried out are such as to create terrible resentment. It will be impossible to achieve the two other – and they are prime – foundations of a contented Germany – namely that it should be politically free in relation to other nations, and that it should be a free, self-governing democracy, with freedom of speech, religion and assembly, while the economic conditions are wanting! But let me quote an expert writer in an English conservative journal as to the effect of the whole transaction so far as the European outlook is concerned:

> The disruption and disintegration of the economic structure of Europe through the shifting of frontiers as have taken place in the East, the unbalancing of its population by the expulsion of many millions of its economically most efficient inhabitants from the homes in which they lived, from the soil which they had tilled and from the towns, factories and workshops which they had built and kept going

---

[8] See Bell's criticism of the Potsdam Conference in the House of Lords on 22 August 1945; Hansard, vol. 137, cols. 141–5.

with their activity and skill, all that cannot but help to affect the political, moral and economic future of the entire continent in the most disastrous way perhaps for generations to come.[9]

Personally I think, as a European, the right policy after a terrible war to a defeated foe is to combine justice with mercy. The terms which Britain made with the Boers after the South African War led to a lasting peace because they were liberal. The Treaty which the Duke of Wellington made with France in 1815 has resulted in peace unbroken for 130 years, because it was generous. But the point I wish to make is that what has so far been determined with regard to Germany's future is unjust to Europe.

But let me speak now to the theme of Germany in Christendom, as a Christian. I hope not to keep you very much longer. But this is crucial. I have had, from 1933 onwards, very close contacts with the Confessional Church. You and I, Mr. Chairman,[10] have had memorable experiences together at Berlin in this connection. From the very start of the Hitler regime, and right through the war, there has been a strong, brave, Christian share in the Resistance movement to Hitler. The leaders of this movement, Niemöller, Dibelius, Wurm, Koch, and many more, and its members, loved their country with a passionate love – but hated the godless regime. They longed to see it freed from the godless tyranny, with all its cruelties, and they did their best, with their spiritual weapons of prayer and resistance to deliver it. But they lacked the material and the military power which alone could accomplish the material liberation. The Christian Church, be it Protestant, Catholic or Orthodox, has a very hard task everywhere, especially in Europe, today. In Germany the Protestant and Catholic Churches both failed to give the nation that strong moral foundation which should have enabled them to make such a regime as the Hitler regime impossible. The Protestant Church in particular has been too detached from interest in social questions, in work, and housing, and peace, and too subservient to the State. And the German people are so docile, so undemocratic by temperament, speaking generally, that the responsibility of the Church in evangelizing the people and insisting on the sovereignty of God over the State and over the whole of human life is all the greater.

But while Christians must work side by side with men of good will and all who believe in spiritual forces, the Christian Church has a special charge for filling the void in Germany today, and for giving the people that faith and that hope without which there can be no recovery.

I believe that the Churches have a great contribution to make; and that without them there can be no inspiration, no genuine education, no liberation of Germany's soul. I have, as I said, just come from the World Council of Churches, where I sat side by side with Bishop Wurm and Pastor Niemöller – brave preachers and fighters both. And we all worked and prayed together in a collegium of many churches, commissioned to proclaim to mankind the one Hope of the world.

The Christian Churches in Germany are but portions of the Christian Church all over the world. You in Switzerland, we in England, Christians in France, in Norway, in

---

[9] Bell provides no reference to this source.
[10] i.e. Koechlin himself.

Greece, in America, in China, in Japan, are members of the same Universal Christian Church. And because of our common belief in the same God and Saviour, we are bound to give them the maximum of support when they as Christians teach the Christian faith and commend the Christian life to their fellow-Germans.

There is a great clash of faiths all over the world. It is in Germany but not limited to Germany. It is the clash between Anti-God and God: between fascism and liberalism: between Marxian communism and real democracy: between belief in spiritual values and nihilism. In this clash Christianity has a decisive role to play. But in order to prevail it is essential that Christians should help one another. It is from Christianity that belief in the human personality is derived. Alas, totalitarianism creeps upon us. The Nazi poison has overflowed from Hitler's cup. Who shall succeed in resisting its influence if the Christian fails? The support of the Christian to his fellow Christians is needed everywhere. It is needed in each nation. It is needed from us all by the Christians who are now oppressed under totalitarian regimes in Poland, and in Yugoslavia, for example. It was needed by and given to the Christian churches in occupied countries during the war. It is needed by our fellow Christians in Germany today, for a different reason. The ghost of Hitler still haunts the nation. And a more dangerous spirit still, the phantom of Nihilism. It rises up from the ruins. It can only be banished by such a faith as that which fired the first Christians, and all true Christians since. By faith, did I say? By faith and by love.

We need the reign of Justice among men. But Justice by itself is not enough. Justice and Mercy must go together. We need to give our friendship to a nation which has done such wrong, and is now overwhelmed. But we need to acknowledge our own faults as well. Christ could say: 'Let him that is without sin among you cast the first stone', when He took pity on the woman taken in adultery.[11] Above all we need to show pity for them as for all suffering people – not only for the good, but for the bad. It is by showing pity – by giving help – by being moved with compassion for the multitudes without a shepherd in Germany, that we do something to follow in the steps of Christ, and something to bring together once again Germany and Christendom.

---

[11] John 8:7.

Bibliography

Bayles, William, *Seven were Hanged: An Authentic Account of the Student Revolt in Munich University*, London: Victor Gollancz, 1945.
Beckmann, Joachim (ed.), *Kirchliches Jahrbuch für die Evangelische Kirche in Deutschland 1933-1944*, 2nd edn, Gütersloh: Güterloher Verlagshaus, 1976.
Bell, George K.A., *A Brief Sketch of the Church of England*, London: SCM Press, 1930.
Bell, George K.A., *Randall Davidson, Archbishop of Canterbury*, 2 vols, London, 1935. Later editions, 1938 and 1952.
Bell, George K.A., *Christianity and World Order*, Harmondsworth: Penguin Books, 1940.
Bell, George K.A., *The Church and Humanity (1939-1946)*, London: Longmans, Green & Co., 1946.
Bell, George K.A., *Christian Unity: The Anglican Position*, London: Hodder & Stoughton, 1948.
Bell, George K.A., *The Word and the Sacraments*, London: A.R. Mowbray, 1952.
Bell, George K.A. and Herbert Waddams, *With God in the Darkness and Other Papers by Eivind Berggrav, Bishop of Oslo, Illustrating the Norwegian Church Conflict*, London: Hodder & Stoughton, 1943.
Bentley, James, *Martin Niemöller*, Oxford: Oxford University Press, 1984.
Bergen, Doris L., *Twisted Cross: The German Christian Movement in the Third Reich*, Chapel Hill: University of North Carolina Press, 1996.
Berlis, Angela, Stephan Leimgruber, and Martin Sallmann (eds), *Aufbruch und Widerspruch. Schweizer Theologinnen und Theologen im 20. und 21. Jahrhundert*, Zürich: TVZ, 2019.
Besier, Gerhard, *'Selbstreinigung' unter britischer Besatzungsherrschaft. Die Evangelisch-lutherische Landeskirche Hannovers und ihr Landesbischof Marahrens 1945-1947*, Göttingen: Vandenhoeck & Ruprecht, 1986.
Besier, Gerhard, *Die Kirchen und das Dritte Reich. Spaltungen und Abwehrkämpfe 1933-1937*, Berlin: Propyläen, 2001.
Besier, Gerhard, *'Intimately Associated for Many Years': George K.A. Bell's and Willem A. Visser 't Hooft's Common Life-Work in the Service of the Church Universal – Mirrored in their Correspondence*, Newcastle: Cambridge Scholars Publishing, 2 vols 2015.
Besier, Gerhard and Gerhard Sauter, *Wie Christen ihre Schuld bekennen*, Göttingen: Vandenhoeck & Ruprecht, 1985.
Bethge, Eberhard, *Dietrich Bonhoeffer. Theologe – Christ – Zeitgenosse*, 9th edn, Gütersloh 2005.
Binfield, Clyde, '"An Artisan of Christian Unity": Sir Frank Willis, Rome and the YMCA'. In *Unity and Diversity in the Church*. Studies in Church History 32, edited by R.N. Swanson, Oxford: Blackwell, 1996, pp. 489–505.
Boegner, Marc, *The Long Road to Unity: Memories and Anticipations*, London: William Collins, 1970.
Bonhoeffer, Dietrich, *Werke*, edited by Eberhard Bethge et al., 17 vols, München: Gütersloh, 1986–96.

DBW 13: *Dietrich Bonhoeffer, London 1933–1935*, ed. by Hans Goedeking, Martin Heimbucher and Hans Walter Schleicher, Gütersloh 1994; or, in English, Keith C. Clements (ed.), Fortress Press, Minneapolis, 2007.

DBW 15: *Illegale Theologenausbildung: Sammelvikariate 1937–1940*, ed. by Dirk Schulz, Gütersloh, 1998; or, in English, Victoria Barnett (ed.), *Theological Education Underground, 1937–1940*, Minneapolis: Fortress Press, 2011.

Boyens, Armin, *Kirchenkampf und Ökumene 1933–39*, Munich: Chr. Kaiser Verlag, 1969.

Boyens, Armin, *Kirchenkampf und Ökumene 1939–47*, Munich: Chr. Kaiser Verlag, 1973.

Bringeland, Hans, *Religion und Welt: Martin Dibelius (1883–1947)*, Vol. 2: *Dibelius in seiner Heidelberger Zeit (bis 1933)*, Münster: Lit Verlag, 2013 and Vol. 3: *Dibelius im Dritten Reich und in der Nachkriegszeit*, Münster: Lit Verlag, 2013.

Buller, Amy, *Darkness over Germany*, London: Longmans, Green and Co., 1943.

Busch, Eberhard, *Karl Barths Lebenslauf: Nach seinen Briefen und autobiografischen Texten*, Zurich: TVZ, 2005. Or *Karl Barth: His Life from Letters and Autobiographical Texts*, Grand Rapids: Wm Eerdmans, 1976.

Butler, J.R.M, *Lord Lothian, Philip Kerr (1882–1940)*, London: Macmillan, 1960.

Chandler, Andrew (ed.), *Brethren in Adversity: Bishop George Bell and the Crisis of German Protestantism, 1933–1939*, Woodbridge: Boydell and Brewer, 1997.

Chandler, Andrew (ed.), *The Church and Humanity. The Life and Work of George Bell, 1883–1958*, Farnham: Ashgate, 2012.

Chandler, Andrew, *George Bell, Bishop of Chichester: Church, State and Resistance in the Age of Dictatorship*, Grand Rapids: Wm. B. Erdmanns, 2016.

Chandler, Andrew, *British Christians and the Third Reich: Church, State and the Judgement of Nations*, Cambridge: Cambridge University Press, 2022.

Christensen, Hilda Rømer, 'When the YWCA Entered the City: The Complexity of Space, Gender and Modernity'. In *Pieties and Gender*, edited by L.E. Sjrup and Hilda Rømer Christensen, Leiden: E.J. Brill, 2009, pp. 196–9.

Conway, John S., *The Nazi Persecution of the Churches 1933–45*, London: Weidenfeld and Nicholson, 1968.

Cresswell, Amos S. and Maxwell G. Tow, *Dr. Franz Hildebrandt. Mr. Valiant-for-Truth*, Leominster: Gracewing, 2000.

Daughrity, Dyron B., *A Worldly Christian: The Life and Times of Stephen Neill*, Cambridge: Lutterworth Press, 2022.

Dentan, Paul-Émile, 'Alphons Koechlin – Schweigen können wir nicht'. In Dentan (ed.), *Nachgeben oder Widerstehen. Schweizer Protestanten gegen den Nazismus*, Zürich: EVZ, 2002, pp. 43–58.

Domarus, Max, *Hitler. Reden und Proklamationen 1932–1945*, vols. 1 and 2, Munich: Würzburg, 1965.

Domarus, Max, *Dokumente zur Kirchenpolitik des Dritten Reiches*, Vol. 1–6/2, München: Kaiser, 1971 – Gütersloh: Gütersloher Verlagshaus, 2017.

Ericksen, Robert P., *Theologians under Hitler: Gerhard Kittel, Paul Althaus and Emanuel Hirsch*, New Haven: Yale University Press, 1985.

d'Espine, Henri, *Alphonse Koechlin. Pasteur et chef d'église, 1885–1965*, Genève: Labor et Fides, 1971.

Fandrich, Heiner, *Carl Stange – Theologe und Wissenschaftsorganisator*, Gütersloh: Gütersloher Verlagshaus, 2022.

Fey, Harold (ed.), *The Ecumenical Advance: A History of the Ecumenical Movement, Vol. 2: 1948 – 1968*, London: SPCK, 1970.

Gailus, Manfred and Clemens Vollnhals (eds), *Christlicher Antisemitismus im 20. Jahrhundert. Der Tübinger Theologe und 'Judenforscher' Gerhard Kittel*, Göttingen: Vandenhoeck & Ruprecht, 2020.
Gerlach-Praetorius, Angelika, *Die Kirche vor der Eidesfrage. Die Diskussion um den Pfarrereid im 'Dritten Reich'*, Göttingen: Vandenhoeck & Ruprecht,1964.
Gerstenmaier, Eugen (ed.), *Kirche, Volk und Staat. Stimmen aus der Deutschen Evangelischen Kirche zur Oxford Weltkirchenkonferenz*, Berlin: Furche Verlag, 1937.
Gieseking, Erik, *Der Fall Otto John. Entführung oder freiwilliger Übertritt in die DDR*, Lauf and Pregnitz: Europaforum-Verlag, 2005.
Greschat, Martin (ed.), *Die Schuld der Kirche. Dokumente und Reflexionen zur Stuttgarter Schulderklärung vom 18/19. Oktober 1945*, Munich: Chr. Kaiser, 1982.
Greschat, Martin (ed.), *Zwischen Widerspruch und Widerstand*, Munich: C.H. Beck Verlag, 1987.
Gutteridge, R.J.C., 'German Protestantism and the Hitler Regime'. *Theology* 27, no. 161 (November 1933): pp. 243–64.
Gutteridge, R.J.C., *Open Thy Mouth for the Dumb. The German Evangelical Church and the Jews, 1879–1950*, Oxford: Basil Blackwell, 1976.
Hansard: Debates of the House of Lords, Fifth Series, London: HMSO, 1933–1939.
Hassing, Arne, *Church Resistance to Nazism in Norway, 1940–1945*, Seattle: University of Washington Press, 2014.
Hauschild, Wolf-Dieter (ed.), *Profile des Luthertums. Biographien zum 20. Jahrhundert*, Göttingen: Vandenhoeck & Ruprecht, 1998.
Heiene, Gunnar, 'Bishop Berggrav's Peace Initiatives at the Beginning of the Second World War'. *Current Research on Peace and Violence* 13 (1990): pp. 210–19.
Heiene, Gunnar, *Eivind Berggrav. Eine Biographie*, Göttingen: Vandenhoeck & Ruprecht, 1997.
Helmreich, Ernst, 'The Arrest and Freeing of the Protestant Bishops of Württemberg and Bavaria, September–October 1934', *Central European History* 2 (1969): pp. 159–69.
Helmreich, Ernst, *The German Churches under Hitler: Background, Struggle and Epilogue*, Detroit: Wayne State University Press, 1979.
Hockenos, Matthew, *Then They Came for Me: Martin Niemöller, The Pastor Who Defied the Nazis*, New York: Basic Books, 2018.
Hoffmann, Peter, *Widerstand, Staatsstreich, Attentat. Der Kampf der Opposition gegen Hitler*, 3rd ed., Munich: Piper Verlag, 1979. Or Peter Hoffmann, *The History of German Resistance 1933–1945*, 3rd edn, London: Macdonald and Jane's, 1977.
Jasper, Ronald C.D., *George Bell. Bishop of Chichester*, London: Oxford University Press, 1967.
Keller, Adolf, *Religion and the European Mind*, London: Lutterworth, 1934.
Kirche Basel-Stadt, Kirchenamt der Evangelisch-reformierten (eds), *Der Reformation verpflichtet. Gestalten und Gestalter in Stadt und Landschaft Basel aus fünf Jahrhunderten*, Basel: Merian, 1979.
Koechlin, Alphons, 'Die Weltkonferenz für Praktisches Christentum in Stockholm 19. bis 30. August 1925'. In *im Auftrag des Schweizerischen Evangelischen Kirchenbundes dargestellt*, Basel: Friedrich Reinhardt, 1926.
Koechlin, Alphons, 'Kundgebung des Deutschen Evangelischen Missionsrates zur Kirchenfrage', in *Die Bekenntnisse des Jahres 1934*, edited by Kurt Dietrich Schmidt, Göttingen: Vandenhoeck & Ruprecht, 1935.

Koechlin, Alphons, 'Oekumenische Konferenz in Utrecht 1938', *Basler Nachrichten*, 17 May 1938.
von Koenigswald, Harald, *Birger Forell: Leben und Wirken in den Jahren 1933–1958*, Witten and Berlin: Eckart Verlag, 1962.
Kraemer, Hendrik, *The Christian Message in a Non-Christian World*, London: Edinburgh House Press, 1938.
Kreutzer, Heike, *Das Reichskirchenministerium im Gefüge der nationalsozialistischen Herrschaft*, Düsseldorf: Droste, 2000.
Kunze, Rolf-Ulrich, *Theodor Heckel 1894–1967. Eine Biographie*, Stuttgart: Kohlhammer, 1997.
Lächele, Rainer, *Ein Volk, ein Reich, ein Glaube. Die ‚Deutschen Christen' in Württemberg 1925–1960*, Stuttgart: Calwer Verlag, 1994.
Landmesser, Christof (ed.), *Bultmann Handbuch*, Tübingen: Mohr Siebeck, 2017.
Lane, Antii, Juha Meriläinen, and Matti Peiponen, 'Ecumenical Reconstruction, Advocacy and Action: The World Council of Churches in Times of Change, from the 1940s to the early 1970s'. *Kirchliche Zeitgeschichte/Contemporary Church History* 30, (2017): pp. 327–41.
Leuschner, Immanuel, 'Pfarrer Alphons Koechlin (1885–1965) – Ein Mann der Oekumene und der Mission'. UB Basel NL 37; VII, 2.
Lilje, Hanns, *In the Valley of the Shadow*, London: SCM Press, 1950.
Lindner, Rudolf, 'Pfarrer Alphons Koechlin-Thurneysen', *The Basler Stadtbuch* 86 (1966): 26–8.
Lindt, Andreas, *George Bell – Alphons Koechlin, Briefwechsel 1933–1954*, Zürich: EVZ, 1969.
Loscher, Klaus, *Studium und Alltag hinter Stacheldraht, Birger Forells Beitrag zum theologisch-pädagogischen Lehrbetrieb im Norton Camp, England (1945–1948)*, Neukirchen-Vluyn: Neukirchener, 1997.
Ludlow, Peter W., 'Scandinavia Between the Great Powers: Attempts at Mediation in the First Year of the Second World War', *Särtryck ur Historisk Tidskrift*, 1974.
Ludwig, Hartmut, *An der Seite der Entrechteten und Schwachen: Zur Geschichte des ‚Büro Pfarrer Grüber' (1938 bis 1940) und der Ev. Hilddtelle für ehemals Rasseverfolgte nach 1945*, Berlin: Logos Verlag, 2009.
Ludwig, Hartmut and Eberhard Röhm (eds), *Evangelisch getauft – Als 'Juden' verfolgt. Theologen jüdischer Herkunft in der Zeit des Nationalsozialismus. Ein Gedenkbuch*, Stuttgart: Calwer Verlag, 2014.
Mallmann, Klaus Michael and Gerhard Paul, *Das zersplitterte Nein. Saarländer gegen Hitler*, Bonn: Dietz, 1989.
Meier, Kurt, *Der evangelische Kirchenkampf. Gesamtdarstellung in drei Bänden*. Vol. I: *Der Kampf um die 'Reichskirche'*, Halle: Niemeyer, licence Göttingen: Vandenhoeck & Ruprecht, 1976; Vol. II: *Gescheiterte Neuordnungsversuche im Zeichen staatlicher 'Rechtshilfe'*, ibid., 1976; Vol. III: *Im Zeichen des zweiten Weltkrieges*, ibid. 1984.
Meyer, Winfried, *Unternehmen Sieben. Eine Rettungsaktion für vom Holocaust Bedrohte aus dem Amt Ausland/Abwehr im Oberkommando der Wehrmacht*, Frankfurt/M.: Hain, 1993.
Müller, Christine-Ruth, *Bekenntnis und Bekennen. Dietrich Bonhoeffer in Bethel (1933). Ein lutherischer Versuch*, München: Chr. Kaiser Verlag, 1989.
Müller, Friedeborg L., *The History of German Lutheran Congregations in England, 1900–1950*, Frankfurt/M: Peter Lang, 1987.
Nicolaisen, Carsten, *Der Weg nach Barmen. Die Entstehungsgeschichte der Theologischen Erklärung von 1934*, Neukirchen: Neukirchener Verlag, 1985.

Niemöller, Wilhelm (ed.), *Die zweite Bekenntnissynode der Deutschen Evangelischen Kirche zu Dahlem (AGK 3)*, Göttingen: Vandenhoeck & Ruprecht, 1958.
Niemöller, Wilhelm (ed.), *Martin Niemöller, Briefe aus der Gefangenschaft Moabit*, Frankfurt/M: Lembeck, 1975.
Oelke, Harry, *Hanns Lilje. Ein Lutheraner in der Weimarer Republik und im Kirchenkampf*, Stuttgart: Kohlhammer, 1999.
Oldham, J.H. and W.A. Visser 't Hooft, *The Churches Survey Their Task*, London: SCM Press, 1937.
Priepke, Manfred, *Die evangelische Jugend im Dritten Reich 1933–1936*, Hannover: Norddeutsche Verlagsanstalt, 1960.
Radcliffe, James, *Proceedings of the Church Assembly of the Church of England*, London: Church of England, 1933–1939.
Radcliffe, James, 'Bishop Bell of Chichester and Non-Aryan Christians: The Role of the Berlin Quakers, the Paulusbund, the Grüberbüro and the German-Jewish Emigration Office', *Kirchliche Zeitgeschichte/Contemporary Church History* 21 (2008): pp. 277–86.
Raina, Peter (ed.), *Bishop George Bell: House of Lords Speeches and Correspondence with Rudolf Hess*, Frankfurt/M: Peter Lang, 2009.
Ringshausen, Gerhard, *Widerstand und christlicher Glaube angesichts des Nationalsozialismus*, 2nd ed., Berlin: Litt Verlag, 2008.
Ringshausen, Gerhard, 'George Bell's Relations to the German Evangelical Church and the Problem of Information', *Kirchliche Zeitgeschichte/Contemporary Church History* 33 (2020): pp. 351–9.
Ringshausen, Gerhard and Andrew Chandler (eds), *The George Bell–Gerhard Leibholz Correspondence. In the Long Shadow of the Third Reich, 1938–1958*, London: Bloomsbury, 2019.
Robertson, Edwin, *Unshakeable Friend: George Bell and the German Churches*, London: CCBI, 1995.
Robertson, Edwin, *Bishop of the Resistance. The Life of Eivind Berggrav, Bishop of Oslo, Norway*, Saint Louis: Concordia, 2000.
Roggelin, Holger, *Franz Hildebrandt. Ein lutherischer Dissenter im Kirchenkampf und Exil*, Göttingen: Vandenhoeck & Ruprecht, 1999.
Rosenberg, Alfred, *Protestantische Rompilger. Der Verrat an Luther und der Mythus des 20. Jahrhunderts*, Munich: Hoheneichen-Verlag, 1937.
Rouse, Ruth and Stephen Neill (eds), *A History of the Ecumenical Movement, 1517–1948*, London: SPCK, 1954.
Rupp, E. Gordon, *I Seek my Brethren. Bishop George Bell and the German Churches*, London: Epworth Press, 1975.
Schilling, Manuel, *Das eine Wort zwischen den Zeiten. Die Wirkungsgeschichte der Barmer Theologischen Erklärung vom Kirchenkampf bis zum Fall der Mauer*, Neukirchen: Neukirchener, 2005.
Schmidt, Dietmar, *Martin Niemöller – Eine Biographie*, Stuttgart: Rowohlt Verlag, 1983.
Schmidt, Kurt Dietrich (ed.), *Die Bekenntnisse und grundsätzlichen Äußerungen zur Kirchenfrage des Jahres 1933*, Göttingen: Vandenhoeck and Ruprecht, 1934.
Schmidt, William J. and Edward Ouellete, *What Kind of a Man? The Life of Henry Smith Leiper*, New York: Friendship Press, 1986.
Schneider, Martin, *Reichsbischof Ludwig Müller. Eine Untersuchung zu Leben, Werk und Persönlichkeit*, Göttingen: Vandenhoeck & Ruprecht, 1993.

Scholder, Klaus, *The Churches and the Third Reich*. Vol. I: *Preliminary History and the Time of Illusions 1918–1934*; Vol. II: *The Year of Disillusionment: 1934 Barmen and Rome*, London: SCM Press, 1987 and 1988.

Siegele-Wenschkewitz, Leonore, *Nationalsozialismus und Kirchen: Religionspolitik von Partei und Staat bis 1935*, Düsseldorf: Droste Verlag, 1974.

Siegmund, Johannes Jürgen, *Bischof Johannes Lilje, Abt zu Loccum. Eine Biographie, Nach Selbstzeugnissen, Schriften und Briefen und Zeitzeugenberichten*, Göttingen: Vandenhoeck & Ruprecht, 2003.

Stöhr, Martin and Klaus Würmell (eds), *Juden, Christen und die Ökumene. Adolf Freudenberg 1894–1994. Ein bemerkenswertes Leben*, Frankfurt/M.: Spener, 1994.

Smyth-Florentin, Françoise, *Pierre Maury: Prédicateur d'Evangile*, Paris: Labor et Fides, 2009.

Tenorth, Heinz-Elmar et al (eds), *Friedrich Siegmund-Schultze (1885–1969). Ein Leben für Kirche, Wissenschaft und soziale Arbeit*, Stuttgart: Kohlhammer, 2007.

Tietz, Christiane, *Karl Barth. A Life in Conflict*, Oxford: Oxford University Press, 2021.

Visser't Hooft, W.A., *Memoirs*, London: SCM Press, 1973.

Vollnhals, Clemens (ed.), *Die evangelische Kirche nach dem Zusammenbruch. Berichte ausländischer Beobachter aus dem Jahr 1945*, Göttingen: Vandenhoeck & Ruprecht, 1988.

Weitz, John, *Hitler's Banker. Hjalmar Horace Greeley Schacht*, Boston: Little, Brown, 1997.

Wright, Jonathan R.C., *'Above the Parties' The Political Attitudes of the German Protestant Leadership 1918–1933*, London: Oxford University Press, 1974.

Index

13-point programme of Gauleiter
    Greiser   28
1933
    April   15–16
    August   18
    Bell to Archbishop Lang, 10 June
        1933   20–1
    Bell to Koechlin, 1 July 1933   29–30
    Bell to Koechlin, 4 July 1933   33
    Bell to Koechlin, 4 November
        1933   51
    Bell to Koechlin, 4 October 1933   40–1
    Bell to Koechlin, 7 July 1933   33–4
    Bell to Koechlin, 10 July 1933   34–5
    Bell to Koechlin, 14 June 1933   23
    Bell to Koechlin, 19 December
        1933   54–5
    Bell to Koechlin, 20 June 1933   26
    Bell to Koechlin, 25 October
        1933   44–5
    Bell to Koechlin, 27 September
        1933   35–6
    Bell to Koechlin, 30 December
        1933   56–7
    Bell to Koechlin, 30 October 1933   50
    Bell to Ludwig Müller, 23 October
        1933   45–7
    Bell to Müller, 12 December 1933   57
    Bell to the Editor of *The Times*, 12 June
        1933   23–6
    Bell to the Editor of *The Times*,
        published 4 October 1933   41–3
    December   19
    February   15
    January   15
    J.H. Oldham to Bell, 8 June 1933   20
    July   17–18
    June   16–17
    Koechlin's secretary to Bell, 12 October
        1933   43–4
    Koechlin to Bell, 1 November
        1933   50–1
    Koechlin to Bell, 3 July 1933   31–2
    Koechlin to Bell, 11 December
        1933   52–4
    Koechlin to Bell, 14 June 1933   21–2
    Koechlin to Bell, 27 December
        1933   56
    Koechlin to Bell, 27 June 1933   26–9
    Koechlin to Bell, 28 October
        1933   47–50
    Koechlin to Bell, 30 September
        1933   36–40
    March   15–16
    May   16
    Müller to Bell, 8 December 1933   55
    November   19
    October   18–19
    Oldham to Koechlin, 16 November
        1933   52
    September   18
1934
    April   59
    August   60
    Bell's Message to the Representatives
        of Life and Work, 10 May
        1934   88–9
    Bell to Bishop Ammundsen, 7 July
        1934   96
    Bell to Heckel, 13 February 1934   70–2
    Bell to Henry-Louis Henriod, 15
        August 1934   103
    Bell to Karl Koch, 18 July 1934   102
    Bell to Koechlin, 1 November
        1934   119–20
    Bell to Koechlin, 1 October
        1934   104–5
    Bell to Koechlin, 2 May 1934   83
    Bell to Koechlin, 3 December
        1934   129
    Bell to Koechlin, 7 July 1934   95

Bell to Koechlin, 8 October 1934   106
Bell to Koechlin, 9 May 1934   87
Bell to Koechlin, 10 January 1934   62
Bell to Koechlin, 10 March 1934   76
Bell to Koechlin, 11 October 1934   110
Bell to Koechlin, 12 November 1934   121
Bell to Koechlin, 13 February 1934   68-9
Bell to Koechlin, 13 October 1934   110-11
Bell to Koechlin, 15 August 1934   102-3
Bell to Koechlin, 15 December 1934   135
Bell to Koechlin, 15 October 1934   111-13
Bell to Koechlin, 17 October 1934   116
Bell to Koechlin, 18 January 1934   65
Bell to Koechlin, 19 July 1934   100-1
Bell to Koechlin, 19 October 1934   116-17
Bell to Koechlin, 23 April 1934   80-1
Bell to Koechlin, 27 February 1934   74-5
Bell to Koechlin, 29 December 1934   136-7
Bell to Koechlin, 29 November 1934   126
Bell to Schönfeld, 17 February 1934   72-3
Bell to the Editor of *The Times*, 16 January 1934   64-5
December   61
February   58
German Church Struggle, from *The Times*, 8 June 1934   89-91
The German Church, 10 February 1934   70
The German Church, from *The Times*, 8 June 1934   91-3
Henriod to Bell, 13 December 1934   132-5
Informal Notes, 9 February 1934   70
January   58
July   60
June   59

Koechlin: Telephone Bishop of Chichester, Wednesday, 17 October 1934   113-14
Koechlin to Bell, 1 December 1934   126-8
Koechlin to Bell, 3 October 1934   105-6
Koechlin to Bell, 5 December 1934   129-30
Koechlin to Bell, 5 July 1934   93-5
Koechlin to Bell, 5 May 1934   85-7
Koechlin to Bell, 7 March 1934   75-6
Koechlin to Bell, 8 February 1934   65-7
Koechlin to Bell, 9 November 1934   120-1
Koechlin to Bell, 9 October 1934   107
Koechlin to Bell, 10 July 1934   97-8
Koechlin to Bell, 11 October 1934   108-9
Koechlin to Bell, 12 December 1934   131-2
Koechlin to Bell, 13 November 1934   122
Koechlin to Bell, 14 July 1934   98-100
Koechlin to Bell, 15 January 1934   62-3
Koechlin to Bell, 15 November 1934   122-4
Koechlin to Bell, 17 October 1934   114-16
Koechlin to Bell, 21 December 1934   135-6
Koechlin to Bell, 22 October 1934   117-18
Koechlin to Bell, 23 February 1934   73-4
Koechlin to Bell, 26 March 1934   77-8
Koechlin to Bell, 26 November 1934   124-6
Koechlin to Bell, 28 April 1934   81-2
Koechlin to Bell, 30 October 1934   118-19
Koechlin (via Secretary R. Preiswerk) to Bell, 19 April 1934   78
Koechlin to Bell. 13 February 1934   67-8
Koechlin to Schönfeld, 19 April 1934   78-80

March 58
Mason to Koechlin, 10 June 1934   89
May   59
November   61
October   60–1
Oldham to Cavert   111
to the representatives of the Churches on the Oecumenical Council   83–5
September   60
1935
    April   138
    August   138–9
    Bell to Koechlin, 3 April 1935   152
    Bell to Koechlin, 4 December 1935   171
    Bell to Koechlin, 17 April 1935   155–6
    Bell to Koechlin, 19 July 1935   161
    Bell to Koechlin, 21 January 1935   143
    Bell to Koechlin, 21 October 1935   161–3
    Bell to Koechlin, 22 May 1935   156–7
    Bell to Koechlin, 25 March 1935   146
    Bell to Koechlin, 26 December 1935   172–3
    Bell to Koechlin, 29 March 1935   149
    Bell to Koechlin, 31 May 1935   160
    December   139
    February   138
    January   138
    July   138
    June   138
    Koechlin to Bell, 1 April 1935   150–1
    Koechlin to Bell, 3 December 1935   170–1
    Koechlin to Bell, 6 April 1935   152–3
    Koechlin to Bell, 7 January 1935   140
    Koechlin to Bell, 12 April 1935   153–5
    Koechlin to Bell, 15 January 1935   141–2
    Koechlin to Bell, 16 November 1935   166–8
    Koechlin to Bell, 22 June 1935   160–1
    Koechlin to Bell, 22 March 1935   143–6
    Koechlin to Bell, 23 December 1935   172
    Koechlin to Bell, 23 October 1935   163–6
    Koechlin to Bell, 24 May 1935   157–9
    Koechlin to Bell, 27 March 1935   146–7
    Koechlin to Bell, 27 May 1935   159
    Koechlin to Bell, 28 December 1935   173–4
    Koechlin to Bell, 28 November 1935   168–70
    Koechlin to Bell, 29 March 1935   147–9
    March   138
    May   138
    November   139
    October   139
    September   139
1936
    April   175
    August   176
    Bell to Koechlin, 5 June 1936   191
    Bell to Koechlin, 5 March 1936   181
    Bell to Koechlin, 7 August 1936   199
    Bell to Koechlin, 8 February 1936   180
    Bell to Koechlin, 8 July 1936   196–7
    Bell to Koechlin, 9 January 1936   177
    Bell to Koechlin, 12 June 1936   194–5
    Bell to Koechlin, 29 April 1936   182–3
    Bell to Zoellner, 23 June 1936   197–9
    December   176
    February   175
    January   175
    July   176
    June   175–6
    Koechlin to Bell, 2 May 1936   187
    Koechlin to Bell, 3 July 1936   195–6
    Koechlin to Bell, 5 June 1936   191–4
    Koechlin to Bell, 6 February 1936   179–80
    Koechlin to Bell, 7 March 1936   181–2
    Koechlin to Bell, 14 January 1936   177–9
    Koechlin to Bell, 28 May 1936   188–90
    March   175
    Mason to Koechlin, 12 March 1936   182
    May   175
    November   176
    October   176
    Zoellner to Bell, 1 April 1936   183–7

Zoellner to Bell, 29 July 1936   200–1
1937
   April   202
   August   202–3
   Bell to Eidem, 11 October 1937   234
   Bell to Koechlin, 4 December
      1937   247
   Bell to Koechlin, 4 October
      1937   227–8
   Bell to Koechlin, 9 November
      1937   244–5
   Bell to Koechlin, 11 November
      1937   245
   Bell to Koechlin, 11 October
      1937   235
   Bell to Koechlin, 13 December
      1937   249
   Bell to Koechlin, 23 August
      1937   219–21
   Bell to Koechlin, 25 October
      1937   239–40
   Bell to Koechlin, 28 April 1937   206–7
   Bell to Koechlin, 28 May 1937   208–9
   Bell to Koechlin, 30 July 1937   213–14
   Bell to Koechlin, 31 December
      1937   250–1
   Bell to Mrs. Koechlin, 6 January
      1937   204
   December   203
   February   202
   January   202
   July   202
   June   202
   Kerrl to the leading officials of
      the German Evangelical
      Provincial Churches, 19 May
      1937   212–13
   Koechlin to Bell, 1 June 1937   210–12
   Koechlin to Bell, 3/4 August
      1937   214–18
   Koechlin to Bell, 3 April 1937   204–6
   Koechlin to Bell, 4 November
      1937   240–4
   Koechlin to Bell, 5 October
      1937   228–9
   Koechlin to Bell, 9 October
      1937   229–33
   Koechlin to Bell, 10 December
      1937   247–8
   Koechlin to Bell, 15 November
      1937   246
   Koechlin to Bell, 16 December
      1937   249–50
   Koechlin to Bell, 20 October
      1937   235–9
   Koechlin to Bell, 25 September
      1937   224–7
   Koechlin to Bell, 26 May 1937   207–8
   Koechlin to Bell, 30 August
      1937   222–4
   March   202
   November   203
   October   203
1938
   April   252
   Bell to Koechlin, 9 April 1938   274–5
   Bell to Koechlin, 11 January
      1938   256–7
   Bell to Koechlin, 11 July 1938   284–5
   Bell to Koechlin, 13 April 1938   276
   Bell to Koechlin, 14 February
      1938   267–8
   Bell to Koechlin, 25 March
      1938   272–3
   Bell to Koechlin, 30 April 1938   278
   Bell to Schönfeld, 30 April 1938   278–9
   January   252
   July   252
   Koechlin to Bell, 5 February
      1938   264–5
   Koechlin to Bell, 5 March 1938   270–2
   Koechlin to Bell, 5 May 1938   281–2
   Koechlin to Bell, 7 January
      1938   254–6
   Koechlin to Bell, 8 April 1938   273–4
   Koechlin to Bell, 8 July 1938   282–4
   Koechlin to Bell, 11 April 1938   275–6
   Koechlin to Bell, 11 February
      1938   265–7
   Koechlin to Bell, 12 January
      1938   257–61
   Koechlin to Bell, 21 February
      1938   268
   Koechlin to Bell, 25 February
      1938   270
   Koechlin to Bell, 28 April 1938   277–8
   Koechlin to Bell, 28 January
      1938   261–3

Koechlin to Bell, 29 January
    1938   263–4
Koechlin to Bell, 29 March 1938   273
Koechlin to Bell, Utrecht, 13 May
    1938   282
Koechlin to Oldham, 21 February
    1938   269–70
March   252
May   252
November   253
October   252–3
Schönfeld to Bell, 28 April 1938
    279–81
September   252
1939
    August   286
    Bell to Koechlin, 8 'December'
        1939   292–3
    Bell to Koechlin, 9 November
        1939   290–1
    Bell to Koechlin, 11 September
        1939   289–90
    Bell to Koechlin, 14 January
        1939   289
    February   286
    January   286
    July   286
    June   286
    Koechlin to Bell, 11 January
        1939   287–9
    Koechlin to Bell, 20 November
        1939   291–2
    March   286
    May   286
    November   286
    September   286
1940
    April   294
    April–June   294
    Bell to Koechlin, 1 October 1940   300
    Bell to Koechlin, 19 April 1940
        296–7
    January   294
    July–October   294
    Koechlin to Bell, 19 August 1940   299
    Koechlin to Bell, 26 March
        1940   295–6
    Koechlin to Bell, 27 April 1940   298–9
    March   294
    May   294
1941–7
    April 1945   301
    August 1945   301
    Bell to Koechlin, 12 December
        1947   303–4
    Bell to Koechlin, 18 March 1946   302
    Bell to Koechlin, 30 December
        1947   306
    December 1941   301
    December 1942   301
    February 1944   301
    February 1946   301
    January 1943   301
    January 1947   301
    July 1944   301
    July 1945   301
    June 1941   301
    June 1944   301
    June 1946   301
    June 1947   301
    Koechlin to Bell, 6 June 1947   303
    Koechlin to Bell, 16 March 1946   302
    Koechlin to Bell, 20 December
        1947   304–6
    Koechlin to Bell, 27 March 1946   302
    May 1942   301
    May 1945   301
    November 1943   301
    October 1941   301
    October 1945   301
    October 1946   301
1948–58
    April 1948   307
    August 1948   307
    August 1954   307
    Bell to Koechlin, 19 February
        1953   309
    Bell to Koechlin, 25 September
        1954   309–10
    January 1953   307
    July 1949   307
    July 1950   307
    June 1948   307
    June 1950   307
    Koechlin to Bell, 15 December
        1950   308–9
    May 1949   307
    October 1958   307

Acland, Richard 206
Aid Organisation of the Protestant Churches of Switzerland 4
Albertz, Martin 258, 261, 262, 291, 292
Ammundsen, Valdemar 95, 96, 101–3, 108, 109, 156, 173
amnesty decree 81
amnesty legislation 79, 80
Anglican communion in India 205
Anglo-German naval agreement 151, 155, 202
Anglo-German theological conferences 5
anti-Christian attitude 220
Aryan Paragraph 7, 16, 18, 19, 21, 35, 37, 40, 44, 46–8, 50, 51, 53–5, 58, 68, 112, 125, 233
Asmussen, Hans 66, 67, 71, 124–6, 148, 173, 178, 216, 230, 258
Attlee, Clement 319, 319 n.7
Aubrey, M.E. 215, 218
Aulen, Gustav 107, 109, 110
Azariah, Vedanayagam Samuel 206

Barber, Melanie 13
Barmen Confession Synod 66, 67, 90
Barmen Declaration 29, 39, 94, 148
Barth, Karl 2, 4, 9, 10, 27, 29, 34, 35, 53, 59, 61, 65, 66, 85, 107, 120, 122, 124–30, 135, 136, 140, 141, 143, 146, 148, 149, 157–61, 169, 170, 173, 178, 188, 193, 208, 210, 255, 256, 258, 284, 290, 298, 313
Barth's Dialectical Theology 3
Basel Mission 3, 10, 28, 66, 71, 94, 105, 107, 150, 151, 157, 187, 192, 204–6, 224, 255, 258, 283–5, 291, 292, 299
basic theological principles 15
Baudert, Samuel 232, 233, 235
Beckmann, Joachim 71, 72
Bell, George. *See also individual entries*
  Anglo-German theological conferences 5
  Dean of Canterbury 1
  executive committee, Universal Christian Council for Life and Work 1

Bell-Koechlin letters
  in 1933 15–57
  in 1934 58–137
  in 1935 138–74
  in 1936 175–201
  in 1937 202–51
  in 1938 252–85
  in 1939 286–93
  in 1940 294–300
  in 1941–7 301–6
  in 1948–58 307–10
Berggrav, Eivind 4, 292, 293, 296–8
Berggrav's promotion of negotiated settlement 4
Berliner Mission 279
Berliner Tageblatt 152, 155
Bismarck, Prince Otto Christian von 111
Bleek, Philipp 259, 261
Blomberg, Werner von 145, 208
Blue Cross organization 2
Bodelschwingh, Friedrich von 1, 7, 16, 17, 21–5, 27, 28, 77, 94, 102, 120, 124, 125, 142, 162–4, 192, 225, 226, 265, 267
body-line bowling 45
Boegner, Marc 4, 113, 114, 133, 303, 304
Böhm, Hans 217, 218, 223, 225, 227, 232, 236–8, 240, 243, 256, 258, 262–4, 266, 276
Bolshevism 27, 45
Bonhoeffer, Dietrich 4, 62, 64, 85, 89, 96, 101–3, 112, 137, 146, 151, 155–8, 221, 244, 297, 301
Boyens, Armin 44
Breit, Thomas 59, 120, 121, 125, 265–7
Brown, William Adams 29, 51, 219
Buchman, Frank 18, 44, 299
Bultmann, Rudolf 233, 287, 289
Busch, Eberhard 140
Büsing, Wolfgang 297, 298

Cadman, Samuel Parkes 30
Canaris, Admiral Wilhelm 4
Cavert, Samuel McCrea 111
Chamberlain, F.J. 80, 81
Chamberlain, Neville 252
Chamberlain, Während 314, 315
Chandler, Andrew 20, 35, 78, 121, 163, 272, 274, 276

Choisy, Jaques Eugène   32, 98, 105–7, 144
Christensen, Hilda Rømer   168
Christensen, Ingolf Elster   296, 297
Christianity and Social Order (Temple)   294
The Christian Message in a Non-Christian world (Kraemer)   280
Christiansen, Nikolaus   150, 151
Christian World   31, 41, 84, 88, 156
chronological tables   14
Church peace   79, 169
church struggle   3, 5, 6, 58, 66, 67, 85, 99, 145, 152
'The Church, the State, and the World Order'   84
Coch, Friedrich   169, 170, 188
Committee of 7   216
Confessing Church (*Bekennende Kirche*)   5–9, 13, 25, 34, 39, 49, 59–61, 63, 67, 72, 82, 95, 96, 99, 100, 103, 114, 115, 121, 125, 126, 132, 139, 145, 148, 149, 156, 161, 163, 165, 166, 171, 175, 181, 183, 190, 191, 201–3, 206, 209, 211–14, 218, 227, 229, 233, 244, 252, 255, 256, 261, 276, 278, 286, 289, 297
Confessing movement   7, 176
Confessing pastors   6, 7, 55, 59, 60, 99, 203
Confessional Synod   90, 91, 95–7, 104–8, 110, 112–14, 117–20, 122–4, 126, 127, 133, 134, 138, 139, 141, 145, 148, 150, 151, 153, 155–60, 163, 165, 167, 178, 179, 185, 195–9, 254, 257
Cooke, Leslie E.   309, 310
Cragg, Roland Herbert   118, 137, 149, 150

Dahlem Synod   165, 179, 180, 254
Danckwarth, Erika   297
Dand, Robert. B.   54
Davidson, Randall   4, 5, 174
Dawson, Geoffrey   62, 201
Day of Potsdam   15
death penalty   72
Deissmann, Adolf   5

de Quervain, Alfred   168, 169
D'Espine, Henri   310
destroyed Churches   157, 173, 250
Deutsche Akademie   165
Deutsche Christen movement   1, 6–8, 16–19, 25, 34, 40, 59, 66, 67, 72, 99, 100, 121, 138, 146, 149, 180, 190, 193, 196, 202, 221, 260, 261, 284, 286
Dibelius, Martin   209, 211, 287–9
Dibelius, Otto   15, 146, 183, 207, 208, 210, 216, 218, 227, 267, 274, 276
Dickinson, Willoughby   51
Diem, Hermann   255
Diestel, Max   246
Dinichert, Paul   116
Dodd, Charles Harold   287–9
Dohnanyi, Hans von   4, 151
Dohrmann, Franz   145
Don, Alan   26, 45
Dožić, Gavrilo   251
Duncan-Jones, A.S.   17, 29, 30, 35, 59, 157, 218, 252
Dundas, Lawrence   290
Dürckheim, Karlfried Graf   208, 209

Ebbutt, Norman   201
Ehrenström, Nils   241, 244
Eidem, Erling   76, 105, 110, 213, 216, 225, 227, 228, 231, 233–42, 245, 247, 249, 250, 263, 264, 266, 268, 296
Elliott, William Thompson   296, 297
Evangelical Christianity   111, 155, 156
Evangelical Church   1, 6, 9, 18, 22–4, 26, 28, 31–3, 37, 40, 41, 44–6, 49, 50, 53, 55, 59, 60, 63, 68–72, 74, 82–4, 88–92, 95, 96, 102, 104, 114, 115, 117, 120, 121, 124–6, 128, 139, 146, 148–51, 155, 162–4, 166, 167, 169–71, 174, 181, 183, 188–90, 195, 197–200, 203, 210, 212, 213, 218, 220, 221, 227, 234, 236, 240–2, 244, 245, 248, 250, 251, 256, 260, 269, 270, 280, 304
Evangelical Youth Movement   19
Évian international conference   285

Faith and Order Movements   3, 8
Fanø Resolution   117, 194, 198
Fausel, Heinrich   255
Fenn, Eric   271, 272
Fezer, Karl   18, 37, 40, 44, 47, 48, 53, 54, 80
Forell, Birger   76, 80, 115, 116, 146, 149, 152, 160, 225, 227–9, 233, 259
Free Church representatives   216
Free Reformed Synod   97, 101, 144
Free Reich Synod   93
Freudenberg, Adolf   258–60
Frick, Wilhelm   15, 17, 35, 61, 97, 98, 128, 131, 133, 138, 145, 150, 155, 158, 159, 202
friendly aliens   290, 291
Führer principle   16, 18

German Christians   20, 24, 26, 27, 29, 31, 34, 37, 39, 53, 54, 64, 71, 72, 78, 79, 93, 99, 120, 133, 134, 148, 150, 162, 169, 185, 192, 230, 231, 234
German Church situation   20, 21, 47, 98, 100–2, 111, 160, 194, 211, 233, 247, 283
German Church Struggle/*Kirchenkampf*   1, 6–10, 89, 96, 176, 256
German Faith Movement   18, 128, 138, 145, 164, 175
Germanos, Lukas Pantaleon   213–15, 232, 234, 250, 272
German Protestant Churches (Deutscher Evangelischer Kirchenbund)   1, 22, 24, 28, 32, 34, 39, 42, 45, 58, 59, 62–4, 103, 151, 170, 183–6, 197, 227, 288, 296, 305
German Protestantism   5, 22, 35, 50
Germany and Christendom   316–22
Gerstenmaier, Eugen   221, 242, 244, 304–6
Gestapo   19, 58, 96, 118, 149, 157, 165, 166, 168, 175, 229, 236, 275, 291, 318
Gethman, Walter W.   50, 51
Gleichschaltung   1, 15, 60, 92, 155
Godesberg Declaration   25

Goebbels, Joseph   15, 35, 86, 87, 131, 150, 152, 201, 203, 210, 224
Gogarten, Friedrich   144, 146
Göring, Carin   87
Göring, Hermann   15, 58, 81, 82, 87, 135, 143, 145, 148, 149
Gossner Mission   277–81
gottgläubig   145
Guillon, Charles   77, 78, 242, 243
Gulin, Eelis   292, 293
Gürtner, Franz   150, 151, 257
Gutteridge, Richard J.C.   50, 51

Hahn, Hugo   66, 67, 71
Handels-Zeitung   152
Hartenstein, Karl   150, 151, 157, 224, 225, 228, 277, 278, 281
Headlam, Arthur Cayley   5, 8, 15, 19, 23, 44, 118, 209, 221, 252
Heckel, Theodor   18, 19, 34, 58, 60, 68–70, 74, 86, 96, 101, 103, 105, 109, 161, 163, 187, 189, 193, 195, 196, 208, 209, 211, 217, 219–23, 225, 231, 232, 234, 238, 240–3, 266, 273, 274, 276, 295, 296
Heckel, Wahl and Co.   232
Henley, V.E.   97
Henriod, Henry-Louis   1, 10, 32, 39, 44, 48, 50, 51, 103, 108–10, 112, 114, 115, 131, 132, 142, 168, 170, 171, 193, 194, 196–8, 205, 208, 210, 238, 240, 242, 246, 264, 272–4, 276
Henselmann, Peter   141, 142
Herde, Georg   85–7
Hess, Rudolf   133, 135, 138, 161–3, 165, 171, 224
Hesse, Helmut   254, 255
Hildebrandt, Franz   111, 112, 247, 291, 297
Himmler, Heinrich   35, 131, 132, 175, 224, 229, 256
Hindenburg, Paul von   30
Hinderer, August   28
Hitler, Adolf   6, 7, 15–20, 22, 24–7, 30–2, 34, 35, 43, 53, 55, 58–61, 63, 65, 66, 72, 76, 82, 109, 113, 118–23, 125, 127, 135, 136, 138, 140,

144, 145, 147, 148, 150, 151, 154, 155, 159, 163, 165, 166, 168–70, 175, 189, 191, 202, 203, 206, 213, 218, 221, 247, 252, 254, 256, 270, 274–6, 283, 286, 301, 313–15, 317, 321, 322
Hitler girls youth movement 166
Hoesch, Leopold von 81, 121, 175
Hollweg, Walter 212, 213
Holy Spirit 84, 88
Hope Simpson, John 285
Hossenfelder, Joachim von 17–19, 37, 39, 40, 44, 47, 48, 53–5, 121, 133, 193, 194
House of Commons 129, 130, 132
Houses of Convocation 91, 92
Hugenberg, Alfred 30
Humburg, Paul 39, 124–6
Hymmen, Johannes 8

Immer, Karl Immanuel 124, 125, 157, 178, 226
'In German Eyes' 19
inter alia 186, 200
Interchurch Aid 9
international Christendom 230
international ecumenical movement 1
International Missionary Council 48, 49, 52, 95, 206, 239, 272, 279, 282
Irinej Ciric 221

Jacobi, Gerhard 114, 115
Jäger, August 17, 28, 29, 35, 58–61, 78, 79, 81, 82, 94, 100, 109, 113, 118–22, 143, 254
Jannasch, Wilhelm 201, 212
Jasper, Ronald C.D. 156
Jewish Mission 284
John, Rosemarie 305
Jung, C.G. 80
Junge Kirche 82, 131–3
Jungreformatoren (Young Reformers' movement) 6

Kapler, Hermann 16, 21, 22, 27, 141
Karow, Emil 77, 78
Kassel-Convention 230, 235, 237, 242, 243, 258
Kasseler Gremium 258, 264–6

Keller, Adolf 78, 80, 97, 98, 101, 105, 128, 144, 172, 205, 277, 278, 281, 285
Kemnitz, Mathilde Ludendorff von 145
Kempthorne, John 23
Kerr, Philip Henry 270
Kerrl, Hanns 7, 8, 138, 139, 161–71, 174–6, 179, 181–3, 187, 192–4, 202, 203, 206, 210, 212–13, 218, 221, 226–8, 230, 240, 241, 244, 247, 249, 250, 252, 254, 265, 267, 287, 288
Kinder, Christian 19, 120–2, 141
Kirchbach, Arndt Friedrich von 67, 71
Kirchlich-Theologische Sozietät 255
Kittel, Gerhard 50, 54, 287–9
Klose, Gerhard 40, 41
Knak, Siegfried 52, 225, 277, 279, 281
Knofe, Oskar 155
Knubel, Frederick Hermann 282
Knuth, Wilhelm 66, 67, 71
Köberle, Adolf 80
Koch, Erich 142
Koch, Karl 41, 58, 59, 96, 97, 101–5, 108, 110–14, 116–18, 120–2, 124–6, 134, 137, 145–51, 155–61, 163, 167, 169, 173, 176, 185–7, 195, 197, 214–17, 225, 239, 256, 258
Koch, P.S. 112
Köcher, Otto Carl 261
Koechlin, Alphons 1. *See also individual entries*
  Aid Organisation of the Protestant Churches of Switzerland 4
  Archbishop of Canterbury 5
  Basel mission 3
  Blue Cross organization 2
  commitment to Christian mission 3
  ecumenism 3
  education 2
  Elisabeth, mother of 2
  eschatological perspective 3
  Faith and Order Movements 3
  Geigy, Johann Rudolf, uncle of 2
  honorary doctorate 3
  Interchurch Aid 9
  intermediary theologian 3
  Koechlin, Carl, father of 2
  leadership 3

Life and Work movement 3
President of Federation of
    Churches 4
secretary of new Church Council 2
Swiss Protestant Refugee Aid 4
Thurneysen, Emilie, wife of 2
Unternehmen Sieben (Operation
    Seven) 4
World Council's Ecumenical
    Commission for the Chaplaincy
    Service to Prisoners of War 4
Kohnstamm, Philipp Abraham 38, 40
Kols-Church 279–81
Kraemer, Hendrik 280, 281
Krosigk, Johann Ludwig von 135
Krummmacher, Friedrich-Wilhelm 69, 194, 195, 197, 226, 227, 230, 232

Lang, Cosmo Gordon 15, 16, 20, 25, 44, 58, 59, 61, 89, 138, 170, 176, 252, 253, 286
Lang, Peter 15, 16, 20–1, 25, 26, 44, 45, 58, 59, 61, 89, 138, 155, 160, 163, 170, 176, 252, 253, 286
Law on Asset Management 165
Leiper, Henry Smith 113, 114, 128, 147
Le Temps 267
Lewek, Ernst 154, 155, 177
Ley, Robert 224
Life and Work movement 3, 5, 8, 28, 87, 97, 224, 272
Lilje, Hanns 36, 39, 131–3, 150, 178, 229–32, 234, 236, 242, 243, 265, 266, 269, 270
Lindt, Andreas 2 n.1, 13, 31, 63
Livingstone, L.M. 227, 228, 282–4
Lord Jesus Christ 33, 43, 55
Lucas, Fräulein 29, 30
Lucas, Gerda 30
Ludendorff, Erich 143, 145
Luftwaffe 145
Lutheran Council 67, 207, 210, 214, 231, 234, 263, 281, 283
Lutheran Pact 181, 195–7
Lutheran World Convention 25, 234, 281, 305

Maas, Hermann 191, 287
Malicious Practices Law 15

The Manchester Guardian 54, 181
Manifesto of Loccum 16
Marahrens, August 8, 16, 24, 25, 35, 99, 109, 120, 125, 128, 132, 139, 141, 146–50, 154, 157, 158, 162–5, 173, 174, 179, 181, 182, 185, 189, 196, 200, 207, 210, 212–17, 219–25, 227, 229–32, 234, 240–50, 252, 258, 262, 264, 266, 273–6, 283, 285, 286, 288, 301
Maury, Pierre 36, 39
McDonald, James Grover 169, 170
Mcder, Oskar 154, 155
Meiser, Hans 19, 35, 58–60, 81, 82, 86, 109, 113, 117–20, 122, 125, 158, 159, 174, 181, 182, 195, 196, 207, 210, 245, 252, 266, 283, 285
Menn, Wilhelm 33, 303–5
Mergenthaler, Christian 193, 229
Meusel, Ernst 32
Michael, Horst 160
Michelfelder, Sylvester C. 305
Moberly, Walter Hamilton 208, 209, 284, 285
Moore, Edward 205, 206
Moore, W.G. 252
Mott, John Raleigh 3, 3 n.4, 48–50, 74, 77, 114, 193, 194, 218, 271, 281
Muhs, Hermann 176, 220, 221, 230, 267
Müller, Ludwig 1, 6, 7, 16–19, 25, 26, 44, 45, 47, 48, 66, 193
Murr, Wilhelm 79, 87
Mutschmann, Martin 155
muzzling order 58, 65
The Myth of the Twentieth Century (Rosenberg) 144

National Christian Council 204, 272
National Socialism 13, 140, 154, 164, 170, 182, 193, 210
National Socialist movement 8, 49, 166, 189, 288
National Socialist Party (NSDAP) 1
National-Socialist revolution 90, 92
National Synod 18, 19, 26, 35–7, 40–4, 46, 97, 98, 126, 146, 149
Nazi regime 4, 45, 64, 209, 309
Neill, Stephen 205, 206, 289

neo-paganism 147
Neurath, Konstantin Freiherr von 21, 48, 144, 210
New York Herald Tribune 30
Niemöller, Martin 6, 8, 10, 58, 65, 112, 118, 119, 124, 125, 134, 139, 141, 148, 158, 173, 175, 178, 183, 188, 189, 196, 202, 207, 208, 210, 212, 216, 218, 244, 252, 254, 256, 257, 259, 262, 266, 267, 270-6, 280, 283-5, 321
Niemöller trial 264-6, 272
Niesel, Wilhelm 173, 174
Niven, Charlotte T. 63
Nowack, Erwin 124, 126

Oberheid, Heinrich 58, 66, 77, 86, 193
oecumenical movements 38, 42, 46, 47, 53, 56, 63, 65, 67-9, 76, 77, 87, 116, 123, 133, 188-90, 192, 195, 199, 205, 222, 227, 230, 236, 241, 242, 245, 247, 263, 265-7, 277, 278, 288
Oeri, Albert 63
Oldham, J.H. 20, 48-50, 52, 59, 60, 80, 83, 105, 110, 111, 116, 129, 135, 156, 160, 194, 199, 208, 218-20, 232, 242, 246, 265-73, 278
Old Prussian Church 6, 8, 26, 125, 155, 183
One Holy Catholic Christian Church 64
Ormerod, Mary 285
Otto Melle, F.H. 216, 218, 239, 240, 244
Oxford Conference 50, 176, 198, 199, 205, 207-9, 211, 218, 220, 224, 225, 227, 231, 232, 242, 243, 245, 256, 260, 265, 272

paganism 90-2, 137, 138, 144-7, 149-51, 153, 154, 159, 176
Papen, Franz von 15, 59, 151
Paton, William 271, 272, 278, 279, 290, 293
Peace Conference 320
Peace Treaties 319
Peter, Friedrich 71, 72
Peters, Hans-Helmut 295, 296

Pfarrenotbund/Pfarrernotbund 6, 18, 19, 58, 65, 100, 112, 125
Phipps, Eric 21, 23
'political conflict' in German Church 24
Pressel, Wilhelm 193
Protestant Church 1, 3, 4, 10, 17, 22, 24, 26, 28-30, 32, 34-6, 42, 45, 58-60, 62-4, 80, 100, 103, 151, 165, 170, 183-6, 195, 197, 221, 227, 230, 288, 296, 301, 305, 310, 316, 321
Provincial Synod of Westphalen 77
Provisional Church Government 100, 121, 125, 154, 159, 179, 180, 183, 189, 200, 202, 206, 211, 212, 214, 218, 243, 254, 258, 261-4, 283
Provisional Committee of the WCC 260, 293
Prussian Synod. *See* Synods of Prussia/ Prussian Synod

Radcliffe, James 228
Rehm, Wilhelm 196, 197
Reichsbischof 1, 16, 17, 24, 45, 46, 53, 56, 64
Reichsbruderrat 141, 173, 178, 196, 197
Reichs-Constitution 47
Reichskirchenausschuss (Reichs Church Committee) 165, 169, 184, 187-92, 212
Reichskristallnacht 288
Reichstagung 231, 240
Reichswehr 60, 123, 137, 143
religious liberty and constitutional rights of the Church 16
Ribbentrop, Joachim von 21, 121, 122, 128, 138, 155, 161, 162, 165, 176, 208, 209, 220, 252, 269, 270, 274
Rieger, Julius 112, 155, 156, 256, 257, 260, 264, 285, 291
Riethmüller, Otto 63, 122, 123, 132, 166-8, 178-80, 190-2, 194
rival to Christianity 90
Rodhe, Edvard Magnus 114, 115
Röhm-Plot 95
Roman-catholic Church 37, 53, 260
Rosenberg, Alfred 143, 144

The Round Table 62, 63, 65, 68, 69, 73
Rouse, Ruth 56, 57
Rumbold, Horace 21
Runestam, Arvid 80, 110, 114
Rust, Bernhard 17, 34, 58, 128, 140, 160, 161, 286

Saar question 141
Sandegren, Johannes 280, 281
Sasse, Hermann 243, 244
Schacht, Hjalmar 274
Scheffer, Paul 152
Schempp, Paul 255
Schian, Martin 28
Schirach, Baldur von 19, 49, 75, 76
Schlunk, Martin 52, 277
Schmidt, K.L. 38, 40, 53, 54
Schmidt, Kurt Dietrich 47, 95
Schmidt, Paul 218
Schmidt, William J. 114
Schmitt, Kurt 30
Schneider, Georg 258, 260
Schoell, Jakob 179, 180
Schöffel, Simon 37, 40
Schönfeld, Hans 10, 20, 21, 25, 33, 34, 39, 67, 68, 72, 73, 76–8, 80, 83, 96, 101, 105, 128, 131–3, 135, 172, 179, 181, 184, 219–22, 232, 238, 240–4, 246, 266, 277–9, 281, 282, 301, 303–6
Schultz, Walther 8, 286
seizure of power 32
Sheppard, H.R.L. 285
Siegmund-Schultze, Friedrich 27, 29–31, 33
Smidt, Udo 49
societas studorium Novi Testamenti 287, 288
Soden, Hans Freiherr von 230, 233
Söderblom, Nathan 22, 80, 87, 105
Sohns, Hans Friedrich 260
Sparring-Petersen, Gunnar 264, 265, 267
Spenger, Jakob 166
spiritual unity 64
Sprenger, Jakob 170
Stange, Erich 38, 40, 43, 49, 63, 65, 74, 75, 85, 106, 108, 142, 167, 172, 211
state-church-system (*Staatskirchentum*) 159

St Michael's Church 40, 277
Stockholm Conference 22, 41, 42, 45, 183, 309
Stresemann, Gustav 152, 153
Strong, Thomas 90, 91
Stuckart, Wilhelm 143–5
Svenska Morgenbladed 170
Swiss leadership 291
Swiss Protestantism 2
Swiss Protestant Refugee Aid 4
Synods of Prussia/Prussian Synod 37, 44, 46, 142

Temple, William 294
Tenorth, Heinz-Elmar 29
Terboven, Josef 299
Thadden-Trieglaff, Reinhold von 36, 37, 39, 207, 208, 243, 244, 261–3, 265
theological training 230
'Theologische Existenz heute!' (Theological Existence to-day!) (Barth) 34
Theology (Bell) 5
Thurneysen, Eduard 2, 66, 74, 135, 140, 224–7, 229
Thurneysen, Emilie 2
Tietz, Christiane 29, 136

Ulm Declaration 82, 83
Una Sancta 47, 239
Unification Work (*Einigungswerk*) 9
United Church 16, 124–6, 148
unity of Evangelical churches 1
Universal Christian Council for Life and Work 1, 22, 41, 44, 64, 70, 83, 85, 88, 95, 102, 114, 197, 244
Unternehmen Sieben (Operation Seven) 4
Utrecht Conference 265, 282

van Asch van Wyck, Cornelia Maria 67, 73–5, 178
Versailles Treaty 130, 138, 161
Visser't Hooft, W.A. 4, 6 n.4, 9, 44, 73, 74, 108, 218, 272, 292, 299, 303–6, 308, 316 n.2
Vorläufige Kirchenleitung ('Provisional Board of the Confessional Church') 186

Wadiyar, Nalwadi Krishnaraja   204
Wahl, Hans   69, 86, 182, 183, 196, 226, 227, 230, 232
Walter, Georg   155
Warnshuis, A.L.   282
Weber, Otto   8
Wehrhan, Fritz   291, 297
Wehrmacht   67, 82, 145, 149
Weizsäcker, Ernst von   128, 205, 261, 296, 297
Werner, Friedrich   8, 213, 257, 260, 283, 285, 286, 291
Western, Frederick   205, 206
Wilamowitz-Möllendorff, Fanny Gräfin   87
Willis, Frank   81
Winterhager, Jürgen Wilhelm   146, 149
Wood, Edward   247
Woods, Theodore   22
Woodsmall, Ruth   172
Word of the Reich Church Committee to the Congregations   201
World Council of Churches   3, 9, 10, 39, 50, 146, 174, 272, 281, 301, 305, 307, 310, 316, 317, 321
World Council's Ecumenical Commission for the Chaplaincy Service to Prisoners of War   4

World's Youth   63
world-wide missionary responsibility   291, 292
Wurm, Theophil   9, 19, 25, 40, 47, 49, 58, 60, 78, 79, 81, 86, 87, 98, 109, 113, 118–20, 122, 125, 131, 157, 158, 169, 179–82, 188, 192–7, 207, 210–12, 221, 225, 228, 229, 239–41, 244, 245, 252, 254, 256, 266, 283, 285, 287, 288, 321
Wurth, Klaus   258, 260
Württemberg Church Synod   78

Young Reformation Movement (*Jungreformatorische Bewegung*)   22, 34
Ysander, Torsten   273

Zahn, Karl Friedrich   74, 86, 94
Zarnack, Hulda   167, 168
Zentgraf, Rudolf   66, 71, 190
Zimmermann, Richard   212, 213
Zoellner, Wilhelm   8, 162, 165, 174, 179, 182, 183, 187–97, 199, 206, 217
Zöllner, Wilhelm   8
'zum Schutz der Volksgemeinschaft' degree   80

www.ingramcontent.com/pod-product-compliance
Lightning Source LLC
Chambersburg PA
CBHW071759300426
44116CB00009B/1141